States of Inquiry

New Studies in American Intellectual and Cultural History
Howard Brick, Series Editor

States of Inquiry

Social Investigations and Print Culture in Nineteenth-Century Britain and the United States

OZ FRANKEL

The Johns Hopkins University Press

Baltimore

The Johns Hopkins University Press
2715 North Charles Street
Baltimore, Maryland 21218-4363
www.press.jhu.edu

Library of Congress Cataloging-in-Publication Data
Frankel, Oz, 1958–
States of inquiry : social investigations and print culture in nineteenth-century
Britain and the United States / Oz Frankel.
p. cm. — (New studies in American intellectual and cultural history)
Includes bibliographical references and index.
ISBN 0-8018-8340-7 (hardcover : alk. paper)
1. Social surveys—United States—History—19th century. 2. United
States—Population—Statistical methods. 3. Printing, Public—
United States—History—19th century. 4. Government publications—United
States—History—19th century. 5. Social surveys—Great Britain—
History—19th century. 6. Great Britain—Population—Statistical methods.
7. Printing, Public—Great Britain—History—19th century. 8. Government
publications—Great Britain—History—19th century.
I. Title. II. Series.
HA37.U55F75 2006
314.1072'3—dc22   2005027400

A catalog record of this book is available from the British Library.

For my parents, Sara and Yair Frankel

CONTENTS

Researching and writing this book was an extraordinary privilege made possible by the magnanimity of family, teachers, colleagues, friends, and institutions. My chief resources have been the unwavering devotion and support of my partner Alyson Cole, my son Tammuz (Muzi) Frankel, my parents Sara and Yair Frankel, my sister Varda Mann, and her family. I dedicate this book to my parents as a token of my gratitude. At the University of California at Berkeley three advisors, Sheldon Rothblatt, David Hollinger, and Catherine Gallagher, were generous with their time, energy, and advice, all of which I have never ceased to avail myself. This project began as a research paper for a seminar I took with Sheldon during my first year in graduate school. His enthusiasm, erudition, and good judgment never failed me. David's rigor, acuity, and encouragement enhanced my work. Cathy graciously acquainted me with the joys and tribulations of literary criticism. Our meetings twisted, bent, and reshaped my way of thinking.

Individuals who read or simply listened to my work over the years often asked questions, made comments, and shared insights that have improved this book. I am especially obliged to Eli Zaretsky, Philippa Levine, Tom Laqueur, Lisa Cody, Ann Laura Stoler, Geoff Goldfarb, Kali Israel, Anne Humpherys, Michael Warner, Seth Koven, and Hans Bak. At Berkeley I am also indebted to Nelson Polsby, Paula Fass, Larry Levine, Waldo Martin Jr., and the late Michael Paul Rogin, as well as to Anna Shtutina, Cornelia Sears, Stephen Cole, Jesse Berrett, Andrea Roberts, and Marc Foster. At the University of Michigan I was fortunate to receive a warm reception and valuable advice from James Boyd White, Rebecca Scott, Bill Rosenberg, Paul Allen Anderson, Robert Self, John Carson, Geoff Eley, Gina Morantz-Sanchez, Richard Candida-Smith, Tom Green, Todd Endelman, Jochen Hellbeck, Tiffany Holmes, and Carla Mazzio. Working in London, England, Peter Mandler, Lawrence Goldman, Michael Thompson, and Anthony Howe provided important assistance, while Dan White, Lara Kriegel, and Jeanette and Alex Byrd provided camaraderie. My colleagues at the New School for Social Research and Lang College have been exceptionally kind. I wish I could list them all. Special thanks are owed to Aristide Zolberg, Vera Zolberg, Arien Mack, Bill Hirst, Claudio Lomnitz, Nancy Fraser, Vicky Hattam, David Plotke, Jim Miller, Richard Bernstein, Jose Cassanova, Elaine Abelson, Andrew Arato, Alice Crary, Orville Lee, Robin Blackburn, Courtney Jung, James Dodd, Will Milberg, Ann Snitow, and Anwar Shaikh.

There is no scholarship without scholarships. At Berkeley, my work was funded by the generosity of the Regents of the University of California, the Doreen B. Townsend Center for the Humanities (whose weekly meetings under Randy Starn's leadership were a source of inspiration), the Mabelle McLeod Lewis Memorial Fund, and the Institute of International Studies (which granted me the Reinhard Bendix Research Fellowship for Social and Political Thought, the Allan Sharlin Memorial Award, and the John L. Simpson Memorial Research Fellowship in International and Comparative Studies). Additional support included a yearlong predoctoral fellowship from the Smithsonian Institution, an international dissertation research fellowship from the Social Science Research Council, an Andrew W. Mellon fellowship from the Massachusetts Historical Society, and an Andrew W. Mellon fellowship from the Huntington Library. A postdoctoral appointment at the Michigan Society of Fellows and the University of Michigan Department of History provided a nurturing environment for further research and writing.

I am also indebted to the archivists, librarians, and staff of the Smithsonian Institution Archives (especially Paul Theerman); the Library of Congress; the National Archives and Records Administration at Washington, D.C., and College Park, Md.; the Massachusetts Historical Society (especially Conrad Edick Wright and Peter Drummey); the Boston Public Library; the Houghton Library at Harvard; the British Library; the Public Record Office, Kew; the Special Collections Library at the University College, London; the London School of Economics; the Doe Library at U.C. Berkeley (especially Phoebe Janes); the Elmer Holmes Bobst Library at New York University; and the libraries of the New School. Finally, my thanks are hereby tendered to the Johns Hopkins University Press, its editors, staff, and readers.

States of Inquiry

Introduction

During the middle decades of the nineteenth century, the U.S. and British governments asserted themselves—with great fanfare—in the arenas of knowledge and print. A few of the instruments elaborated for that purpose are familiar to us today, two of which stand at the center of this book: the function of the state as an energetic gatherer of facts about (or investigator of) social, economic, and other aspects of national affairs, and the role of government as a prolific publisher of policy reports and official documents. In Britain, royal commissions of inquiry, inspectorates, and parliamentary committees famously investigated myriad social problems and sites, such as child labor, poverty, sanitary conditions in urban slums, and the safety of mines. On the other side of the Atlantic, the U.S. government surveyed Indian tribes (and, through expeditions and explorations, the West in general) as well as the condition of the South during and after the Civil War. The two states also printed, bound, and circulated numerous accounts about these and additional topics for the perusal of legislators, bureaucrats, and ordinary citizens. The British study and depiction of the lesser regions of society shared important features with the U.S. exploration and publication of reports on the West and the South.

The nineteenth-century state justified its new informational tasks in diverse terms. The list is long and includes policy making, transparency and accountability, public education, and even archive keeping and memorialization. This book argues that investigations and reports in effect constituted a new form of politics that interlaced communication with representation. Beyond declared goals and the façade of "information," legislatures and governments sought to represent their citizens and the national (or, sometimes, imperial) sphere in ways that exceeded conventional modes of political representation, namely, electoral politics. They engaged in unprecedented scientific, literary, and aesthetic documentation of the country, its social circumstances, economy, and history as well as its natural environment. Concurrently, the British and American states in-

vested heavily in documenting and publicizing their own actions and deliberations. In other words, official reportage facilitated the representation of the centralized, modern state *to* its publics and, in turn, the representation of the nation
by (and *to*) the government itself. One consequence was that investigations and
reports incorporated less powerful groups into the national conversation by rendering them presentable and representable political subjects. This was the case
with American Indians and freed slaves in the United States and the working or
unemployed poor in Britain. Exchange of knowledge and texts thus operated
through multifarious paths, implicating governments and legislatures, the disenfranchised populations—now the object of national attention—and diverse
communities of readers who recognized the state in its published documents.
Conversely, through fact-finding enterprises, the state conjured up its subjects,
publics, and spheres. It also fashioned itself a target of observation and scrutiny.
I term this field of communication between the state and its constituencies *print
statism* (following Benedict Anderson's notion of *print* capitalism).

From the vantage point of the mid-nineteenth century, it became incumbent
upon governments to enhance their capacity to communicate, and tools were put
in place to enable the state to serve as its own medium. Individuals as well as
groups became vigorously involved in this new field as speakers and readers—
as informants and witnesses, on the one hand, and as interpreters, collectors, and
"poachers" of state-issued documents, on the other. Knowledge as well as tangible objects such as reports and books changed hands. The full dimensions of this
vibrant commerce are somewhat obscured today by the contemporary culture of
information and its preoccupation with matters of utility and facticity—the
quality, veracity, and comprehensiveness of state proclamations and official data.
These evaluative standards do not account for the dynamics and meanings of the
traffic in knowledge and its venues. Knowledge is not only a tool of government
but also a currency of explicit and tacit transactions between the state and its citizens.

Governance may be intrinsically tied to some forms of knowledge and communication, but the mediated exchange described in the following chapters is a
specifically historical phenomenon. It emerged before the modern regime of information reshaped, at the turn of the twentieth century, journalism, public science, and politics. By the progressive era (in the United States), citizenship would
become intertwined with possessing information, as in the notion of the "informed citizen." The nineteenth-century state's declared wish to enlighten lawmakers and citizens served often as a pretext to manage public debate and master public perception. Official circulation of knowledge betrayed even greater

aspirations of power and regimentation: building state institutions, curbing social unrest, forging citizens, fostering a national spirit, and even spawning em-
pires. However, the trope of the state as a monolithic and ever-ascending entity,
whose knowledge brims with power and whose power always knows, is at best an
oversimplification. Too much of the recent scholarly discussion about knowledge
and the state has been haunted by the specter of the panopticon, the Foucauldian
paradigm for the coercive power of post-Enlightenment knowledge. My study
shifts attention instead to the place of the state/knowledge nexus within a larger
dynamic of exchange and substitution. This is neither to reject Michel Foucault's
art of seeing—including his "insight" into the capacity of particular discourses
to mint subjectivities—nor to embrace the nineteenth century's other apparition, its public sphere (or "public opinion") ideology that uncritically trumpeted
its own supposed inclusiveness and rationality. Governments and legislatures certainly capitalized on their capacity to launch investigations and publish reports.
Nevertheless, the specific political effects of this series of performances were uneven and inconclusive. For one, chronic gaps existed between the sometimes fantastical and totalizing ambitions of bureaucrats and legislators and the reality of
daily governance. Recall also that the nineteenth-century state was neither the
only receptacle of authority in society nor the sole author of imperious taxonomies and categories of knowledge. The relationship between state power and
knowledge is complex and in need of historicization. It is further complicated if
we turn our focus from abstract discourses and their hierarchy-making potentials
to the actual sites and scenes where the state and its constituencies encountered
each other for the ostensible purpose of producing and consuming knowledge.
As this book demonstrates, rather than simply empowering the modern state,
official publications and investigations facilitated unforeseen encounters and
dealings between governments and legislatures and their local interlocutors.

The state could not exercise full mastery over the process of inquiry, the behavior of its emissaries as investigators or authors, or the fate of its printed reports once they were issued and promiscuously circulated. The contingent, inter-
personal nature of the exchange between official agents and studied populations
often determined investigative field experiences. While government occasionally
initiated inquiries at the behest of vulnerable communities, in other instances,
commissioners had to contend with acts of resistance such as demonstrations,
boycotts, attempts at counter-investigations, or witnesses who simply chose to
"talk back" rather than to answer questions. Massive social surveys also revealed
confusion over matters of discourse due in part to competition among systems of
measurement and observation; contests that involved different disciplines such

as modern physiology and city planning, besides older protocols of deciding facts that rested on judicial and legislative procedures. Irrespective of discourse, in the locales of investigation, facts and knowledge proved elusive and occasionally ungovernable. Likewise, official reports were subjected to practices of critical reviewing and other elements of modern print culture that constricted the power of government.

At times, it seemed that the American and British states were not ascending as much as fumbling through the economy of facts, social and otherwise. Always costly undertakings, investigations and publications required resources and skills the state found difficult to muster. Inquiries often revealed friction among bureaus and accentuated the fault lines between the executive and legislative branches of government. Print culture afforded state officials and legislators the cultural capital entailed by authorship—sometimes at the expense of the unified, commanding voice of the state. We still frequently label major governmental and legislative reports after their nominal "authors" rather than the bodies that actually craft them, and the state expresses itself through the voices of individual officials.

Other questions of voice suffused the nineteenth-century project of policy investigation as well. In common parlance, having a voice subsumes the difference between political agency (if only through entitlement to electoral franchise) and the public articulation of opinion. We conceive of the lack of voice as signifying endemic oppression. Consequently, Karl Marx's often quoted assertion that French peasants "cannot represent themselves; they must be represented" seems symptomatic of the predisposition, even among nineteenth-century radicals, to deny the other agency.[1] Equating voice and power should not be taken for granted. In the mid-nineteenth century culture of social inquiry, marginal populations did speak and represent themselves rather frequently. The state, in fact, invited them to make claims about their condition. Yes, government often sought to commandeer these voices. Public inquiries modified indigenous voices by eliciting particular responses. Officials selected and edited self-representations and on rare occasions even forged them, less by falsifying evidence than by counterfeiting voice, by speaking for or instead of, by ventriloquizing the other. (Giving voice to the voiceless—a recurrent refrain in modern historiography—is always a suspect endeavor.) These investigative ventures were even less benign when representation—a form of substitution or "standing in"—resulted in complete occlusion or erasure. For instance, federal efforts to capture and commemorate indigenous Indian life were integral to the policy of removing and "civilizing" the Indian. The testimony committed to writing and print is already muffled,

Voice
(...voicelessness)

"voice"-less. No longer aural and immediate, it becomes merely a simulacrum of presence. This point however can be carried further, for the state itself was also somehow left voiceless by official reportage. At the conclusion of the investigative sequence, when oral exchanges and other types of evidence were translated into printed reports, not even the mighty state could speak for itself—its voice had to be modulated and mediated; published documents subsumed the multivalent tasks of representation.

This book thus takes as its main topic, and documents in some detail, two fundamentals of modern public culture. First are the procedures of investigation, meaning the set of tactics and performances developed to select the location and timing of the encounter and then to acquire and authenticate information, particularly the experience of individual government envoys in the "field" of investigation and that of their interlocutors. Second is the factual report as a unique type of text, its authorship, publication, distribution, and uses, which this study situates within the entire print output of the state and the history of the book. The full dimensions of the traffic between the state and its public (or publics) become apparent only if we follow the thread of investigation throughout, to explore how the publication of reports completed, complemented (or undermined) the aggregation of knowledge. The rest of this introduction briefly describes the fields that the new medium of investigations and official reportage, "print statism," linked and reconfigured: society, print culture, representation, and the state.

Society

A panoply of circumstances prompted the early nineteenth-century concern with "society": novel methods and locations of production, urbanization, fresh humanitarian discourses of care as well as new calculi developed to manage the populace and to restructure government, such as utilitarianism. This engrossment with the social domain, still more by way of contemplation than extensive inquiry and reform, originated in Britain and other European countries during the concluding decades of the eighteenth century when a need arose for efficient strategies to mobilize entire populations. Such efforts corresponded to the demands of the new market regime but historically became imperative chiefly under circumstances of war, in the aftermath of the French Revolution. In the early nineteenth-century United States, urbanization, new modes of organizing labor, migration and immigration, and cycles of economic recessions inspired awareness about the social sphere, or society. As significant were the presence of (and ongoing exposure to) distinct racial groups and, once again, the experience of war, in this case the Civil War and the social turmoil that befell the country in its wake.

Society was open to diverse interpretations as an autonomous system, an organic body, a realm of grouping and affiliation, or, alternatively, a site of great vulnerability and strife, in need of intervention, assistance, or regimentation. For the purpose of this discussion, the most important aspect of the newly rearranged social scene was that distinct social blocks lived completely ignorant of each other, or so argued some contemporary observers. The social sphere, spatially conceived, had grown thoroughly divided between segments that were known and familiar and those that were designated hidden. The *social* enters public consciousness in times of crisis: war, riot, major accident, epidemic, or natural disaster. Otherwise, it is highly factual and endemically elusive, requiring recurrent explorations and discovery.

Social inquiries were consequently devised to uncover the circumstances or "condition" of weaker or disenfranchised populations. During the early decades of the nineteenth century, investigations came to define British political culture as well as the frantic reform drives in the American Northeast. In Britain, government dispatched commissioners and inspectors to the mills and mines of the industrializing Midlands and the North, while Parliament and numerous reform societies, philanthropists, and journalists amassed testimonies and statistical data on the impoverished. This information fed the grand debate over the social predicament of Britain, which Thomas Carlyle termed the "condition of England" question. Cycles of legislation centralized poor relief and inaugurated state regulation of new industries by restricting child and female labor and imposing safety and education measures upheld by periodic inspections. These early steps overlapped with a protracted campaign that was given added impetus in the early 1830s to remake the British polity, its electoral system, local government, and ancient institutions such as the military, the Church of England, and the old English universities.

Critical reforms on a national level corresponded to the sensibilities of a middle class whose contours were now defined by a new franchise replacing an antiquated mélange of urban voting privileges with a £10 yardstick (1832). This class shared the investigative perspective according to which the condition of the poor encompassed moral and physical dimensions. Paid agents of the popular Statistical Associations, for example, frequented the houses of the poor, counted the number of rooms and inhabitants (the habit of sharing beds always produced anxieties about sexual permissiveness), tabulated the possession of books, recorded the command of skills such as knitting among women and mending furniture among men, and even evaluated the competence of parents to sing a "cheerful song" to their children. Other organizations dedicated their energies to more immediate targets, for instance, the suppression of vice and vagrancy. Such reforms and invasive philanthropy contributed to this new class's self-conception. However, the British middle classes did not escape public inspection either. Reform campaigns and official inquiries targeted factories and mills that were largely owned by newly arrived entrepreneurs. Proprietors protested what they considered intolerable intrusions into their private affairs.

The United States had not yet experienced the Industrial Revolution in full. Nevertheless, Boston, Philadelphia, and especially New York were among the fastest growing urban centers in the world, contending with tenements, squalor, prostitution, crime, and abandoned children. Antebellum reformers emphasized the perfectibility of the individual (a concern manifested, for instance, by temperance and hygiene campaigns), but that goal, of course, always had social dimensions as well. Prisons and asylums were sites of experimentation. Observers from Europe visited the Eastern Penitentiary in Philadelphia and other innovative institutions. A burgeoning literature on penal practices followed the great controversy brewing around the "silent" versus the "separate" prison systems of Pennsylvania and New York. State governments, organizations such as the Boston Discipline Society, and reform crusaders like Dorothea Dix—celebrated as a "voice for the mad"—published research about incarceration and confinement. The 1830s heralded a watershed for American reform. The decade witnessed an unprecedented drive for the abolition of slavery and the proliferation of reform organizations. One consequence of this ferment was the creation of state-supported public school systems, beginning with Massachusetts.

The conflict over slavery in the United States shared significant properties with the debate over the social crisis in Britain. Abolition, with other modes of early nineteenth-century social investigation, attempted to penetrate isolated, inaccessible sites—the factory, the prison, the workhouse, the plantation—in an effort to learn the true situation of their inhabitants. To give one example, the publication of Harriet Beecher Stowe's *Uncle Tom's Cabin* (1852) inspired Frederick Law Olmsted to launch a one-man commission of inquiry into the South's social and economic arrangements. With the Civil War and Reconstruction, the federal state replaced abolitionists in rendering the South an object of numerous fact-finding enterprises. Another field of social inquiry that was uniquely American addressed the condition of the Indian tribes. Before the Civil War, native nations were the only social group directly cared for by the federal government, perhaps with the minor exception of federal attempts to ensure healthy conditions aboard immigrant ships. Indian policy, namely, the policy of removal west of the Mississippi, triggered national controversy that spawned reports and counterreports. The federal government accumulated information about the tribes within (and sometimes outside) its territorial confines and launched research projects into Indian culture and history.

Print Statism

Rather than exploring these landmarks of early nineteenth-century social history in the familiar contexts of reform, policy, history of scientific discourse, or "government growth," this book pursues a different tack. Society was conceived to be autonomous but its discovery took place in the public sphere and the realm of politics. After all, conventions of accumulating and diffusing knowledge did not necessarily emanate from the social crises they addressed. They were primarily rooted in expanding electorates of voter-readers, the bureaucratization of public life exemplified in the proverbially gray world of commissions and committees, the rise of professional authors, and the symbiosis between politics and printed texts through, for instance, party platforms or (in the United States) party newspapers. During the first three decades of the century, the last hurdles to universal white male suffrage in America, usually property requirements, were removed. Research into immigrant neighborhoods or female and child laborers often targeted those outside the voting citizenry. Inquiries that focused on African Americans during the Civil War and Reconstruction and Native Americans addressed the prospects of their inclusion in the polity. In Britain, where the populace consisted of subjects rather than citizens, Parliament and the ministry conducted intensive social studies under the penumbra of discord over the expansion of the electorate, from the early 1830s conflicts over the Reform Bill to the 1840s threat of violence leveled by the Chartist movement. Particularly in Britain, early nineteenth-century social inquiries appeared to expand the representative functions of government beyond the franchise. In the United States, the electorate was proportionally much larger and the gap between voters and nonvoters even more pronounced.

The history of print and literary culture provides another context for print statism, especially the growing literacy rates, the burgeoning daily press (the American penny press furnishes the best example), popular magazines, and the technological breakthroughs that enabled cheap mass printing and distribution of documents. The quantity of state publications was soaring at the same time that stereotyping, electrotyping, the steam press, and the rolling press—the most notable cluster of innovations in print technology since the invention of moveable type in the fifteenth century—further mechanized the print shop. This study highlights the contribution of state reports as well as other state-published ephemera to the culture of print. Social reports have been often studied as platforms for the inculcation of ideas and transmission of information, as vehicles of policy and propaganda. The medium itself—its physical properties, its aesthetic signification, and the consequences of its unhampered circulation—has been overlooked. The entire course of investigation was geared toward the publication of factual documents. Bureaucrats and lawmakers deeply engaged in the preparation of reports, their content, design, and production as artifacts and, consequently, allocated immense resources for that goal. The state interjected itself into the literary marketplace by distributing and even selling documents and by paying attention to the reading habits of its citizens. In this regard, print capitalism often served as a template for the manner in which print statism circulated texts in society.

Government manufactured its papers with an eye to literary genres, as well as to the formats of review or scholarly journals. They shared with them not just sensibilities and language but also publishing strategies, such as serialization. Recently, there has been a lively critical interest in the embodiment of social and political discourses in nineteenth-century literary texts. My analysis contributes to this discussion by addressing the textual quality of official documents and their ossification into identifiable, self-referring genres. The textuality of government itself is highly significant in this regard, not just its susceptibility to multiple interpretations but its public presence in tangible printed documents and the possibilities it offered for mass reading.

One historical genealogy connects print statism dialectically with the permutations of the eighteenth-century political discourse that demanded government accountability, open debate, and public scrutiny of the affairs of the state. Michael Warner recently demonstrated how American colonial print culture sustained an imaginary public sphere whose discursive rules fused citizenship and democratic action with the reading and writing of printed texts. Print culture and republicanism became mutually constitutive. The voluntary networks of the American "republic of letters" or the kind of intellectual milieu of critical discussion that thrived in late eighteenth-century London—both long gone by the mid-nineteenth century—left decisive imprints (pun intended) on modern public sphere ideologies. Still, we should not regard nineteenth-century state reportage merely as an embodiment of the Enlightenment desire for political and social transparency. As we shall see, print statism flourished in a new cultural order and served differently conceived states, publics, authors, and readers. It is nevertheless of some importance that the early Victorian and Early Republic governments appropriated and further expanded the function or the posture that had been initially codified in the previous century to critique the British *ancien regime* at home and in the colonies. Public inquiries opened a space for the modern state's self-invention and self-reflection, however limited.

Viewed another way, the state's print output comprised a vast archive, an archive in print. The archive designation here has literal and figurative connotations: the archive as a comprehensive repository that is classified, catalogued, and periodically updated; the archive as a body of knowledge the state generates, aggregates, and sustains; and the archive as a place, a site of registration and retrieval or memory. Over the last 150 years, social historians and social commentators have repeatedly visited parliamentary papers. Among the first to do so, Karl Marx and Friedrich Engels scanned this treasure trove for their own purposes. It remains one of the chief sources for nineteenth-century British historiography. In some ways, however, the print archive functioned as a counterarchive, for unlike historical state repositories it was not shielded and kept in a concrete interior space. Rather, it was exteriorized, reproduced, and circulated for general commentary. The state could not retain the exclusive power of perusing its own record, and the print archive could be made to divulge more than one sort of truth. But even with its celebrated openness and publicity, the state print archive was sporadically a volatile place, raising suspicions of concealment (if not within its own confines, then elsewhere, in other, better-guarded state archives) and deception. In addition, its existence raised the problem of consignment: what should be published and what should remain secret, private, or merely unpublished, and, by implication, whether the state or its officers have a protected sphere of private writing. The print archive also became symptomatic of the state's "inner" truth, betraying its appetite for the printed page, its gluttonous consumption of paper, its compulsion in creating the archive.

Large-scale research projects did not merely archive but also "made" history. Major public hearings and other forms of official investigation often amounted to remarkably visible, dramatic, attention-grabbing events and occasionally engendered momentous (hence, historic) turning points in policy, legislation, and public perception. This historical movement followed two different trajectories. While reform was predicated on notions of progress and historical linearity, the concept of social discovery—at the heart of reform and investigation—entailed repetition and circularity. The persistent urge to open previously enclosed spaces or other locales of perceived violation and abuse for inspection required (then and ever since) the recurring identification of old regimes and horrifying Bastilles. Sequences of discovery and rediscovery have been inscribed into post-Enlightenment public discourse. It has been therefore one element in the cultural work of social investigations to literally and figuratively write history. At the same time, they have sustained the ghost of the unreformed order of things.

The print archive was an archive of facts. The following analysis describes several techniques employed to verify information and to represent reality (social and other) on the printed page. In the early decades of the nineteenth century, facts were expected to be "authentic" rather than "objective." These concepts support somewhat different notions of factuality. Objectivity became a predominant quality, as in "objective journalism," only later in the century. (At the turn of the twentieth century, the role of "objectivity" in the fields of social knowledge—social work, social science, reform—was in fact contested as it would be again by the end of the century.) Social observers incessantly employed the adjectival modifier *authentic* to describe factual matter. In addition, they toiled hard to convince readers that they were presenting facts in their immaculate form, precisely as they were uprooted from their original soil—as if smidges of earth were still hanging from them as a measure of authenticity. Nineteenth-century social inquiries were formalized in a culture that had already been conditioned to associate print with the rendering of facts, either in journalism, science, or, as importantly, the law.

From its inception, modern science was inseparable from the printing press. This intimacy is evident whether one subscribes to the argument that the invention and spread of movable type during the Renaissance stabilized scientific intercourse by affording what Elisabeth Eisenstein termed *typographical fixity*, or to the more historically textured approach according to which only in the seventeenth century and later—when the state regulated the book market and institutions such as the Royal Society established publishing procedures—could a culture of credit rather than a technology of print guarantee truth in the scientific text, as Adrian Johns recently contended in *The Nature of the Book* (1998). Johns's view that in order to become a successful author of scientific tracts in the early modern period one had to be savvy about the machinery, the labor, and the professions of print also might be applicable to the world of the Victorian social reporter and certainly to the work of the naturalist or western explorer. Nineteenth-century social inquiries fueled public debates with printed texts of varying sizes and authority; these were embellished by genres of representation categorized as facts, among them statistical charts, testimonials, social maps, personal journals, and illustrations. These reports, along with a freer and more vitriolic press and new types of literary expression, battled and dialogued in an effort to document social predicaments and, simultaneously, to argue for specific solutions. The production of social facts took place in particular sites—factories, slums, prisons, the South—each bolstering micro-economies of knowledge, a textual wealth of journalistic reporting, travel accounts, fiction, and social inquiry.

An expansive notion of an economy of knowledge is necessary here. The commerce of knowledge in society and of social knowledge followed diverse procedures. On occasion, it hinged on the rules of the marketplace itself, where information was bartered or sold as a commodity (as books and newspapers are traded), but information changed hands by other means as well. It could be obtained by authority, deception, appropriation, surveillance, or sheer theft. A few of these methods might be rather innocuous, for instance, the custom of newspapers to excerpt each other or to lift passages of government documents without the need for permission. Legislatures and governments (as well as political parties, especially in the United States) assumed primary roles in the configuration of this new public culture. The state was certainly not the only agent trafficking in social facts or seeking reading constituencies. Indeed, government entered into a few fields of knowledge quite late. Regardless of timing, it always had to compete with enterprising reform associations or individual philanthropists and journalists who churned out countless treatises and annual reports on the underprivileged. Voluntary public associations, which proliferated after 1830, had at their disposal an impressive publishing apparatus. In the United States, this means of public education had emerged in previous decades as waves of revivals, known as the Second Great Awakening, propped up a book-making infrastructure driven by demand for Bibles and religious tracts.

Nevertheless, by the 1830s, the British state sponsored the most comprehensive social surveys, and in the United States, state and local governments began to engage in social policy. Many reform causes sought legislation or state sponsorship of one kind or another. Reform associations took upon themselves the task of representing the poor and their circumstances—an assignment that sooner or later, directly or vicariously, the state itself assumed. Also bear in mind that the state regulated the circulation of printed matter. One way or another, the social report always had the state on its horizon and, vice versa, the state had society (or policy) on its horizon.

Patterns of investigation and publication in Britain and the United States reflected the temper of these representative governments and typified public arenas nurtured by a series of tense conflicts that were devised as discursive exchanges or debates. After the turn of the twentieth century, peppering public deliberation with factual matter became an even more essential task for the state but increasingly was done under the signs of science, information, and expertise. While one way to evaluate the historical importance of the practices described in this book might be to regard them as precursors of the modern, knowledge-laden public sphere, there were significant breaks between the nineteenth-century and the twenty-first century informational states. In the middle of the nineteenth century, for example, the production of knowledge was not dominated by a strong, institutionalized, social science. In fact, the difference between social science proper and the kind of investigative work performed by government agencies, presidential task forces, royal commissions, or legislatures endured into the twentieth century. I maintain that state-sponsored social and policy reportage constitutes a distinctive political-discursive form that predates and coexists with professional social science. This distinction rests, in part, on the representational capacities of official investigations and their affinity with traditional legislative inquests, the type of inquiries performed by congressional or parliamentary committees as part of oversight responsibilities. These procedures are closer to common law methods of determining facts than to the modalities of modern science. Many official investigations, regardless of subject matter, adopt courtlike practices in line with parliamentary or congressional traditions.

This study also highlights aspects of public life that became less visible with the additional systemization of knowledge production but never really disappeared, for instance, the modern state's predilection to enhance its extraparliamentary representational faculties in times of crisis. New Deal documentary projects of the 1930s spring to mind. Franklin D. Roosevelt's administration sponsored these efforts to depict Depression-stricken social groups and to record and commemorate authentic regional culture.

Representation

Print statism was central to the new politics of representation. But what is "representation," and how is it tied to exchange, communication, and substitution? At the outset of her classic study *The Concept of Representation* (1967) Hanna Pitkin maintains that despite its elusiveness, the concept of representation in politics and in the arts, "taken generally, means the making present *in some sense* of something which is nevertheless *not* present literally or in fact . . . in representation something not literally present is considered as present in a nonliteral sense."[2] Three applications in Pitkin's typology of representational functions are especially relevant to our discussion. First, the notion that representation is (or should) be descriptive; a person or thing stands for others by being acceptably like them, and therefore the absent is made present by "resemblance or reflection as in a mirror or in art." In politics, this approach conceives of the legislature as a miniature version of the people. In the name of achieving a more precise likeness, its proponents frequently call for proportional representation. Second is the idea of symbolic representation or representation through symbols where no resemblance or reflection is required, as in the manner by which the king or other leaders represent the nation or a flag represents the state. Both approaches regard representation in terms of "standing for" something else. Third is the application of representation in the sense of "acting for," performing duties and functions on behalf of somebody else. This notion foregrounds the function of representative bodies in making law or policy for the people rather than merely operating as a mouthpiece for the unmediated wishes of voters. (Pitkin's classification is pertinent even if, unlike her, we accept that the process of representation partakes in constituting subjects rather than simply substituting for them.)

Explicit and implicit aspects of representation were manifest at every stage of investigation and reportage in nineteenth-century Britain and the United States. Commissioned individuals who conducted social surveys acted for government as its delegates—usually equipped with a detailed list of instructions—but in the field they also stood for the state. They symbolized the state and even attempted to deliver government messages or to explain its measures and policies to their local counterparts. Conversely, investigators represented investigated populations or environments, either by producing accounts that depicted these groups or places as part of their commission, by taking upon themselves to speak on behalf of the downtrodden, or, more rarely, by cultivating strong resemblance to the societies under investigation either as a means to acquire information or because of a deep-seated identification. In the field (slums, factories, Indian reservations, the conquered South), investigators were also on the lookout for representative witnesses. Here too we may recognize diverse modes of representation. First, the "representative" stood for the typical or average. Her ordinariness could be vouched for by the randomness of the encounter (as in sampling), or she might be the composite persona conjured through the power of statistical representation. Second, inquiries attempted to engage the actual leaders or representatives of the local population (as in trade union leadership or Indian chiefs). The third understanding invokes the conception elaborated in Ralph Waldo Emerson's essay *Representative Men* (1850): inspiring models of self-sufficiency, self-making, heroism, and social climbing, or, the representative man's double, an individual who could attest to particularly extreme forms of suffering and deprivation.

A plethora of representational tasks surrounded the official report and its distribution. Reports described in great minutia the social strata or the institutions under inspection. State publications in general were also expected to represent government descriptively (by detailing the course of the investigation) or symbolically (for instance, in the physical attributes of reports as books). Circulating these tomes, government offices and legislators endeavored to satisfy the demand for accountability—another dimension of political representation. As mentioned earlier, the project of social investigation itself was sometimes conceived of in terms that imply virtual representation, giving voice to those otherwise not politically represented. Recurrent public allegations of misrepresentation were another telltale sign of representational work. On occasion, these charges were leveled at government accounts. In other instances, the cry of "misrepresentation" prompted formal investigation.

Wide expectations that state-initiated reportage, print statism, would represent local society became evident when such an endeavor failed to deliver. An extreme example involves the infamous 1847 Commission on Education in Wales. Its report portrayed Welsh society in derogatory terms and blamed the Welsh language in particular for hindering progress. These insults coming from the pens of English (and Anglican) commissioners and from the printing press of government in London incensed Welsh public opinion. The report became known as the "treachery of blue books" and lingered in Welsh popular memory as an atrocious violation, akin to Cromwell's seventeenth-century massacres in Irish national imagination. For the purpose of this discussion, the most striking aspect of this episode is that before the nineteenth century such comparison between mass slaughter and a slighting official report would not have made much sense. One of the report's staunchest critics, Henry Richard, opined in 1868, more than twenty years after the fact, that the real Welsh nation was comprised of those who had not been heard by the commission and consequently remained without a voice.[3] The commission thus did not misrecognize or misrepresent the modern Welsh nation as much as inadvertently call it into being.

These and other intertwined and multivalent representational tasks, accents, expectations, and ambitions were greatly shaped by the strong involvement of representative legislatures in unleashing investigations or supervising the publication of official documents. It is also of some importance that a few of the most influential political thinkers of the period conceived of democracy in terms of descriptive representation. Writers required that the legislature be a mirror of the nation, that it reflect the people, the state of public consciousness, or the transformation of social and economical forces in the nation. In John Stuart Mill's view, in addition to watching and controlling the government, Parliament is also the state's "Congress of Opinion, an arena in which not only the general opinion of the nation, but that of every section of it, and as far as possible of every eminent individual whom it contains, can produce itself in full light and challenge discussion; where every person in the country may count upon finding somebody who speaks his mind."[4] Other visions about the mirroring function of government were articulated in the United States. For instance, John Adams argued that a legislative body ought to be "an exact portrait, in miniature, of the people at large, as it should think, feel, reason and act like them."[5] The essence of proportional representation (which was not the principle of representation in the two polities) is the idea of being present through one's voice.

Regardless of specific theories of representation or the particularities of national institutions, the representative work of representative regimes (and arguably of other regimes as well) should be recognized to be multifaceted and historically contingent. The politics of representation described in this book collapses the difference between political and aesthetic representation. Curiously, the term *representation* itself rarely surfaced in nineteenth-century discourse in conjunction with the state's informational mission. How might we account for this absence? One point to consider is contemporary public sphere ideology and its tendency to emphasize presence. The key concept of "public opinion" served to efface political mediation, to fill the gap between the public and its substitutes— elected representatives—by supposedly endowing all citizens of an opinion-based polity with a voice in national decision making. Likewise, the analogy that was sometimes established in Britain between official social investigations and the summoning of the entire public to partake in parliamentary-style grand debate sidestepped the difference between representative and direct democracies.

In this spirit, government reports were crafted to be transparent to both the field of inquiry and to the process of political decision making. The claim of transparency was buttressed by the employment of various representational techniques, including novel ones like high-quality lithography and, later, photography. Authenticity of facts denotes presence, while the notion of objectivity—usually associated with the ethos that guides the institutions and individuals that present those facts—acknowledges mediation. (Similarly, the mirror metaphor itself indicates presence rather than mediation or representation.) This ambivalence about political representation was not necessarily propelled by a strong democratic impulse. In fact, it often typified great concerns about electoral politics and majoritarianism. Early Victorian Britain grappled with unrest over the Chartist demand for universal suffrage. Antebellum reformers in the United States often grumbled about the excess of Jacksonian politics and its leveling effects. By the 1850s, many reformers held the rowdy, conspicuously corrupt, party politics in utter contempt. Social reportage was therefore sometimes a way to supplant electoral politics rather than merely supplement it.

Investigative activities and publications intermediated between government and the citizenry (understood as the reading public) but also between the "center" and the "periphery," between the state, expansively understood, and unknown or remote regions and people—making present what was, or appeared to be, absent—government and the nation's extremities. Mediation operated in a polity that appeared more cohesive (or even more democratic), while society, progressively shaped by the marketplace, became more differentiated and fragmented. Through the range of printed matter it offered the public, the state anticipated the reading subject to be a citizen—voter, lawmaker, or participant in national conversation—but also an actor in the marketplace, further bridging the gap between itself and "civil society." Ultimately, the state performances described here constituted only one form of communication in modernizing societies in which communication in general became increasingly mediated.

The new communicative field was replete with ambiguities. First, the state assumed contradictory positions as both subject and object of representation and investigation. Its dual role as a social reporter and a topic of reporting became at times a double-mirror entrapment. The investigated populations were also caught in seemingly opposing positions as subjects and objects. Social investigations in both countries questioned the subjectivity of the dependent population, their autonomy as individuals, their ability to make decisions, to sustain themselves in the market, to render an opinion, to be citizens. But specific investigative procedures often presupposed or even ensured this subjectivity. Thus, for instance, the U.S. Civil War investigation (see chapter 6), which looked into whether the newly emancipated freedmen could be full members in society and the polity, already guaranteed in a way their political subjectivity by allowing slaves and former slaves to give full public testimony, hitherto forbidden to them. Similarly, the project of social investigation in Britain (state-sponsored and otherwise) worked through the friction between the panoptic desire to forge or reform subjects according to middle-class models, and foundational middle-class assumptions about the autonomy of the subject or the notion of noninterference that guided the marketplace, where subjectivity was a priori assumed. Racial differences in the United States complicated both the wish to make the other and assumptions about his or her market suitability.

Beyond (and sometimes, instead of) the subjectivity of individuals, nineteenth-century social investigations recognized and even reinforced the collectivity of social groups. This was a collateral of the inquiry's representational work manifested in efforts to classify communities or to create typical or comprehensive descriptions of conditions and views. The drive to incorporate indigenous organizations and leaders into the investigations also acknowledged the group as a group. The representation of populations, regions, and communities in social reports paralleled the function of constituencies in electoral politics. As political theorist Melissa Williams observes, regardless of the current emphasis on the principle of one-man-one-vote (a relatively recent phenomenon), historically, doctrines of representation have been based on assumptions concerning groups and, therefore, "in most senses in which we use the term, *political representation* means the representation of a constituency, an aggregation or collection of citizens."[6] A third realm of ambiguities involved the very ambition to make the absent present. The project of social research was attached to the notion of discovery, of making known, present, or visible (as in bringing light to) previously hidden or suppressed social realities. As we shall see, common techniques of investigation and reporting militated against this sensibility by estranging or othering the field of inquiry and consequently sustaining it at some distance.

Notwithstanding its expansionist tendencies, the state enjoyed great authority but had limited power over this medium of mediation and exchange. It was ensnared, as much as its citizens and dependents, by these efforts at representation (i.e., rendered a subject and questioned as a subject). Many of the investigative projects and publication schemes described in this book resulted in failure or at least fell victim to the law of unintended consequences. There was much that was unpredicted, unplanned, and out of control in the state's accumulation and distribution of knowledge, projects that were often governed more by the political/bureaucratic unconscious than by well-articulated policies. To give an example, because of its new task as a social researcher and its decision to sell its official documents in the open market—the British state confronted in the late 1830s a liable suit (*Stockdale v. Hansard*) instigated by a casual remark made in a "blue book" on the condition of Newgate prison. The suit pitted Parliament against the courts, threatening a constitutional crisis. In the wake of this episode, the state was forced to reposition itself with respect to what Roger Chartier labels the "order of books," the legal/cultural system that governs the making, selling, and reading of books and prescribes, among other things, the range of rights and liabilities that are associated with authorship. Parliament had to reassert by law its speaking and publishing privileges.

Structure

The comparative component of this book serves as a form of organization and interpretation. It points to developments that exceeded national particularities, and yet the two cases are presented in some detail to avoid losing local flavor as well as the contingencies and intermittencies that are essential features of the historical record. The material is not forced into unbending variables, however. Exhibiting the American and the British experiences side by side allows them to serve as each other's context or frame. Thus, for example, the concurrence of the U.S. case highlights the conspicuous nation-building, or even patriotic aspects that were somewhat muffled in the British project of domestic social exploration. (The fissures described in this project were clearer in the British domestic sphere than in the colonial context. Royal commissions worked in the empire, but the national focus in the 1830s and the 1840s was much closer to home.) At the same time, the British state's systematic role in documenting society assists us in finding greater coherence within otherwise seemingly disparate projects on the American scene. In the realm of similitude, the comparison demonstrates, for instance, the unsurpassable importance of legislatures in shaping public culture in self-described democracies. In the contemporary scholarly focus on state formation, bureaucracies take center stage while the continuing effects of parliamentary or congressional culture often go unnoticed.

Although unequal in their size and reach, the British and American governments were rather weak relative to state institutions in continental Europe. Neither nation had a very large or strong bureaucracy or any other organization that could generate widely acceptable knowledge about society. There were, however, important differences between the objects of inquiry and between the manners in which government documents traveled in the two nations, a dissimilitude that yields insights into divergent systems of power. The British government offered its papers for sale and thus, inadvertently, limited their actual circulation, relying on the press to disperse much of the information included in blue books and other such products. In the United States, for much of the period, the distribution of official documents was integrated into the relationships between lawmakers and their constituents. Massive numbers of officially published books and reports were sent gratis directly to voters.

The comparative approach is an analytical tool as well as a feature of the historical narrative. Social knowledge in the nineteenth century was garnered and generated in comparative contexts. Comparing groups, institutions, regions, and countries was a common strategy for gauging and categorizing social phenomena. The comparative style rhetorically placed public issues within particular frames of reference and sometimes borrowed from the vocabularies of other societies, for example, the notion that the American racial hierarchy was akin to the caste system in India. There was a lively interchange of reports and social explorers between the United States and Britain in addition to other strong professional and personal ties, especially between the coterie of Boston reformers and their British counterparts. In the fields of print and publication, the British Parliament and the U.S. Congress were not merely aware of each other's contributions but, in an ironic twist, took each other as role models.

Since print culture undergirded the new politics of representation, the first part of the book focuses on the operation of governments as publishers. Here social reports are discussed among remarkably diverse print products. Chapter 1 explores Parliament's enormous publishing output on the social arena as well as on trade, law, administration, and other aspects of British public life. The chapter follows efforts made at the beginning of the nineteenth century to overhaul and rationalize the British knowledge policy and the subsequent schemes proposed to find readers for official papers. Chapter 2 analyzes large-scale publishing projects supported by the U.S. Congress and congressional disputes concerning the state's informational mission. Chapter 3 examines the publication of expedition accounts during the 1840s and 1850s. Through a discussion of select case studies, I show the development of a particular sense of authorship among government officials, the emergence of generic rules in western reporting, and finally (using a collection of close to a thousand applications for volumes of the 1850s Pacific Railroad expeditions) the great public desire to acquire or even collect state documents. All three chapters engage the relationship between governments, authors, and readers.

The second and third parts of the book examine more closely the work of social investigators in the field and at their writing desks. Chapter 4 focuses on a uniquely British institution, the royal commission of inquiry, and its relation to other types of official probes, namely, the workings of inspectorates, which were established to supervise new laws regarding poor relief, child labor, and mine safety, as well as parliamentary investigations conducted by select committees. The chapter delineates the course of action taken by a host of commissions, in particular the exertions of petty officials who populated the lower rungs of the new bodies. It describes the techniques devised to elicit cooperation, and the complicity or resistance exhibited by the lower classes, the object of official attention. Investigative practices offered the investigated communities numerous possibilities of mimicry and parody, but investigators could also use imitation or impersonation to obtain or to authenticate information. Field investigators in both countries occasionally assumed a precarious position as mediators between the scenes of social malady (or remote peoples and lands) and respectable society.

Chapter 5 considers the making and the diffusion of the literary products of British officials, their "bureaucratic poetics." It follows the process of crafting official reports, including the interaction among officials/writers of what were in effect multiauthored documents. Whereas chapter 2 scrutinizes the state's preoccupation with readers and reading, this discussion details strategies exploited by readers to intercept and appropriate official publications. Here, as in the previous chapter, I examine in what ways the investigation as a practice and the report as a text functioned to incorporate the investigated population into society, and under what terms.

Chapter 6 focuses on a single case study of social investigation. The American Freedmen's Inquiry Commission was a three-man board appointed in March 1863 by the Secretary of War to explore the condition of and future policy toward former slaves. The Freedmen's Commission traveled to the South and Canada to examine in different settings the "aptitude" and wish of former slaves to live under freedom. A profound ambiguity concerning the status of these freedmen as either racial others or products of slavery (the free market's other) dominated, in fact, overwhelmed the commission's work. This chapter describes these and other conceptual and practical conundrums that emanated from the decision to define the freedmen question as a problem of knowledge under official state investigation. My case study exemplifies the tension between government's desire to master social knowledge and knowledge's endemic ungovernmentability.

The third part of the book explores a few 1840s and 1850s studies of American Indian tribes, research that was conducted during a time of great public dispute over the federal removal policy, the future of the native peoples, and even the status of the aboriginal as fully human. Chapter 7 examines Henry Rowe Schoolcraft's two state-sponsored projects, first his study of the Iroquois nations on behalf of the state of New York, a survey that coupled a census with ethnographical work, and second, his mammoth work for Congress on the Indian tribes of America. Schoolcraft's work demonstrates how the preservation and representation of aboriginal culture turned into a state mission, justified either as a duty for the Indian or as an effort to create a new American identity. Chapter 8 analyzes Lewis Henry Morgan's own pioneering research of the Iroquois, some of which he conducted under the auspices of New York State. The chapter follows Morgan's membership in the New League of the Iroquois—a group of young professionals who "played Indians" as a pastime—to explore the relationship between racial masquerade and social investigation.

As for the period selected, the origins of the investigative routines described here may be traced to the end of the eighteenth century, if not earlier. Nevertheless, during the 1830s this new political culture received its fullest expression following the Reform Act in Britain and the emergence of the two-party system in the United States. This study focuses on the middle decades of the century through the late 1850s in Britain and the early 1870s in the United States. The concluding third of the nineteenth century was characterized by increased focus on the results of industrialization and labor disputes (in the United States) and the colonial world (in Britain), a succession of political reforms in Britain (with additional expansions of the national electorate in 1867 and 1884–85), and a more controlled production and growing transmission of information with the rise of expert institutions.

This book is based on archival research and draws upon current theoretical debates over knowledge, print culture, and the state, as well as over the nature and the history of the "public sphere." In addition to state reports and other official papers, sources include private and official correspondence, unpublished papers of governmental departments or congressional committees, records of congressional and parliamentary debates, and review magazines (or daily newspapers) where many reports were excerpted and critiqued. Some informational projects are not included in this study; arguably, the most important are the ambitious national censuses both governments conducted. This topic has already received ample scholarly attention. Furthermore, the census seems closer in nature to conventional forms of representational politics rather than the politics of representation described in this book. The census came into being as a device to organize and maintain the electoral system. This was certainly the case in the United States, which inaugurated its national census in 1790, a decade before Britain. Heads were counted in order to outline electoral districts, and although not every individual enumerated was entitled to vote (e.g., women, minors, and particular minorities), they were, through some means, represented in national institutions. The census and social investigations therefore involve somewhat different elicitation of voice. Census enumeration is conducted under conditions of anonymity. The identity of individuals is kept from public view and is largely irrelevant to the purposes of this undertaking, but the census leads to the expression of the aggregate political voice of the nation through the ballot. Both modern techniques of voting and the census schedule are linked to periodicity, anonymity, and result in "bounded totals."[7] In contrast, in public investigations where the inquiry itself was expected to produce representations, voice and representation collided.

A word about terminology: this study calls attention to the institutional diversity of the state, especially the division between the legislative and the executive branches. In most cases, I circumvent the confusion inherent in the concept of *government* that connotes either the executive branch or a comprehensive political system, which includes the executive branch, by assigning the term *government* to the administration in the United States or to the "ministry" in Britain.

PART I

MONUMENTS IN PRINT

The State as a Publisher

The first report of the Royal Commission on the Employment of Children (1842) prompted outrage. Its depiction of child labor cruelties in mines and collieries shocked Britain. In the United States, John Charles Frémont's accounts on his first two expeditions to the Rocky Mountains and to California (1842–44) dazzled the public mind and heralded the age of the "Great Reconnaissance." Free of copyright restrictions, the two documents were reprinted by private publishers looking for a quick profit and then circulated in more than ten thousand copies each. Emigrants riding on the trails to the American West had copies of Frémont's reports in their wagons. In Britain, the Employment of Children report—probably the most widely read document of its kind—created a sensation, in part because it featured illustrations of half-naked females laboring in dire conditions. As alarming, the document alleged that work encouraged promiscuity and illegitimacy among women, rendering them dangerously unfit for their domestic duties as wives and mothers.

Social investigations and expeditions had much in common, and their similarities did not escape contemporaries. Edwin Chadwick, the famous Victorian reformer, saw in the mines investigation the unearthing of previously unknown human tribes in remote lands. In the *Quarterly Review,* he enthused that "modes of existence" were revealed to the reading public "as strange and as new as the wildest dreams of fiction."[1] But these distinct enterprises on opposite sides of the Atlantic—western expeditions and social investigations—were even more alike than most Victorian observers realized, and shared much beyond the affinity between natural history and the nascent social sciences. Both projects featured central governments dispatching commissioned investigators to visit lesser-known locales. Both supposedly deployed modern tools with which to devise pol-

icy but were actually driven by comparable and rather straightforward political purposes. Through investigation of the employment of children
and similar inquiries, the British state defined social problems and specific groups of people as under its national jurisdiction. Extension of a
somewhat different kind propelled Frémont's expeditions. The U.S. government endeavored to study and consequently to Americanize the West,
its rocks, mountains, and native peoples. Frémont's explorations were in
fact a ploy of the Democratic Party led by Frémont's father-in-law, Senator Thomas Hart Benton from Missouri, to justify further expansion anchored in "manifest destiny." In Britain, a Tory member of parliament,
Lord Ashley (later, the Seventh Earl Shaftesbury), initiated the mines inquiry not so much to accumulate new information as to promote the short
workday by restricting child labor in industries not covered by previous
factory legislation.

Both projects were invested in concurrently discovering and estranging their respective subject matters, rendering them familiar, almost
tangible, and at the same time removed and in need of representation.
They correspondingly betrayed a sensibility of being on the edge of
something formidable. In one of the best-known passages of his first expedition narrative, Frémont described himself standing next to an American flag he had just hoisted on what he mistakenly thought to be the
tallest summit in the Rockies. There, he contemplated the sublime while
peering over the majestic yet terrifying abyss. The silence was inter-
rupted only by a single bumblebee, which was duly captured and put into
a book otherwise used to dry botanic specimens.[2] The British royal commissioners crawled in damp tunnels deep into the belly of the earth, risk-
ing their own health, gathering chilling stories of little children laboring alone in the abiding darkness of narrow mine shafts. These reports
also shared a style that coupled scientific measurements (meteorology,
botany, zoology, and geology in one case; pediatric medicine, morphol-
ogy, and geology, in the other) with anecdotal, on-the-spot experiences of
investigators retold in the languages of marvel, terror, and disbelief. Statistics and spectacle worked side by side in these texts. The British report
contained unprecedented illustrations of mining procedures and child
laborers. Frémont's accounts featured engravings of novel landscapes and
of fossils, plants, and animals. Although Frémont's main narrative proceeded chronologically, while the mine report was edited thematically,
the two documents recorded a continuum of men and environment:

John C. Frémont plants the American flag on top of the Rockies during his 1842 expedition. This heroic rendition of an episode documented in his enormously popular official report appeared in an 1856 campaign biography of Frémont by John Bigelow. That year the soldier-explorer became the nascent Republican Party's first presidential candidate.

miners' bodies deformed by life in the pit, and people hardened by life in the West. The latter featured Frémont's colorful entourage, most notably that paradigmatic Rocky Mountain rough Christopher "Kit" Carson (another "discovery" of Frémont's expeditions) as well as indigenous peoples.

For our discussion, the most significant aspect of these two ventures is that both yielded documents produced by officials assuming the mantle of authorship and by states that sponsored protracted publishing processes. The publication of official documents became part of governance in the nineteenth-century United States and Britain. Publication constituted an arena of action in which the state could demonstrate its might or, alternatively, as we shall see, expose its incompetence. Reporting protocols were essential to the dynamics of commissioning. They completed the field execution of investigation or exploration. Nonetheless, there was never a simple linearity between government actions and the volume or design of its publications. In Britain, the proliferation of blue books certainly exemplified legislative activism and the collateral short bursts of bureaucratic growth. But even there, debates over the publication of official reports displayed a panoply of views concerning the role of the state in the market of information, expectations that exceeded the simple task of official reportage. The comparison between the two national cases further accentuates the point. Despite its steadily growing tasks the federal apparatus remained, until the Civil War and beyond, small and largely nonintrusive in matters of social policy. Yet, the U.S. government invested in lavish publishing projects incommensurable with its size and scope. Compared with Parliament's dreary and cheaply bound blue books, some of the great exploration reports were exceptionally well-crafted volumes featuring dozens of vividly colored lithographs and woodcuts beside expedition narratives, statistics, and scientific monographs. (In the United States, the term *blue book* was reserved for registers of government officials.)

The first part of this book explores the intersection of print culture and political culture. The British state (in the early modern period, predominantly the crown) had been involved with printing ever since Caxton set up his press at Westminster in 1476. By the end of the eighteenth century, government sponsored extensive legislation that regulated the work of printers as well as stationers, booksellers, and authors. In the early modern period, the British state maintained as its prerogative the right to issue authorized translations of the Bible, Acts of Parliament, the *Book of Common Prayer*, almanacs, and more—all profitable workhorses of the book industry that were dispensed by patents and grants to a Byzantine universe of privileged printers. In antebellum America, public printing also became a notorious domain of political patronage. Our discussion, however, presents the state in a new role, not merely as a dispenser of printing assignments or a regulator of print culture but as an actual publisher responsible for much of the document's life cycle: production, including printing, binding, and sometimes embossing, engraving, and lithographing; promotion; and circulation. The British and American states published printed documents that were often packaged as books and peddled as news or information, in line with other vehicles such as newspapers, magazines, and political pamphlets.

The state's reinvigorated presence in the arena of books and information was in part due to the entrepreneurial spirit of government officials. But the production itself was largely controlled by the legislature at least until late in the century. Blue books occupied a niche in the vast array of parliamentary documents, and Congress initiated and supervised most federal publications. This is particularly important since in the two countries the labor of the legislature (floor debates as well as committee work) molded public discourse in terms of content and modes of conversation. Communicating details about, and arguing over, parliamentary exchange constituted a key element of the print-based public sphere in Britain. The press assumed much of this task and habitually used state publications as its source. In the United States, a wide diffusion of political information, including news about congressional debates, relied on the privileges Congress conferred on newspapers, supplemented (in the early decades of the century) by circular letters congressmen sent back to their home districts.

The vast distribution of Frémont's and the Employment of Children's reports beyond a small group of decision makers served strong evangelical (rather than merely utilitarian) agendas, whether the aim was to draw public attention to the grandeur and promise of the soon-to-be-conquered territories or to the misery of mine work. Circulation of official reports had other objectives as well. In the case of explorations, the conventions of science required publication. Moreover, the printed document, or its consumption, simulated or reproduced the act of discovery itself. Whereas Chadwick compared the effect of factual reports to the power of fiction, Senator Benton made an analogy between the explorer and the reader. In yet another rendition of the archaic "book of nature" metaphor, he wrote that Frémont was anxious to investigate the large terrain between Salt Lake and the Sierra; it was "a sealed book, which he longed to open and read."[3]

A few congressional publishing projects had explicit patriotic ratio-

nales. These included the "founding fathers'" papers and, by the late
1840s, reports of explorations of western routes, nature, and peoples. National aspirations underlay the desire to record and to appropriate Indian
culture as an expression of a distinct American identity. Such motivation
was paramount in congressional support for Henry Rowe Schoolcraft's
six volumes on the Indian tribes of America (1851–57) or, to give another
example, in the particular details of the American flag that Frémont employed in the Rockies, which featured at the center of its circle of stars
an Indian peace pipe. Britain seemed keener on building the state than
defining the nation. But the latter task was implicit, ostensibly an effect
rather than a driving force in investigative enterprises, and always appeared in some equilibrium with the meticulous effort to contemplate
and register the social sphere. In comparison with congressional print
products, parliamentary papers were more uniformly executed albeit less
elaborate documents. Still, in their enormous size and scope these publications provided a medium of representation as monumental as the famously ostentatious congressional publishing enterprises.

We should also keep in mind that by the nineteenth century print culture was inextricably tied to national cultures. In the eighteenth century,
culture emerged as a connecting tissue between the state and its citizens.
The idea of an indigenous literature rooted in national languages epitomized this function. By the mid-nineteenth century, the state itself became a cultural force, producing official literature that, in turn, shaped
genres of fiction and nonfiction. One example was the affinities between
characters and plots that appeared in official blue books and in Victorian
novels, especially the genre of the industrial novel, which documented
the social upheaval brought about by the new industrial regime. About
the now largely forgotten author Charles Reade, it was said rather dismissively that his great gift was to convert parliamentary reports into
works of fiction. "No man but he can make a blue-book live and yet, be
a blue-book still."[4] Subgenres of print statism thus resonated particularly
well with recognizable discourses of national expressions: social novels
and political economy in Britain, and the frontier novel and later the
"western" in the United States. Similarly, Schoolcraft's Indian project inspired Henry Wadsworth Longfellow's enormously popular *The Song of
Hiawatha* (1855), while bits of Charles Wilkes's *Narrative of the United
States Exploring Expedition* (1844) found their way into Herman Melville's *Moby Dick, or, The Whale* (1851). It was not a coincidence that the

federal government's accelerated production of books and reports occurred during the mid-1840s through the late 1850s, which historian William Charvart labeled "America's first great literary boom."[5]

The steady outpouring of state-originated documentary reports could
bolster or configure national sentiment, either by their content, their materiality, or by the virtue of their repetition. This is analogous to the implicit distinction in Benedict Anderson's analysis in *Imagined Communities* between the imaginary function directly tied to the discursive
particularity of a text, an institution, or a ritual—a specific novel, for instance—and the imaginary work performed by the regularity or repeti-
tiveness of publishing a text or performing a ritual. The paradigm for
the latter is the newspaper, which fosters a community of readers by facilitating an affiliation that is renewed each and every day in a manner
independent of the content of the paper—but not independent of the
boundaries of its circulation, language, format, and readership. Frémont's report could thus partake in nation building through the celebration of specific views about the American empire in an official report
published concurrently by the House of Representative and the Senate
and dispatched from the national Capitol to constituents across the land.
In addition, it inaugurated a long chain of similar efforts to explore and
report the West in what became a defining project for the national government.

The imaginary work of the state's official print output, however, was
polyvalent rather than merely propping up a unified nation as a site of
identification. Ironically, making the American West an object of imperial desire awakened sectional rather than national sentiments and ex-
pedited the disintegration of the Union. The census, which Anderson
regards as emblematic of national self-imagination for its claims to
represent the nation as a whole and as one, also fueled the sectional conflict between North and South (especially the controversial 1840 census).
Moreover, can anyone claim that the enumeration of African American
slaves according to the infamous three-fourths formula could possibly secure them a place in the American national consciousness? In Britain, the
documentation of society did not obscure but accentuated and normal-
ized class differences and class hierarchies. In both countries, production
of official reports was symptomatic of an increasingly segmented and
belligerent political arena. Perhaps, therefore, the community that print
statism helped cement was that of its reading public, or the "public

sphere" itself, which was now nationalized to a degree (but otherwise comprised of multiple communities or publics) and yet was neither a national "imagined community" of the kind theorized by Anderson, nor the classical bourgeois public sphere depicted by Jürgen Habermas. Dispensing information was also entangled with strong didacticism, which nineteenth-century governments embraced. In the United States, the pedagogical drive paralleled the emergence of the public school system, also supported by the states. In Britain, the notion of instructing the populace had a stronger paternalistic timbre, separating those who could partake in the national decision-making process, including the franchise, from those who were deemed deficient in this regard. In both countries, the complexity of issues that modern legislatures faced necessitated tutoring their members about topics such as the advanced machinery of production in cotton mills or the techniques of building railroads in the West.

The British and American states paid incessant tributes to the informative value of their publications, whether the knowledge released was expected to guide the decision-making process in the national legislature or the choices individual citizens had to make in the marketplace. But the modern concept of information was new to mid-nineteenth-century public discourse. What is information? How should we understand its association with print culture? (Turn of the twenty-first century anxieties over the demise of print culture in the digital bowels of cyberspace appear to invest these questions with novel poignancy.) The linguist Geoffrey Nunberg recently pointed to the role of the state in what he otherwise calls the "phenomenology of information." Nunberg's critique of information emphasizes its historicity and, as significantly, its materiality. Information is an impression, an effect that is experienced at the confluence of a routinized form such as the page of a newspaper, its recognizable authoring institutions (e.g., the *New York Times*), and other encoded daily practices like buying or subscribing to a newspaper. "The material properties of information, then—its morselization, its uniformity, its quantifiability—are the reifications material properties of the documents that inscribe it—their layout, their boundedness, the collective presence that establishes them as fixed places. By contrast the semantic properties that we ascribe to information—its objectivity and autonomy—are the reflexes of the institutions and practices that surround the use of these documents."[6]

Institutions and artifacts such as libraries, museums, daily newspapers, and card catalogues impose a specific matrix of registration on their content and concurrently strive for self-effacement. One aspect in the creation of such informational genres was therefore the suppression of explicit authorship in the document (and the suppression of the subject in the language of the document) and its subsequent replacement with institutional or phenomenal authorship. Many of the informational genres recognizable to us today appeared or were radically refashioned in the nineteenth century. Debates over official production and diffusion of documents alluded to information as a guiding principle, although the word *information* was employed at times in its old sense, to denote education, instruction, or *bildung* rather than in the ethereal, objective, and ubiquitous sense of the late-twentieth-century, fully blossomed "age of information." Nevertheless, by the middle of the nineteenth century, the concept of information in its modern use became a feature of public discourse.

The modern state indeed purposefully created important apparatuses to provide mass, uniform, transparent, and authorless facts. Most of the state's textual output, however, could not generate corresponding material and semantic properties to enable bodiless "information" as characterized by Nunberg. For one, in numerous documents knowledge was not and could not be arranged in any morselized, uniform, and easily accessible template (for instance, long transcripts of interviews). The form/authority nexus fell apart for other reasons as well. The materiality of public documents never ceased to attract notice. Likewise, government sponsorship of texts could never fully suppress either a personal authorship in the document or overt subjective language in the text. In this point the two national cases differ somewhat. The production of knowledge in blue books assumed the consistency of a standardized state project. By contrast, U.S. institutional authorship was weaker and the individuality of authors more pronounced. Observers in both counties contended that individuals exploited the power of the state to fulfill their personal ambitions. At certain moments, the state appeared to dissolve into the subjectivity of office holders and lawmakers, who simply could not resist the opportunity to be authors.

These and other dissonances and cracks in the state's informational performances occupy the following discussion. Such disjunctures demonstrate that the state's informational duties were often overwhelmed by its representational ambitions; in other words, the commitment to provide usable, accessible, and governable knowledge often proved incompatible with the state's desire to represent the populace or the national space, as well as with the penchant of national institutions and public officials to sustain vast public archives in print. As the next three chapters demonstrate, the value and utility of government-made knowledge as information and the separate question of the merit of official publications as books were persistently at issue in Britain and the United States. Early on and before the actual onset of the age of information, there was a lingering impression that state-sponsored knowledge was multiplying at a Malthusian pace, threatening to deluge its consumers. In both countries, official printing was deemed excessive in terms that foreshadowed twentieth-century fears about information explosion.

The problematic of double authorship—one associated with corporate institutions and the other attached to individual subjects—unfolded somewhat differently in distinct branches of government. Individual lawmakers wrote and signed documents (and famously lent their names to reports and pieces of legislation), but as the two episodes with which we began this introduction exemplify, the state official, whether a royal commissioner, inspector, or an officer in the Army Corps of Engineers, had a particular claim to authorship that was closer to the emerging nineteenth-century market understanding of this construct, albeit not similarly protected by law. The state official frequently wrote about his tasks and performance and, by implication, about himself. The degree of independence he enjoyed in the field, where the power of the central government was not entrenched, translated into a measure of autonomy he exercised in crafting a document. Furthermore, the power of the field investigator as an author seemed to parallel his authority as an intermediary between society and its margins.

Authorship as a social, political, and historical construct is among the insights my analysis borrows from the rich scholarship on the history and sociology of the book. The following discussion is also attentive to additional methods and emphases that guide contemporary studies of print culture: first, an awareness of the tangible dimensions of printed texts and how physical attributes generate and occlude meaning (sometimes in correspondence with, in other times in opposition to, the range of meanings that flow from the contents of texts); second, a holistic view of print culture that situates books within circuits of transmission in which authors and readers occupy various links in larger networks of production and consumption; third, a nuanced approach to the practices of actualizing texts (including the rituals and sites of reading) as well as other uses to which books are put, including collecting, recycling, and discarding.

As a subgenre in the history of the book, the report merits extended commentary here. Despite the indiscriminate application of the label *report* to designate diverse types of collated information, accounts, news, or even gossip, the act of reporting within a hierarchy marks or even determines its asymmetrical structure and the reporter's position within it. Paradoxically, then, the subjectivity of the official author was to a great extent an effect of his rather modest place in government, that is, his relative lack of authority and the consequent demand that he report to his superiors. Beyond the responsibility and vulnerability shared by all authors of texts, the government emissary's dual role as a reporter and an author indicated subjugation (reporting to authority) and control (over the text). These incongruent positions became harder to maintain when a report broke the chain of reporting and was interjected into public discourse where authorship was held in high esteem. The public career of Chadwick and Frémont as officials, authors, and official authors evidenced these contradictory paths.

The report, by its very nature, is always already in some kind of movement, changing hands. It was cited on its way to some department, sent to Congress, or presented in the House of Commons where bills were often reported and therefore were in their "report-stage." (*Reporting* is also commonly employed in parliamentary parlance to denote an account or a bill made by a segment of the whole, a committee to the entire chamber.) It is not surprising, therefore, that many reports were phrased or framed as letters. The epistolary feature brings the reporter closer to a genre of eighteenth- and nineteenth-century political pamphlets that were crafted as open letters. It also separates the report from modern informational genres. In contrast to the common understanding of information as a multitude of details that reside in inanimate receptacles independent of human exchange, for instance, computers—a perception, which is sustained today by content-blind Information Theory—informative reports, as a genre, are always addressed to institutional or individual recipients. The obligation of an administration or a ministry to report to the legislature was part of intricate power relations between the two branches of government. A prime minister could be caught reporting, too, although the monarch presented documents to the Commons "by command" and the president was often expected to send a "message." (The president's annual message epitomized the duty of the head of the executive to report routinely to the legislature and the people.) When a report concluded its travels in the corridors of power, it was moving again, integrated into the relationship between government (i.e., lawmakers and officials) and a host of social institutions, constituents, and the reading public. It was only when it no longer circulated—becoming more like yesterday's paper rather than the unsold book to which it was often compared—that the report lost most of its value. It was then that the print archive was consigned to the brick-and-mortar archive.

Although this study identifies the report as a form of mediated communication, in a few of its uses *report* denotes presence, as an officer is ordered to "report for duty," or employees are expected to "report themselves," which the *Oxford English Dictionary* defines as, "to make known to some authority that one has arrived or is present at a certain place." In one way or another, the report has retained a certain oral surplus. Rather than solely a manifestation of an emerging print culture, it is arguably a vehicle of *orature*. Orature—a term I borrow from postcolonial aesthetic theory—is a hybrid category that transcends the dichotomy between literature and orality. "[Orature] acknowledges that these modes of communication have produced one another interactively over time and that their historic operations may be usefully examined under the rubric performance."[7] The report is enveloped by a set of performances. The ceremonial air with which major policy reports are submitted to their initiating authority (a president, a secretary, a prime minister, the security council) is familiar today. Importantly, the transmission of the text is now usually accompanied by the presentation of the report to the public, often through the venue of a "press conference" where the authors of the report summarize their findings and recommendations and respond to questions. Presentation of reports included, at times, the public reading of the document or of specific segments. Here we may recognize the enduring influence of parliamentary practices on the culture of official reportage. Regardless of the fusion of print culture and politics, so much of the operation and so many of the traditions of Congress and Parliament had evolved around the spoken word. In the early nineteenth century, political culture on both sides of the Atlantic celebrated eloquence and oratorical flair, albeit in a somewhat different manner. (The British

Parliament's emphasis on orality has been so complete that it all but prohibited reading from prepared notes on its floor.)

Lastly, the centrality of "voice" to the political process and the potential of print statism to serve as a platform of opinion further tied oral expression and print culture. John Stuart Mill's famous testimony during an 1852 House of Lord's select committee hearing on India seems to embody the reliance of modern governments on technologies of record keeping. Mill boasted that the East India Company ruled India benevolently through an unsurpassed system of writing and reportage, for "no other [government] probably has a system of recordation so complete."[8] However, for Mill this modern apparatus of writing separated the colonial world from domestic governance. It was merely a necessary but flawed substitute for the kind of open and inherently oral and aural exchange that generated, in his conception, a regime of general public interest and public opinion back home in Britain.

CHAPTER ONE

Blue Books and the Market
of Information

The poor-law investigation (1832–34) ushered in one of the most drastic social reforms of nineteenth-century Britain. It also inaugurated or perfected modes of public persuasion that coupled the employment of a royal commission of inquiry with a massive circulation of printed texts. The publication of the Poor Law Commission's material began in late 1833, long before the investigation was completed. For the price of four shillings, the public could purchase a compilation of titillating "exemplifications" culled from assistant commissioners' notebooks. In that spirit, Commissioner Nassau Senior strategized, "We should make a gradual attack in public opinion. First, [publish] our instructions and queries. Then, the specimens of our evidence. Then, 6 weeks after, the full evidence. Then, two months after, the report, and then, measures could be prepared during the vacation and brought in at the beginning of next session."[1] After ten thousand copies of the report were sent to the parishes gratuitously, between four and five thousand copies of the abridged version and between nine and ten thousand copies of the report itself were sold to the public. Looking for even more compelling narratives, the Society for the Diffusion of Useful Knowledge (SDUK), one of the most prolific publishers of the 1830s and 1840s, commissioned Harriet Martineau to write four stories on the operation of the old poor law. Each tale in her *Poor Laws and Paupers Illustrated* (1833) corresponded to one of the four main questions that guided the commission's investigation. The tales purported to demonstrate the supposed abuses and corrupting effects of parish relief and the benefits of reform.

The collaboration of government with reform organizations, private booksellers (especially the commission's publisher Charles Knight, who also worked for the SDUK), parliamentary printers, and a novelist yielded an impressive spectrum of texts, from the thirteen-volume encyclopedic and impenetrable official report, to abridgments and pamphlets as well as popular fiction, all claiming to represent social reality. When criticized by SDUK members for the explicit nature of a murder scene in one of her narratives, Martineau invoked the official report. "It is singular that the incidents and expressions which [are] marked by my critics as questionable, are precisely those which are taken without alteration from the Poor Law Evidence, & from real life."[2] The diverse documents spawned by the poor-law investigation targeted different constituencies in what was—beyond an attempt to promote a particular reform—an effort at mass education, propagating the principles of political economy for the benefit of the entire nation, including Westminster lawmakers, poor-rates payers, and the laboring or nonworking poor.

A decade later, the Employment of Children investigation would also initiate massive distribution of an official report, which private publishers seized and reissued in edited versions. From the beginning of the century, booksellers often produced octavo editions of the most popular official documents, for instance, the Bullion Report of 1810 and the Mendicity and Vagrancy Report of 1815. Such market appropriations of official publications were permitted or even encouraged, for it was argued that Parliament published these documents for the sake of their wide diffusion. The policy of a sweeping permit to reproduce government reports, which usually were not shielded by copyright, was altered only at the end of the century when a private printing of Army Regulations caused public embarrassment.[3]

Regardless of their actual influence, large-scale, spectacular propaganda campaigns became staples of nineteenth-century political culture. Several of these episodes are stories often retold to demonstrate the manipulative character of Victorian reform and the Victorian palate for printed matter. For future generations, the poor-law crusade and its later renditions enhanced the (somewhat inaccurate) perception of a utilitarian takeover, most succinctly articulated in S. E. Finer's concept of "suscitation" to describe Jeremy Bentham's disciples' gift for exploiting public tools to peddle their ideas. The suspicion that official investigations are relentlessly exploited to market preconceived schemes also dates back to the nineteenth century. Still, in the Victorian mind, especially its liberal and utilitarian lobes, state knowledge had an intrinsic value beyond its immediate application. Victorians had great pride in the scope and apparent growing scientificity of the public record. Domestic and foreign observers noticed that the accumulation of social knowledge was an endeavor in which the British excelled, or a project that was particularly British.[4]

Known as command papers because they were presented to Parliament at the command of the monarch, royal commissions' reports were the most conspicuous in what became by the mid-nineteenth century an enormous production of parliamentary papers. Select committees of both houses also examined aspects of British society and issued blue books appended by long transcripts of hearings and additional documents. In comparison with the pomp of royal commissions, parliamentary inquiries constituted a rather mundane investigative pattern. Still, they attracted much attention. As in the case of royal commissions, the publication of select committees' reports turned, at times, into a public event.

This chapter surveys early nineteenth-century campaigns to reshape the British state's publishing apparatus. Reform targeted the production of blue books and other parliamentary papers as well as their promotion and dissemination. Market principles such as efficiency, value, competition, and frugality guided these perennial efforts. Most importantly, reformers reconceived of the British public sphere as a system of exchange commensurable with the dynamics of the marketplace and often took the commercial press as their paradigm for circulating knowledge. Beyond facilitating publicity, they vied to rearrange state knowledge itself, its accumulation and modes of registration. They envisioned a universally accessible great body of knowledge that would address every facet of British public life, a representative mirror image of the nation.

By the early 1850s, after more than two decades of hectic debate and reform, the celebratory view of knowledge-based legislation seemed to be fully in place and so were the technologies of gathering and disseminating information. In 1852, Benjamin Disraeli, then the chancellor of the exchequer, maintained that blue books attested to the intellectual development of the era. "If we looked to manners, if we looked to the means of Government not only in this country but its dependencies, and indeed, to all those subjects which ought to afford the materials whence the true history of a country was drawn, we should find that in the Parliamentary literature, which had grown into importance within the last half-century, resources were placed in the hands of the public writers, such as never had been before possessed in any time or country."[5]

The historian, Disraeli suggested, would judge the age not just by its known achievements but also by the thoroughness of the official record that was inscribed and left behind. Nevertheless, despite self-congratulatory declarations of the kind Disraeli offered and the appearance of normalcy in the production of official knowledge, there was a lingering confusion and division among lawmakers and state officials over parliamentary publications.[6] Recurrent debates concerning seemingly technical issues—number of documents to be printed, their size, and cost—betrayed greater dissatisfactions enhanced by the public's

uneven response. Government and Parliament were (desperately) seeking readers for their publications.

Many of the clefts in what otherwise appeared to be an article of Victorian
faith were linked to a dissonance between the ideology and the actuality of "information." This chapter demonstrates that the increased expectation that state
knowledge preserved in blue books would be regimented, transparent, and autonomous was disrupted by the diversity of purposes implicit in official reports,
their material dimensions, and the symbolic weight of printed texts. After all,
Parliament was not just gathering and dispensing information but, in reality, was
producing printed documents that were often labeled books (as in blue books,
named so for their blue paper covers). In the professional parlance of printing,
the publication of commissions' and committees' reports was known as "book-
work" while that of printing ledgers and other forms was known as "job-work."[7]
The printed medium—bulky, expensive to print, and difficult to utilize—had a
significant presence that sometimes obscured and even subsumed its content.

Tension emerged between clashing representational assignments. Victorian
lawmakers' and bureaucrats' ambition to provide useful information and to communicate with the public coexisted uncomfortably with their insistence on registering in great minutiae all aspects of British society and the governing process.
The concept of usable information denoted succinct, naked, out-of-context facts.
At the same time, officials deemed it necessary to render visible for observation
the process of accumulating information. In the liberal state, procedures of investigation, as other dimensions of government, were to be exposed to public
gaze. For example, reports of select committees' hearings had to include the entire course of witnesses' questioning, regardless of utility or readability. This resulted in a growing distance between the notion that information was vital for
political actors, lawmakers, and voters alike, and, as we shall see, the perception
that government was manufacturing reams of purposeless, or worse, self-indul-
gent printed matter. For some, government had become an incontinent printer.

Policy of Knowledge

Extensive deployment of royal commissions of inquiry was one element in a
new set of practices and institutions that shaped the modalities of the British
public sphere from the very beginning of the nineteenth century. This process
assumed a clearer form after 1830, when aristocratic Whigs, with their middle
class, utilitarian "fellow travelers," gained power. These innovations constituted
a comprehensive yet tacit policy of knowledge. For instance, reformers vied to

further open Parliament to press coverage and to unburden newspapers of the stamp duties that restricted their circulation and were now deemed "taxes on knowledge." (In 1836, the Stamp Tax was reduced to one penny, and in 1855 it was eliminated.) Another host of initiatives aimed at improving the accuracy and volume of state knowledge. An effort that was initially prompted by the exigencies and turmoil of the Napoleonic wars resulted in the creation of new tools to measure social and commercial phenomena through the census and the Board of Trade's statistical department. Parliamentary printing was a third domain of reform initiatives fueled by similar aspirations, the desire for more exact, comprehensive, and better-circulated information, dispensed by the cheapest and most efficient forms. One indication of the unifying principles underlying these efforts was that they were sponsored by the same small coterie, among them Edward Bulwer, Thomas Spring Rice, Joseph Hume, and Lord Brougham.

Two trends characterized this vortex of reform: first, the gradual consolidation of social research by central government in London at the expense of the periphery where such information had been previously accumulated by clergymen, magistrates, physicians and other local observers; second, the eventual guarantee of an unhampered diffusion of information to the largest number of readers by way of the press. The liberal state engaged in projects that, while they seemed to enhance each other, were contradictory. It assured the free flow of knowledge (in accordance with the principles of what Jürgen Habermas termed the bourgeois public sphere), while, at the same time, it was eager to control the quality and production of some of its most important fields. Disguised by the absence of a full separation of government branches, the new policy of knowledge intruded into the traditional methods of parliamentary inquest. The poor-law reform furnished an excellent example of how the Whig government resorted to extraparliamentary methods (a royal commission instead of a select committee, a private publisher instead of the official parliamentary printer) to promote its particular interest in Parliament. A year later (1833), a royal commission was instituted to modify the far-reaching child labor reform that had been charted by a select committee headed by the cabinet's foe, the Tory M.P. Michael Thomas Sadler. Contemporaries construed the Sadler Report and the Factory Commission's report as foot soldiers in a political battle.

The dynamics of parliamentary culture can empower individual members. Introduction of petitions, requests for particular information (or Returns), initiation of select committees, and participation in debates have been methods for the promulgation of views and promotion of causes beyond their actual weight in terms of political representation. Such practices, at times employed to shift attention to the margins of society, were somewhat restrained by 1830s reforms. It may not be surprising that two of the most vociferous critics of royal commissions of inquiry were, at one time or another, reporters of parliamentary deliberations: William Cobbett and J. Toumlin Smith. Cobbett saw in the entire process that yielded the new poor law—from investigation to publication—a deviation from accepted and proper practices. "These *commissioners* sit in London, it seems, and send forth roving deputy-commissioners to collect information about the country. These rovers give in written accounts of the result of their inquiries. A parcel of *extracts* from these accounts have been collected together, printed in the form of an octavo book, and sold at *price four shillings,* "PUBLISHED BY AUTHORITY"; and, the members of the House of Commons have each then been furnished with a copy of this book. This is a new way of doing the nation's business."[8]

Never before had members of a public board turned into authors and sold their books. A few months earlier, Cobbett quipped that the purpose of the commission was "to muster up a parcel of stories from the people, picked out for the purpose, to justify more severe measures against the working people."[9] Cobbett's concerns, it appears, lay less with the purity of the print marketplace and more with the autonomy of the radical public sphere (of which he was a prominent citizen) now threatened by an avalanche of cheap, manipulative literature.

Smith, who offered the harshest attack on the ascendancy of fixed and investigative commissions, further developed this critique. Commissions not only infringed upon old freedoms by assuming functions that were historically performed by local authorities but also departed from accepted modes of inquiry by eradicating the adversarial dimension that was at the core of the parliamentary hearing. The access of commissioners to the printing press was therefore particularly worrisome since "all evidence is taken in secret; and so much published as, and when, they like; and with such an accompanying *gloss* as they please to give it."[10] Manning an inquiry with like-minded individuals skewed the results by accentuating similarities in the body of evidence marshaled in front of the commission, while neglecting disagreements (dissimilitude). Smith invoked Bacon's warning against "anticipation," in other words, preference for similitude. Political rivalry in Parliament guaranteed that committees confronted contrasting evidence. According to Smith, the outcome of frequently appointed royal commissions was mass indoctrination, or, the "dwarfing of the minds of the people and reducing them to that state of only half-development that they shall be unable to know the difference between a sham and a reality, between truth and falsehood."[11]

The Matter of Facts

In the realm of parliamentary printing, reform offered yet another challenge to the inefficiencies and small corruptions of the old regime. It especially targeted Luke Hansard (and, after his death in 1828, his descendants), the official printer of the House of Commons. Hansard was the most important among a host of printers who, according to a decidedly antiquated system, controlled different shares of the printing tasks commissioned by the two houses of Parliament and the monarchy. However understood by rivals and reformers, Hansard's role in parliamentary printing was not a symptom of the British *ancien regime* but a response to the needs of the modern state. As did other innovations of the Victorian period, it dated back to the emergencies of the late eighteenth century and was the fruit of collaboration between Hansard and the future House of Commons' speaker Charles Abbot (1802–17).[12]

The papers on the abolition of the slave trade, East India Papers, and reports on finance and on the commercial intercourse in Ireland were among the most sought-after documents of the 1790s. The political crisis of the decade also made it necessary to improve communication between London and its provinces. In 1797, Abbot, then an M.P., initiated a plan for the dissemination of the statutes, assuring that a printed copy of every new act of Parliament would be sent to the courts of justice and public offices as soon as the legislation was completed. Previously, local justices of the peace had to rely on incomplete, and in many cases dated, private collections. Interestingly, Abbot's committee noted that with the advent of print new legislation received less publicity. The ancient mode of informing the public of new laws through sheriff's proclamation—in other words, through the local crier—had been discontinued, and the printed copies of the acts were confined to a limited number of individuals. Abbot was also involved in a committee to inquire into the state of the national record (1800) and, in the same year, introduced the bill that led to the first census. With the first Union Parliament in 1801, parliamentary printing accelerated. Despite efforts to restrain what seemed even then to be an avalanche, the printing capacities of the legislature and government only increased. By the 1820s, twenty-five committees might be working concurrently in the Commons. Sessional papers (without the bills, votes, and journals) amounted to more than twenty-five folio volumes. In 1799, the expense of printing the journals, votes, and all other papers was £8,000; in 1827 it rose to £46,184, exclusive of the journal, and by the 1850s it would more than double to £100,000 a year.[13]

Carrying printing proofs under his arm, Luke Hansard became a fixture in the halls of Parliament. Abbot considered his knowledge of printing, in its intricacies still very much a craft rather than a modern industry, indispensable. Hansard was also responsible for preserving and storing official documents and dispensing advice to the speaker on every aspect of publication. In the 1790s, the printer introduced a new template of printing, inaugurating the use of side annotations that led the reader to particular questions in the appendix or to previous acts, reports, and other official documents. He added indices, created his own system of abbreviates, and made decisions concerning the size of type, margins, and division of the page. These efforts set standards where there had not been much precedent. The disparate handwritten documents that arrived at his printing plant did not conform to any regular layout. Hansard selected a title for each manuscript. Then he drew a table of contents and added information in the margin. The printer was thus the de facto editor of parliamentary papers, even if he did not alter a single word in the body of the original texts. He gave parliamentary publications uniformity and the material appearance of a serial publishing project. Hansard was quite proud of the form parliamentary papers assumed, maintaining that they were printed "to the complete satisfaction of the Members who rejoiced at seeing unintelligible broadsheets brought into convenient reading pages."[14]

Previously, printers of official documents toiled hard to provide printed facsimiles of the original text. The Poor Returns of 1787, for instance, were printed page after page on wide sheets of paper that required folding. Printers were not allowed to deviate from the form or even the size of the manuscript. Hansard forsook the hopelessly clumsy attempt to simulate the authentic document, substituting one principle of fact rendering (fidelity to original form) for another (the claim of parliamentary documents to a corporate, commanding authorship). Official documents thereafter derived their authority in relation to each other and from their consistent adherence to a standard of printing. Embedded in the new materiality were assumptions about these documents' prospective use as reading material. Hansard avoided layouts that obstructed fluent reading, such as printing long lines across two pages.[15] Late eighteenth-century Encyclopedia-inspired ventures may have been his inspiration. He certainly did not take as a model the condensed page and small font of early nineteenth-century newspapers. Fonts were large and the page uncluttered. It was easy to read and, despite efforts to economize, expensive to print.

Reform

In the wake of the Napoleonic wars, parliamentary printing attracted hostile attention. The call for greater equity, efficiency, and economy had a particular resonance when the legislature was busy overhauling old institutions, including the poor-law apparatus, military appointments, and the Anglican Church. When it came to parliamentary literature, reform was self-referential and exemplary. The entire system of official printing, with its convoluted procedures and privileges, was an invitation for a reformist probe.[16] For example, sessional papers appeared in bound volumes and in appendices to journals. Some documents were printed concurrently by both houses (usually as "communicated papers," a custom that was finally abolished in 1886).

Patronage, sinecures, and fees were to be eradicated. Reformers now demanded competitive contracts in public printing. As revealed by repeated investigations, a few unelected officials of the Commons accepted copies of printed material for their personal gain. The custom of copy money was an equally unacceptable residue of the old system. The clerk of the Commons was entitled to a certain fee for all copies of papers ordered from his office. Every M.P. could receive an entire set of all the journals of both houses, more than 120 folio volumes. Many of these tomes resurfaced at local booksellers. The important 1835 Committee on Printed Papers recommended that M.P.s receive journals only for the years they served in Parliament.[17]

Lawmakers were joined by government officials who were habitually anxious about monitoring and restricting public expenditure (Treasury) or who simply wished to extend their authority over parliamentary printing (Stationery Office). Eyeing that most lucrative field of public printing, Hansard's commercial rivals also pushed for reform. In a long succession of select committees, M.P.s received lectures on the technical details and jargon of printing. They explored new printing patents and immersed themselves in the nitty-gritty of pica, columns, paper weight, and typesetting. Between 1831 and 1835, five committees explored every dimension of public printing. Heralding a new era of governmental takeover, the Treasury decided in 1831 that the Stationery Office would supply the paper used by parliamentary printers. There were also schemes to save money by introducing alterations to the layout of parliamentary reports by compressing the print and using double columns. Many lawmakers, however, became fond of Hansard's signatory page design. The printing status quo was perhaps harder to undermine when the speaker regarded many reform ideas as incursions into his power. Even after the appointment of a printing committee in the mid-1830s, the order of print remained with the speaker. Still, the Hansards had to be constantly on the defensive. In 1825, they responded to criticism about the long delays in printing by citing the enormous evidence taken on the question of Catholic emancipation, the large volume of copies printed, and the difficulty of hiring help in a busy industry. New types of information necessitated distinct printing skills. Many typesetters refused to handle statistical tables, finding this particular task too perplexing. In some publishing projects, individuals employed in arranging statistical tables had to be paid double.[18]

The controversies over the mechanism of printing and the disputes over the method of inquiry (royal commissions versus select committees) pitted the executive departments (Treasury, Stationery Office) against the Commons. (Hansard was supported by the Speaker's Office.) From 1791 until 1835, the House of Commons printer was responsible for everything except the votes. After that, many of the command papers, including the reports of the royal commissions (perhaps the most profitable of parliamentary printing) were executed by special contracts under the immediate supervision of the Stationery Office. In 1886, select committee reports were contracted out and in 1890 the journals.

Another dimension of reform addressed the growing recognition that parliamentary papers provided rich but inconsistent, patchy, and difficult-to-access knowledge. In 1833, a select committee alleged, "It has long been a matter of complaint with those who wished to become acquainted with the Statistics of the British Empire, that information was not given in Public Documents with the regularity and perspicuity which are indispensable in all inquiries of this nature."[19] Much of the statistical information was gathered as a response to private initiatives in the Commons. These returns corresponded to the queries and sometimes to the views of the individuals who had requested them. A Treasury official testified that a particular return on corn requested by an M.P. for the benefit of a single constituent took four clerks six weeks to prepare. Its printing cost no less than five or six hundred pounds, and, "when the Return was produced, I would defy any one to make one single practical point from it."[20]

John Marshall, a publisher of a statistical compilation, criticized the accounts provided for the House of Commons as truncated and puzzling. Parliamentary documents covered incommensurable periods and inconsistently blended figures from Britain and Ireland.[21] In assuming responsibility for the accumulation of complete and accurate statistical knowledge, government was engaged in a decidedly national project. It was also emulating a few continental countries that had already created advanced institutions with similar aims. For several reformers, abandoning such a vital task to private entrepreneurs was a stigma on the British state. The indefatigable radical Joseph Hume argued that in any other country government would undertake a project such as Marshall's compilations. Nicknamed by Harriet Martineau "the plodder of Parliament," Hume spearheaded the reform campaign and chaired four committees on printing. He was an avid supporter of the freedom of the press and fought for the repeal of the tax on newspapers and against government prosecution of pamphleteers.

A minute but typical element of the new knowledge policy was the decision to curtail the number of petitions slated for printing. The formal pretext was the unbridled proliferation of petitions sent to Parliament. Their number had risen from 880 in 1787 to 4,498 in 1815 and 24,492 in 1831.[22] Other calculations crept in as well. The clerk of the Commons argued that petitions became a way to disseminate views rather than merely call for legislative action: "There are many cases of Petitions which are more like Pamphlets than Petitions."[23] Indeed, William Cobbett urged his readers to pester Parliament with petitions in order to secure free publicity: "If you would have anything generally known, or any principle generally discussed, you cannot do better than embody it in a petition to Parliament. This is the only effectual way of drawing attention to it."[24]

In 1833, a select committee was appointed to classify petitions and arbitrate the merit of their publication, which was to be done mostly in the form of abstracts. The number of printed petitions declined sharply. The new regulations exemplified a trend to restrict public access to the exchange that took place inside and through Parliament. Parliament denied any intention of restraining the expression of public opinion. "The House ought to refrain from printing, at the public expense, such Petitions of individuals as are more in the nature of general disquisitions upon subjects of controversy, which ought rather, in their opinion to be given to the Public through the medium of the Press at the expense of the Author."[25] Unsolicited opinion had to comply with the rules of the market. The value of information and opinion could be signified, although not fully measured, by monetary exchange. It was the function of newspapers to represent public opinion. Importantly, it would also become the mission of state publications.

Another contemporaneous reform addressed the country's past rather than current record and led to the creation of the Public Record Office (1837). The PRO replaced the Commission of Records, which since the beginning of the century had been entrusted with preserving, indexing, and publishing historical documents. A cardinal charge against the commission was that only a small fraction of the money that poured into the project, more than £600,000, was dedicated to the actual conservation of records. Lavish publishing projects drained much of the rest. There were signs of mismanagement, and the commission was £20,000 in debt. The public record campaign demonstrated, in a field other than parliamentary printing, how a large publication project could be associated with the vagaries of an unreformed state rather than with the information and mnemonic technologies of modernity.

Charles Buller described in graphic detail how ancient documents rotted, scattered in damp vaults—one of which was reported to grow a stalactite—among the remains of rats and skeletons of dead cats, while the commission translated into a host of continental languages a document that acknowledged all commissioners by their full titles. Holding the Portuguese version, Buller mocked the commission (some of its members were present) for making their names known from Lisbon to Hamburg. "Even the Secretary to the Commission is immortalized in the printed proceedings as 'Viro illustri, excellentissimo, clarissimo, doctissimo C. P. Coopero equiti Anglo.'"[26] Other commission-sanctioned printing endeavors were riddled with horrendous typographical errors, duplications, and omissions. As it turned out, the commission sponsored the publication of modern essays and not just ancient documents. Meanwhile, the condition of the state's historical documents was truly appalling. Some of them were stolen and sold in local curiosity shops. The public record, contended Buller, was enormously valuable for ascertaining private property such as grants, leases, and conveyances by the crown to individuals and corporate bodies, and as a reliable source for history writing. Buller consequently chaired a select committee that proposed the creation of a centralized body to protect valuable documents, arrange them methodically, and render them easily available for public use, mainly for judicial and property purposes.

The familiar principles of efficiency and frugality determined both public record and parliamentary printing reforms. The establishment of a national repository indicated a preference for maintaining a collection of irreplaceable objects as facts for special consultation over a policy of mass reproduction of original documents. As we shall see, despite attempts to apply similar criteria to their preparation, blue books remained archival in their individual and collective comprehensiveness, detail, and immensity, as well as in their capacity to stand for or represent an era to posterity. In addition, they were archivelike because of the propensity to reproduce within them smaller papers, transcripts, notes, and other documents verbatim and to present these objects side by side in long appendices. The print archive functioned as its own literal archive, in the sense that once committed to print there was no incentive to retain the particular documents that had comprised it, for example, subcommissioners' notes. In many respects, the printed form was even more retentive than the repository archive. Much of what was consigned to it would have probably been otherwise discarded.

Marketplace

One of the most radical novelties of the new knowledge policy was the sale of parliamentary papers to the public at large, thus expanding and formalizing a custom previously applied mainly for parliamentary votes. The decision to sell the entire yield of the Commons' printer was proclaimed to be part of the new knowledge-saturated, censure-free public sphere. Previously, there was no clear policy for distributing parliamentary papers. M.P.s and privileged officeholders received a certain number of papers. Others had to apply. Hume envisaged a rational system unencumbered by the remnants of old privilege lists or official favors. Moreover, in contrast to early nineteenth-century circumstances, there was no crisis-born exigency that mandated the free-of-charge diffusion of statutes or other documents. Statutes too were to be sold. In August 1835, the Commons resolved, "Parliamentary Papers and Reports printed for the use of The House should be rendered accessible to the public, by purchase, at the lowest price they can be furnished; and that a sufficient number of extra copies shall be printed for that purpose."[27] Besides an attempt to ameliorate an unsatisfactory mode of dispensation, the decision to sell papers was embraced with an eye to limiting expenses.

The immediate result of the new policy (supposedly devised to increase the flow of information to the public) was to curb the volume of publication. According to one calculation, there was an immediate reduction of 5 percent in the number of copies printed. By the late 1830s, a typical run—previously between 1,000 and 4,000—shrank to between 1,000 and 1,250 copies and rarely exceeded 1,500.[28] It was argued that beforehand individual members could hardly exercise any judgment in the distribution of papers. They were pressured to respond to demands from their respective districts regardless of their actual merit. The new regulations avoided ineffectual examination of applications and made the documents accessible to everybody. They guaranteed that those in need of specific information indeed received it. This argument hinted at a gap between considerations of public knowledge that emphasized maximization of information, and an efficiency calculus that attached certain information to particular functions and agents in society. Ultimately, it seems that the prospective consumer was presumed to be a middle-class individual for whom the benefit from government information, legal, political or commercial, could be immediate and material.

Selling documents may have prevented a nuisance for members who had had to respond to tedious requests, but the sale policy reduced the power of individual M.P.s by completely seizing the allocation of documents from their hands. Not all legislators were satisfied with the novel arrangement that required them to pay for copies of every printed report or bill exceeding the single copy allotted to each of them. In early 1836, William Tooke, an M.P. from Truro, vented his frustrations after he had applied in vain for two copies of the Accidents in the Mines Report, which he thought his constituents in Cornwall should have. He intended to dispatch the report to two libraries in his district but was told that the documents had to be purchased. Tooke remarked wryly that it was easier for Hume, who represented Middlesex, to send his constituents to the shops where documents were sold, but when requests came from the country, only a few members would have the nerve to do the same. M.P.s should not be put to the expense of purchasing papers vital for their districts. He further complained that there was no place in the Commons to buy documents and members had to go to shops and ask for them as would any other customer. In response, the speaker, J. Abercromby, trumpeted the fairness argument. If these reports were to be granted to libraries in Cornwall, other institutions in all parts of the country would make similar requests. Libraries were among the establishments most likely to become extensive purchasers of documents, as they should. These papers, he reminded, were sold for only a halfpenny a sheet.[29] This was not the only incidence in which M.P.s expressed their anger at Hume and his crusade. Hansard's son, Luke Graves Hansard, whose diary detailed his painstaking efforts to maintain the family hold on the Commons' printing, saw in the new set of policies the spirit of cheap public projects. "There seems too much of the 'Diffusion of Knowledge' new scheme in this," he remarked.[30]

Nevertheless, the sale of parliamentary papers was initially celebrated as a success and was broadly advertised. Hansard had two London offices for the purpose of the sale, one close to the Inns of Court. Offices were set up in Dublin and Edinburgh as well. During the first years, the public purchased 29,715 copies of bills, reports, and accounts. While Hume planned to introduce into parliamentary business what were seemingly free-market principles (e.g., open competition), with the sale of documents, Parliament itself became a participant in the marketplace as a publisher of blue books and other printed ephemera, indiscriminately (although nonprofitably) offered. The Commons' involvement in the economy of printing was already evident in other aspects of the trade. The volume of official printing burdened the market for paper as early as the 1820s. Hansard, in fact, became a paper merchant, maintaining a £20,000 inventory to eliminate sharp trends in the market following sudden demands for parliamentary printing. The presence of Parliament in the marketplace also had some unexpected consequences. In January 1837, a mapmaker, James Wyld the Younger, threatened to pursue legal action for damages due to piracy. A map of Australia he had prepared appeared in an August 1836 report on transportation, a document that was printed and sold. Hansard had purchased and published the map by the order of the committee on printing. Wyld's silence was procured for £105, paid through Hansard.[31]

The most damaging repercussion of the decision to disseminate public documents was a constitutional crisis instigated by the Stockdale versus Hansard litigation. The affair began when prison inspectors William Crawford and the Rev. Whitworth Russell claimed, in their 1836 report on the state of discipline in Newgate prison, to have found in one of the cells (which they meticulously scanned and inventoried) a pornographic publication "of a most disgusting nature, and the plates are obscene and indecent in the extreme." The volume was nominally a medical book on human anatomy, titled *Robinson's Account of the Structure and Diseases of the Generative System* (1827). Subsequently, John Joseph Stockdale, the book's small-time publisher, sued Hansard for libel and found a sympathetic ear in the courts.

Selling the inspectors' report to the public was not the sole basis for the legal action. Nonetheless, in his suit Stockdale described himself specifically purchasing the libelous document in a bookstore, implying that the public sale of parliamentary papers rendered Hansard susceptible to his legal challenge. This affair developed into a constitutional blunder that lasted for more than three years and featured at its height a somewhat comic grandstanding between the House of Commons and Lord Denman, the Lord Chief Justice of the King's Bench. Less amusing was the plight inflicted upon the two national institutions' proxies: eleven of Hansard's presses were confiscated by the sheriffs of Middlesex, who carried out Lord Denman's orders only to be put in Newgate by the Commons' Sergeant of Arms. Stockdale himself was committed to prison for contempt.

The House of Commons' printer did not write the report or sanction its content, but the litigation ascribed him the responsibility commonly associated with authorship. Ultimately, it was the state that was entrapped on the web of authorial liabilities that are at the foundation of modern print culture, a culture the state had created and inscribed in law. This suit threatened to impair Parliament's (and the ministry's) ability to publish material that features strong criticism of individuals or corporations, directly challenging the function of the legislature as a body of inquest and deliberation. Any parliamentary publication and possibly any utterance made by lawmakers or public officers could prompt similar suits against printers, shorthand writers, and clerks. To disentangle itself, Parliament had to adopt new legislation designed to reassert its speech and print privileges.[32]

The Stockdale case highlighted and problematized the new functions of the legislature in a time of hectic social reform when the Commons and the nascent bureaucracy were frantically engaged in scrutinizing institutional wrongdoing. Significantly, the offending remark was made by prison inspectors (representing government in a new capacity) ostensibly evaluating the moral condition of inmates but primarily passing judgment on the performance of the warden and guards. An 1837 committee determined that if put to the same critical scrutiny, much of what had been published by parliamentary committees and commissioners on treatment of slaves, charities, poor law, and municipal corporations, or even what had been asserted in bills presented in the Commons, could be similarly termed defamatory.[33] The affair prompted much debate on the floor and in committees established to address the consequences of the convoluted legal events. While Hume's committee had supposedly opened a new era by bringing parliamentary documents to the public, select committees, defending the ancient privileges of Parliament as the "Grand Inquest of the Nation," presented historical evidence to demonstrate that diffusion of printed documents was an integral part of the Commons' operation for the previous two centuries.

Despite the anchoring of parliamentary privilege in new legislation, the House of Commons resolved to arrest the seeping of incriminatory material into its published record and in the process subjected its members to greater discipline. An 1840 committee was especially concerned with the printing of the minutes and proceedings of select committees. Since committees inquired into abuses, a certain latitude was inevitable. "It is essential to the due performance of the functions of The House that criminatory evidence should be admitted," determined the committee, "but it is no less incumbent on the Committees . . . to examine the evidence so taken, and sift it of all that appear wantonly malicious or even needlessly offensive to the feelings of individuals."[34] A few alterations had to be introduced into the format of committees' reports. For the first time, minutes of evidence included before each and every question the name of the member who asked it. Each day's attendance was registered, as well as the name of members in every split vote. The Stockdale case also occasioned further restrictions on the printing of petitions to Parliament. It was observed that petitions featured "much incriminatory matter."

A measure of self-censorship was already in place prior to the eruption of the affair. It guided the prison inspectors' decision to omit in their unfortunate account the title of the controversial publication and to substitute it with two blanks. This was a common practice. At the same time, the two officials named the publisher and specified the year of publication and the number of plates featured in the book. Lord Denman criticized what he referred to as "mysterious blanks." Apparently, their use contributed to his decision to side with the plaintiff. He wondered why the inspectors mentioned any book or the publisher's name when the aim of this passage was to indicate that jailers allowed prisoners to read questionable material. The gratuitous blanks conveyed even a worse impression than the actual title. The episode demonstrated, therefore, not merely the potential consequences of governmental reportage but also the meaning invested in conventions of official printing. It was not the power of the printed word but the insinuations generated by its absence, signified by two straight lines, which made Parliament vulnerable to a libel suit.

Other policies instituted in the late 1830s further assured the accuracy of the printed record and its fidelity to the oral exchange in committee rooms. Sir Robert Peel challenged the practice of allowing witnesses to go over their testimony after it had been given to a committee and before it was sent to the printer. Apparently, witnesses were permitted to revise their evidence. Some took improper liberties with the shorthand copy under the pretext of a legitimate correction. In one incident, a witness not only altered his original answers but also inserted guiding questions that created the impression that his responses were solicited by likeminded parliamentarians. In another case, a witness claimed to have lost the copy of his testimony, which he had received for revision. The report had to be printed without it. Peel maintained that correcting minor errors or grammatical mistakes was fine, but the privilege tended to undermine the public's confidence in the parliamentary record: "The undoubted superiority of parol over written evidence in eliciting the truth was destroyed by the system of deliberate alteration, and the spirit of a witness's verbal testimony, when thus retouched and reconstructed, could be traced no longer."[35]

In Peel's view, the precise reproduction of the oral exchange was of greater value than any attempt to assure the accuracy of witnesses' testimonies. Efforts to smooth the rough edges of the record compromised the reader's access to the procedure. Charles Buller proposed to prevent altogether the correction of evidence, and, "whenever an unguarded word was let fall, allowance would be made for the imperfection of unstudied style."[36] William Wynn concurred but thought it was unfair to deprive witnesses of the opportunity to rectify errors. Mistakes were made, and witnesses "misrepresented." By the early 1840s, modifications of the official record were severely restricted. Whatever small corrections were allowed always took place after the evidence was already in printed form.[37]

Octavo Versus Folio

While some official documents were enormously popular with the public, much of parliamentary literature was not in great demand. Interested citizens satisfied themselves with press reports and pamphlets. The apparent apathy of the public towards informative publications puzzled officials. There were doubts about their use. Should they be easier to inspect? Were they readable at all? Was reading their proper function? Edwin Chadwick's actions exemplified this uncertainty. An aide of Bentham who launched his public career by authoring the poor-law report, Chadwick believed that his reports made for great reading. In 1860, he sent the ailing Florence Nightingale a copy of his rural constabulary investigation (1839). Chadwick wrote: "Observing from your . . . attack on the writers of novels that you do read such things, it occurs to me that you want amusing reading occasionally . . . Murray, the bookseller, told me that he thought [the constabulary report] as interesting as a novel and he proposed to republish it. In it you would find the history of the adventures of young thieves as recounted by themselves."[38] Chadwick further advised Nightingale to publish an abridged private edition of her royal commission report on sanitation in the army so it would be more widely read. He even took the liberty of contacting a publisher of cheap "railway books"—Routledge—on her behalf.[39]

At the same time, implicit in Chadwick's dissemination of his own reports was the expectation that some or many of their recipients would never bother to peruse them. He therefore habitually recommended to his interlocutors to read a small number of passages (which he indicated by page numbers) and, in addition, summarized the most important points of his reports. In contrast, J. Toumlin Smith argued that royal commissions' reports were deliberately devised to be read only in part. "The pictures of horror artfully put together in the pages of blue books are greedily devoured, and serve as food for the sentimental philanthropy of the reader; while the reports themselves are accepted as infallible gospel."[40] Government designed blue books for the lazy reader, who consumed the easy-to-digest part but, deterred by its enormity, never bothered with the rest of the report.

By the end of the 1840s, it became evident that the public at large remained rather indifferent to the opportunity of purchasing parliamentary documents. Speaking in the Commons, Thomas Emerson Headlam complained that even those who could afford these papers did not know how to get them. Booksellers were not interested in their sale because there was no profit for them in the transaction. In addition, official printers—there were five by the mid 1850s—also printed state documents for private profit in a slightly different design, circumventing the official sale of papers. The Queen's Printer, for instance, produced an octavo edition of the acts of Parliament in addition to the folio and quarto forms which he printed for government.[41] Hume found himself defending the policy he had sponsored some twenty years earlier. He pointed to the meager charge for the papers (by then, a penny a sheet). He maintained that still the best way to guarantee more publicity was the removal of the tax on newspapers, explaining that "he was willing to give information cheaply, but not to throw it away; for things given away were too often regarded as of no value."[42]

Hume's 1830s vision was of individuals purchasing official papers out of interest and therefore paying for them as they would for other platforms of information, like newspapers. The new argument, however, militated against his initial belief in the inherent value of parliamentary papers, as their worth seemed now to be derived, at least in part, from the fee charged. There was a didactic element in selling documents to the people. Beyond exposing them to knowledge, it taught them (as children are told) that objects that cost money were valuable and therefore should be respected. Indeed, if in the 1830s the question was how to give a rising middle class access to official papers, debates in the 1850s touched upon the allocation of papers to local officials for the performance of their duties and to the public, especially working-class readers, as a means to facilitate self-improvement.

Several reformers argued it was incumbent upon government not merely to satisfy demand but also to ensure that important information would reach its destination. As authors, officials also betrayed an urge to see the documents they produced widely circulated. They became impatient when the dispensation of their blue books in the literary marketplace seemed sluggish. By the late 1840s, the communication know-how of members of the Board of Health, including Lord Ashley and Chadwick, converged with the urgency of instructing local authorities and the public in the details of the cause célèbre of the decade, sanitation.

Claiming emergency—outbreaks of cholera seemed to justify the claim—the board had its reports printed and reprinted by the thousands in the smaller octavo format. Members of the board regarded the circulation of their reports part of their public duty. Once the board (and a few other departments) was able to publish in the smaller format, they wished to transform government publishing altogether. The board launched a campaign to print all parliamentary documents in the octavo rather than in the large folio size, promising a savings of 20 percent in printing expense. As important was the argument that the octavo page was far more convenient. The board maintained that reading a folio page induced fatigue. The lines were too long to follow, and the volume had to be read flat on a table or set up on a stand. Due to the size and weight of folio documents, readers could not hold them close to the eye. Reading statistical tables was also best done in a compact form. The board anticipated great advantages for the busy lawmakers who could "carry copies with them, and read them in their carriages or in railway traveling." "Parliament, by permitting the continuance of the printing of Reports in the expensive, cumbrous, and comparatively useless form, limits injuriously the extent of its own influence."[43] In their zeal for the octavo size, Chadwick, Ashley, and their colleagues went as far as arguing, quite seriously, that excessive public printing was encouraged by the value of folio as wastepaper. Since it could easily wrap up large commodities, it could always be resold. Printing in an octavo format made for worthless packing material, which, they reasoned, would deter large inventories of government documents. What is striking about this petition beyond Chadwick's insistence on blue books' textuality (in the sense that they constitute reading material and should be restyled accordingly) is that he conceives of the citizen reader as an embodied individual with vulnerable eyes and posture. There is little here of the abstract, bodiless rationality that the Enlightenment associated with print culture, knowledge, and opinion.

The Board of Health's proposal was followed by a long, slightly nasty, correspondence between the board, the Treasury, and the Stationery Office, in which the latter attempted to refute in great technical detail all arguments about the great savings of printing in the octavo. As for the convenience of reading, the Stationery Office claimed it was dependent on the function of particular books. Reference works like Bayle's *Dictionary,* Thurloe's *State Papers,* and the *Encyclopedia Britannica* were more desirable in the folio or quarto size, while magazines such as the *Spectator, Tatler,* and works of literature like Scott's novels or Pope's poems were more suited to the octavo size. The Stationery Office regarded parliamentary literature as closer to the first than the second category. "In a Folio, the eye can take in a much larger space at once. There is a greater facility of comparing one passage with another, and of making annotations. His would be a peculiar taste who should prefer having the *Times* done upon in an Octavo pamphlet."[44] The office conceded that for very popular reports, the octavo would be more adequate, then added that those were quite rare. Octavo publications would be easier to hold and read but much of parliamentary printing consisted of relatively small numbers of pages.

The octavo panacea was repeatedly invoked in debates on the floor and in committees' hearings. Sir George Grey argued in the Commons that the octavo-size sanitary report was less bulky, more portable, and easily sent by post. He predicted that it would boost circulation.[45] Another supporter argued, "A person wishing to write upon, or read up to a particular subject, might like to take a Blue Book with him into the country, or abroad. At present that must be out of the question."[46] There seemed to be a correspondence between the desire to make blue books more transportable and the movement inherent to the phenomenology of the "report." Chadwick's bureaucratic reveries put blue books in constant transit. When the Commons did not show strong enthusiasm, Chadwick tried to recruit Brougham's help in the Lords, reminding him that under his leadership in the early 1830s, abridged poor-law reports were issued in octavo. He maintained that the compact size of the document was responsible for its popularity. Conveniently, Charles Knight, the publisher of the Poor Law Commission, became in the 1840s the Board of Health publisher.[47]

Despite the experimentation with the octavo, the folio remained the standard size for most parliamentary literature. The speaker maintained that when reprinted in octavo, reports ran into too many volumes. It was impractical to deliver the daily evidence to committee members in that format, and they objected to the small type used in the octavo page. Richard Monckton Milnes complained, "The good old large orthodox folio had been abolished, and a little, thick, dumpy volume substituted, which was far less convenient, for by turning over a folio page you could see at a glance whether there was anything in it which you wanted to read, while in a small volume you took twice the time in finding it out."[48]

Finding Readers

Many schemes were floated to find readers for state publications. Edward Morton, a journalist and shorthand writer, argued that the public learned about parliamentary debates in the morning papers but knew very little about committee hearings where some of the more interesting "statistics on health, crime . . . and facts and opinions on the social condition of important classes" were divulged.[49] This information arrived in the public domain only at the end of the session and in a cumbersome, hard to read, form. Committees should be opened to the public through the press by allowing the publication of frequent reports on their dealings. Under the present system, Morton poeticized, "Parliament dams up its water until the dry season is over, and then lets them out in a flood which inundates, not fertilises."[50] Parliament was thus encouraged to manage the temporal release of information to satisfy a fleeting collective interest and to indulge specific public appetites. This material would be of interest to commercial people and professional men, and would have a devoted readership in the colonies, in particular India, Australia, and Canada. It would set people's minds' to work, enthused Morton, and the Commons might get in response facts or suggestions on the subjects under discussion. Information begets information.

Morton's proposal had a precedent in parliamentary practice. In a few cases, committee chairmen decided to release their transcripts piecemeal while investigations were still taking place. The Select Committee on Combination Laws (1824) was a model for such publication strategy, unprecedentedly issuing frequent accounts that occupied many columns in the press and fueled public debate. (The committee's work concluded with a wide consensus over the repeal of the acts.) Numbering fifty-two M.P.s, a decade before committees were limited to fifteen members, this select committee functioned as a miniature Parliament or a national court. The publication of the weekly evidence opened the process to public rebuttal.[51]

Morton thought that for the collective edition of committee hearings a book the size of the *Edinburgh Review* would be the most pleasant to read. Individual documents might follow the format of the *Economist* or the *Spectator* and be printed in double columns. He thus proposed to emulate another genre that was literary and informational, the periodical review. As to the style of the reports, Morton thought them readable as they were without radical editing. "I am inclined to think that on subjects of interest the public would not be content with the substance, and that the form of dialogue is not unpopular; it gives a dramatic interest to the evidence; the only objection is, that the examination is sometimes conducted in too discursive a style; there is a want of continuous interest, from one subject not being followed up and exhausted before another is started."[52]

From the 1830s to the 1850s, the concept of information gradually replaced the term *knowledge*—for instance, "taxes on knowledge" or the "Society for the Diffusion of Useful Knowledge"—as a designation for the type of intelligence

purveyed by newspapers and government publications. There were also more frequent allusions to *reference* (as in the later expression *reference work*) to describe
the function of those documents. This understanding evoked a tightly registered
body of facts whose usefulness depended on organization. At the same time, there
was a continuing concern over the readability of the parliamentary record, a concern that informed Hansard at the beginning of the century, and Chadwick, Morton, and others in midcentury. Allusions to literary and journalistic genres in the
attempt to gauge the possible use of blue books were typical of the debate over
parliamentary papers. These documents (blue books in particular) were the subject of multiple inscriptions as archives, records, and books in a cultural order
where reading was ubiquitous but "information retrieval" had not yet become a
formalized practice. Once they were crafted and marketed as books or pamphlets,
it was presumed that blue books would be similarly consumed.

Morton's testimony was given to a committee that deliberated over a plan,
which gained some popularity at the time, to allocate parliamentary documents
to the burgeoning Mechanics' Institutions. Indeed, the spirit of the SDUK lingered on. Henry Tufnell, the M.P. who sponsored the scheme, reported that the
230 or so Mechanics Institutions throughout the country were a great tool for the
"mental improvements" of their membership, estimated at between sixty and
seventy thousand. In order not to overwhelm the institutions with massive quantities of papers, Tufnell suggested selecting the most important documents on
finance, colonization, and other great subjects of national concern so that "full
information" would be placed in the hands of the people. Lawmakers appeared
familiar with the reading sensibilities of the laboring classes. Another M.P. remarked that it was commonly understood from the decline in the circulation of
Chambers's Journal, the *Penny Magazine,* and similar publications that the
working class had altered its reading tastes and now preferred political material.
If this was the case, they should receive the best political literature, the documentary legacy of Parliament.

The dispersion of these papers had a purpose beyond educating or informing
the populace. "They would show . . . that the representatives of the people, besides their attendance and debates in that House, were arduously engaged
throughout the Session in the development of information essential to the public service."[53] John William Fortescue concurred that "more was done in the
House than mere talking and debating, and the information contained in [par-
liamentary papers] would tend to correct many crude and mischievous ideas."
There was a degree of defensiveness in this and similar statements. Witnesses alleged that working people were dismissive of the gentlemanly debating-club

character of the parliamentary exchange, and lawmakers opined that they should better represent their labor to the people. Joseph Brotherton was convinced that laborers were fully able to appreciate the information conveyed to them. "If the people were seeking political power it was important that they should have the best political education."[54] This idea could be articulated more comfortably a few years after the collapse of Chartism, when the incorporation of workers into the political classes was unlikely to be done abruptly, violently, or immediately.

The initial sign that the members of Mechanics' Institutions in fact coveted parliamentary papers was given at a conference held at the office of the Society of Arts in May 1852. Eventually, 272 petitions containing 15,281 signatures arrived in Westminster. The select committee concluded that its witnesses uniformly agreed that diffusion of the "most interesting and instructive" documents would dispel ignorance, correct misrepresentations, and enable "the mass of the people to form for themselves a just opinion upon subjects of legislation and other important questions of the day."[55] Witnesses recommended that in choosing material regional interests should be addressed, citing diverse reading preferences in agricultural and industrial areas, maritime towns, and inland districts. Reportedly, workers were particularly interested in the report of the Committee of the Privy Council on Education as well as the accounts of the Board of Health, Department of Practical Arts, and the Government School of Mines. Despite the select committee's recommendations and comparable schemes that resurfaced throughout the 1850s, these ambitious ideas did not yield legislation. While retrenchment was certainly an important factor in the plan's failure, another major obstacle was the Commons' inability to agree on the mechanism of selecting specific segments of the enormous printed record for distribution. Profoundly reluctant to make such choices, M.P.s claimed that reducing the size of the record impaired its capacity to represent fully the range of opinion and information brought before Parliament.[56]

Lord Stanley (M.P. for King's Lynn) promoted another scheme: allocating important blue books to newspapers, popular journals, and magazines. In a pamphlet titled, "What Shall We Do with Our Blue Books? Parliament the National School Master" (1854), he agreed that the annual sixty or seventy volumes of parliamentary papers were the most important tools for adult education, especially in remote regions, but opined that the work of digesting and diffusing official knowledge should be left to the press. In his view, the provincial editor functioned as a schoolmaster of sorts. Stanley had little concern about bias. Journalistic bias was not radically different from the way opinion shaped parliamentary exchange and the public arena in general. Besides, "opposite exaggerations elicit truth."[57] He even predicted that press reports would encourage individual readers to purchase blue books and thus increase revenues from the sale of parliamentary papers.

In the Maze

The paternalistic benevolence of lawmakers wishing to employ blue books as schoolhouse textbooks and the ambition of diligent public servants encountered a skeptical and ever more frugal bureaucratic culture, best represented by the comptroller of the Stationery Office, the political economist John Ramsay McCulloch. With wit and sarcasm that preceded the author of Parkinson's Law by a century, McCulloch mocked the zeal of commissioners and other officials to keep the printing machines running amok. As a prime example of "an abuse of printing," he gave a report by a committee on wine duties that contained 231 pages on the "Vatting of Wine in the different Docks . . . There is not, I believe, a sane person in the empire who ever read one line of it or ever will."[58] Only a small number of documents, such as the one on marriage with a deceased wife's sister, were widely purchased by a curious public.[59] McCulloch dismissed the customary allocation of complimentary government reports as wasteful and unfair. Why should government give documents to some and not to others? He pointed to the mounds of papers that languished in government warehouses. The Stationery Office had instituted a policy of selling printing surplus as wastepaper to recover at least some of the expense. Asked about Mechanics' Institutions' requests, he quipped, "If you could get a Sir Isaac Newton to cull out of the million of pages of trash, the 5 or 10 per cent of good that there is in them, and circulate that through the country, it might be useful; but as it is, it would merely involve an enormous additional expense."[60] He was willing to sell at cost but not to supply wastepaper gratis. McCulloch believed that parliamentary papers could be made more interesting to the public but only by severe editing.

As early as the 1820s, lawmakers complained that official publications contained excessive material of dubious utility. In an 1828 debate in the House, one participant pointed to the appendix of a slavery report that featured nothing but the names of slaves and their masters and mistresses together with evaluations of the slave owners' moral qualities. The select committee on printing similarly criticized the wastefulness of documenting individuals by name.[61] The second report on education in Ireland featured 1,331 pages, nearly all filled with the names of schoolmasters. Papers relating to the slave trade included 938 pages populated with the names and character evaluations of slaves. Appendices to a report from the Chancery Commission featured 600 pages of suitors' names.

These were among the first instances in which the effort to print every detail in the state's record was subjected to overt ridicule. Massive registration of personal names and assessments of individuals' moral rectitude possibly indicated the controlling drives behind accumulating social knowledge. However, the publication of such minutia in a national document printed in London was considered excessive, perhaps improper or even ludicrous. This knowledge was removed from its locality (where it was first gathered and collated) and the context of dominance and subordination outside of which proper names were all but meaningless. The mindless reproduction of such details brought to absurdity the Baconian imperative for aggregation of facts. This is not to say that government could not exercise social control by publishing individual names. For example, the official *Police Gazette* that in the late 1820s replaced the older *Hue and Cry* was expected to arrest crime by prevention rather than punishment. Its originators maintained that the Achilles heel of policing society was the lack of effective means of communication and publicity. The new publication was an unstamped, franked publication and therefore accessibly to many. It featured information about military deserters, runaway apprentices, and "parish absconders," as well horse thieves and other offenders. It was argued that if hung in public houses the *Police Gazette* "would afford amusement and instruction to two millions of readers."[62]

By midcentury, public officials competed in telling anecdotes and coining metaphors for the seemingly rampant production of printed matter. One critic defied any busy M.P. to even try to turn the leaves of all the papers printed for the Commons. Royal commissions of inquiry were ripe targets for such criticism. Parliamentarians complained about the unlimited printing power given to royal commissioners. "Upon the appointment of a Commission by the Crown, the Presses of a Government Printer are placed at its disposal."[63] In an attempt to slash expenses, officials proposed that instead of printing mammoth appendices to commissions' reports, the raw evidence in manuscript form would be deposited in the library of the House of Commons or in the Home Office. In other words, the evidence's appropriate place was the repository archive rather than the print archive. Sir George Cornewall Lewis remarked that members of both houses and the public did read reports but rarely consulted appendices.[64] However, while the speaker and the printing committee kept the run of ordinary documents low, public board and commission reports varied from 1,750 to 5,000 and even 10,000 copies.[65]

Commissioners were accused of printing long documents for their own edification. To the frustration of M.P.s, the printing committee had no clear jurisdiction over the publication of royal commission reports in matters of content, quality of production, or number of copies. McCulloch also objected to the glut of minutia in reports from the poor-law, prison, and other inspectorates. Government issued elaborate statements on the poor of every parish that repeated themselves every year. This material should be published every five or ten years, he opined. Sardonic statements from public officials betrayed a measure of sobriety in the midst of the Victorian cult of the fact. Thomas Vardon, the secretary of the printing committee, thought that select committees' reports were also burdened by the "dead weight of that which the public would not even desire to know."[66]

Lawmakers became accustomed to describe themselves as being swarmed with printed matter without recourse. They even seemed ambivalent regarding the importance of blue books for the parliamentary process. When a delegation of Chartists enters Charles Egremont's library in Disraeli's novel *Sybil*, they notice on a side table his arranged parliamentary papers and piles of blue books, a detail that attested to the young statesman's dedication and sincerity.[67] The statesmen in Anthony Trollope's parliamentary novels, known as the Palliser series, also devour blue books into the early hours of the morning to educate themselves about matters of the world or, alternatively, to escape its woes. Thus, in *The Eustace Diamonds*, "Lord Fawn has suffered a disappointment in love, but he had consoled himself with blue-books."[68] (Trollope's heroines read novels, of course.) Mr. Gradgrind's library in Dickens's *Hard Times* is crammed with blue books (a manifestation of this tyrannical schoolmaster's belief in the superiority of facts over sentiments). The volumes are so numerous that the profusion of blue reminds the narrator of Bluebeard's infamous den and by implication suggests, tongue in cheek, that this repository of government reports is in fact a chamber of utilitarian horror.

In contrast, the libraries of actual (rather than literary) parliamentarians, according to a few depictions, were hopelessly cluttered with blue books. Members such as V. Scully, remonstrated against getting lost in the labyrinth of their own textual production. "[I] object to having tons of papers which are never opened sent to my lodgings. [I have] been out of town for a few weeks, and on my return, instead of being able to go to "The Derby" . . . had to wade through a mass of Parliamentary papers. [I] put away 1 lb and threw away 2 cwt. [I] could not sell the residue; . . . could not exchange them for books, for that would be selling them; . . . could not burn them, for that would be voted a nuisance. Why should these tons of paper be thrust on unwilling members?"[69]

"A duti-ful subject, or, 'The man wot never interferes in any business over which he has no control.'" The Duke of Wellington is surrounded by mounds of state papers and parliamentary reports (mostly in loose sheets) on every conceivable topic of domestic and imperial affairs. John Doyle drew the caricature shortly after the aging Wellington, then a member of Robert Peel's cabinet, added the army commander in chief to his duties. By the mid-nineteenth century, the labor of bureaucrats, legislators, and statesmen became synonymous with the perusal of parliamentary papers or "blue books." (H. B. [John Doyle], July 27, 1843, the Tabley collection at the University of Manchester.)

William Ewart declared in another debate, "It had rained blue-books—Pelion had been piled on Ossa, and Ossa on Olympus. It had been sarcastically remarked that if you wanted to hide a question the best plan was to bury it in a blue-book—you might then defy anybody to excavate it."[70] (The print archive could therefore also be a place of concealment.) For the benefit of M.P.s and the public, Ewart suggested two sets of blue books, one in full, another in digest. He thought that the statistical department of the Board of Trade should prepare this carefully abridged and condensed edition. Since they had done so stupendously, presenting valuable volumes of figures in the *Statistical Abstract*, they should be able to do the same with other types of facts. Joseph Warner Henley contended that even for the purpose of a digest information had to be printed in full. Besides, committees and commissions could not be trusted to select evidence without introducing their own opinions and biases. Because M.P.s sought information simultaneously in diverse directions, full-scale blue books brimming with details were essential. Ewart's proposal thus faced an insurmountable chicken-and-egg problem, and the motion was withdrawn. Once again, lawmakers felt they could not compromise the completeness of their published record.

They also guarded jealously their blue book privileges. Before the late 1850s, all papers were delivered to every member, but it was decided that certain papers would be left in the Votes Office and dispatched only upon request. Members grumbled. When he did not receive a document concerning the prevention of smallpox, Sir John Pakington determined, "If there was one thing of more importance than another in the performance of their functions as Members of that House, it was that all possible information should be accessible to them on all occasions."[71] Members also complained that the commercial press received official reports before they did.

Despite somewhat quixotic efforts and even temporary successes, reducing the overall size of parliamentary printing proved to be, in the long run, all but impossible. The same was true of the length of royal commissions' reports. There was some correspondence between the gentlemanly status of commissioners and their publication privileges. It was tacitly assumed that reining in those who made such an effort at collecting and sifting evidence without pay would encounter much resistance. One of a commissioner's few tangible rewards was to see his entire work in print regardless of utility. Some M.P.s were concerned that removing the evidence from printed reports would eliminate the basis for evaluating commissioners' work and recommendations. Commissions of inquiry reports would continue to provoke derision for their size, as the commissioners themselves would be mocked for their absurdly long tenure, for, it was popularly remarked, royal commissions, "take minutes and last for years." The *Globe* sneered at the 1833 Factory Commission, complaining that "it was not necessary that 12 gentlemen should be sent on a voyage of inquiry and produce . . . a large blue book 14 inches by 9 and weighing about 9 lb." Lytton Strachey would write that royal commissions "achieve nothing but a very fat blue-book on a very high shelf."[72] The trail of heavy volumes, a feast for historians, became for contemporaries an allegory for the aimlessness of bureaucratic rituals. The tension between blue books' cumbersome, overbearing, and yet measurable physicality and their alleged uselessness as reading material (or as a basis for policy making) was endlessly employed for poking fun at government. Under the title "The Book of the Month," a 1930 caricature in the *Evening Standard* depicts a Gandhi supporter in national garb attempting to purchase the Simon Report on colonial policy in India, a report that Indian nationalists had soundly rejected. The clerk exclaims, "A million copies, Sir? Certainly, Sir! Excellent reading, Sir!" "Oh! I don't want them to read—Just to throw at policemen."[73]

Despite that such ridicule became a leitmotif in British public life, royal commission reports did not get shorter. The 1894 report of the Labour Commission was sixty-seven volumes. The 1909 Royal Commission on Poor Law would wrap its findings in merely fifty-three. By then the term *blue book* inspired expressions such as *bluebooky, bluebookish,* and *bluebookishness,* to denote dry, tediously factual texts and individuals.

Further into the nineteenth century, blue books became increasingly self-referential, featuring more and more details extracted from other parliamentary papers and covering previous investigations and resolutions, in effect delineating the historical trajectories of policies, institutions, and social predicaments. Official publications served thus as a comprehensive memory receptacle. The British state could now be conceived of as a historically determined unified "subject" propped by institutionalized memory. This apparent stability, continuity, and visibility emerged, at times, as a liability rather than a source of power. Parliament and government became entangled in their own self-representations, as was evident in the Stockdale affair. A similar form of entrapment involved the new publication *Hansard's Parliamentary Debates.* With this reliable record, M.P.s had at their disposal yet another archive that created coherent subjects—themselves. Members who abandoned old positions too obviously were confronted in floor debates with their own previous utterances, which had been faithfully registered. By the end of the nineteenth century this practice would become a verb, to *hansardize. Hansard* vouched for continuity but somewhat curbed the free-flowing exchange in parliamentary debates.[74]

The official print output was concurrently a source of pride and embarrassment. In authoring and printing blue books, Parliament and the ministry launched a medium for their own self-representation. Reports of commissions, committees, and inspectorates were particularly important in Victorian political culture for their discursive and physical commemoration and celebration of reform and the new bureaucracy. The obliteration of secret procedures in politics and administration (which obviously was never to be fully achieved) related to the ideal of a democratic public sphere. The shift from the old regime to the modern state involved the opening up of the state's hidden sphere of decision making. However, elephantine government reports also testified to the compulsiveness of the state (as well as of individual bureaucrats) to write about itself. Official reports—the state's diaries—were construed in terms compatible with graphomania, megalomania, or other bureaucratic and personal pathologies. Uncommonly large documents (Iraq's 12,000 page 2002 report on its unconventional weapons or—to give a radically different example—Hillary Rodham Clinton's 1993 Health Reform Report, which was derided for occupying 4,000 pages) unless clearly organized as information (e.g., the *OED*, *Encyclopedia Britannica*), can leave an impression of excess, impropriety, and even cover-up. These mammoth documents subvert the demand for transparency by complying with it excessively. The state is supposedly telling us everything it can in order to deceive us not by lying but by divulging the truth in its unreadable entirety. (Of course, it also tells actual lies and omits material, as critics of royal commissions in the 1830s and beyond alleged.) Calling attention to either symptoms of bureaucratic lack of self-control or tricks of deception, this impression emanated from an apparent misplacement of the state's archive outside its proper interior space. In this reading, the distinction between the state's repository archive and its print archive was analogous to contemporaneous notions of "private" versus "public" spheres.

The efforts to create alternative modes for representing the nation descriptively (which also featured the representation of opinion) was bound to collide with traditional parliamentary and extraparliamentary forms of political representation. By the mid-nineteenth century, the Victorian state was sweeping away most of the old constraints on the circulation of knowledge (and opinion) through the press. Concurrently, government and Parliament attempted to intrude upon this freedom by, for instance, assuming a pedagogical posture that was previously the domain of free associations such as the SDUK. Moreover, at this historical moment, the state collaborated with private publishers in various campaigns to sway public opinion, and Parliament entered the market by selling off its printed documents. Macaulay wrote that "a government can interfere in discussion, only by making it less free than it would otherwise be . . . Government can bring nothing but the influence of hopes and fears to support its doctrines. It carries on controversy not with reasons, but with threats and bribes."[75] Whiggish thundering proclamations about the freedom of the press all but ignored the Whig governments' own conspicuous and intrusive "contributions" to public discussions.

In our times, Habermas's work rather than lingering Whiggism perpetuates the veneration of turn-of-the-nineteenth-century British public culture. In

Habermas's early writings, the state was largely ignored in favor of an ideal of bourgeois liberation and rational exchange that reached its apex with the first election platform, Robert Peel's Tamworth Manifesto of 1834. In this view, the model bourgeois public sphere began to unravel toward the later part of the nineteenth century, a transformation closely linked to economic differentiation manifested in the emergence of large industrial and financial conglomerates, governmental regulation of the market, the rise of consumerism, and the consequent emphasis on the advertising capacity of the press at the expense of a learned, rational debate.[76] However, the lines between the public theater of discussion and the state began melting much earlier. This transformation was largely due to the state's increasingly aggressive role in generating and distributing knowledge as well as in representing public opinion. By instituting the sale policy in the name of greater accessibility, the early Victorian state collapsed the difference between the Enlightenment demand for an unimpeded circulation of ideas and the dynamics of the marketplace. It further restricted access by curbing the range of "authors" that were allowed admission to print statism (e.g., writers of petitions) and giving power to bureaucrats—rather than legislators— in allocating official publications. Most importantly, the state emulated the classical public sphere by partaking vigorously in the critical review of itself and, as we shall see, became a model of appropriation by working-class organizations that mounted their own social investigations. In contrast to Habermas's rather monolithic view of the public sphere, his critics have demonstrated the plurality of communities of exchange (including oppositional counterpublics) in early nineteenth-century Britain and elsewhere. The state endeavored concurrently and indiscriminately to colonize them all, as was evident to Cobbett and others. To some extent print statism indeed contributed to the convergence of these divergent publics.

Finally, the episodes described here epitomized not just the publishing ambitions of the modern state but also its great desire to communicate, to be read. By the middle of the twentieth century, the state ventured into more popular branches of publishing. The Stationery Office (HMSO) ran its own chain of stores, where it has displayed books, leaflets, periodicals, maps, folders, wall charts, transparencies, and microfilms on almost every conceivable topic, including war history, social history, archaeology, English art, museums and galleries, photography, and technology, in addition to the immense output of government departments and parliamentary papers. Publishers watched, with much concern, HMSO shops offering fancy Christmas cards and titles such as *The ABC of Cooking* (1954) or *The History of Light Cars* (1958). More traditional staples such as

The Rents Act and You (1957) sold 1.3 million copies. By the early 1960s, there were forty thousand titles in print and about six thousand new titles every year. One of the most celebrated best sellers, Sir Ernest Gowers's *Plain Words* (1948), sold more than 1.25 million copies worldwide and was published as a paperback by Penguin. The question of the archive's readability was circumvented. The bureaucracy, at the height of its twentieth-century self-confidence, produced books that were crafted and circulated as any other commercial books. Once again, as in the days of William Cobbett, government undersold the competition. In 1962, the Council of the Publishers Association protested what it considered to be government's invasion into a commercial field. Two years earlier, Cyril Northcote Parkinson famously remarked, "Continents are being de-forested, pulping-machines worn out and paper-makers kept working night and day to keep up with this appalling output of literature."[77] As our survey demonstrates, the ability to arouse interest, awe, or scorn has accompanied official publications since the early decades of the nineteenth century.

CHAPTER TWO

The Battle of the Books

Citizens as Readers

With some ambivalence, Victorian lawmakers looked to the European continent for models of stupendous elaboration of state knowledge through statistical
bureaus and other scholarly institutions. As for publication projects, examples of
state abundance increasingly came from across the Atlantic. Parliamentary debates about official publications often referred to the United States. Thus, members of the 1853 select committee on allocation of parliamentary papers to public institutions heard, with a touch of envy, the testimony of Henry Stevens Jr.,
an agent for the Smithsonian Institution in London. This position also put him
in charge of negotiating the exchange of official printed documents between the
two countries.

In the early 1850s, the federal government issued each of its papers in 1,500
copies, but in every session, Stevens told the committee, about ten to twenty documents received publicity unmatched by any parliamentary literature. Printed
in large editions of between 5,000 and 100,000 copies, they were allocated
through congressional representatives and senators to hundreds of libraries,
learned associations, and athenaeums. As a matter of law, Washington sent some
of its most lavish print productions to state governments, colleges, and incorporated literary institutions, mostly historical societies. Government made no demand upon these institutions. Only the *Statutes at Large*, published by Little and
Brown, was designated government property. An act of Congress required that
office holders transmit those copies to their successors. The federal legislature
also funded, fully or partially, books on historical or scientific topics. Congress
usually owned the manuscripts and subscribed for perhaps one or two thousand
copies. The publisher could sell as many additional volumes as he chose at the
price paid by Congress.[1] British parliamentarians heard that their counterparts
in Washington regularly received multiple copies of the reports on congressional

debates prepared by the privately owned and federally sponsored *Congressional Globe*. Interest in the Westminster committee room rose even higher when it turned out that in the beginning of every legislative session, U.S. lawmakers were entitled to thirty dollars worth of subscriptions to periodicals and newspapers of their choosing, including foreign publications. (The witness claimed that many selected the *London Times*.)

A few states engaged in massive publishing enterprises of their own. In 1842, the New York legislature launched a natural history survey. It issued fifteen volumes in more than twenty thousand copies, which were either granted to public institutions or sold for a subsidized price of one dollar per volume. In order to prevent this publication from becoming the object of booksellers' speculations, the state obtained a copyright, and individual purchasers had to guarantee their good faith. The New York legislature issued about ten or twelve volumes of official papers a year (as much as half of roughly twenty-five volumes produced by Congress), with the exception of unique undertakings such as the *Natural History Survey* or the *Atlas of the State of New York*, and special reports on schools, canals, and other public undertakings. Members of Parliament noticed that some of the controversies that haunted British blue book production were absent from the U.S. scene. For instance, congressional select committees seldom printed their proceedings in full, doing so mostly in cases of great controversy such as election disputes. Many committees conducted their business without a stenographer. They did not print evidence daily for the use of committee members. Legislators publicized their disagreements by authoring minority reports, not through a full transcript of the proceedings. Stevens claimed that he had never heard complaints about the partial nature of the printed record. "The system pursued there is quite different from the system pursued here; our reports are very much fuller being more like an essay upon the subject; the authorities are frequently fully quoted but the evidence is not given in full."[2]

In its report, the select committee cited federal and state governments as paradigms of liberal diffusion of knowledge. Even the ever-frugal Hume did not recoil at the idea of a massive gratis distribution of official documents. "Public papers of America circulate information much better than we do, and a deal of information is communicated to distant parts, and of those distributed by order of the Congress, many of them are well taken care of."[3] This somewhat unexpected appreciation was guided by the impression that, rather than gratifying political needs, the United States was building a comprehensive educational apparatus in which the distribution of documents was only a single element, supplemented by vast public school systems and official support to libraries and aca-

demic institutions. In this respect, the state of New York in particular drew the
parliamentarians' admiration. It also occurred to them that in enterprises such
as the natural history survey, the New York legislature had taken upon itself tasks
that in continental Europe were reserved for national governments.

Stevens's testimony, however, prettified the reality of congressional printing.
True, there was a degree of openhandedness in the production and dissemination of official papers, and sponsorship of books, all of which were justified in
endless tributes made to the spirit of republican education, democracy, and useful knowledge. Nevertheless, it was also evident that many of the textual products prepared or funded by Congress served concrete political needs and that, besides allocating important documents to learned institutions, members of the
two houses dispatched them to loyal constituents. Moreover, at the turn of the
1850s—while British lawmakers were debating the fate of their official publications—the Senate and, to a lesser degree, the House of Representatives were
holding heated debates over similar concerns. Charges of excess and abuse surfaced. The entire field of printing was, until the establishment of the Government Printing Office in 1861, one of the most notorious arenas for party patronage.

Recurring questions concerned the duty of government to provide its citizens
with information and the type of knowledge that lent itself for such circulation.
Since Congress was often sponsoring actual books rather than blue books (a term
used in U.S. bureaucratic parlance for lists of office holders), doubts over federal
involvement in the business of publishing were even more acute than in Britain.
Was congressional largess indulging a cadre of authors by funding their private
ambitions? Befitting the republican ethos, this concern was articulated in terms
not of a danger to the purity of the free market but of a threat posed to individuals' autonomy by an overbearing authority. Congressmen often simply asked
whether a particular document was what their constituents wanted to read or to
own, making the desires of the population the leading criterion. While in times
of economic depression the notion of retrenchment gained popularity, proponents of restraint in official publications were not as victorious (or as sincere) as
were British reformers. The Jacksonian revolution that was lauded as an attempt
at retrenchment (more a campaign to curb privilege than to save money) seemed
only to intensify federal splurging on public printing.[4] Political exigencies and
the absence of an emerging bureaucratic ethos—together with the inherent for-
eignness of utilitarianism to antebellum political culture—insured that in comparison with Britain the production and circulation of knowledge in the United
States would be less systematized or constricted.

The following discussion first situates federal publications within the contours of the American "knowledge policy." Through a range of congressional debates over specific publishing ventures, it explores congressmen's response to the reading preferences of the electorate and how the Jacksonian politics of representation (rather than merely party politics) converged with the publishing capacities of Congress and the executive. This chapter also examines publishing initiatives that were grounded in uniquely American circumstances: debates over offering official documents in foreign languages (especially Spanish) for the benefit of non-English-speaking residents and citizens, and the efforts to commit to print the works of "founding fathers."

State Culture

There was an apparent incongruity between the relatively small tasks of the antebellum federal government and Congress's engagement in large-scale publishing projects. Clearly, official printing was not a collateral of any grand administrative expansion, or an indication of rampant legislative activism. Certain publications, however, did suggest growth in the pale of government. For instance, the practice of Indian removal became during the Jacksonian period a matter of highly publicized and hotly debated public policy. The administration used the annual reports of the commissioner of Indian affairs to justify and promote the removal schemes. Westward expansion in the 1840s, the war with Mexico, and the addition of Texas and California to the Union involved federal action and surges of public contention, exploration, and publication.

In the 1850s and 1860s, Congress intensified its fact-finding initiatives. In 1856, a full congressional inquiry examined the Kansas crisis, and in 1859, a Senate committee investigated John Brown's raid in Harper's Ferry. The onset of the Civil War triggered an unprecedented burst of investigative projects for Congress and the administration. With Reconstruction, the two branches of government found themselves feuding, and the later years of Andrew Johnson's administration amounted (at least according to Woodrow Wilson's interpretation) to "congressional government." Indeed, the aftermath of the war occasioned massive congressional inquiries into the South, including examining events such as the race riots in Memphis (1866) and New Orleans (1866), and culminating in 1872 with a comprehensive investigation into the condition of the "former insurrectionary states." While congressional investigations drew national attention, their reports grew in size and included lengthy appendices populated with documents and strings of interviews. The Kansas Committee, the Memphis riots Committee, and the Doolittle Committee, which examined the condition of the Indian tribes (1865–66), featured fieldwork performed by senators and representatives. In the absence of an institution comparable to the British royal commissions of inquiry, Congress retained a hold on large-scale fact-finding missions.

Beyond investigations, the publication of documents occasioned struggles between Congress and the executive, as was famously demonstrated in the December 1865 congressional decision to publish Carl Schurz's report (as well as a shorter document by Ulysses Grant) on the situation in the South. President Johnson had dispatched Schurz to tour the former Confederate states. (Radical republicans also assisted. Senator Charles Sumner arranged for his friends to pay the high premium for Schurz's life insurance.) But concerned about his emissary's apparent support of massive reconstruction, Johnson later advised Schurz against publishing his report. The Senate insisted that Johnson submit the report and subsequently printed and circulated tens of thousands of copies. This was not the first time that Congress snatched a publication project from the hands of the executive. In the 1840s, it had taken charge over the publication of the results of the ground breaking naval exploring expedition to the Pacific (1838–42).

The two-party system and later the worsening sectional rift also accelerated the production of printed matter. Western expansion articulated national sentiments, and official expedition reports served as vehicles for imperial as well as empirical aspirations. Allusions to American grandeur were easy to provoke and did not necessitate either momentous events or extraordinary undertakings. They reappeared in mundane congressional debates over, for instance, the quality of the paper and binding of official publications. A particular dimension of the craving to demonstrate American competence was the concern over the states' image abroad. Like Chekhov's characters, antebellum statesmen and intellectuals constantly asked themselves: what would "they" think of us? But instead of worrying about future generations, these Americans were preoccupied with the gaze from the east, from the capitals of Europe.

Federal publishing schemes also point to a comparatively more intimate relationship between state and culture. British reflections on culture and the state largely aimed at implicating the latter in an effort to educate disenfranchised populations. Later in the century, Matthew Arnold and others would introduce "culture" as a mechanism for controlling the encroaching threat of mass society. Allocating federal documents to libraries, literary societies, and colleges may be construed as a pedagogical mission consistent with the individual states' initiation of public school systems.[5] There was, however, little resemblance between the political education (or, more precisely, market education) of the kind the

British Society for the Diffusion of Useful Knowledge (SDUK) sponsored and the American notion of "republican education." Congressional debates revealed ambivalence about the pedagogic predilections of the state. The usefulness of "useful knowledge" had a more immediate and egalitarian resonance on the American side. Our understanding of culture here should not be confined to education. The book-making federal government directly engaged in aesthetic production long before the New Deal or the advent of the National Endowment for the Arts (NEA) and the National Endowment for the Humanities (NEH). This aspect was particularly discernable in the official literature about the West and Indian tribes, which habitually and consciously featured aesthetic surpluses manifested in either visual depictions or narrative structures. The subject matter as well as its complex relations to the United States, required representational strategies of a different order than those employed to describe child laborers and the poor in Britain.

The antebellum period witnessed the concurrent flourishing of print and oral culture. The spoken word was central to the localized public sphere that evolved around town meetings, public assemblies, and stump speeches. Political antagonists often confronted each other in the public arena. The famous Lincoln-Douglas debates of 1857 come to mind. Politics was marked by a remarkable oratorical quality, from Henry Clay and Daniel Webster's Senate floor rhetoric to the elegant yet accessible "Saxon eloquence" of Abraham Lincoln. One of the unique aspects of congressional debate was that some printed reports (such as Schurz's and Grant's) were read aloud, simply for effect. Yet, while rhetorical force seemed an essential aspect of the democratic polity, print culture invaded the U.S. political process in far more radical ways than in Britain. The size of the electorate and the enormity of the country necessitated a large-scale system to disperse information. From the late 1830s on, every national election was accompanied by hectic production of ad hoc party papers, official biographies of candidates, and bric-a-brac print matter, including party almanacs, handbills, pamphlets, caricatures, and even congressional publications recruited for direct political purposes. Participatory political culture, freedom of expression, and high literacy rates further encouraged the relentless diffusion of political literature.

Government propped an intricate network of communication. Untaxed, cheap, and constitutionally protected newspapers flourished everywhere. Beyond their primary local function, they served as a mighty infrastructure, utilized in implicit and explicit ways to circulate information emanating from Washington. The arbitrary relocation of the federal Capitol at the turn of the nineteenth cen-

tury necessitated new vehicles of information. While in Britain the presence of
the state in the provinces was assured by itinerant government officials (tax collectors in the eighteenth century, commissioners and inspectors in the nineteenth), in the United States the congressional representative was most likely the
only person in his district to travel with any regularity to Washington, D.C. Until communication improved during the second and third decades of the century,
congressmen (especially from remote districts in the South and the West) dispatched to individual constituents and local newspapers hundreds of copies of
printed circular letters in which they summarized federal news largely excerpted
from government documents. Much of the information came from officially published documents such as presidential messages (the first of which was printed in
1803) and reports from cabinet members, especially the secretary of the Treasury.

The state extended invaluable support to the press that amounted to a subsidy.
Newspapers enjoyed especially low postal rates. Postmasters collected subscriptions. Publishers could exchange newspapers for free and used this privilege to
traffic in news reports. A significant portion of the news segment of antebellum
papers was comprised of excerpts lifted from other papers around the country.[6]
Selected newspapers close to the administration were given direct official assistance and particular printing tasks, including the production of executive and
legislative documents ordered by Congress. Beginning in 1789, the State Department, custodian of the acts of Congress, assigned the publication of "authentic copies" of laws and resolutions to newspapers in every state and territory.
In the following decades, government further extended the promulgation of the
laws through papers, which it assigned to political friends. By the 1870s, the number of designated newspapers reached a few hundred. Congress utilized other
means besides newspapers to transfer information from the Capitol. The "franking" privilege of representatives and senators permitted them to send mail without charge. This advantage endowed federal lawmakers with a centrifugal might
and facilitated the dispensation of an enormous mass of printed matter from
Washington to the rest of the country.

The dissemination of federal laws and the publicity of congressional proceedings occupied the legislature early on. An 1822 House committee declared,
"The Government of the United States being a Government which essentially
depends upon public opinion, it is a consideration of the first importance that the
course pursued by the immediate representatives of the people in Congress
should be impartially presented to public view."[7] Congress and the executive
sought to advertise legislation and government action, but, most importantly, the
arteries of the nineteenth-century information superhighway would remain

wide open in order to maintain the contact between congressmen and their districts, senators and their states, and parties and their voters.

The Constitution prescribed that each house keep a journal of its proceedings and publish it occasionally. In 1789, Congress decided to print six hundred copies of the congressional acts and seven hundred copies of its journals. By the early years of the nineteenth century, the newly established *National Intelligencer*, edited by Samuel H. Smith, positioned itself as the public organ of the administration. Smith was allotted State Department law patronage and was asked to print 350 copies of evidence in Aaron Burr's trial at Richmond. Joseph Gales Jr. and William W. Seaton soon overtook the *Intelligencer*, arguably the first national paper. It published abbreviated reports of congressional proceedings, usually weeks after they had taken place. In 1794, the Senate had opened its debates, hitherto conducted behind closed doors, for press reporting. Gales and Seaton would become important public figures in Washington, D.C., and both served as mayor.

Beginning in 1817, Congress launched a serial publication of bound volumes, largely in the octavo format, that featured congressional papers and reports, presidential communications, accounts by executive departments, and other official and nongovernmental documents (including, later, annual reports by the Boy and Girl Scouts, the American Historical Association, the Daughters of the American Revolution, and additional, similarly charted, civic organizations). This ongoing series would become known as the *Congressional Serial Set*, or, until the turn of the twentieth century, the *Sheep Set*, for the expensive sheep skin that bound individual volumes.[8]

Early in the century, both houses established a system of contracting out printing to the lowest bidder. Congressional printing expanded but was notoriously inaccurate and slow. Important documents were not printed, and occasionally they simply got lost. In late 1818, a joint committee visited printers in New York and Philadelphia and eventually rejected the lower bidding system. Despite its ostensible economy, the pressure to underbid competition incurred cheap, low-quality productions. The committee reminded Congress that documents were sent to Europe and "are executed in such an inelegant and incorrect manner, as must bring disgrace and ridicule on the literature, and the press of our country."[9] In order to achieve promptitude, uniformity, accuracy, and even elegance, it was recommended that a national printing office be established. Another forty years passed before government implemented the idea. Meanwhile, in 1819, Congress decided to institute a fixed schedule of prices. Each house was to elect a printer. Congress thus reversed the trajectory of free market ascendancy by terminating an open contract system. Fixed rates made official printing especially profitable, and it became even more so when the introduction of new technologies considerably lowered expenses. Gales and Seaton were the first to enjoy the largess of the new arrangement.

Printing would become emblematic of Jacksonian patronage. Even before the 1828 elections, the Jacksonians were strong enough to assist their paper, Duff Green's *United States Telegraph.* In late 1827, the Senate selected Green as its printer. On the eve of the elections, supporters of Jackson in Congress far surpassed their foes' efforts by a massive franking of forty thousand copies of Green's paper. Simultaneously, they attacked previous forms of patronage. An 1826 committee headed by Senator Thomas Hart Benton charged, "The Government press is, to all intents and purposes, effectually established . . . for the purpose of purchasing the joint and harmonious action of one hundred papers, in the uncompromising vindication of those in power, and in the unsparing abuse of those who are not."[10] This campaign seemed to echo anti–*ancien regime* sentiments from the other side of the ocean but also appropriated rhetorical strategies from America's revolutionary past. Ultimately, the Jacksonian solution to the problem of patronage was not its abolition but its redistribution in accordance with the political will of the people as manifested in election results. Soon after the new administration assumed office, it replaced 70 percent of the newspapers on the list. When the Whigs came to power in 1841, they followed the same pattern. Jackson's ultimate break with the *Telegraph* introduced a new organ, Francis P. Blair's *Congressional Globe.* When Jackson decided to remove government deposits from the Bank of the United States, he gave a statement of his reasons to the *Globe* for publication five days before issuing the official order of removal.

In the next two decades, Gales and Seaton, Force, Green, and Blair and Rives played musical chairs in the world of congressional printing. Throughout the period, congressional committees scrutinized printing profits and abuses while parties and factions negotiated the selection of printers for both houses. Printers were obviously exploiting congressmen's ignorance of their craft. It was also alleged that they funneled money to help elect friendly representatives. Hosts of incremental reforms led eventually to the resumption of the contract system in 1846. Each house appointed a committee on printing and subsequently formed a joint committee on printing. Once again, the bidding system failed. Fierce competition eliminated revenue, and in the early 1850s Congress returned to the practice of electing House and Senate printers under rates fixed by laws. A superintendent of public printing was appointed.

During President Franklin Pierce's tenure, government printing exploded.

For printing, binding, papers, and related processing, the Thirty-third and Thirty-fourth Congresses paid $3,899,000, more than the total cost for all the previous sessions since 1819. Select committees exposed new abuses, including printers subcontracting to others for a substantial profit. The House 1860 investigation of public printing became a Republication campaign document. Extracts were published as a pamphlet called "The Ruin of the Democratic Party."[11] In 1860, three committees began hearings that would lead to the creation of the Government Printing Office, preceding the British Stationery Office's takeover of printing assignments by at least half a century (but behind the French *Impremerie National* by two centuries). Lincoln's administration also signaled the end of a single presidential paper in Washington. Printing became a government function, but Reconstruction would demonstrate that Congress retained much of its control over the domains of publication and knowledge production.

Citizens and Readers

The public-funded printing press was recruited for political purposes in diverse ways that exceeded patronage to printers and newspapers. For example, Congressman Abraham Lincoln wrote in May 1848 to a constituent, "I will place your name on my book, and send you such documents as you desire, when I can get them. The entire [Mexican] War correspondence is in course of printing, and will be the best electioneering document, when completed. I will then send you a copy of it."[12] Senator Sumner from Massachusetts corresponded regularly with numerous Boston-area reformers, many of who habitually asked for and duly received public documents and reports. In February 1860, Sumner informed a C. F. Smith in Boston that he had forwarded him the eighth and ninth volumes of the Pacific Railroad Surveys under his frank. Since there was reason to believe that the valuable reports were often stolen from the post office, he asked him to confirm that the volume indeed arrived. At the end of that year, Sumner wrote to a constituent that he could not obtain the first volume of the Pacific Railroad report although it was available in the bookstores. However, "I have great pleasure in sending you the others. In the distribution of this valuable work I act as a trustee for the good of science, to which you tell me you are devoted. I congratulate you upon the career of study before you."[13]

Sumner provided many congressional papers to the abolitionist Theodore Parker, including documents on Cuba and Haiti and other material concerning the slave trade. This exchange took place shortly after the publication of *Uncle Tom's Cabin*, when Parker was assisting Harriet Beecher Stowe in collecting anecdotes to defend the veracity of claims made in her novel, an effort that led to the factual *Key to Uncle Tom's Cabin* (1853).[14] Samuel Gridley Howe, a long-time friend of Sumner, was particularly keen on amassing government publications. He often asked Sumner to supply him particular volumes and concurrently requested other Massachusetts members of Congress to complete the missing parts of the series. Responding to such requests was part of a lawmaker's daily routine, and not only political friends solicited for documents. A representative from Virginia received a letter from a Harper's Ferry resident who somewhat apologetically (describing himself "a stranger and a Whig") asked for a copy of David Dale Owen's geological survey and promised to reciprocate the favor if the congressmen would ever visit his area.[15]

A fall 1850 Senate debate on the purchase of a compilation known as Hickey's edition of the Constitution demonstrated the senators' attentiveness to constituents' reading tastes. The resolution called for purchasing ten thousand copies of Hickey's primer, which, in addition to the Constitution, featured George Washington's inaugural and farewell addresses and some statistical matter, "illustrative of the genius of the American Government, and the development of its principles." Congress had ordered this work before in thousands of copies. To those who questioned the legislative aim of the purchase, Senator George E. Badger, from North Carolina, replied that the object was simply wide distribution. "I know of no books which either House of Congress has at any time circulated which is so valuable, and so generally acceptable, and so much desired by our constituents as this very book."[16] David Rice Atchison (Missouri) contended that the Constitution was more diffused and more easily obtained than any other document. It served as the preface of every state constitution and appeared in numerous digests of laws. The Constitution could be purchased in every bookstore across the land. "Who will get these books?" he asked. Only a few among 20 million people.

Atchison's skepticism did not dominate the discussion. Thomas Jefferson Rusk (Texas) argued that Congress paid much more for inferior documents. "If congress never goes into extravagance till it does it in circulating the Constitution of the United States among the people, we shall be a very economical Government, indeed."[17] Senator M. Gwin from California suggested that if Atchison had tired of franking his books, then he was willing to take charge of the extra share. Gwin's county (San Francisco) had not received the compilations last time they were given away, and his constituents certainly wanted their due allowance. Isaac P. Walker (Wisconsin) reported receiving letters from those in favor of the abolition of the franking privilege who, nevertheless, still wished the government to put Hickey's book in the hands of every U.S. citizen. "I believe I can say that in Wisconsin it has had a good effect on the sentiments and political opinions of the people, and has introduced a high feeling of patriotism wherever it has been read."[18] The resolution was accepted twenty-two to nineteen.

The most popular nineteenth-century official publication was arguably the Agriculture Report of the Patent Office. In 1849, the commissioner of patent issued the first report as part of his annual communication. Congress printed more copies of this report than any other official document, and congressmen sent it to voters, especially during campaigns. It was an illustrated volume featuring a medley of articles and correspondences on field cultivation and animal husbandry, better seeds, improved grafts, and other such useful or simply interesting details. The 1858 report, to give one example, was a 552-page octavo affair that opened with a series of woodcuts, the first of which was a large drawing of the Tibetan yak. A rather inconspicuous essay contemplated the introduction of the yak to the Great Plains as a mean to improve the condition of the Indian tribes and to expedite their civilization, "for the possession of property is a strong bond of society."[19] The decision to display the yak at the beginning of the report had less to do, it seems, with the gravity of the proposal than with the illustration of the impressive humped mammal.

In addition, the reader could find a potpourri of practical and not so practical information: an article on farming and education, agricultural statistics, a piece on the classification of Midwestern weasels, a discussion of new brands of grapes and apples, and more than a hundred pages dedicated to short descriptions of local agricultural societies. The volume featured a continent-long list, exceeding 1,700 items, of statistical queries for readers who would like to volunteer information. The questionnaire (a commonly used device) was an invitation for an exchange of information between government and its readers, a nineteenth-century form of interactive media. The Patent Office also declared that it initiated the importation of seeds from foreign countries (an agent was sent to bring tea-shrub seeds from China) and the gathering of farming knowledge in Europe. The binding displayed an intricate design of a female figure (probably Cornucopia herself) sitting on a plow shaft by a head of wheat and a mound of fruits, holding a sickle in one hand and a shorter head of wheat in the other.

In March 1850, Congressman William McWillie (Mississippi) presented a resolution on behalf of the House printing committee to issue thirty thousand copies of the mechanical portion of the Patent Office report and seventy thousand of the agriculture report. There were more farmers than mechanics, he explained, and since the document was too long for a single volume, there had to be a corresponding difference in the number of printed copies.[20] Some were uneasy about the need to choose among constituents. For instance, Robert McLane, a Democrat from Maryland, calculated that one hundred thousand copies of the two parts of the report would give four or five hundred to each member for distribution. Constituents would be aware of that and congressmen could not limit the allocation only to institutions. After all, members received private requests for these books daily. Robert A. Toombs (Georgia) questioned whether it was Congress's business to teach the people what their interest was. The purpose of public printing was to inform the people of the actions of their government and legislature. In a constituency of twenty thousand only one in every forty would receive the report, the cost of which would ultimately be paid by everyone. David K. Cartter (Ohio) countered that regardless of distribution rates government owed information to the people. There was in his argument a trace of regional animosity. "West of the mountains, the people got nothing from the Government but intelligence. Of the $30,000,000 which were annually taken from the people, to supply the Treasury, why should they not be permitted to receive back five mills on the dollar, in the way of information?"[21] Government established the Patent Office to guarantee the fruits of inventive genius and to inform the people of the latest inventions and mechanical improvements

But another Democrat, Albert Gallatin Brown (Mississippi), argued that if the reason for printing was informing the people, why wasn't the representative from Ohio suggesting printing the House journal in tens of thousands of copies? The real target was evident. "We all know very well what an effect might be sometimes produced by sending a book to some particular constituent, in a doubtful part of the district, in securing his exertions in favor of the member who had sent it."[22] Despite these and other reservations, the number of printed copies of the agriculture report grew dramatically. By 1877, orders rose to 300,000 with 224,000 to the House, 56,000 to the Senate, and 20,000 for the Department of Agriculture. The 1884 edition had 400,000 copies. In 1894, the report was replaced by the *Agriculture Yearbook*, which survived well into the twentieth century. In 1880, the commissioner of agriculture complained that while the number of copies was larger than that of any annual book ever published, it was not yet half large enough to meet the "reasonable and pressing demand."[23]

Binding and Boundlessness

In another congressional debate, the House considered producing an extra ten thousand copies of a report from the Treasury on statistics of commerce and navigation. Representative John A. McLernand, a Democrat from Illinois, suggested reducing the number of copies by half. The report, he explained, was probably a valuable document but as a source of practical information it best suited the interests of navigators, merchants, and boards of trade. "It was such a document as the mass of the people would neither have leisure nor taste to trace into its arithmetic details."[24] Moreover, he saw political motivation behind the printing proposal. Purporting to be the patrons of internal improvement and commerce, Whigs promoted the report. In the same spirit, Congressman Jacob Thompson, a fellow Democrat from Mississippi, remarked that the report would be particularly valued in the districts along the seacoast, where the shipping interest was strong, but less so in the interior among farmers. Since none of his constituents had ever asked him for the document, he assumed that they were not concerned with the details of trade and were satisfied with "aggregates." "Some to whom I might send it, when they find it only a book of figures, might take up the conception that I only sent it to them to puzzle their brains."[25] The *Globe*'s stenographer heard someone in the hall exclaiming, "Perhaps your constituents cannot read?"[26]

John Houston, a Delaware Whig, was surprised to hear that constituents took no interest in this account. From what other source would Mississippi farmers derive information about the export of their greatest staple, cotton? The report was important for the South. Another representative computed that the proposal would leave about three hundred copies for each of the thirty-four states and territories, five copies per county. His colleagues from Mississippi would surely find five interested persons in each county of his district. It was Thompson's duty to encourage them to get interested in these figures and to make "a wise and patriotic use of them."[27] Eventually, the House decided to authorize publication. Beyond its panoply of sectional and political considerations, this debate offered two market-driven approaches to the diffusion of state knowledge; one emphasized constituents' stated needs, and the other saw a role for the representative in eliciting grassroots demand.

At times it seemed that the task of sending official publications back home overwhelmed American lawmakers. On the last day of 1850, the House busied itself with the question of whether to issue the president's annual message in one or two volumes. The document stretched over almost one thousand pages. Representing the Printing Committee, Thomas J. D. Fuller argued that the larger number of volumes would mean they could be sent to many more constituents. Alas, some congressmen saw in the endlessly multiplying volumes too much of a good thing. Dividing the reports would make it difficult to follow their exact distribution. Congressmen would have to keep a list and send the second part to all of those who received the first, otherwise they would face disgruntled voters. Congressman John Wentworth confirmed that in the previous year, when the message was bound in three parts, he got into trouble, for he sent different parts to different people and was subsequently deluged by requests for the two missing volumes. The amendment to print only one volume passed.[28]

The debate over the president's message took place while a new practice was rendering governmental publications ever closer to actual books. Large executive reports (over 250 pages) in the octavo *Congressional Series* were to be bound with hard cover as a matter of policy anchored in renewable legislation. Representative McWillie obtained for the inspection of the House specimens of alternative bindings. We could bind for less, he explained on the floor, but the committee figured that if congressional documents were to be properly treated, the work would better be performed in half-morocco style. That December a resolution was proposed to bind in a "superior manner" the forthcoming three thousand copies of the "Reconnaissances of Routes from San Antonio to El Paso." The estimated cost was thirty cents a copy, more than double the ordinary binding expense. Senator Solon Borland (Arkansas) explained that these reports were brimming "with a large number of beautifully executed plates; and the committee deem them of sufficient excellence and value to have them bound in better style than such documents have been bound heretofore."[29] Senator Hannibal Hamlin (Maine) likewise praised the document. "It is indeed an ornament, and adorned with some of the finest specimens of engravings that I have ever witnessed."[30] Lawmakers wished, therefore, that official documents could be judged by their covers. Endowing reports with a booklike exterior opened a new expanse for aesthetic signification. Several senators noticed, however, that with the clamor over binding, congressional committees became entrapped in commercial activities. Senators Badger and Benton declared that committees should not engage in the business of trading, dealing, and making bargains.

Once again, official publications tempted a legislature to become an agent in the marketplace, not through legislation, policy supervision, or patronage but as a consumer or producer. By binding its documents, Congress was transcending its own boundaries. Commissioning its printing tasks, Congress either set the price or offered the job to the lowest bidder. In the case of binding, it appeared that congressmen were negotiating special deals with merchants and literally bringing the marketplace to the floor by presenting there various commercial products. Benton thought that the Senate's administrative staff should handle those matters. But his remarks demonstrated how preoccupied senators were with the minute details of printed documents, for he argued that if binding was to improve, stitching should be taken into consideration as well. Books fell to pieces while their bindings stayed intact. He predicted future abuses driven by jealousy and competition among governmental departments to get their reports bound in the "superior" style.

In tedious debates over binding, lawmakers increasingly sounded like booksellers, comparing the value of muslin to other forms of binding and bickering over the best methods of preserving books that were destined to make long journeys in postal bags. Countering the presumption that without binding the documents would be useless, Senator John P. Hale, representing an increasing public sarcasm toward congressional publications, could not resist the opposite idea that the binding was their only valuable part. "Now, if it is worth while to print these documents to send to our friends, it is certainly worth while to put upon them this ninepenny binding; for instead of tearing them up, as they would inevitably do if they were not bound, they allow them a place on the shelves of their libraries, there to remain, sir, like many of our documents here, never to be opened and read again."[31] In contrast, Alexander Evans (Maryland) complained that, with all the attention given to binding, congressmen overlooked the production quality of the texts. The paper was inferior, "being such as was used in the grocer's shops for ordinary wrapping, full of blurs, blemishes, and impurities."[32] State printing done in Virginia, South Carolina, and, above all, Massachusetts and New York was far superior. Better still, he suggested his colleague examine the papers produced for the British House of Commons. They would blush with embarrassment at the poor quality of the documents Congress dispatched in exchange. "Mr. Speaker . . . it does not become a great and prosperous nation, interested in preserving the records of its greatness, and its prosperity, and in imparting to the people the fullest degree of information in the most durable and imperishable form, to submit any longer to the present style of public printing."[33]

Americanization

The American scheme that was closest to the British plan to prepare workingmen for participation in the polity by encouraging them to read parliamentary literature involved the prospect of nationalization rather than the question of enfranchisement. In December 1850, the Senate deliberated over printing two thousand copies of the president's message in Spanish. Senator Gwin presented the motion as a measure to instruct the Spanish-speaking population in his new state of California as well as those residing in New Mexico territory.[34] The ensuing debate centered on government obligations toward specific cultural com-

munities and the means available to the state to insure the assimilation of foreigners into the United States. Predictably, several senators warned, if Congress
were to agree to translate a document into a foreign language, it would eventually have to underwrite many other translations. Senator Badger demurred. This
was not a precedent-setting gesture. The United States had acquired, partly by
the sword and partly by treaty, a large piece of land inhabited by Spanish-speaking people. "We have brought them into the Union, and I think that, under such
circumstances, it is wise and just and reasonable to present them this document
in their own language."[35]

James W. Bradbury (Maine) reminded the chamber that the acquisition of
Louisiana with its French-speaking population, or Spanish-speaking Florida,
had not prompted a similar initiative. All American citizens should be induced
to speak one language, he asserted. Senator Henry S. Foote (Mississippi) claimed
to be mortified by this reasoning. Refusing to translate was comparable to the behavior of the Roman tyrant who hanged his edicts so high that the citizens might
not be able to read them. "I thought we had determined to do all we could speedily to Americanize those persons . . . I thought we were all disposed to supply, in
the most liberal manner, facilities to those people to acquire a knowledge of our
institutions and the *modus operandi* of our Government, and to acquit themselves
honorably in all respects, as doubtless they are ambitious of doing, in the dis-
charge of their duties as American citizens."[36] In order to defeat the proposal,
Senator Walker motioned to print a similar number of documents in German
and Norwegian. There were about ninety thousand immigrants in Wisconsin
who spoke little else, but they did not expect such a gesture from government
and instead had established presses of their own. "They [the Spanish-speaking
Californians] are now a portion of our fellow-citizens; their destiny is ours; and
it is their vital interest to speak the common language of the country."[37]

In response, Senator Gwin raised a new set of arguments. There was no paper in the Spanish language printed in California at that moment. The new citizens did not have the same facilities to obtain this message as did the constituents
of the senator from Wisconsin. The Mexican population was concentrated in the
southern part of the state, isolated from the English speakers of the North. They
were "natives of the soil," brought under this government without either their
knowledge or consent, unlike the immigrants in Wisconsin, who had come purposefully to enjoy the institutions of this country. This prompted Augustus
Dodge from Iowa to suggest that Congress should not make distinctions between
immigrants and those who became Americans by territorial expansion, but if
special treatment was warranted, then immigrants from Europe had greater

claims, for they had left their homes and traveled far to become "a part and parcel of our people."[38] Another midwesterner, Salmon P. Chase from Ohio, thought that many Germans would probably welcome a German version of the president's message. Each case should, however, be decided on its own merit. If there was a large enough group that wished for a translation, it should be offered. Similarly, Senator Badger allowed that government should engage in a legislation that would "fuse" foreigners as quickly as possible but considered the newly annexed population of the Southwest a special case. They were secluded, "shut out from all the ordinary benefits which those who can read these public documents can attain."[39] The resolution was tabled and not discussed further. Still, this debate is significant not merely for the way it prefigured major themes in late twentieth-century controversies over bilingualism in education, but for the unchallenged conviction that reading the president's annual message regardless of language would have an "Americanizing" effect. In all of these cases, proponents spoke in terms of pedagogical (or assimilatory) efficacy and fairness (towards "accidental Americans" or children); foes objected to government-sponsored cultural heterogeneity and saw the English language, rather than the polity or education, as the medium of integration.

Two years later, New Yorker Eugene Plunkett offered Congress a Spanish-language compilation of the Declaration of Independence, the Constitution, Washington's farewell address, and additional documents of similar stature. In his memorial, Plunkett reiterated arguments made in the Senate debate in favor of translating foundational documents for the benefit of Spanish-speaking citizens. Other immigrants could scatter among the masses "and speedily imbibe from association not only a knowledge of American principles but a sympathy with American feelings."[40] The annexed Spanish population remained immobile and retained its social fabric and contacts. Congress therefore had to intervene (literally compensating for lack of social intercourse) and enlighten the new population "with a thorough knowledge of the rights and privileges they enjoy under our government." The committee endorsed the proposal but no further action was taken.[41]

Archives in Print

One conspicuous class of private initiative that did receive federal support was serial compilations of historical documents, a popular undertaking among congressmen. The first systematic attempt to gather such documents was recorded as far back as the War of Independence, when Ebenezer Hazard sent a memorial to the president of the Continental Congress soliciting official patronage for a collection of state papers in order to document the country's birth. The Continental Congress granted its approval and provided one thousand dollars as an advance. Hazard privately published two volumes. There were comparable ventures following the war of 1812. In January 1816, the firm of Thomas B. Wait and Sons requested Congress to extend its patronage to the second edition of its *State Papers and Public Documents*, eight volumes of which had been already issued. The publishers promised an enlarged edition that would include previously confidential papers. Consequently, Congress passed a law authorizing the secretary of state to subscribe for five hundred copies of the improved edition. Two year later, Congress sanctioned the publication of the *Diplomatic Correspondence of the American Revolution* and the *Journal of the Constitutional Convention of 1787*. Jared Sparks conducted the former project. By 1829, he completed ten volumes of diplomatic exchange.[42]

In later decades, such projects would become more ambitious and costly. Gales and Seaton initiated the largest of the antebellum documentary projects, the *American State Papers*, which Congress financed in its entirety. After losing their congressional printing contract to Green in 1829, they contemplated alternative projects that would keep their press working. In March 1831, after two years of intensive lobbying, they finally succeeded by a narrow vote. Gales and Seaton claimed that manuscript copies of state papers were subject to mutilation from overuse and constant reference, and that beyond their utility for the statesman and the student, state papers should be saved by print "as a monument of the past, and beacons of the future. A proper National pride demands that they shall be rescued from oblivion."[43] The role of the British government (in the days before the public record reform) in preserving documents by publishing not merely printed versions but actual facsimiles of historical records was invoked as an example of a nation committed to salvaging and preserving its documentary heritage. The enterprising duo emphasized that written law and doctrine were of greater consequence in the United States than in Britain. The *American State Papers* stretched over thirty-eight folio volumes that required thirty years to complete (1861). The work was divided thematically into ten series (e.g., Finance, Indian Affairs, Public Lands), and included documents from 1789 up to 1832. It was the first consistent attempt to publish documentary history according to a rigorous plan. The clerk of the House and the secretary of the Senate assumed a role in selecting the documents.

Another historical project that Gales and Seaton launched in 1834 was the *Annals of Congress*, which they were soon forced to abandon but then resumed in the mid-1850s. Its forty-two volumes included debates, proceedings, and other documents from 1789 to 1824. It was devised to complement the *Register of Debates in Congress*, a venture born in 1824 as the first publication entirely devoted to transcripts of congressional debates. The scramble to publish the records of Congress in full was thus to move simultaneously forward and backward in time. Gales and Seaton also conceived and promoted the *Register* as an effort at history writing. In the preface of their first volume, they proclaimed, "It is a History which cannot deceive, because it reflects, in the faithful mirror of Truth, not only the motives of public acts, but also the grounds on which those acts were opposed. Its impartiality may defy the most fastidious scrutiny."[44] Twenty-seven volumes were issued until the *Register* was eclipsed by the *Congressional Globe* and finally lost support in 1837. What started as a commercial venture received official subsidy when each house subscribed for five hundred copies. In their attempts to revive the *Annals of Congress* in the early 1840s, Gales and Seaton extolled the importance of print in preserving history. It was the only device to arrest national amnesia. "Already, hardly any traces of the doings of the early Congresses are to be found except in the skeleton remains which the Journals of the two Houses have preserved from decay.... Unless immediate means be taken to perpetuate it, the History of Congress will come to be almost as little known as that of the World before the flood."[45]

The historical knowledge the printers were so keen on preserving was the original intent of the union's founders. Securing this wealth of political knowledge would enable the present generation to comprehend constitutional theory as expounded by its framers. By an act of March 1833, the secretary of state contracted another printer and entrepreneur, Peter Force, and the former clerk of the House of Commons Matthew St. Clair Clarke for the publication of *The Documentary History of the American Revolution*. The planned twenty volumes were projected to cost half a million dollars. The series, eventually titled the *American Archives*, was fraught with difficulties from its inception. Nine volumes appeared, but in the 1850s, for reasons that remain unclear, the project fell out of favor with the administration and was practically terminated.[46] From the 1820s on, there were also efforts in the South and New England to collect documents and prepare state histories. North Carolina, Georgia, South Carolina, Rhode Island, and the American Antiquarian Society each attempted to secure access to British repositories in London in search of relevant historical documents. Collecting Americana became a hobby of sorts among the well-to-do. Henry Stevens, Jr. (with whose testimony in the House of Common we began this chapter) arrived in London in 1845 as a representative of a group of affluent

New England collectors like John Carter Brown of Providence and Governor William Slade of Vermont.[47]

Contemporary reviewers considered the republication of historical papers the best method for archiving history. Gales and Seaton's lobbying effort also indicated the emergence of a cultural field dedicated to the interpretation of the Constitution and nurtured by judicial review and recurrent public discord over the proper reading of the constitutional. As Michael Warner has remarked, the U.S. Constitution and the hermeneutics it inspired bonded public life and print culture in America in novel ways. Importantly, the U.S. documentary legacy, as national memory itself, was to be arranged around the symbolic presence of the nation's founders. The veneration of founding fathers—the American version of hero worship—was prompted, in part, by the demise of the 1776 generation, so powerfully symbolized by the death of Thomas Jefferson and John Adams on Independence Day 1826. Regardless of their commercial underpinnings, historical publishing projects should be understood in the context of this particular generational shift, which coincided with the rise of Jacksonian politics to generate a collective perception of a historic watershed.

Congress decided (1846) to purchase the papers of James Madison from his widow, with the tacit understanding that by doing so the federal government would also be giving her an informal pension. A select committee of the House reported, "It is a natural and commendable desire [to procure and publish these documents], considering the agency which Mr. Madison had in the formation of the Constitution which binds together these States in one great and powerful confederacy."[48] The committee predicted that any legal challenge to Congress's engagement in such publishing schemes would fail. Congress had established a library that held printed work and manuscript collections. In the same year, Elizabeth Hamilton petitioned Congress to sponsor the publication of her late husband's papers. "The subjects contained in the proposed publication are intimately blended with the vital interests and permanent prosperity of the American people, presenting the conduct and character of General Hamilton, on all national questions."[49] Since she did not have the means to publish the work herself, she asked Congress to purchase one thousand copies of the planned five volumes, Alexander Hamilton's *Works,* with the understanding that the original correspondence, documents, and papers would be deposited in the library as a national property. The Senate accepted the offer.

Three years later, Congress received a petition from Samuel L. Gouverneur, the executor of James Monroe's will. The petitioner promoted Monroe's correspondence and papers during the war with Britain as "explanatory of [the war's] ori-

gin, progress, and termination, [and] would afford efficient aid in the future eluci-
dation of its history, and a fair distribution of justice among those who took part
therein." The petitioner had been busy selecting material and organizing documents for the publication. "*The History of the Life of James Monroe* would be, if
executed on a proper scale, for that period of time, *a history, essentially, of the country which gave him birth.*"[50] He made another interesting bid for the purchase. Congress already lent its support to similar endeavors. The published papers of other
presidents addressed many of the issues that occupied Monroe. Some of the most
important letters of the time were exchanged among Monroe, Jefferson, and Madison. If other presidential paper projects would be executed rightly, the commercial
value of the independent publication of Monroe's papers would inevitably decline.
Financially unfeasible, the project would not find private support. Congress, he implied, was morally responsible for the public consequences of its intervention in the
business of publishing. Support was therefore not just a matter of national memory but an issue of fairness as well. (While the printed form of monument building became a routine, the capital city endured the ungainly sight of the unfinished
Washington Monument. For more than two decades after its cornerstone was
placed (1848), that obelisk stood unfinished—a decaying stump among the herds
of sheep and cows that roamed what is known today as the National Mall.)

The Battle of the Books

As we have seen, 1850 was a frantic year for congressional printers and binders. That summer, Senator Foote proposed in the name of the Foreign Relations
Committee that the Senate assist the publication of a study by Aaron H. Palmer
entitled "A Comprehensive View of the Principal Independent Maritime Countries of the East." Foote notified the chamber that the work was warmly recommended by the secretary of state.[51] Like Henry Rowe Schoolcraft, who a few
years earlier convinced Congress to support his Indian project, Palmer was an intellectual entrepreneur. He had already lobbied and petitioned for other similarly oriented projects and had been temporarily hired to examine the diplomatic
correspondence on China and the East. The former administration had unsuccessfully pressured for an appropriation of ten thousand dollars to dispatch
Palmer to conduct research in Asia. Foote's proposal prompted one of the most
thunderous Senate debates over the role of the federal state in sponsoring the
publication of books.

The motion specified three thousand copies to be purchased by the Senate,
each to cost no more than two dollars and include no less than five hundred oc-

tavo pages. Congress expected a measurable return for its money. Anticipating a strong partisan sentiment, Senator Hamlin argued for a political quid pro quo. He recalled that during that session, Congress ordered ten thousand extra copies of a report of the secretary of the Treasury on American industry although they were obviously tracts for protectionism, a doctrine favored by "the other side of the chamber." Nevertheless, he had supported that publication "on the ground that error may be promulgated where truth is left freed to combat it." Now, when a different kind of document serving commercial interests was offered, should not these views and information be spread as well before the people, and for the sake of commerce? Senator William Dayton, another of Palmer's supporters, maintained that Congress already sponsored the project. For all purposes, Palmer was a congressional employee, and the remaining question was how to present his manuscript to the public. If the aim is "to make it readable, if I may be allowed the expression, or attractive to the public mind, it is necessary to give some aid in this form to the attempt to secure the benefits of those labors."[52] Senator Pierre Soulé (Louisiana) concurred. He read the book and thought its value would more than compensate for the expense. He also noticed reviews in the French press praising the research. The United States was "in the dark" regarding prospective relations with Asian countries.

Apparently, the untiring Palmer had already presented an early version of the new manuscript to the library committee under the title "The Geography and History of the Unknown Countries of the East."[53] Jefferson Davis quoted St. John as saying that the world could not contain all the books that might be written. If Congress were to publish all the books deemed beneficial to the country, the Capitol would not be able to contain them. Only original research conducted by individuals engaged directly by Congress ought to be published. Senator Rusk declared that theirs was "the age of books and the age of discovery." If a precedent were established, every similar book on phrenology, mesmerism, biology, and other topics that might attract the attention of the European reviewers would be deemed to merit the Senate's subscription.

Despite caustic remarks, Palmer's supporters appeared initially to garner enough support. In late August, however, after two floor discussions on Palmer's book, Senator Benton made his harshest assault to date. In the late 1840s, Benton emerged as the most vitriolic opponent of lavish publication projects. He alleged that the abuse of public money by supplying senators with books commenced seventeen years earlier, when Congress consented to publish Peter Force's *Documentary History of the American Revolution*. The books obtained ever since were useless, or worse, dangerous. As an example, he furnished Robert

Greenhow's *History of Oregon and California* (1844). Congress had purchased the book a few years earlier under the pretext that senators needed information to form their opinion on the dispute with Britain. It was better to seek advice in a fountainhead, he quipped. Senators had at their disposal all the necessary documents on the history of the negotiations between the two countries, as well as plenty of books on western explorations. He was now convinced that because of abridgments and omissions of important aspects of the historical negotiations between Albert Gallatin and the British government over Oregon, the book almost brought the United States and Britain to the brink of war. Instead of guiding the federal legislature, it misled lawmakers on issues of cardinal importance in a time of international tension. The omissions, he implied, were intentional and served a purpose.[54] Benton's illustration provides another instance of a legislature entangled in its own print product as well as a warning against history books that purport to replace actual archives.

Palmer's project did not address any prospective legislation. Moreover, the resolution granted Palmer his own copyright. Since when did Congress award copyrights? Why was the text, merely a humble paper, dignified by the resolution as an official "document"? Palmer's paper turned into a document by a process of "filtration," Benton sneered.

> This "document" after having been spun and wove by Mr. Palmer, not out of his own bowels, like the spider's web, but out of other people's brains and books, was carried to the Department of State and asked house room. There are a great many good men in this world, and many of them have been Secretaries of State. Many things have been carried and left there, and kindly cared for. The bantling is left and, and when it is wanted, he who put it there knows where to find it. As the boys say in the street, the fox is the finder; and in this case, I presume there was a deposit of this paper with the Secretary of State, and that Aaron H. Palmer was the finder . . . Well, members of Congress get their feelings excited, and call for the paper. It comes down with great dignity. It comes down from the Secretary of State, stopping in at the President's for his private secretary to bring it up to Congress. Hence it must be dignified; it must be deemed very respectable. It comes upon us imposingly. It is then referred to a committee. The committee brings it back to the House. By then it has ripened into *"a document,"* and not only ripened into a document, but it has undergone so many filtrations and received so many *imprimatures* that its value can scarcely be calculated.[55]

There was a vicious streak in Benton's remarks but also, arguably, an insight into the nature of authority and authorship. In his reading, Palmer's authorship was dubious, for he merely hauled bits and pieces from others' work. The manuscript needed a surrogate author, which was found in the form of the State Department. Never really lost, it was rendered a document by the virtue of its fictitious retrieval, which set the text in endless motion. Once "found," it went "down" and "up," and was then "referred" and brought "back." Endowed with a deconstructive edge, Benton's critique addressed not just Palmer's manipulations but also the easily excitable, ignorant behavior of official power. The history of the document as document could be easily culled from "the face of the paper" by reading its title, which swelled considerably, accumulating parts at all the stops made by the paper along the way. By the conclusion of Benton's speech, the author of the study on the "unknown" countries of the East appeared to be the worst of conspirators. "He is here; he is levant, couchant, and cormorant here. And he undertakes to make a book for us without our leave." Benton believed merchants did not wait for Congress to tell them where to look for trade. He even quoted Christophe, the emperor of Haiti, who reportedly said, "hang up a bag of coffee in hell, a Yankee would go and bring it down without being singed."[56]

Benton's satire was echoed in others' comments on congressional publications. A few years later, during the debate over the printing of John Bartlett's report (see chapter 3), Senator Hamlin charged that every person who had the wish to publish a book attached himself to some expedition or survey. By doing so, he had an opportunity to report to the department that had dispatched him and thus was guaranteed a book at the expense of Congress. In other words, once an individual subjected himself to the official hierarchy, what seemed an imposition to report on his assignments in fact enabled him to rise as a writer. It was not that government commissioned individuals to perform tasks, but individuals harnessed government to help them achieve their personal ambitions. Senator Robert Hunter (Virginia) saw in the printing of books at government expense two hazardous desires: the craving of private authors for personal fame, and the consequent demand of the public to have books for nothing, an appetite that government would never be able to satisfy.

Taking its cues from Benton's rhetoric, the Washington press labeled the dispute over Palmer's manuscript "The Battle of the Books," following Jonathan Swift's famous satire. Swift's story featured a war between two camps of adversarial books ensconced in the King's library. The battle reenacted the conflict between modern experimental science and classical scholarship, a rivalry that found Swift firmly on the side of the "Antients." Benton's attempt to conjure the image of the spider alluded to one of the most repulsive "Modern" characters in Swift's piece. Offended by the manner in which his friend Palmer was maligned and ridiculed, Senator Foote read on the Senate floor long passages from Swift. Palmer, he protested, was not the offending spider but his bitter enemy, the diligent honey-producing bee. The tone of the exchange became unmistakably personal. Admittedly, the hatred between the two Democratic senators may have predetermined the course of the debate. A few months earlier, in the heat of an argument over the "Compromise of 1850," Foote, responding to a threat, drew a pistol on Benton; others intervened before he could shoot.

Foote quoted at length Swift's description of the deity called Criticism, whom the Moderns enlisted for their cause, along with her decaying father (and husband) Ignorance; her mother Pride, dressed in scraps of paper; her sister Opinion, headstrong yet giddy; and her equally unattractive children, Noise, Impudence, Dullness, Vanity, Positiveness, Pedantry, and Ill-manners. But Foote had a stronger weapon than Swift's acid pen. He recalled Benton's enthusiastic support for the printing, lithographing, and binding of his son-in-law John Charles Frémont's reports. Benton vehemently denied the comparison, ignoring his own political maneuvers in the early 1840s. Frémont was an officer in the topographical engineers. He had nothing to do with congressional decisions on the printing of his account and nothing to gain from it. Senator James A. Pearce joined with the project's foes and announced he would vote against publication. "There is a great disposition throughout the country to depend too much upon the Government," he warned. This inclination was not confined to any class. Government patronage of books was so often sought after that unless checked Congress would become "a great publishing establishment, that authors and editors may avoid the risk of trade."[57] A weary Senate decided eventually to postpone the debate on the topic indefinitely.

The Traffic in Books

The exchange between authors and government was not the only fictitious transaction in the traffic in congressional books. By the early 1850s, congressmen enriched with official documents not just select group of constituents but themselves as well. After all, the entire practice of purchasing privately published books thrived under the pretext of assisting lawmakers in their duties. In each session, new representatives and senators received a package of official books at least as large as the one voted for in the previous session. In the case of an ongoing series (such as the *American State Papers*), lawmakers were entitled to receive their share for years after they left Washington, as long as there were still new volumes. When in December 1847 the Senate decided to furnish books to new

members, one senator remarked that his colleagues were ostensibly voting themselves a seven or eight hundred dollar pay increase. However, lawmakers in both
chambers found it difficult to abandon this practice, which was steadily becoming costlier. The monetary value of these books rose so much that letters arrived
from deceased congressmen's widows and children requesting the remaining volumes of various publishing projects as their due.[58]

In late 1848, the clerk of the House of Representatives, Thomas Campbell,
had to exercise ingenuity in providing those volumes because the House had decided not to commission expensive new printing but instead to obtain existing
copies. The Clerk was forced to orchestrate a somewhat strange series of exchanges. He commissioned booksellers to purchase official publications from current and previous congressmen so other members could receive them. For example, William Morrison, a merchant from New York, was engaged to furnish
the House with more than one hundred copies of the *American State Papers,
Diplomatic Correspondence,* and *American Archives* in "a clean unmutilated and
perfect condition."[59] Morrison wrote to Thomas Stall in North Carolina offering
him $160 cash for papers that he was entitled to as a member for the Twenty-
third Congress, provided Stall would transfer to him his right to all documents
still owed. The clerk himself received letters from former representatives who
offered (sometimes through proxies) their books.[60] The congressman's library for
that session comprised a mixture of legal, historical, and reference works: *Congressional Globe, Revised Statutes, Register of Debates, Contested Elections,* W.
Hickey's *Constitution, Senate Land Laws,* Peter Force's *American Archives,* Gales
and Seaton's *American State Papers,* and Blair Rives's *Diplomatic Correspondence.*[61] Six years later, the expense for supplying the new 154 members of the
Thirty-third Congress with books and documents rose to $151,949.87; the value
of each individual package climbed to $1,043.85. Besides old staples such as
American Archives, members were now entitled to *Annals of Congress* (forty volumes at $200), as well as Hamilton's *Works* and President John Adams's *Works.*[62]

This circulation of books, as absurd as it was, rested on the multiple roles of
legislators as publishers, book peddlers, and readers. In addition, the idea that
every lawmaker should have his own reference library corresponded with the acknowledgment of authorship in federal documents, for both relied on notions of
individuation and privacy. For Benton, however, this routine brought the abuse
of the book-buying system to its preposterous apex. "It is a fact beating fancy-
furnishing books backwards, retrospectively, retroactively, to the dead, and to the
moved-away, and to the left-out of Congress. It is like pensioning members—
pensioning with books, transmuted into money."[63] The framers of the Constitu-

tion never expected senators, men over thirty, to need "horn-books" to instruct them in their duties. Benton assumed in these congressional debates the role that John Ramsay McCulloch, the comptroller of the Stationery Office had in Britain—gadfly against federal graphomania and frivolous allocation of books.

In the Labyrinth

In 1858, the *New York Herald* declared, "The government printer and his claque in both Houses of Congress are always ready to appropriate money for the 'dissemination of intelligence amongst the people' in the shape of ponderous and costly books."[64] A Senate report blamed printers' greed. For instance, the Pacific Railroad report was originally ordered in an octavo form. The practiced eye of the printer allegedly saw the profit potential in enlarging the format. Under the pretext that it would be easier to fold maps into quarto volumes, the octavo books, already presented to senators, were withdrawn, and the quarto saga commenced. The establishment of the Government Printing Office eradicated numerous printing abuses. In 1873, the process of centralizing public printing and federal information accelerated following the decision to replace commercial reporters of congressional debates with government employees and to establish the official *Congressional Record*. Neither development resulted in a reduction of the volume of printing, which had also greatly increased because of the Civil War. Reconstruction demonstrated the political advantage of publication privileges. Congress seized from the administration the newspaper patronage. An 1869 committee headed by Senator Henry B. Anthony, a Rhode Island Republican, proposed to cease publishing laws in the papers, which cost $100,000 annually. He claimed that it was "questionable whether the dominant political party should thus aid those newspapers which only reflect its partisan views instead of being mirrors of public opinion."[65] The practice was finally abolished in 1875.

Anthony became the most ardent voice for rationality and frugality in government printing. He argued that heads of bureaus had become aspiring "book makers." They kept clerks working year-round obtaining material with which to inflate their annual accounts to the heads of their departments. These communications, originally merely memoranda to assist secretaries in compiling reports to the president, became more substantial than the documents to which they were appended. "It is not essential that the public should be informed how many books of manuscript are filled, how many letters are received or written, or how many cases examined in a bureau, nor can those numbers give a definite idea of the actual labor performed. Neither should the head of a bureau utterly disregard the specific province of his labors, and invade other subjects entirely foreign to those committed to his charge, in quest of material wherewith to form a ponderous report."[66]

Thus, report critique in Washington increasingly resembled the charges leveled against blue books in Westminster. The committee complained about useless details that presented obstacles for those searching for specific information. Congress should consider, it asserted, discontinuing the distribution of all public documents, except the register of congressional debates and the report of the commissioner of agriculture. Anthony was certainly looking to Britain as a model. "For a quarter of a dollar one can purchase a folio 'Blue Book' of a hundred pages or more, containing diplomatic or parliamentary information of the most valuable character."[67] Indeed, in June 1864 Congress launched the sale of public documents by authorizing the superintendent of public printing to sell at cost documents printed at the Government Printing Office. However, early attempts to sell public documents yielded disappointing results, and official publications were still allotted to representatives and senators in large numbers.[68]

Poking fun at the pointless splendor of public documents remained a theme in congressional floor debates in the postwar years. In January 1872, Senator John Sherman estimated the cost of each volume of Professor Hayden's geological report to be twenty-five dollars and remonstrated that Congress was not consulted in printing a book, "which is only useful to be shown occasionally for the pictures in it."[69] By then, however, the sheer size of official printing became an object of mockery. In *Washington: Outside and Inside* (1873), George Townsend, the Washington correspondent of the *Chicago Tribune,* portrayed in great detail the mounds of printed matter stored in the bowels of Capitol Hill. Under the supervision of the doorkeeper of Congress, a one-hundred-member staff filed and distributed books, reports, and memorials from a series of twenty-six rooms in the cellars of the old Capitol building called the Folding Room. Townsend observed layers of books twelve deep, "the fall of a pile of which would crush a man to death."[70] (This was yet another rendition of the theme that government publications might present a danger.) Just the 260,000 copies of annual agriculture reports would take, he calculated, 225 double-horse wagons to move. Each member of Congress could dispatch up to one thousand volumes of the report to "corner grocers and gin-mill proprietors."[71] Boys packed the reports in sturdy, two-bushel canvas bags. "It is a busy scene in the depths of the old Capitol building, to see wagons come filled with documents, long rows of boys sealing envelopes, and others working with twine, and the custodians and directors of the work are generally free to admit that here is much unnecessary printing done, and that many of the books printed are stored away and forgotten, in the vaults of the mighty labyrinth."[72]

These passages evoked a subterranean universe of waste and corruption. Townsend's gothic portrayal was also reminiscent of contemporary depictions of oppressive night labor in factories and mills. Meanwhile, in a different set of rooms called the Document Room, Congress stored 2 million annual copies of bills and documents for the daily use of members. Townsend further computed that the $180,000 spent on the agriculture report every year were enough to pay the combined annual salary of the president, vice president, the cabinet secretaries, the speaker of the House, and two-thirds of the high-ranking diplomats. All of this splurging occurred while 800,000 copies of reports from previous years were lying in the vaults of the Patent Office, a "decaying mass of agricultural knowledge, manuring the ground instead of the yeoman intellect."[73] Townsend also paid a visit to the Government Printing Office; in the bindery he found four thousand Russian leather skins, 760 packs of gold leaves, and nearly twenty thousand dollars worth of twine.

Another target of Townsend's scorn was the industrious commissioner of the Land Office, Joseph Wilson, who each year prepared a voluminous report on the condition of the public domain, new surveys, and accounts on topics that extended far beyond his call of duty, from the history of gold to, as Townsend wrote, "other problems of empire and extension."[74] Despite reform, the publication appetite of officials and politicians died hard, if it can be said to have ever perished. In 1870 another publishing dispute erupted on the Senate floor, this time over the Land Office annual report. The Senate addressed a proposal to issue an extra eight thousand copies beyond the usual run for domestic purposes, and an additional five thousand copies in German, Swedish, or French for dispensation through the State Department.[75] The controversy focused on the printing of new maps prepared specifically for the report. The printing committee suggested using an already engraved U.S. map, but Senator James Harlan objected to the omission of the new maps, which demarcated surveyed public lands. Whatever cost they incurred would be a "drop in the bucket" in comparison with their service. "It is a great advertising medium. A wholesale merchant would spend that much in advertising his goods. There is not a railroad having a land grant in the whole country that would hesitate a moment in thus advertising the lands it had for sale."[76] Harlan was conceiving of the federal government as a full actor in the marketplace and thus in need of market techniques to promote its merchandise. However, in this document there was a measure of grandiosity that belied any possible utility, for the most expensive map appended was that of the entire globe.[77]

Townsend formulated two opposing arguments concerning such publication. One was that the land commissioner's diligence should be greatly appreciated. "The nation rejoices to see itself in the light of its rivals, and to see the century in the light of the past . . . the Federal State ought to waste no expense to understand and properly represent itself, both before its own citizens and the world." The opposing argument was that economy should take precedent, and "the Republic is not a high school, and a Land Commissioner is not a Professor of History."[78] Townsend, of course, took the latter position. Government should leave the people alone to make their own maps and produce their own books. The state did have a role, however. It should create the market conditions for authorship rather than assume this function itself. How? By signing an international copyright law, which would not cost a cent but "will at once raise authorship to a profession here, and out of authorship will come maps, facts, excursions, discoveries."[79]

Regardless of his specific prescription, Townsend, it seems, properly grasped one of the main drives behind federal publication efforts: self-representation. Beyond the vast possibilities of reading, official publications offered multifaceted monument-making opportunities evident in their content as well as in their materiality: engraving, embossing, printing, and binding. Representational needs intersected with another institutional dimension of representation—dispatching delegates to represent the people and the states in Washington. Senator Benton wrote to Frémont before he embarked on his western journey that it was crucial that the person in command of the expedition appeared to the Indians as the representative of Washington, not as the officer of a bureau. "To them he represents the government, and as such he must make presents, or bring both himself and his government into contempt . . . All savages expect them: they even demand them; and they feel contempt & resentment if disappointed."[80] A somewhat similar observation could have been made on the traffic in public documents. In this respect, congressmen were not only the representatives of their districts and states in the nation's capital. They represented the federal government to the periphery and in doing so had to dispatch small printed trinkets, tokens, back home. Viewed through the lens of the history of the book, gratis circulation of reports harked back to (and yet inverted) early modern modes of disseminating books as gifts of knowledge, often from the writer to a ruler in exchange for patronage.

The last grand federal enterprise of publication in the nineteenth century was the enormous project *War of the Rebellion*, which commemorated the Civil War.

Congress made the initial decisions in 1864. Seventeen years later, after a long hiatus, the first of seventy archival volumes appeared. The last installment of the $2,858,000 undertaking was issued in 1901. It was early on decided not to limit the project to official military reports but to publish the entire military record, "verbatim and literatim copies, arranged in chronological order, of every report, dispatch, letter, and other documentary paper relating to the rebellion on file."[81] The idea of publishing an entire archive caused some concern. One senator asked whether the project should publicize embarrassing items, such as courts-martial and records on deserters. Even Sumner, the relentless supporter of large-scale scholarly projects, advised caution. Once again, citing the experience of imperial Europe, Sumner recommended taking notice of the work conducted in France under Louis Bonaparte to publish all the writings of his uncle Napoleon—military, diplomatic, and personal—an effort that had reached fourteen or fifteen volumes.

The volumes of the *War of the Rebellion* were devised as receptacles of collective memory for the perusal of army veterans and their families in particular. The publication was compatible with the public culture that thrived from the mid-1870s over the commemoration of the war. Perhaps its most important work was not so much to signify the conflict as celebrate the Union or the "birth of a nation" at the conclusion of bloody fratricide, for the series incorporated the documents of the defeated Confederacy. The War Department even employed former Confederate general Marcus J. Wright to collect documents and hired other former Confederates for the editorial staff. In its content and scene of compilation, the seventy-volume series symbolized and reenacted national reconciliation.

Despite the persistent critique of the state's publishing excess and the cynicism of Townsend and Benton, among others, the volume of federal government printing increased during the remainder of the nineteenth century. Production of government-sponsored publications would greatly intensify in the 1930s. The Depression prompted the self-inspection and self-documentation of the American past, culture, and regional differences, manifested most notably in the famous output of the Federal Writers' Project. During the same decade, government deluged the public with official advice guides, such as *Infant Care,* of which 1,735,066 copies were sold and 8,233,558 given away, or *Keeping Fit* (by the Public Health Service), a fifteen-page affair that sold 572,119 copies. These publications were symptomatic of the rise of social service experts under state auspices.

CHAPTER THREE

The Bee in the Book

Expeditions and Explorations

During the two decades that preceded the Civil War, government support for expeditions, explorations, and comparable scientific enterprises amounted to between one-fourth and one-third of the total federal budget.[1] This astounding investment epitomized the transformation of antebellum public life (to borrow a famous title by historian John Higham) "from boundlessness to consolidation," but American scientific curiosity was boundary-less and went far beyond the West, encompassing projects in Latin America, the Pacific Ocean, the Arctic regions, and even the Jordan River. Official assistance also coincided with the elaboration of American science from a gentlemanly club pursuit to an increasingly institutionalized undertaking. This shift manifested itself, for example, in the scholarly leadership assumed by the Smithsonian Institution almost immediately after its establishment in 1846. A small scientific cadre emerged. Academically trained and narrowly specialized, it emulated the ethos of the European scientific establishment and shared an obligatory contempt for whatever it considered speculative and amateurish. Indeed, one subplot of the story of explorations and expeditions was the rise of the eastern seaboard expert whose authority superseded that of field explorers. This tiny coterie of scientists—for example, Asa Gray, John Torrey, and Spencer Baird—were often assigned to the arrangement, classification, and presentation of specimens that they had not collected themselves. As a venue for the promotion and display of scientific findings, natural history projects facilitated the creation of an intellectual hierarchy, notwithstanding recurrent tributes to republican, accessible, useful science. Science, however, was only one motive, at times a pretext, among a plethora of interests. The guiding forces behind expeditions included commerce, farming, whaling, emigration, and national expansion, which was the subject of considerable controversy.

These drives also converged in the printing and publication process. The publication of exploration reports and other scientific texts (the Patent Office annual report comes to mind) satisfied the communication exigencies of science (articulated in the "diffusion of knowledge" slogan of the Smithsonian), the farmer's need to be acquainted with the latest agricultural techniques and meteorological knowledge, the seaman's and the emigrant's wish for better maps, and sometimes even the statesman's attempt to make policy. Yet, publication was not merely a completion of government action in the market of information. Once again, breaks occurred between the ideology and actuality of information. First, rather than simply being the concluding phase or the realization of expeditions in print, the publications of a few famous reports became expeditions in their own right. Publication was a complicated and somewhat risky assignment that demanded great financial resources and manpower, an endeavor that could go awry, or simply subvert the conventional equilibrium between action and reportage. It sometimes seemed easier, let alone cheaper, to send ships to remote oceans or a unit of soldiers to uncharted deserts rather than to publish a book describing those ventures. The preparation of Charles Wilkes's exploring expedition reports stretched over more than thirty years after the conclusion of the famous four-year voyage. The publication of the Pacific Railroad surveys was reported to cost at least twice as much as conducting the expeditions themselves. Political wrangling, bureaucratic inexperience, the incredible number of specimens that were truly impossible to classify in a short time, and the enormity of the printing volume contributed to what seemed occasionally to be ineptitude.

One way or another, publication exposed government to observation and criticism. The Pacific Railroad Report, for example, exhibited another malfunction of the bureaucratic digestive system, an inability to edit, summarize, and separate the important from the trivial. Government ran the risk of going astray in its home-brewed books. At the same time, the trajectory from explorations to the world of print accentuated the patriotic signification of expeditions and explorations. This sentiment was articulated in the tangible dimension of government documents. National grandeur could be measured in type of binding, size of font, and quality of engravings. These books were roving monuments dispatched across the nation (and, as importantly, to Europe) for inspection and admiration. Accordingly, they were sometimes collected merely for their aesthetic value.

Here we examine the publication of expedition reports through four case studies: John C. Frémont's 1840s accounts on his travels to California, documents that became paradigmatic in terms of content and production; the perennial printing project of Charles Wilkes's Exploring Expedition to the Pacific (1838–

42); the debate over the publication of John R. Bartlett's report on his journeys as head of the Mexican Boundary Commission in the late 1840s; and the dissemination of the bulky reports of the 1850s transcontinental railroad survey. The tension between national and personal ambitions connects these episodes. Explorers—army officers and civilians—shared a particularly enhanced perception of themselves as authors. They understood authorship as a duty and as a privilege that emanated from the state's commission. The state was often considered to have an obligation to publish the accounts of its emissaries and to document their respective areas of study. Besides discussing issues of authorship—social status, commercial and political aspects, and the development of recognizable writing styles—this chapter gauges a range of public responses to exploration reports, most importantly through hundreds of applications—many of which written by ordinary citizens—for volumes of the transcontinental railroad report.

Scene of Writing

In October 1842, at the conclusion of his travels in the West, Frémont returned home to his wife Jessie in Washington, D.C. Introducing another gesture into this already symbolically burdened odyssey, he soon presented her with the American flag that he had hoisted on a summit in the Rockies. In the following weeks, he faced the seemingly uncomplicated task of producing an official account of his expedition. As prescribed by convention, the report was to be organized chronologically according to the expedition's itinerary. In the middle decades of the nineteenth century, much of the West was perceived via the trails that cut through it. Together with the appended maps, detailed descriptions of western routes rendered reconnaissance and exploration narratives doubly useful as guidebooks for prospective emigrants en route to the Pacific coast. Correspondingly, expedition reports were often illustrated with not-to-be-missed orifice-like passes at crucial points along the way.

Preparing such a document was a collaborative work that involved, in this case, Charles Preuss, the expedition's cartographer, and John Torrey, the pioneering botanist who was entrusted with the botanical and zoological specimens. Frémont was responsible for the narrative segment, but the task of translating his personal journal into an official record proved taxing. Three strenuous days of work yielded only a tremendous headache and a nosebleed. At this point, his wife entered the scene of report writing. Jessie Benton Frémont, Senator Thomas Hart Benton's daughter, volunteered to sit by the desk to record her husband's words. Initially dictating from his notes, Frémont soon moved into a more conversational tone, reportedly "forgetting himself" in his oral retelling. According to one of Jessie's biographers, "freed from all self-consciousness, unhampered by the nagging thought of the mechanics of writing, [he] happily recounted the story of his adventures to the woman he loved. In answers to her eager and adroit questions, he simplified, clarified, and dramatized his experience."[2] This account of the making of the narrative suggests a notion of transparency different from that offered by the maintenance of daily field journals. It was the safety and warmth of the domestic sphere that allowed Frémont to be "himself," a natural raconteur rather than a writer, and to communicate the supposedly unadorned yet engaging narration of his travels. (This and other versions of Frémont's homecoming were part of the cultural work that Frémont's travels performed in nineteenth-century America as enterprises and texts that triangulated the modern self, nature, and American nationalism.) Future scholars would disagree about the respective contributions of the husband-and-wife team. Jessie Frémont was apparently an avid reader in the classics and familiar with famous expeditions' accounts. Although in later decades she would write and publish under her own name, she regarded this particular collaboration as her "life's work."[3] As important was Frémont's wish to produce a popular, readable document. His political backers and the press expected no less of him.

Beyond its patriotic and sentimental tone, Frémont's first report has been noted for the narrative's visual properties, vividness, and power to conjure images, which was enhanced by the illustrations. Following Alexander von Humboldt's wish for "truth in representing nature," Frémont also took a camera on his first two expeditions, hoping to make daguerreotypes, but he was never able to use the new technology successfully. When the first report was presented to Congress, Senator Lewis F. Linn, another Missourian, moved to print an extra thousand copies. The War Department was supremely content. Col. John James Abert, the commanding officer of the Topographical Corps of Engineers, wrote Frémont, "I should express my great personal as well as official satisfaction with your report which has now been printed, reflecting credit alike upon your good taste as well as intelligence."[4] Following the second expedition, the two reports were coupled with a general map and printed in more than ten thousand copies by Gales and Seaton and Blair and Rives for the Senate and the House, respectively. They also printed lengthy extracts of the report (to which they had early access) in their *National Intelligencer* and *Congressional Globe*. The second report completed the first in delineating the route beyond the Rockies to Walla Walla and then California. The combined document made Frémont a national celebrity.

These reports were so coveted that a controversy brewed over whether members of the previous Congress, if not reelected, could still receive their share. Publishers issued different versions for profit, at times omitting the maps or the illustrations. Excerpts from the narrative would be liberally used for the campaign biographies of 1856, when Frémont ran as the first Republican Party presidential candidate. Several diaries and autobiographies of emigrants to the West cited the text, and it was widely read abroad. There were, however, critics. Ralph Waldo Emerson noticed that Frémont was busy glorifying his place in nature and in history while the expedition was still taking place. For Emerson this tendency signified that "Our secondary feeling, our passion for seeming, must be highly inflamed" for all the famine, depravation, and terror of facing a vast, hostile land "could not repress the eternal vanity of *how we must look!*" Historian Bernard De Voto, a twentieth-century observer, would label the reports "adventure books" and "charters for manifest destiny."[5] Frémont's subsequent assignments were even more controversial. His next mission, which ended unexpectedly in California, has been often considered among the causes for the Bear Flag Revolt and the war with Mexico. A dispute with Gen. Stephen Watts Kearny led to a court martial for charges of mutiny. Afterward, despite a presidential pardon, Frémont decided to resign his military post. A select committee established in 1848 to look into the publication of Frémont's report on his third expedition to California and Oregon offered an analogy between his momentous tasks and Lewis and Clarke's earlier explorations. "Reason tells a nation, as it does an individual, that when it has acquired a new and distant possession, the first thing to be done is, to learn its value, and the means of getting to it."[6] Of course, in Frémont's case, this trajectory was reversed, first exploration and only then acquisition.[7]

Frémont's early reports became templates for the expeditions of the next two decades. In the aftermath of the war with Mexico, the genre grew more patriotic, inspiring documents such as Lt. Col. William Emory, Lt. James W. Abert, and Lt. Col. Philip St. George Cooke's "Notes of Military Reconnaissance from Fort Leavenworth in Missouri to San Diego in California" (1848). (The House authorized the printing of 10,000 copies of these reports, out of which 250 copies were granted gratis to each of the authors.) The particular narrative strategies of these texts are certainly beyond the scope of this discussion, but the creation of stylistic continuity under the auspices of Congress and government is not. This fidelity of style was not exhausted by the characteristics that are typically associated with Frémont's reports, namely, chauvinistic emotionalism and detailed, graphic descriptions. More intriguing was subsequent documents' tendency to reproduce uncanny moments of the kind that brought together Frémont and the wandering bee on the top of the Rockies (see introduction to part I). Without directly alluding to the concept, Frémont's account on his ascent to the top of the Rockies is a rather conventional rendition of the sublime motif in nineteenth-century literature, employing one of the sublime's most common tropes, an individual overlooking a magnificent, almost transcendent and yet deeply threatening scenery from a mountain's top. Peril was signified by the danger to his person posed by climbing enormous rocks and by the topography of the Rockies, which evoked a mightier force. Arriving at the peak, Frémont encountered absolute stillness and silence, no trace of animated life. The strange (indeed uncanny) appearance of the buzzing bee prompted ambivalence; a sense of identification with the path-breaking insect, which was probably "the first of his species to cross the mountain barrier, a solitary pioneer foretells the advance of civilization." Nevertheless, the bee provoked a burst of aggression. "I believe that a moment's thought would have made us let him continue his way unharmed, but we carried out the law of this country, where all animated nature seems at war."[8] The bee's demise was inevitable. It found itself between the leaves of the book that held Frémont's flora collection.

Emory's journal began in August 2, 1846, when he described himself standing alone looking at the direction of Bent's Fort. While watching an enormous American flag flapping forcefully, he noticed that it was waving against the direction of the wind, threatening to break the ash pole on which it was hoisted. "The mystery was soon revealed by a column of dust to the east, advancing with about the velocity of a fast walking horse—it was 'the Army of the West.' I ordered my horses to be hitched up and, as the column passed, took my place with the staff."[9] Lt. Abert's narrative commenced with his arrival at Bent's Fort, the author ill and suffering from fever and hallucinations. "At this time, my disease had obtained such an influence over my senses, that days and nights were passed in delirium and a mental struggle to ascertain whether the impressions my mind received were true or false. Even my sight was affected, and when I gazed on Bent's Fort, the building seemed completely metamorphosed, new towers had been erected, the walls heightened, and, as I then thought, everything put in readiness to resist an attack of the New Mexicans."[10]

The proclivity of physical objects in Bent's Fort to defy the rules of nature when military scouts (as the nation they represented) were stupefied, restless, or feverish, further developed Frémont's estrangement motif. The misplaced bee on the mountain is substituted here with strangely animated buildings and a flag. All three moments seemed to displace onto the natural and man-made world the anxiety originating from the presence of expeditions in the alien vistas of the West. Strangest of all was that these anecdotes found their way into official military accounts. Nevertheless, the moment of capturing the bee in the book, the bee that Frémont regarded a competitor as well as a reflection of himself, was also to be the point in time when the West was "won" and rendered American.

Production

Frémont's explorations were perhaps a "national work," but, as his mentor Senator Benton indicated in his memoirs, the federal executive had little to do with them. Government was unquestionably innocent of the first expedition's "conception," he wrote, merely permitting it to take place and "therefore, not entitled to the credit of its authorship."[11] In general, congressional committees and staff, as well as the authors themselves, supervised the publication of expedition reports. The little that has survived from early nineteenth-century congressional manuscript record reveals how complex was the production of these elaborate books, a process that necessitated an army of printers, engravers, map makers, and binders in Washington, Baltimore, Philadelphia, and New York. During the 1840s, the secretary of the Senate and the clerk of the House of Representatives managed directly many of the publication projects. The making of Frémont's reports also demonstrated the extent to which western reporting centered on palpable objects: maps and illustrations of varying degrees of cost and sophistication, ranging from woodcuts and lithographs to steel and hand-colored copper engravings. In the report-making industry, these artifacts were the most expensive and complicated to produce and the most sought-after objects. They were considered to have great knowledge value, for they were labeled facts, material facts that represented other tangible facts. This multifaceted designation of value corresponded to the notion expressed by an 1848 select committee that Frémont's achievement culminated in a collection of employable objects that was "brought home," including minerals, birds' plumage, and drawings of scenery. Another dimension of the objectification of the West through official reports emanated directly from their particularities as books.

The narrative part of Frémont's report was ready within two months of the House's decision to circulate the document, but the production of the entire report was to become a long-term endeavor. When questions about delays arose the following year, the somewhat apologetic clerk of the House informed representatives anxious to receive their copies that ten thousand sets of engravings would not be completed for another three or four months. He claimed that Frémont had made the contracts for engraving the plates and the large map with Endicott in New York and Edward Weber and Co. of Baltimore without consulting him. To make things worse, Rives, the House printer, reported that the five hundred sets that he already had received for binding were all "imperfect." Meanwhile, the Committee on the Library of the Senate investigated rumors that congressional staff was clandestinely selling copies instead of delivering them to senators. The committee pointed to difficulties with printing the lithographs and the binder's broken embossing machine but exonerated the Senate's employees.[12]

Secretary of the Senate Asbury Dickins assumed a special role in the world of governmental printing, coordinating publishing efforts and demonstrating great understanding of the intricacies of the numerous crafts involved. In one episode, Dickins advised the Navy Lt. William Lynch to divide the map adjoining his report on his travels to the Jordan River and the Dead Sea into sections to avoid the difficulty of engraving a narrow but elongated map on a large plate. In late 1848, he ordered twenty thousand copies of Frémont's map of Oregon and California on thin, tough paper so they could be folded and sent by mail. He asked for roughly one thousand on a thick, strong paper easier to preserve in portfolios or mount in frames to be hung on walls.[13]

A correspondence with Alexander Dallas Bache of the Coast Survey showed the secretary again preoccupied with the production of executive reports. He pressured Bache to produce the introduction to his report on the magnetic observation of Girard College, admonishing him that the delay had already caused embarrassment since many senators and representatives had made inquiries about the report "as necessary to complete their series of documents."[14] Dickins also arbitrated in questions such as the design of the title page of the annual report of the Smithsonian Institution, and the use of copper rather than other types of plates for engraving the 4,800 maps of the territories between the Mississippi and the Pacific.[15] All of these admittedly trifling matters give us a glimpse into Congress's involvement in managing large-scale, chronically behind schedule, publishing projects. Some of the decisions Dickins and other congressional staff made were more editorial than technical. In the case of Gales and Seaton's *American State Papers* and other documentary projects, the clerk and the secretary were given explicit editorial discretion. Beginning in the early 1850s, the executive departments gradually assumed some of these functions. The navy and the Department of the Interior supervised expedition reports while the War Department was in charge of printing the Pacific Railroad surveys.

Expedition Lost

The U.S. Exploring Expedition (1838–42) was the first naval operation of its kind. Roaming the Pacific, it established the existence of Antarctica as a continent, charted almost three hundred islands, conducted ethnological observations, discovered hundreds of new species of flora and fauna, and accumulated measurements on navigation, meteorology, and magnetism. The changing political scene at the turn of the 1840s greatly determined the path of the report's publication. Lt. Charles Wilkes, the famously short-tempered commander of the expedition, was a Democrat and a Van Buren appointee. When he returned to Washington in June 1842, the Whigs were in power and seemed to want either to entrust the expedition's results to someone else or not publish it. Wilkes found an ally in a fellow Democrat, Senator Benjamin Tappan from Ohio, setting a pattern by which an agile Congress occasionally snatched a publication project from the hands of a reluctant administration. Tappan and Wilkes peddled the publication as a national undertaking and an expression of naval pride. Wilkes popularized his expedition in a series of lectures at the National Museum in the city. He wrote privately, "the reputation of our country is at stake." Unless the work was finished, "all will be ruined and we shall become the laughing stock of Europe and all the praise that has been lavished on our Government for its noble undertaking prove but satire in disguise."[16] Some were doubtful about the federal government's ability to handle a project of such magnitude. The naturalist John James Audubon commented to his protégé Spencer Baird (later the second secretary of the Smithsonian) that government probably could not dispense with the half million dollars he thought were necessary. It would take the wealth of the Russian emperor or the French king, he opined, associating the prospective project with the opulence of monarchical power. If only he could, he would "address the Congress of our Country, ask of them to throw open these stores of National Curiosities, and Comply with mine every wish to publish, and to *Give Away* Copies of the invaluable Works thus produced to every Scientific Institution throughout our Country, and throughout the World."[17]

Wilkes's greatest achievement was probably his success in convincing Congress to employ in the publication effort the individuals who participated in the expedition. He similarly established a continuum between his command on the high seas and the administration of the publication project, a principle based on a notion of deservedness that linked field exertions with the rewards of authorship. Wilkes was to write the narrative history of the voyage. According to the law enacted in August 1842, this illustrated account would follow in form the report of the voyage of the Astrolabe that France had just issued. For the *American Journal of Science and Art*, the French example was the proper choice. "France has outstripped England in the liberality with which her expeditions have been fitted out, and in the magnificence of her publications. The many folio volumes of plates, published as the result of the voyages of Freycinet, Duperey, and D'Urville, and those of Napoleon's expedition into Egypt, are among the most splendid productions of the age. They are a noble gift of France to the world."[18] The article implied it was a matter of fairness, if not justice, that government should not keep the knowledge accumulated in the voyage for the few but share it with the public at large, for the people bore the expense of the journey. Likewise, members of the expedition should control publication. "Each will prepare his own report, reap his own honors, and be held responsible for his own facts."[19] (In a similar fashion, Frémont's supporters would argue in the late 1840s that government owed Frémont the opportunity of publishing the report on his third journey to California for his expeditions "only want the finishing hand of their author to erect a monument of honor to himself and of utility to his country."[20])

These notions of popular science seemed incongruent with Congress's somewhat atypical decision to issue the reports in a minuscule edition of one hundred. The State Department distributed the volumes among the states and foreign countries. Ultimately, despite their publicity, actual public access to the volumes was severely limited. The Library Committee decided to permit each author to print from the typeset 100 to 150 copies for three-fifths of the contract cost, provided the writers would sell them at a low price. All authors except Wilkes declined. Booksellers, who received the offer next, seemed as reluctant, but for Lea and Blanchard, who paid for copies of two volumes.[21] Eventually, most volumes appeared in some form in unofficial and rather small editions. Only the popular (and less scientific) Wilkes's *Narrative* was republished under various commercial guises, the last issued in 1858. Reviewing the volumes on the ethnology and zoophytes reports in 1846, C. C. Felton and Asa Gray wrote in the *North American Review* that unless Congress decided to expand the edition, the books would become "forbidden fruit" to those interested in science in the United States and in Europe. "Such niggardly publication is only tantalizing the votaries of science. It is moreover, particularly unjust to the authors of these works."[22] In this case, authors masquerading as reviewers purported to speak for readers (the "votaries of science"), for Gray was to be one of the scientists employed to write on the expedition's results. Petitions to Congress from the Georgia Historical Society and the president of Amherst College failed to increase the number of printed copies.

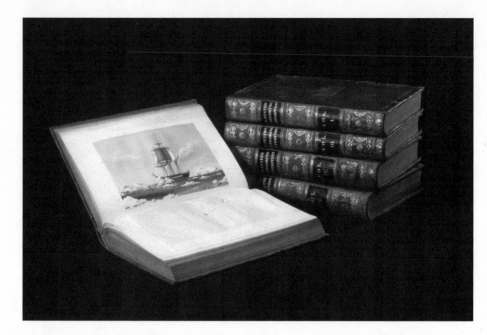

Charles Wilkes was criticized for publishing his *Narrative of the United States Exploring Expedition in the years 1838, 1839, 1840, 1841, 1842* (1844) in a private edition and for issuing a copyright for an account that was ostensibly a public document. The open volume of this sumptuous edition shows an engraving of the USS *Vincennes* in Disappointment Bay, Antarctica, following Wilkes's own illustration. Wilkes led a squadron of six ships, 346 seamen, and a team of nine scientists and artists in the milestone expedition, which among other feats proved that Antarctica was a continent. (Smithsonian Institution Collections)

Tappan and Wilkes developed a small publishing apparatus under the supervision of the Joint Committee on the Library of Congress. At first, it was estimated that the publication would take merely a year. The committee appointed Tappan as its agent, responsible for setting the criteria for contracting and proofing as well as the general layout of the volumes. The project would be often disrupted by tension and scandal. In some respects, this was merely a continuation of rifts that occurred first aboard the ships in the Pacific. There were also persistent rumors that shells and other specimens surfaced in private collections. Matters got worse, and in the spring of 1846, the committee ordered Tappan to stop the departure of specimens and cease making contracts. His subsequent resignation was accepted.

Wilkes completed publishing his five narrative volumes in January 1844. Public reactions were mixed. The *Southern Literary Messenger* noted that Wilkes was often wrong in quoting Spanish words. In the *North American Review,* Charles Davis remarked that much of the *Narrative* was acquired in the library and not in the Pacific. "It would be ridiculous to deny, that a large portion of this work was prepared by Captain Wilkes, or his friends, in the closet at home,— that, in short, it is to a certain extent a compilation."[23] Wilkes's habit of copying material from general histories and lifting passages from journals of crewmembers endeared him to neither reviewers nor his men. Government officially claimed all notes taken by participants during the expedition. This had been common practice since the eighteenth century (for instance, Captain Cooke's journey in the Pacific) but seemed unfair to American sensibilities. In fact, officers were obliged to keep daily journals and to record even trivial incidents on board ship or on shore that "tend to illustrate any transaction or occurrence which may take place, or afford any information in regard to the manners, habits, or customs of natives and the position and characters of such places as may be visited."[24] Wilkes had at his disposal his subordinates' work, which he relentlessly mined.

Further infuriating his critics, he issued a copyright on his own name for future commercial editions of the project. He explained that the *Narrative* was not the original report he had sent to the Navy Department but a distinct document written specifically at the request of the library committee. Ostensibly a reward for a naval officer conducting extra work, he chose to explain the unusual copyright for a government publication in terms of personal integrity. "My object in so doing was to protect my reputation, being unwilling that a garbled edition should be printed by others."[25] The committee had an ambiguous role in the copyright matter. Initially, it supported congressional legislation that would give Wilkes the privilege. When Congress did not pass such legislation and Wilkes issued a copyright through the usual procedure, the committee opined that this copyright might not stand a court challenge. Ordinarily, individuals could not issue copyright on government publications. The court denied copyright to one of the artists in Commodore Perry's expedition, holding that by publishing the drawings for the benefit of the public at large, Congress had given it to the public. Wilkes also notified the committee that because of his "desire to diffuse a full knowledge of the result of the expedition," he was about to publish a complete edition of the work without many of the illustrations and at a reduced price.[26]

In the ten years following Tappan's resignation, Wilkes was in charge of the contracts with authors. Joseph Drayton, one of the expedition's artists, supervised the material aspects of the production, and John S. Meehan, the congressional librarian, provided administrative services. They contracted more than one hundred authors, artists, illustrators, and engravers. Wilkes wrote, "the country is greatly indebted to [Drayton] for the style and beauty of the publication."[27] Drayton lived most of the time in Philadelphia, where the printing and binding were done. His role in executing the production and setting the format exemplified the importance of the material aspect of the work and the absence of other editorial authorities. Surviving proofs of colored engravings display his pedantic dissatisfaction with unrealistic shades of color in the depiction of animals and plants, to the point that, in one case, he preferred to abandon color altogether for it called attention to itself rather than to the actual animal. Arguably, hand-colored plates—not early photography—were the ultimate mid-nineteenth-century technology with which to represent reality in nature. The zoology and many of the botany plates were to be colored "to represent the objects in life."[28] Drayton had to overcome a shortage of engravers prompted, in part, by frantic official printing activities. Scarcity engendered competition with other publishing projects—such as Schoolcraft's, also printed in Philadelphia, Amos Binney's natural history project, and the Pennsylvania State Survey—as well as with a thriving magazine business in New York. Abiding by the library committee's determination to keep the project in the United States, Drayton refused to consider sending work to Europe, although it could be performed there for a moderate cost. In 1856 the committee's chair Senator James Pearce was eager to replace Wilkes, who did not cooperate with his retrenchment policies. Drayton was his obvious choice. Soon after, however, Drayton passed away.

Meanwhile, a battle was brewing between Wilkes's crew and a hostile scientific community. James Dwight Dana wrote three official reports, but he was the only participant in the voyage to acquire a reputation as an important scientist. Others were not considered up to the task. Key publications were eventually taken away from expedition members and given to acknowledged experts. One of the first controversies evolved around the volume on shells. Wilkes fought with Joseph P. Couthouy, the naturalist originally in charge of shells, over his expedition journals and drawings. He wanted another, Drayton, to write the conchology volume instead, but it was an outsider, Augustus Addison Gould, who was commissioned. In the preface to his volume, Gould acknowledged the difficulties of classifying somebody else's collections. Some of the original notes, made by Couthouy, simply got lost, "repeated searches had failed to discover them among the masses of documents pertaining to the Expedition."[29]

Titian Ramsay Peale, an expedition artist and son of the famous museum founder in Philadelphia, decided against scientific convention to record in his report observations on already known animal species, arguing that the spread of animals was as important as the discovery of new species. But it was the belligerent introduction he wrote for his report on birds and insects that earned him Wilkes's ire. Peale criticized and labeled as young and inexperienced the expedition's naval officers, and Wilkes retaliated. In 1848, Peale's zoology report was renamed *Mammalia and Ornithology* and published without the introduction, while the author never completed the adjoining atlas. The Philadelphia ornithologist John Cassin rewrote the entire project. Asa Gray agreed to take charge of the publication of the botanical material only after he was guaranteed a trip to Europe at government expense and a five-year contract at $120 a month.[30]

Since the early 1850s, Senator Pearce was pressuring Wilkes to end the chaotic project. By 1859, $279,131 had been spent.[31] Senators lost patience. Senator Clement J. Clay from Alabama charged that Wilkes had become rich at the government's expense. John P. Hale from New Hampshire alluded to Dickens's *Bleak House,* comparing Wilkes's enterprise to the infamous, everlasting Chancery suit. "I think, really, that Wilkes's exploring expedition has performed a thing of romance that will tax credulity vastly more than Jarndyce vs. Jarndyce." Senator Robert Toombs of Georgia suggested simply throwing the entire project into the Potomac River.[32] This was not the first time that animosity toward the project assumed an antiscientific (or anti-intellectual) flavor. Six years earlier, when Senator Pearce explained to a less than sympathetic chamber that the project did not exceed norms established in similar endeavors sponsored by other countries, Hale quipped, "What, sir, do you suppose that these exploring expeditions do? These explorers take a great oyster-rake; they take the bottom of the ocean, and bring some bugs, shells, plants, and creeping things of all sorts, and then enlist the literary and scientific *recherche* all over the country to pour them over and explain and analyze them to the public and make picture-books."[33]

In 1862, another modest appropriation was made for archiving the archive: preserving the plates of the exploring expedition and the collection that was deposited in the Smithsonian as well as other Washington institutions.[34] Until Wilkes's death in 1877, there would be additional small appropriations for the preservation of the collections and for publication. The project ceased for the duration of the Civil War when Wilkes's recklessness almost brought the United States and Britain into battle. In 1876 Senator Timothy O. Howe, chairman of the joint committee, rejected Wilkes's appeal to proceed with the publication effort. He viewed the continuation as unjustified political patronage. Overall, Congress issued eighteen volumes and twelve accompanying atlases; a few more were prepared but never printed.

The Royal Geographical Society of London awarded Wilkes its Founder's Medal in 1847 for his Antarctic achievements. He never received a similar honor from the U.S. government. Senator Pearce defended the publication as an enterprise with no parallel in the United States or Europe, a "great work" that honored American science. Louis Agassiz saw the expedition's reports as "surpass[ing] in scientific importance the publications of all the exploring expeditions issued by European government taken separately."[35] While the majority of these volumes were produced between 1842 and the Civil War, there were fourteen other naval expeditions, partly in response to maritime commercial interests and the whaling industry, which demanded accurate nautical charts. Still, one should bear in mind what the English botanist Joseph Hooker wrote to Gray in 1861: "Who on earth is to keep in their heads or quote such a medley of books—double-paged, double-titled, and half finished as your Government vomits periodically into the great ocean of Scientific bibliography."[36]

Boundary Demarcation

The exploring expedition investigated the west of the West, traveling, at one point, along the soon to become U.S. Pacific coastline, gazing eastward. (Frémont's second expedition to Oregon and California was formally intended to complete Wilkes's project from the continent's direction.) To the South, the Mexican Boundary expedition demarcated the new postwar borderline following the 1848 peace treaty of Guadalupe Hidalgo. It presented an opportunity for the Army Corps of Topographical Engineers to launch an unprecedently large survey of the trans-Mississippi Southwest. The controversy over the publication of a report by the third commissioner of the survey, John Russell Bartlett (1850–53), foregrounded, once again, the question of authorship in official documents.

In 1850, President John Tyler's administration was looking for a candidate to fill the recently vacated position of boundary commissioner. Bartlett, an ethnologist, publisher, and a Whig from Providence, Rhode Island, stumbled upon the appointment while in Washington, D.C. (He had wished to be nominated minister to Denmark.) Bartlett had limited knowledge of the West and no previous experience in this kind of operation. His tenure was marred by raucous relationships with hostile military subordinates, all southern Democrats. Accusations concerning mismanagement of supply and general incompetence were not entirely unfounded. Quarrels over food, pay, and instances of sabotage by disgruntled former employees abounded. The expedition's first astronomer, Lt. Col. John

McClellan, claimed that George Bartlett, the commissioner's brother who was in charge of purchasing supply, was busy defrauding the government.

Nevertheless, the dispute that eventually terminated Bartlett's appointment touched directly upon the marking of the border. The U.S. and Mexican surveyors who collaborated in the effort faced a hurdle of a legal as well as of a curiously representational nature. Which element in the treaty's map, known as Distruntell's Map, should take precedent: its description of geographical features and their actual location on the terrain, or, the map's delineation of imagined parallel and meridian coordinates that turned out to be misplaced by half a degree to the south and two degrees to the west? The Mexicans demanded to follow the faulty coordinates in selecting the survey's Archimedean point; the Americans preferred to employ the actual location of tiny El Paso, which, as the treaty stipulated, was to be eight miles south of the border. Bartlett was willing to compromise with the Mexican general Pedro Garcia Condé's position. According to his foes in Congress, this amounted to a betrayal of U.S. interests. (The difference between Gray's interpretation of the treaty and Bartlett-Condé's compromise was a territory 35 miles wide and 175 long, or six thousand square miles, that became known as the Mesilla Strip.) The commission's surveyor, Andrew Gray, who refused to sign the Bartlett-Condé agreement, was summarily dismissed.

At stake was not just a piece of desert and some cacti, as Bartlett alleged, but a cause that became dear to the hearts of southern senators. They hoped that the future railroad to the Pacific would pass through Texas to south California along the thirty-second parallel. For two years, Whigs and expansionist Democrats debated the issue in Washington while Bartlett was feuding with his men in the field. Eventually, a new treaty and a land deal had to be concocted between Mexico and the United States (General Gadsden's Purchase of December 1853), after which the current boundary was agreed upon and much of southern Arizona became a U.S. territory. But before that the commission's work was suspended, and Bartlett and William Emory, who replaced Gray and Col. James D. Graham (the commission's chief scientist who was also demoted after a row with Bartlett), were recalled back East.

Arriving in Washington in early 1853, Bartlett faced a hostile Senate and a new Democratic administration that soon revoked his appointment. Bartlett submitted a report on his expeditions to his superiors in the Department of the Interior. However, he still entertained the ambition of authoring a grand report, which he hoped would combine his journal with scientific findings and be adorned with the illustrations of the expedition's artist, Henry Pratt. In April of that year, Senator Sam Houston (Texas) proposed on the floor that Bartlett and Gray "be authorized to furnish a report . . . on the topography, geography, and natural history of these regions adjacent to the line, with such information as was collected relative to the Indian tribes through Texas, California and New Mexico."[37] Demonstrating the degree of discretion senators enjoyed in the production of executive reports, Houston offered editorial guidelines. He proposed that the presentation of the aboriginal subject matter would follow the example set by Schoolcraft's Indian volumes, and the natural history part would take as a model an account that had become an exemplar of the genre, David Dale Owen's *Report on the Geology of Lake Superior.* He further suggested limiting the length of the report to two volumes and a thousand pages, and to pay for it from the contingency fund. Houston's support of the publication raised a few eyebrows. As had many southern senators, he had been critical of Bartlett's position on the boundary question.

The ensuing debate featured the customary attacks on congressional printing. Senators alleged that official publications were exorbitant and that their scientific or informational value was inexcusably low. Subsidized books were resold at D.C. stores, or, worse, their leaves were torn out to wrap loaves of bread. It did not escape participants that the proposed publication circumvented the fundamental rationale of reporting, for evidently the Department of the Interior, its addressee, was quite uninterested in such a document. Senator Solon Borland reminded his colleagues that the publication of the first three volumes of Schoolcraft's project cost a staggering $100,000. Only Owen's geological report was relatively cheap to produce (less than four dollars a volume as against twenty-five for Schoolcraft's). Still, $30,000 were spent on its printing.

Senator James Mason (Virginia), one of Bartlett's chief enemies, maintained that Bartlett had deliberately chosen routes that deviated from the vicinity of the border. "The commissioner—God knows where—[was] exploring the interior of Mexico, perhaps, and collecting material for a book."[38] Senators complained that they were asked to edit a book whose contents were unfamiliar to anyone and its authors were as yet unknown. The Senate should not do it without endorsements from "some literary persons." Defensively, Houston resorted to circular reasoning. To those who maintained they should not publish a book about which they knew nothing, he answered that that was exactly why the book should be printed—so they could learn something about it. "He may give us a very entertaining lecture upon the manners, customs, and peculiar habits of Mexico." This rather fragile argument relied, once again, on the ambiguity of the Senate's

role as producer and consumer of books and the further conflation between lawmakers, voters, and readers.

Houston claimed the entire country between California and the Atlantic was
interested in the report. In the wide distribution of Owen's geological account,
many of the volumes did not reach their destinations because they were stolen
right out of the mailbags. The Texan's allegation prompted chuckles in the
chamber. For Houston, however, the reported thefts demonstrated "the great
value of the work and the great desire of the people for intelligence, and is a co-
gent reason for an urgent necessity of having the supply of books increased." In
order to guard his own shipment he claimed to have spent hundreds of dollars
protecting them in boxes, at least until they reached Texas. "I am not afraid of
the mails being robbed in Texas," he proclaimed over another round of laughter.
Senator Butler from South Carolina defended the good name of his state and its
neighbors but jokingly allowed, "there may be a greater literary mania upon the
route than in the state of Texas itself. How that is I do not know."[39]

Despite his folksy Texanisms (or because of them) Houston was not the most
persuasive advocate for Bartlett's report, for the senator ultimately conceded that
the only book published by Congress he had ever read was the Patent Office report, and from that only the agricultural volume. He had no great desire to read
any other documents. Things did not improve when he further confessed that he
supported the publication in part because of Gray, a fellow Texan, who, he felt,
had been dismissed unfairly. Senator Borland may have hammered the last nail
into the project's coffin when he said that after talking with Bartlett, it became
evident that the manuscript was incomplete. Bartlett probably sought to secure
a contract for his publishing venture.[40] The Senate decided not to pursue the proposal. This was due partly to Houston's mannerism and, in larger part, to Democratic animosity towards Bartlett.

Bartlett had to satisfy himself with a commercial publisher. His two-volume
account *Personal Narrative of Explorations and Incidents in Texas, New Mexico,
California, Sonora, and Chihuahua* (1854) would be among the more popular and
certainly among the most readable expedition reports to come out of the Great
Reconnaissance. Perhaps this quality was the serendipitous result of the imposition that prevented him from publishing an official document. Rather than emulating Schoolcraft or Owen, he apparently took as his model his friend John
Lloyd Stephen's *Incidents of Travel in Central America, Chiapas and Yucatan*
(1841). The narrative was accompanied by ninety-four woodcuts and sixteen lithographs but no metal engravings. A somewhat diffused notion of an American
border emanated from the book. This was partly due to the social heterogeneity

it featured through multiple actors: German settlers, Mormons, Mexican villagers, Indian warriors, Bartlett's own troublesome unit, miners, ranchers, governors, and officials of the Mexican government. Bartlett regarded General Condé and his staff as peers. Rather than the marked and re-marked border between Mexico and the United States, the nondemarcated and receding western frontier emerged as a deeper divide. In the tradition of travel writing, the road itself was rendered foreign. Despite the great empathy Bartlett harbored for Indians, his encounters revealed a tension between his East Coast ethnographic expectations and native people's actual customs.

Ultimately, in Bartlett's travels there was yet another expansionist desire not to draw but to eliminate or cross the border, although in a different manner from that of his Democratic adversaries. In June 1851, Bartlett came upon and released a kidnapped adolescent named Inez Gonzales. She was held by three men who had purchased her from Piñol Indians in Mexico and were about to resell her in Santa Fe. Extending U.S. protection over Inez and her innocence, and safely returning her to her parents, became a peculiar preoccupation that would draw Bartlett deep into Mexico, where he traveled and convalesced much of the following year. With General Condé's blessing, he arrived in Santa Cruz in September. Returning the girl guaranteed her purity and the integrity of her family. Once he found the Gonzales family, Bartlett discovered these Mexican villagers in their full humanity. "Tears of joy burst from all; and the sun-burnt and brawny men, in whom the finer feelings of our nature are wrongly supposed not to exist, wept like children, as they looked with astonishment on the rescued girl."[41]

Bartlett continued traveling as far as Acapulco (one thousand miles south of the border) where in February 1852 he took a boat back to San Diego, California. A few months later, and to his great disappointment, he found Inez in Tubac (south of Tucson) cohabiting with a Mexican officer far away from her parents. In another episode, Bartlett released Mexican children from Apache captivity. The Apache were angered, and Bartlett explained to them at length that he was merely following the treaty between the two countries that made each government responsible for acts of depredation committed across the border. The United States was now obliged to protect its Mexican friends and could not renege on her promises. There was a didactic "Americanizing" dimension to these incidents. At the same time, liberating enslaved children could have implicitly drawn the most important borderline of Bartlett's commission, that between his northeastern, middle-class sensibilities and those of his southern foes.

The publication heralded a new round of controversy. The *National Intelligencer* expressed its wish to see Congress present the geographical, mineralogical, zoological, and ethnographical dimensions of the commission's work to the public in "a suitable manner."[42] The *Union* objected. Bartlett elected "to embark it in the chances of 'the trade;' and if a failure in the anticipated profits, or any other cause, should now make it convenient to saddle Congress with the venture, we respectfully suggest that it is too late."[43] The article claimed that according to "the best authority," there was not a single contribution in the book to science, the mapping of the country, or the illustration of its physical geography. Bartlett rebutted that upon returning to Washington he looked for the collections gathered by the army officers. To his dismay, the specimens had been sent to New York, Boston, and elsewhere for examination and possibly publication as well. He issued an order to members of the expedition to prevent the appropriation of government property. But the secretary of the interior, Robert McClelland (who happened to be the brother of one of Bartlett's chief rivals in the expedition) invalidated his instructions and soon afterward, Bartlett was out of office. "No public officer has ever before met with the treatment that I have." All reports of American surveys and explorations, whether domestic or otherwise (including expeditions to the Amazon), were officially published and distributed without charge. The public should judge who was wronged, government or him.[44] Colonel Emory (his successor and great rival) rejoined in the *Union* that despite Bartlett's disclaimers, the former commissioner was still in possession of government property, including sketches made by the commission's artist. Unlike objects of natural history, which interested few, these illustrations were property that had "both intrinsic and mercantile value-property . . . property easily transferable, and convertible into money."[45]

The title "Personal Narrative" did not hide the fact that Bartlett's book was an account of an official assignment. Still, the *New York Quarterly Review* regarded it mostly as a travel book and the best of its kind. "The style of this work is a model of descriptive writing, simple, unambitious, quiet and in racy, idiomatic terms, it presents a lucid and animated narrative."[46] The *New York Times* joined the chorus. It would have been to the credit of any government to present these facts to the world. "How differs this from sowing freely and reaping sparingly?—appropriating liberally for the prosecution of the work, yet, by refusing appropriations for publishing, reaping no other fruits rather than the Commissioner's *Personal Narrative*."[47] The *Times* expressed its hope that the commission's post-Bartlett finding would not languish in governmental "dusty closets" or be left to private enterprise. "Next to the folly of keeping [explorations' results] entirely out of the popular reach, is the folly of postponing their publication until all the novelty of the enterprise has worn off, and the story becomes an old one before it is ever told."[48] The *Churchman* recommended the book as excellent summer reading for those vacationers who, "while enjoying the easy luxuries of Saratoga, West Point, or Newport, would enhance their satisfaction by the survey of distant portions of their widely-extended country, traveled over under less agreeable circumstances."[49] This was probably the most telling statement on the function of the book. For much of its eastern readership, it served as a form of entertainment and food for the occidentalist imagination. Congressman Benjamin Babcock Thurston from Bartlett's home state of Rhode Island asked that ten thousand copies of his books be published for the use of the House, but his request was in vain.

The Boundary Commission supplied its own version of the "Battle of the Books." The dispute between Emory and Bartlett resumed when Emory's report came out in 1857. In a reversal of roles, the *Herald,* a Bartlett supporter, attacked the first volume of Emory's account as one of the Congress-sponsored extravagant print projects that instead of providing useful information were meant to glorify their authors. It was duly labeled "a ponderous volume," brimming with more expensive illustrations than any similar government work—no less than ninety-nine steel, copper, and stone engravings and twenty woodcuts. "Never have we seen so many illustrations presenting so few features of interest, sixty-four of them being views of the desert directly on the western portion of the boundary, and consequently offering little variety."[50] The article poked fun at Emory's arrogance in calling a mountain near the Rio Grande after himself. The mountain was illustrated in the report and on its binding. By embossing on the cover the mountain he had named after himself, Emory was able to sign his report twice. The fact that the document could be read from its exterior further enhanced its capacity as a monument, although its national signification was clearly threatened or dwarfed by Emory's own sense of grandeur.

The *Herald* added sardonically that America had a Mount Washington in the East and a Mount Emory on its southwestern border. "How slight is the step from the sublime to the ridiculous." (The article reported that the cost of printing Emory's reports was $233,000, while the expenses for the scientific crew were estimated to be only $70,000.) Should we expect next to find Emory Toads and Emory Vipers? By inserting into his official reports remarks on his dispute with Bartlett, Emory became even more vulnerable to criticism about wasting public money for personal purposes. Another burst of open letters between Bartlett and Emory rehashed accusations of neglect and self-aggrandizement. One newspaper compared the high cost of Emory's report and its moderate "literary or scientific" value with Congress's refusal to print Bartlett's account in the simplest form.[51] It was an illustration of the military influence on government. If Bartlett had been a colonel, his report would have featured enough engravings "to make a whole picture gallery." The writer did not neglect to mention that the engravings for the Emory report were executed in Paris and that foreign artists were preferred to Americans in rendering this service. "Possibly the French may beat us in the toads and lizards, but we do not believe that anything is gained by sending away the engraving of the botanical illustrations."[52]

Northwestern papers' support of Bartlett should not come as a surprise. He was a member of various learned societies and well connected with the Yankee intellectual establishment. Those reviews, however, gave ample evidence to prevalent notions concerning the duty of government in providing the public fresh information, scientific and otherwise. Bartlett's campaign for the publication of his report demonstrated contested notions of ownership that pitted government against individuals over texts, specimens, and knowledge. In addition, it betrayed the weakness of the antebellum state. Government was not simply speaking from the pens of its commissioned officers but was occasionally eclipsed by their individual voices registered in exuberant documents.

Bartlett's book was so extensively used that there are no known copies of the original text without missing pages. One is left speculating whether removing pages of expeditions' accounts (perhaps for an illustration or for a particular detail on a part of the route) was a common practice. The report also received some vicarious official recognition. When the postmaster general chose the southern route to San Francisco (the Butterfield Mail), his decision, he claimed, was based on three documents: Captain Randolph Marcy's *Reconnaissances*, Bartlett's *Narrative*, and the Pacific Railroad Reports.[53]

"Very Desirous to Complete My Set"

It is difficult to measure actual readers' response to government publications. Press reviews of explorations and legislative reports tended to reflect predictable views of contending literary, scientific, and political cliques. However, in the records of the Department of the Interior there are roughly one thousand requests for volumes of the Pacific Railroad surveys.[54] They were received between 1854 and 1861 from newspapermen, businessmen, army officers, government officials, educators, amateur scientists, civil engineers, and ordinary citizens who were simply collecting government documents. This is admittedly a rather crude gauge with which to assess who was interested in government documents and for what purposes. Those who wrote thought that because of their public status, personal interest, friends in high places, or actual need, they stood a better chance to receive them. In all likelihood, many more requests were directed at individual members of the two houses. What this repository does reveal is the range of interest and curiosity. Requests came from all over the country, including regions far removed from the West. The single largest group was that of officials or other individuals close to the administration. Other petitions evidenced the grassroots reach of science in the antebellum United States (as also manifested by the cooperation the Smithsonian achieved in enlisting private citizens across the nation to participate in its meteorological and natural history projects).

The Pacific Railroad surveys (1853–54) were a cluster of expeditions conducted to identify the most practical route for the transcontinental railroad. Ostensibly introducing a scientific approach to policy making, Congress and the administration were seeking a way to detour what was in effect an uncircumventable political hurdle. Every possible route (usually variations of about eight alternatives) had a loyal group of politicians, developers, promoters, and speculators who were puffing its merit. Jefferson Davis, then the secretary of war in the Pierce administration, together with a group of Deep South and Texan congressmen, wanted the route to pass along the already-surveyed Mexican border. Many of the leading officers of the Corps of Topographical Engineers, like Abert and Emory, were also fiercely devoted to the far southern route. A few of them harbored strong southern loyalties; others succumbed to a growing institutional attachment to an area that had been repeatedly observed and examined. The Army Corps of Engineers' gaze was fixed on the Southwest and refused to be diverted.[55] The surveys initially evolved around four main expeditions, for which Congress appropriated $150,000. Despite enormous efforts, there was no conclusive answer to the question presented to the explorers. The competition only intensified when it turned out (to the genuine surprise of Davis and others) there were several fine alternatives for the transcontinental route. Lack of rigorous standards and somewhat dubious calculations also made it all but impossible to compare with any precision assertions about economy and practicality. Davis and Captain Andrew Humphreys, Chief of the Bureau of Western Explorations and Surveys, who was put in charge of a small apparatus in the War Department to supervise the project, produced controversial summary evaluations of the surveys.

These expeditions, with their mixture of sectional politics and engineers' calculations of curves and heights, engendered another enterprise that took years and great resources to accomplish. It was the ultimate product of pre–Civil War U.S. imperial aspirations: twelve volumes featuring expedition narratives and writings on geology, zoology, botany, and ethnology. A century later, the Pacific Railroad surveyors still impressed historian William Goetzmann as the largest congregation of scientists and technicians to go on a national campaign of exploration and conquest since Napoleon entered Egypt (an imperial project that was also followed by a lavish publication). More than a hundred scientifically trained men in the field and in the East participated in the effort of collecting, classifying, and publishing. Leading antebellum scientists Torrey, Gray, and especially Baird at the Smithsonian cast a long shadow over the expeditions, selecting field scientists and then supervising and authoring many of the reports. The national project was typically wrapped in universalistic scientific language. Another boundary-defying gesture was the use of *North America* rather than the *United States* in the titles of volumes such as *Mammals of North America* or *Birds of North America*. Moreover, the scientific team was cosmopolitan and included Europeans such as Baron F. W. von Egloffstein, a Prussian illustrator; Frederick Creuzefeldt, a botanist who lost his life in the Gunnison massacre; and Jules Marcou, a French naturalist. Marcou somewhat spoiled the semblance of an international cooperation under the American flag. Claiming illness at the conclusion of his labors, he attempted to leave the country with his geological specimens and without submitting a report. Forced to produce an account, he eventually returned to Paris, where he composed a private document and completed a geological map of the United States, further incensing his American colleagues. The race between exploration leaders and their underlings for the printing press was a feature of these enterprises. It happened first in the aftermath of Lewis and Clark's homecoming, when to Meriwether Lewis's great annoyance and alarm, Sergeant Patrick Gass, a member of the "Corps of Discovery," was quick to publish his journals, prompting Lewis to assault in the press "unauthorized . . . spurious publications."[56]

Government issued the reports in two editions. A three-volume octavo accompanied by a folio of maps was published in 1855 before a few of the last surveys were entirely completed.[57] The second edition was a luxurious twelve-volume (in thirteen parts) quarto that represented the apex of the genre: encyclopedic and in disarray, populated by authorial fancies (in one case a long lecture, provided by a junior military officer, over the importance of government involvement in setting a network of railroads), and retentive. A commemorative volume summarized western explorations since Lewis and Clark and included twenty-four maps and profiles, plus four older maps pointing to historical discoveries.[58] The prospect of publication was so tempting that collections made outside the surveys were appropriated, including the private aggregation of cacti

Stanley .Del   Sarony,Major & Knapp,Lith.? 449 Broadway,N.Y.

The annual allocation of goods to the Assiniboine Indians by government officials at Fort Union (North Dakota) was illustrated by John Mix Stanley, who accompanied the 1855 exploration of the prospective route for the transcontinental railroad from St. Paul to Puget Sound. A cluster of such expeditions led to the thirteen volumes of *Reports of Explorations and Surveys, to Ascertain the Most Practicable and Economical Route for a Railroad from the Mississippi River to the Pacific Ocean* (1855–61), the most comprehensive and lavish western reports of the antebellum period. (Three-tone lithograph by Sarony, Major and Knapp after drawing by Stanley, c. 1855; additional coloring was added later).

and rocks by Major H. Thomas at Fort Yuma featured in the eighth volume. Congress authorized the printing of ten thousand copies of the reports, which were issued simultaneously by the Senate (leatherbound) and the House (cloth).

One group of applicants for these volumes consisted of entrepreneurs who wanted to participate in the rush to build a railroad to the Pacific or who contemplated other real or fantastical business schemes. Several were particularly anxious to promote the southern route. Edgar Conkling from the *Railroad Record,* published in Cincinnati, reprinted government reports and other articles, documents, and pamphlets in order to popularize the thirty-second parallel route. He asked Jefferson Davis to send his synopsis of the surveys and maps as well as duplicates of any other material on the topic. He promised to publish approximately twenty thousand copies of Jefferson's synopsis for gratis circulation all over the country.[59] Dr. Levi Jones from New York also presented himself as a supporter of the southern route, "the line of the 32 parallel is altogether the best which can be taken from the interest of this Union or the world." He had obtained a charter in Texas for a railroad from Matagorda Bay to El Paso and was trying to raise money for the project. Jones asked for a copy or two of the abridged official report as well as for any information that would point to the advantage of that route, such as the discovery of new artesian wells in the Rockies.[60]

Dr. Christian Raub developed a new type of "desert locomotive" specifically for the railroad to the Pacific. The inventor wished to know the precise distances between points of water and coal supplies to help him optimize the performance of the machine. August Harvey, a civil engineer from Nebraska City, was planning to make a survey in the upper part of the territory early in the spring of 1857 and asked for the second volume of the project to use as a guide. A Kentucky applicant intended to visit the Oregon and Washington territories and wanted every detail pertaining to that part of the country. Another petitioner needed expedition reports for a literary work he was busy preparing.[61]

David Wyrick, an Ohioan, came up with a highly ambitious or outlandish project, which he described as "a most admirable work of a Meteorological character, of such feature as has not yet been attempted by any one." His meteorological guide, he claimed, would be valuable in settling new countries and solve some of the severest problems facing American farmers. "I do most abominably hate to beg, but my love for science and the impossibility to buy such works, excites me to that I would not, were those explorations published for sale . . . The way they are distributed (to ranting Politicians) they do not do the good intended—or would do, if the right kind of persons got them—but I would pay something than depend in this way and then lose them."[62] Exploration reports that were available commercially, he added, were "garbled and mutilated." Publishers did not bother with the less commercially desirable scientific portions and eliminated them.

Requests from schools and libraries cited pedagogical purposes. The librarian of Marion College in Missouri wrote that their senator supplied them with various documents, but they received only the second volume of the *Explorations* and wished to have the first. "We have a high appreciation of the value of these most interesting works and feel deeply the loss of the missing volume."[63] J. Gibson had a reading room in which he placed more than three hundred volumes of his private library "for the benefit of the youth in this vicinity. Any aid you can give me will be thankfully received."[64] An applicant from Weymouth, Massachusetts, solicited installments of the report for the local Young Men's Debating Society.

It is difficult to know with certainty which requests met with positive responses. Clerks inconsistently applied departmental markings on the letters. One category of petitioners that appeared to be particularly successful were representatives of the press. Charles Lanman from the *National Intelligencer* desired two volumes for a review, which he hoped would please the department. Editors and publishers were also responsible for numerous requests for maps, particularly sought-after items. The scientist James D. Dana, by then editor of *Silliman's Journal*, requested a map, which he planned to add to a thirty-page long abstract of the reports. A publisher of school geography books was also among the applicants. A St. Louis publisher who had received a map of the West wanted an additional five hundred to one thousand copies for Germans who were expected to migrate to Missouri. Somewhat arrogantly, he specified that he was interested in the maps without their original titles but on the same kind of paper and with eight-inch margins from every direction.[65] The editor of the *San Diego Herald* applied for general maps and reports. "This matter of the Pacific Rail Road is of great importance to us here," he wrote.[66] A letter from Alexandria, Minnesota, carried a request from Samuel Cowdney, who had seen Lieutenant Warren's map on his explorations of the fifty-fifth and fifty-sixth parallels and wished to have one so he and his neighbors might know where they stood as far as government "improvements" were concerned. Finally, a correspondent from Philadelphia asked for three of the latest maps of the surveys. "My object," he explained candidly, "is to have them mounted and hung in my library for study or reference, as I am reading."[67]

Many applicants attempted to play the party card, albeit with varying degrees of success. Party affiliation probably drove them initially to contact the administration, which was Democratic throughout the decade. George M. Fowle from New Haven concluded his request with "you would greatly oblige a good Administration Democrat."[68] New Yorker Thomas M. Howell enclosed a letter of introduction from Governor Seymour. A friend had given him the fifth volume and suggested that he might be able to get the rest from the War Department. "I urge no claim upon your kind consideration, in the matter, other than the fact, that, I have been a Democrat all my life and have had the misfortune to reside in a Whig region and have had no opportunity to procure the work through a Democratic Representation."[69] Two residents of Mount Vernon, Ohio, complained that the local Republicans got the sixth volume of the Pacific Railroad report while they, good Democrats, were not able to get hold of it. An applicant from Liberty, Virginia, simply promised Secretary Floyd that if granted two volumes he would return the favor.[70] Numerous requests included well-wishing platitudes; others featured bits and pieces of local political gossip. The political component of these solicitations, including distinct animosity toward the emerging Republican Party, only grew toward the conclusion of the 1850s.

Individuals involved with the expeditions or the preparation of the reports regarded their contributions worthy of gratis volumes. (In several expeditions, the authors' entitlement to a certain number of copies was prescribed by law.) The War Department received a request from Torrey (through his Congressman W. B. Maclay), who had written 250 pages on florae for the survey. Torrey, then the assayer of the New York Port, complained that he could not receive the report beyond the second volume after his friend Governor Marcy (a former secretary of war), had left office. Since he labored for the project for two or three years, he thought he deserved an entire set. He also wished to supply copies to his colleagues in Europe. Asa Gray wanted one copy to sent to Sir William Hooker of the Royal Botanical Garden and another to Professor Gandille of Geneva. Spencer Baird of Smithsonian fame (and the leading non-field scientist of the expedition) asked for spare copies of the second, third, and fourth volumes. He had a full set of the entire project at home but wanted another one "for reference" at the Institution.[71]

More often than not, those who asked for specific volumes already had others in their possession. Many letters implied that completing the set was a worthy enough cause to merit government cooperation. The ambition, or compulsion, to complete the series was sometimes accompanied by an indiscriminate drive to collect official reports. Thus, a pastor of the Baptist Church at Schulerville, New York, gathered a library of public documents and applied for four volumes of the Pacific Railroad project as well as any other text that would enrich his library.[72] John Fitch wrote that "for years [I] have endeavored to compile a library of public works and to a great measure have succeeded."[73] Another correspondent, J. W. Cott, received all of the first five volumes and now was anxious to get the sixth. Alas, his representative in Congress stopped answering his letters. Cott figured that the congressman could not deliver anymore so he decided to apply directly to the department.[74] Fred E. Cannon declared he was "very desirous to complete my set."[75]

There was a tale in every request from ordinary people. Citizens (all men) told government stories in an exchange for books. After declaring he had always been not just a Democrat but a Buchanan Democrat, John McKiernan wrote about his experience in the Mexican War. After serving as a volunteer under a famous commander who died in battle, he crossed the plains to California. He acquired some knowledge of the "countries" through which the prospective railroad would pass and was anxious, therefore, to read the report. McKiernan had already seen a part and was eager to read them all.[76]

Several writers employed ingenious excuses to obtain volumes. Captain W. C. Palmer received a circular that warned prospective readers that a segment of a naval report was inserted by mistake into the first volume and promised copies of the part that was omitted to recipients of defective reports. Palmer was not entitled for the first volume but regarded the circular letter a pretext to solicit for it.[77] An applicant from Texas (describing himself as an old Mississippian) wanted government-issued studies of the West. The writer had a large family of boys, and the volumes would teach them the geography of that part of the country, information about which could not be acquired in any other way than through reading about government explorations.[78]

The letters contained much flattery, not just of the personal or political kind (including excessive name dropping) but also adulations of government action and official generosity. A letter from Monterey indicated that the fifth volume on California by Williamson and Blake "is received in our state with the highest favor as it is the most valuable work yet published on California and is considered a great honor to the Government and its scientific officers."[79] A representative of the Polytechnic College of the State of Pennsylvania in Philadelphia wrote, "We feel therefore that nowhere more than here will the influence of Government in the publication of the Reports aforesaid be more fully appreciated and the facts therein contained be more profitably studied."[80] H. W. Wood declared himself Secretary Floyd's political adherent and a member of a large secret club in New York whose members were politically united. "The work I should praise (as I am an amateur naturalist) for the scientific information it contains, and which could never have been obtained but through the just appreciation of yourself of the needs of the scientific portion of the vast population of our noble republic." The writer wanted either a set or whatever was still in print.[81]

Some were convinced that their great appreciation of scientific knowledge was enough to guarantee a positive response. B. F. Stein from Easton, Pennsylvania, wanted an entire set. For the previous fifteen years, he had been an educator in various institutions. Unfortunately, he had failed to submit his application to his congressman on time. "Much of the information contained in those volumes is of but little interest to the general reader and can only be appreciated by those whose minds have been trained to scientific investigations." His petition was apparently denied.[82] J. N. Hurd from Rochester had been on a seven-year tour conducting missionary work at Madras, India. Home on a vacation, he had the chance to examine the report and wrote, "The desire to possess a copy and to take it back with me to Hindustan is very great . . . As an exposition of the geography and natural history of the western portion of the continent as well as an illustration of the enterprise of our government and race it is extremely valuable." Besides the information and the joy of reading it, Hurd saw a great opportunity in showing the volumes to officers of the British Army in Madras. "As an American citizen separated by the nature of my pursuit from my countrymen, the reading of works of this description afford me a degree of pleasure the resident would hardly experience."[83]

The many applications for the volumes of the Pacific Railroad expeditions confirm the great public appetite for official publications. In the citizens' reading preferences, the need for personal gain and self-aggrandizement (so much of official print ephemera targeted commercial interests) coalesced with strong national sentiments. But commercial aspirations or nationalism did not always account for the drive to obtain, read, and collect books, a craving that the state volunteered to satisfy or at times toiled hard to cultivate. The American "imperial self" was voracious also as a reader. Moreover, the awareness of congressmen and officials to the citizen-reader's material, market-driven interests was not necessarily rooted in the practices of laissez faire. The federal state had few qualms about infringing upon the absolute freedom of the market, including the market of information. It facilitated patronage for authors, dismantled the open bid system in contracting for printing, and dispatched free books to public institutions and individuals. Before Senator Anthony became so impressed by British printing practices in the 1860s, the antebellum United States looked not so much to penny-wise London as to continental Europe, especially France, for models of generous state support of stupendously executed "national works." (In Britain, social inquiry featured less by way of nationalism and individualism.) Lawmakers crafted a knowledge policy that rested on marketplace awareness of product promotion and customers' demands as well as on republican sensibilities, nation-building aspirations, and the crude needs of the two-party system. Another feature of western explorations was a heightened sense of authorship. The project of discovering the West involved specialized knowledge and unique skills. The incessant expressions of subjectivity in expedition narratives, no less than the explicit authorial ambitions of explorers, were officially sanctioned and were emblematic of the culture that evolved around the conquering of the West.

Expeditions and explorations yielded a print archive that was predicated on a strong sense of temporality, since the recorded world disappeared at the moment of registration. This effect was most clearly articulated in ethnological projects. Collecting facts about native peoples rested on the assumption that the subject matter was fated soon to disappear. As a latter-day version of the Zeno paradox, the Indian was imminently vanishing and yet always still there, a living presence and at times a threatening one. The western frontier, no less than the Indian subject, was a receding object in the American imagination and American reality as well. The West would vanish as a consequence of its own discovery, as railroads, settlers, and towns took over the land. Another impetus for western archivization came directly from science and the logic of scientific discovery, especially in natural history, which in the middle of the nineteenth century still focused religiously on description and classification of previously unknown plants and animals. When in the 1840s Congress decided to publish the exploring expedition's findings, it stipulated the reports engage only newly discovered species. Differentiating between old and new became one of the points of contention between the professional scientists and the expedition's crew. Augustus Addison Gould, a Boston physician who was put in charge of writing the mollusca and shells volume, acidly remarked that by *new* scientists meant not what was new to naval officers and politicians in Washington, D.C., but what was new in Boston and for scientists abroad. It was exceptionally important for him to expedite the printing of his report for, as he alleged, "It is not the date of the *discovery* of an object which gives precedence to it . . . but the date of the *publication*."[84] The cult of the new designated the moment of publication as the moment of discovery and its concurrent archivization. (In contrast, social inquiries, notwithstanding their own logic of discovery, purported to represent the field of investigation in toto.)

Curiously, through these projects of investigation and publication the United States was looking at itself, from its outskirts, from removed vantage points, from its past, from its borders, and in the eyes of others as they read its textual products. As statements on the American nation or the federal government, these projects functioned allegorically or by extension. In contrast, parliamentary literature seemed to represent British society directly, almost as a mirror image. This was not merely an expression of distinct national agendas. The United States faced a grave social, constitutional, and moral crisis that would eventually tear it asunder. But the factual literature that accompanied the rift between North and South was predominantly written outside Washington. With a few important exceptions, such as the 1830s congressional debates over antislavery petitions and the gag rule, the plight of slavery was a blind spot in the federal government's gaze. Admittedly, the British state's preoccupation with the more titillating aspects of child labor or with environmental issues—sanitation reform, for instance—could also be perceived as an effort at deflecting attention from the most insidious aspects of the new industrial regime.[85]

There were substantial variances in the experiences of these two nations, the issues under national discussion, and the relations between the executives and the legislatures, lawmakers and voters. It is in light of these distinct national histories and cultures that some of the similarities are so striking. Both regimes of knowledge were fraught with contention and dissatisfaction. Questions concerning the value, cost, and purposes of official documents were quite similar, and the legislatures in both countries were central to the production of knowledge and its circulation. Most importantly, to return to this discussion's starting point, both countries concurrently experienced the emergence of a print-based national arena distinct from the eighteenth-century bourgeois public sphere. An important dimension of this development was the role of the state either as a producer of knowledge, a publisher, a printer, a librarian, and an archivist, or, as facilitator of the rapid movement of information through the press, either by active assistance (through the postal services) or by removing obstacles such as "taxes on knowledge." Even the harshest critics of congressional publications after the Civil War acknowledged that print had become an indispensable part of the political and legislative processes, "nearly the whole of the vast business of Congress is done by aid of printing,—the bills, acts, etc., being on the desk of every member at the moment of debating them."[86] Lawmakers and officials did not just peddle printed matter but were inundated with it themselves.

PART II

THE CULTURE OF THE SOCIAL FACT

Emerging from the battles over the electoral Reform Act (1832), Earl Grey's Whig cabinet, hesitantly at first, initiated large-scale investigations into poor laws, child labor, and municipal governments. These were formative experiences for the British state. Royal commissions of inquiry, often laboring for years and producing massive documents and policy recommendations, became by the mid-nineteenth century a fixture, even a cliché, of British politics. Chapter 4 examines commissioners' fieldwork, while chapter 5 follows officials through the process of producing and disseminating their reports. Chapter 6 brings us to the Civil War labors of the American Freedmen's Inquiry Commission. Dispatching individuals to conduct surveys for the federal and state government was not foreign to the American experience but instituting a panel to devise major federal policy raised overt criticism in Congress. The national government did not have in its administrative arsenal any institution comparable to royal commissions of inquiry. (In Britain, the modern function of royal commissions was largely an early nineteenth-century invention.) Indeed, the Freedmen's Inquiry, sponsored by the secretary of war, represented an effort by members of Lincoln's administration and the Republican Party to appropriate British or French models of scientific fact gathering in order to forge policy.

Part two of the book addresses therefore the culture of the social fact and its institutionalization. By the early decades of the century, accumulating social information, previously the largely voluntary preoccupation of reformers, physicians, and clergymen, was assumed by a host of official bodies, commissions, committees, panels, and inspectorates. While commissioned work provided for many individuals a venue for authorship and a public career, these tiny outfits, the creation of bureaucratic culture dispatched to study society, were themselves riveted by social relations, hierarchies, collaborations, and strong tensions. The following discussions explore the work of these small units in the field and their contributions to print statism.

These case studies suggest that while the U.S. government was busy grappling with problems of race—What to do with the freedmen? How to civilize the Indian?—the British government focused on matters of class. This distinction should be qualified. First, British and American investigators arrived in their fields armed with a wide array of measuring tools that included disciplines forged to assess racial and cultural differences as well as those that addressed the effects of industrialization. Thus, while the American Freedmen's Inquiry Commission vacillated between labor and racial categories in its efforts to conceptualize the freedmen question, British laborers were often the subject of ethnic taxonomies or casual "racial" commentary. The mines investigation of the early 1840s furnishes an excellent example. For instance, Subcommissioner Samuel Swain Scriven, observing men working in remarkably small subterranean crevices entirely in the nude, remarked, "Black and filthy as they are in their low, dark, heated, and dismal chambers, they look like a race fallen from the common stock."[1] Ethnography was at play in many social investigations, but the same is true of political economy and neighboring disciplines. In the early Victorian languages of difference, race and class where remarkably close idioms, imbricated, entwined—although not interchangeable. At the same time, concepts of race and class were endowed with neither the coherence nor the consistency they would acquire by the end of the century, and there was nothing inevitable in the particular ways in which these categories ultimately congealed.

Second, the race-class divide may be a product of the emphasis, on the American side, on the exertions of the federal government. Otherwise, state and local government, especially in the Northeast, became increasingly involved in social policy and social research before the Civil War. In Britain, issues of race were obviously more pronounced in imperial contexts, but ethnic or cultural classifications did not necessarily rely on imperial reference points. Society in the British Isles was often conceived of through distinctions of region, language, culture, denomination, and ethnos. Finally, in many of the investigative case studies explored here, questions of representation and citizenship, autonomy and propriety, subsumed the distinction between class and race.

CHAPTER FOUR

Scenes of Commission

The triumphalist view deemed royal commissions' work to be the embodiment of science and impartial expertise in the service of policy making. Herman Finer wrote about 1830s social investigations, "An apparatus of exploration was invented for the social field, mightily influential in its sphere as the invention of the microscope had been in physics and medicine."[1] Another admiring observer remarked: "They touched with one hand the ancient machinery of forensic inquiry, with the other hand the new methods of inductive and experimental science."[2] A more skeptical approach, originating in the period and further articulated in the works of Beatrice and Sydney Webb, regarded royal commissions first and foremost as a political tool. Commissions, they reminded us, were often manipulated to promote preconceived policies or to put thorny issues on the shelf, peddling official passivity as action. As early as 1834 the *Quarterly Review* opined that commissions of inquiry served two purposes: "First, that of gaining time— which is everything to indolent or incapable men with a load of business before them to which they feel themselves unequal—secondly, the creation of pleasant and profitable jobs for a dozen or two of friends and retainers."[3] Either way, students of royal commissions have been primarily interested in their contribution to the extension of government and their role as vehicles for the dissemination of discourse, utilitarian ideas in particular.

This chapter examines instead the practices of official investigation, starting with the question of standpoint and proximity to the actual sites of labor and poverty, and then proceeding to investigators' travels, visits, and meetings with witnesses and the populations under investigation (including these communities' own attempts at counterinquiries). Special attention is given to the mundane experiences of low-level bureaucrats entrusted with the routines of inspection and interview. Their exertions have been neglected by the historical literature that paid great attention to celebrity reformers, the Edwin Chadwicks, James Kay-Shuttleworths, and Thomas Southwood Smiths of the Victorian world. Beyond their stated assignments, official emissaries engaged in rather complex representational work, acting (and standing) for government, under the guise of the crown, in various localities and concurrently representing the investigated population, predominantly but not exclusively through written reports. Another representational aspect was embedded in the performances that characterized many encounters between investigators and subjects, including acts of reenactment, masquerade, substitution, and mediation.

Representational work often involves a strong ocular dimension, for—to follow the conceptual underpinnings of representation—making visible is one way of rendering the absent present. In Michel Foucault's writings, observing a "population" is one of the radical innovations of the Enlightenment, an expression of its desire for social transparency. This visibility was symptomatic of the spatial reconfiguration of power along lines that separated the visible and the invisible, the observed and the hidden. The panopticon was the quintessential product of the new technologies of government. In this model prison, power was to be endemic yet unverifiable; its gaze objectified and disciplined inmates, making them autonomous "self-governed" subjects. The panopticon seems particularly pertinent to our discussion for, in the early Victorian period, social research brought an ambitious state together with a few of Jeremy Bentham's most diligent disciples. However, as against the privileged status that Foucault bestowed on this utopian model—the house that Jeremy envisaged but never built—state-sponsored inquiries afforded numerous opportunities for observation (and, importantly, conversation). These were conducted from different viewpoints and involved alternating gestures of the eye, from close focus to panoramic view, from wondering glance to temporary blindness—beyond the imperious gaze, that intense and fixed look that controls and subjectifies. The complexity of these ocular strategies rested on the un-panopticonlike exchange relationships between investigators and the investigated, the (rather verifiable) visibility of government itself, and the ways in which the state had to internalize the gaze from below. The scene of inquiry was saturated with actor-viewers beyond government and the poor. Social investigations featured parties that were powerful participants in the field of inquiry as well as objects of investigation—mill owners and overseers, prison wardens, schoolmasters, and local surgeons. At times, ocular power was a feature of scuffles among a diverse group of poor-spotters themselves rather than a means to control the poor.

This chapter draws mainly on the experience of royal commissions that operated during the so-called angry 1830s and hungry 1840s, especially commissions that addressed child (and female) labor, such as the Factory Commission (1833), and the Employment of Children Commission (1840–43) (which focused on mines and other branches of manufacturing not covered by previous child labor legislation).[4] The labor of royal commissions is examined here in tandem with the investigative work of the inspectorates that supervised the implementation of new policies and laws regarding factories, mines, and workhouses. In many fundamental features, the inspectorates followed in the footsteps of royal commissions. There was a significant overlap of personnel between the two institutions and, at times, a causal link between a particular investigation and the establishment of an inspection apparatus.

Royal Commissions

A few of the informational institutions that were launched in the early part of the nineteenth century, such the Statistical Department of the Board of Trade, do support the impression of increasingly scientific and centralized state mechanism (notwithstanding echoes of old historiographical Whiggism), of modernity at play. In contrast, the royal commission of inquiry was a particularly and peculiarly British institution. Instrumental in what may be described as a tacit effort to dismantle or reform the British ancien regime—local government, the military, the Church—this investigative body was itself a remnant of the old regime. Its power rested, at least nominally, on the royal prerogative to delegate power to a group of subjects, a practice that may be traced back as far as the Doomsday Book of 1086. Participation on such a commission was ostensibly a gentlemanly and mostly unpaid endeavor. In the eighteenth century, royal commissions were still associated with Stuart tyranny and rarely appointed, but by the beginning of the nineteenth century, the exigencies born out of the French wars eventuated their revival. Historically, royal commissions were often perceived as a challenge to parliamentary power.

The early Victorian state remade royal commissions to accord with the immensely important tool of parliamentary inquest, the select committee. For instance, in their terms of reference, commissions were often equipped with the authority to summon witnesses and to take evidence under oath. Both privileges were, at the time, a figment of political imagination, an effort to appropriate the legitimacy of parliamentary inquiry.[5] Commissions were often installed to feed, perhaps manage, public debates, but also allowed the liberal state to replicate and expand its representational bodies, to make itself visible or observable, and, at the same time, to disguise itself behind an antiquated, privileged, and seemingly autonomous institution. Forty-five such royal commissions were appointed between 1830 and 1850 for England and Wales alone, out of which fully one-third dealt directly with social and urban problems. Others investigated administrative, legal, and fiscal matters, as well as the army and navy.

The home secretary appointed royal commissions "to inquire and to report" either by a letter patent under the Great Seal or by a warrant under the royal Sign Manual, and following a decision by cabinet or Parliament. Historians Hugh Clokie and Joseph Robinson maintained that the advantage of commissions over parliamentary committees rested on their ability to carry out research independently of the time constraints imposed by parliamentary sessions. Unlike overpopulated parliamentary committees, commissions were led by small groups of individuals who rather than merely interviewing witnesses could conduct or supervise fieldwork. An 1865 *Daily Telegraph* article asserted that in cases of political dispute, parliamentary inquiry would be preferable for "eliciting the truth in all of its national bearings," but in ascertaining facts a royal commission was advantageous. "Anybody who has compared the results of both systems of inquiry must be convinced of the superiority of the commissions; the evidence taken before them being always much more full of local colouring, more elaborate, more exhaustive, and more minute."[6] Royal commissions and select committees were therefore complementary and rival ways to perform inquiries; friction between the legislature and government was a catalyst for investigation.

A mélange of (mostly titled) dignitaries headed royal commissions, but they were also an important venue for the newly arrived, young, middle-class reformers (as well as other office seekers), who would make their careers marching in and out of the corridors of government. This arrangement reflected the changing composition of the British ruling elite. Commissions also mirrored society, or at least its upper echelons, in their internal hierarchy of senior commissioners who comprised a "Central Board" and a body of paid field workers, subcommissioners, or assistant commissioners.[7] The two-tier structure (somewhat different from the division between scientists and fact collectors that would dominate western explorations) featured its own version of "social mobility," as demonstrated by Chadwick's meteoric rise from the ranks of the English poorlaw assistant commissioners to a prominent place among the senior commissioners as the author of the final report. (He later became the secretary of the poor-law inspectorate, which was in effect a permanent commission).

Vantage Point

Dividing labor between those who procured information and those who "digested" it accentuated the tension between native expertise and knowledge produced from afar by individuals unfamiliar with local peculiarities. A standard criticism against government investigations was that "foreigners" in "roving commissions" could not possibly grasp the condition of a locality. In the same vein, Bishop Doyle challenged the economist Nassau Senior's (a key participant in reshaping English poor law) ability to devise social policy. "Is he, buried in the dens of the inns of court or vending political economy to beardless youths at a coterie in the 'west end,' or I, visiting the hovels and communing with the hearts of the Irish Poor—is he or I the better judge?"[8] Discounting such praise for the immediate, up-close knowledge of the resident observer, subcommissioner William Rayner Wood, who traveled for the Employment of Children Commission among the iron works of Bradford and Leeds, complained about the ignorance among the local middle and higher classes about the actual condition of the mining community. "Benevolent wishes and vague information are very common, but of accurate and sound knowledge upon the subject the instances are very rare."[9] As a "striking proof" for his allegations, he cited a well-meaning proprietor who in the previous five years had been living among his employees. He initially stated to Wood that literacy was common among the poor in his neighborhood, but when careful research demonstrated otherwise, he asked that his testimony be stricken from the report.

The merits of detachment over close proximity were acknowledged in diverse ways. During an early 1840s sanitation inquiry Chadwick sustained a physical as well as symbolic distance from the scene of inquiry by interviewing his own subcommissioners and incorporating these exchanges into his report. Thus, he could guarantee a semblance of an impartial remoteness and utilize his agents, quite safely (and deceptively), as though they were authentic field witnesses. The commissioners of the Irish poor-law inquiry decided to abstain from touring the countryside altogether. They obtained information exclusively by reading reports from traveling assistant commissioners. If each member of the central board would inspect specific districts, they reasoned, personal observations would outweigh the results of inquiry in other regions. Working in pairs, assistant commissioners were required to follow instructions rigorously and dispatch reports to Dublin at the conclusion of each parish visit.[10] The pressure to transmit reports constantly was necessitated by the body-mind split between the facts gatherers and their recommendations-framing superiors.

Social inquiries were immersed in similar acts of writing and reading. Many decades later, Sidney and Beatrice Webb would maintain that only in the process of perusing and reshuffling previously collected written evidence could actual discoveries occur. The social investigator's notes, not the slum or the factory, were comparable to the scientist's laboratory, blowpipe, or test tube. It is the distance from the fieldwork and the capacity to view the entire body of evidence concurrently that enables researchers to break up the mineral conglomerate (the Webbs used a geological metaphor to describe society), "revealing new co-existences or sequences ... [that were] capable of literary or statistical expression."[11] This commentary implies that while within eye's range of the object of study, the fact collector loses his sight.

In the early decades of the nineteenth century, however, local observers were among the most scientifically astute commentators on the social scene. The rivalry between local knowledge and state-produced knowledge was often articulated in terms of competing vantage points rather than the epistemological superiority of science versus the limited, experiential knowledge of locals. Similar tension was sometimes prompted by disciplinary rivalry defined in spatial terms. G. Calvert Holland, a physician in the Sheffield General Infirmary and a social observer, wrote in the early 1840s that a legislator could see only "the tendency of the various springs which modify the elements of society." His reasoning, therefore, was "general rather than particular—comprehensive rather than accurate." The political economist was also ignorant of the actual process of manufacturing. "He looks upon the busy field of industry from a distance, through the medium of previous inquirers." In contrast, Holland's own attempts at social exploration were based on "frequent intercourse with the artisan, [and] have afforded many opportunities of penetrating to the foundation of evils, which are altogether unnoticed by the political economist."[12] Royal commissions' investigations were preoccupied with capturing and defining the local. It was the field investigators' task to record indigenous knowledge. Alternatively, they could generate it themselves, substituting for local knowledge by relying on their own physical and emotional field experiences, and in the process equipping the commission with a bifocal gaze.

A wide, panoramic—rather than panoptic—view and the consequent ability to compare and contrast were the advantage of the remote observer over the immediate knowledge of the squire and the magistrate. Statistics, which in the 1830s were in great public vogue, endowed comparisons with a particularly visual tool. Perusing statistical tables, the reader's eyes could instantaneously glide over localities, trades, wages, and ages. The imperative to compare invaded every facet of commission work. Even lesser field agents devised taxonomies of classification and comparison, sometimes excessively. Evidently, comparisons superimposed cognitive coordinates on the social terrain. Employment of Children subcommissioners, to give one example, compared the size of children employed in the pits and the collieries to those who worked in other occupations, a step that seemingly corresponded to the purposes of the investigation. However, one agent introduced a national and ethnic component into his comparative typology. He reported that the Welsh stature did not reach the standard of the English and the Scotch, which he explained by the "little intermixture of foreign blood."[13] The Employment of Children report also demonstrated how pervasive the comparison between African slaves and British child laborers became in the British mind. It was one of the main rhetorical assets of the Factory (or Short Time) Movement, which sought the curtailment of child labor and a shorter workday. Mill owners also suggested particular comparisons and contested others. They, for instance, adamantly demanded that child laborers be examined side by side with children who engaged in farm work rather than with middle-class children. "Do not attempt to compare them with those from whom their situation is wholly different, and ever must be different."[14]

Outside the confines of official research, the comparative imagination occasionally offered even more far-reaching (and far-fetched) parallels, introducing stronger racial or sexual accents to social exploration. Some comparisons were driven by a strong cultural propensity to employ estrangement as a strategy of persuasion. For Peter Gaskell, for example, the working conditions in the mills produced an equatorial breed of females in the middle sections of the British Isles. In his 1833 book, Gaskell argued that the high temperature in the machine halls, among other factors, resulted in early puberty and increased female sexual activity. He even employed ethnological literature on the sexual promiscuity of warm-climate tribal societies to demonstrate the increased sexual appetite in the factories of Britain. Implicitly drawing another parallel between the antislavery movement and the demand to reform the factory, Gaskell claimed that mill owners encouraged and even abused this enhanced sexuality "calculated for the gratification of their satyr-like feelings, and the baseness of their own minds."[15]

Social predicaments were to be defined comparatively, concurrently accentuating the universality of social phenomena and their concrete local (or national) manifestations. Investigators were looking sidelong at the social and legislative experience of other countries. On their comparative pallet were, in addition, domestic regional differences enhanced by the divergent legal systems, social stratification, and policy traditions in Ireland, Scotland, England, and Wales. Commissioners and inspectors traveled occasionally to the European continent and even the United States to examine first-hand parallel developments in different settings. When the four members of the Handloom Weavers Commission were permitted to appoint five additional assistant commissioners, they chose instead to nominate only four and to use the rest of the money to meet the expenses of sending two assistant commissioners to the continent.[16] Delegates of laborers' organizations visited the continent for similar purposes.

At home, the comparative drive served to expand the reach of investigative projects beyond working men, women, and children to cover a less clearly defined lower class population, and, consequently, to affirm this group's status as under national study. Partly to conciliate mill owners, factory commissioners instructed their agents to include in their survey poor individuals outside the factory system and to explore the possibility that the material conditions of the factory and working-class neighborhoods—rather than long hours of working by machines—were at fault. This practice constituted an early attempt to divert attention from labor relations to work and living environments. With the sanitary campaigns of the 1840s, controversies over Chartism and the factory system were displaced onto the physical squalor of slums, mills, and cemeteries. The sciences of spatial organization, such as city planning, sewage engineering, and architecture, focused on the lower class's surroundings and habitat, not their place in the polity or the economy. Likewise, social researchers trained their probing eyes to wander from their subjects in order, ultimately, to judge them better, to gauge their subjectivity. This sensibility yielded enormously detailed observations in which the poor were seamlessly integrated into their immediate extensions (rags, odor) and settings (tenements, prison cells). These descriptions were "thick," although decidedly not "thick descriptions."

Another twofold strategy for measuring society pitted the "average" against the "exceptional." While statistics (and to a degree, literature) sought to represent a composite profile of society or capture what typified social reality (a sensibility that gave birth to the everyman persona of John Doe), social imagination and political rhetoric were propelled by the exceptional, the tantalizing, and the scandalous in need of exposure and retelling. Working for the Employment of Children Commission, Subcommissioner Wood acknowledged these as two distinct targets of his mission. "It appeared to me also very important to ascertain the ordinary and general condition of the children rather than to search in the first instance for any special or extraordinary cases of ill-treatment or suffering, not neglecting, however, as a separate and subsequent branch of the investigation, to search for such special cases."[17] To access the ordinary together with the extraordinary, Wood visited fewer coalpits (which he selected at random) than he might have, but once there he interviewed in private every child on the premises and occasionally every adult as well.

Social Reenactments

Royal commissions functioned as small outfits, bureaucracies, or expeditions moving in space and time. The Factory Commission completed its work in three months. It took the Employment of Children Commission almost eighteen months to submit its first report, and an additional nine months for the second report—on collieries—to come out. Commissioners rented offices, hired stenographers, printed circulars, advertised in newspapers, and, equipped with a host of maps, toured remote regions of the British Isles. Commissions' expense lists provide a glimpse into the scope of their labor. At the conclusion of the English poor-law inquiry, the Treasury in London received bills for books, cleaning charges, candles, a plumber, sewage rates, land tax, carpentry, rugs, bricklayers, and even poor rates.[18] These were rather expensive operations that did not always yield viable results. The Irish Poor Law Commission, whose recommendations were rejected by the cabinet after extensive surveys that stretched over two and a half years, cost the British taxpayers £25,565. The Home Office then sent George Nicholls, an English poor-law commissioner, to Ireland at a fraction of the cost for a three-month tour that eventuated in the first poor-law legislation for Ireland.[19]

Following the preparation of "heads of inquiry"—a set of themes and queries—investigations were ordinarily launched with a massive circulation of cumbersome questionnaires to local informants. Mill owners were asked to fill out tables describing their employees' well being. Sheriffs wrote back to London about ways to curb crime. Clergymen answered questions on education. The Irish Poor Law Commission mailed roughly 7,600 forms, of which about half were returned.[20] Most of the research for the rural constabulary inquiry of the late 1830s relied on thousands of circular letters, which were complemented by a few interviews and modest fieldwork, mostly conducted by a paid agent. Reflexively utilized as a cheap and quick way to acquire basic preparatory information, questionnaires produced partial and dubious results. In most cases, field investigators followed the trail of the printed questionnaires and conducted the bulk of the inquiry. In 1833, the Factory Commission inaugurated the custom of printing and disseminating the inquiry's foundational document, the instructions to the field commissioners. Published instructions, another manifestation of the prevalence of print culture in public investigations, also allowed government agents to introduce themselves to potential interlocutors.

The factory commissioners' decision to make its instructions public was part

of a relentless campaign to combat suspicions that their inquiry was solely instituted to accommodate the masters' interests by aborting popular child-labor legislation. (In the previous year, a powerful report issued by a select committee
headed by Michael Thomas Sadler had supported the Ten Hours Bill.) Indeed,
Chadwick, who became one of the chief commissioners of this inquiry, would
maintain that the breathless six-week factory inquiry altered the "conditions of
the question" and provided new principles of administration that circumvented
previous plans. As a token of impartiality, the instructions stipulated that "it
should be distinctly understood that the Inquiry is in no respect to be narrowed
to the views of any class, or any party or interest."[21] But what was made visible
by the publication of the instructions was ultimately the commission's proximity to power. By drawing attention to their instructions, commissioners accentuated the essence of their labor as representatives of official authority.

The instructions specified that upon arriving in a new town, commissioners
would obtain a room for interviews and announce in the local papers "that all
communications addressed to His Majesty's Commissioners, and left in the post-
office before [a certain date] will be met with attention."[22] In a transparent effort
to undermine Sadler's investigation, commissioners attempted to reinterview
witnesses who had given testimony to his select committee, especially working-
class leaders. In Manchester, they also asked the laborers' Short Time Committee to nominate three witnesses for each branch of manufacture: a current employee, a former laborer who had left for a better job, and another who had quit
for ill health. This principle of witness selection presupposed a certain typology
of experience and opinion. Employers, who were slanted to give evidence next,
were also required to provide "some public assurance or pledge that [laborers]
shall in no way be prejudiced by any evidence which they may give."[23] Commissioners questioned children unaccompanied by their employers or parents.
Every precaution was to be taken "to diminish the chances of inaccuracy of statement, from timidity, or from the confusion to which children are subject when
spoken to by a stranger."[24] These instructions thus attempted to script not merely
the scene and the content of the investigation but also the sequence of interviews,
allowing the ostensibly more vulnerable party the right to testify first.

Despite these and other gestures to placate the working classes, laborers and
employers often spoke under different conditions and environments. Most importantly, commissioners solicited the opinion of workingmen by addressing
them in large groups. The Employment of Children Commission's investigators
either initiated or witnessed mass meetings of workers. One of the subcommissioners was present at a gathering of more than 350 held in the courthouse at

Bransley. The miners' resolutions, among which was a call for the abolition of female labor in the mines for moral reasons, were passed with only five dissenting voices and were recorded in the report. Disparate interviewing circumstances were predicated on the disproportionately large size of the laborers' population as well as on different notions of privacy and individuality. Subcommissioner Charles Barham measured grades of education by asking a body of approximately four hundred miners to divide according to those who could sign their names and those who could not. Contrary to this public display, much was done to protect the commercial privacy of manufacturers and mine owners in acknowledgment of market competition and proprietary industrial techniques. Concerns that industrial intelligence might seep through inquiries prompted factory owners to bar inspectors from entering guarded areas, duly designated "secret rooms."[25]

Hugh Seymour Tremenheere, a mine inspector who in 1854 served as a one-man commission of inquiry into extending the Factory Acts to bleaching works, also employed dissimilar methods in collecting evidence from employers and employees. He often walked for an hour or so with a proprietor through his factory asking for facts and opinions. At the conclusion of the tour, they sat together in the manufacturer's office where he put only the substance of his host's testimony in writing. Such clubhouse informality was absent from his dealings with the laboring men. When recording their testimony he had to read it back to them immediately to seek their confirmation. "I did not think it necessary to do so with a gentleman."[26] This statement was ever more striking, for Tremenheere's investigation was accused of being, and probably was, biased toward the operatives.

For a small group of working-class individuals, testifying to one's life experience could become a career path. William Dodd, an English laborer whose legs were severely twisted after working in the cotton factories since early childhood, was often designated a representative of the factory handicapped. He gave testimony to parliamentary committees on child labor and safety in factories; besides narrating his personal history he literally presented his body for inspection. Dodd also wrote his memoirs and investigated the conditions in the factories himself as an agent for the reformer-legislator Lord Ashley (later Earl of Shaftesbury) but was finally removed from public view when severe doubts were raised as to the veracity of his autobiography.

Another contingent of witnesses much sought after in the industrial regions was the ostensibly disinterested bystanders, such as clergymen, magistrates, and surgeons. Commissioners appropriated these interlocutors' own attempts at small-scale social reporting and at times incorporated them into their blue books.

Their local standing allowed investigators to balance or triangulate competing interests and to generate a full representation of local opinion in accordance with the inquiry's tasks. The commissioners of the Scottish poor-law inquiry (1843) assured the readers of their report: "The witnesses whom we have examined may be considered as representing every class of society. There will be found amongst them Members of Parliament, Clergymen, Country Gentlemen, Lawyers, Medical Practitioners, Farmers, Manufacturers, Tradesmen, Artisans, and Labourers, differing in education, feeling, habits, and interests, and exhibiting, as will be seen, a great variety of opinions."[27]

The significant aspect of this otherwise unexceptional statement is the correspondence it insinuated between, on the one hand, diversity of position and diversity of opinion regardless of their actual share in the general population and, on the other hand, accuracy or comprehensiveness of representation. Class is typically understood here in terms of specific notches on a highly differentiated social incline rather than as a few monolithic social blocks.

Regional or local elites were at times themselves an object of investigation. During the English poor-law inquiry, to give one example, government solicited advice from provincial officials and allowed them a voice in shaping national policy while planning to snatch power from their hands by eliminating local control of poor relief. This exchange, substituting knowledge for acknowledgment, characterized the entire effort to aggregate facts and opinions about society. When Chadwick urged Lord John Russell to establish a commission to look into the formation of a rural constabulary (which, if instituted, would have clearly undermined the gentry's control of the farming hinterland), he invoked the experience of the English poor-law inquiry. "By sending circulars asking for opinions as well as information," he remarked, "a great proportion of the public were brought as it were to a council and enlisted in support of measures which appeared to be, and in some degree were, the results of their deliberations."[28] For the purpose of inquiry, the entire social hierarchy had to be (at least symbolically) visited. Chadwick asked wardens and chaplains of prisons to interview inmates for the constabulary inquest. In return, he received some of the most astonishing documents of his career as a social investigator. One prisoner had written a lengthy model study on vagrancy that featured colorful anecdotes on the practices of horse thieves, pickpockets, and burglars and their lives on the margin of society. Another substantial document, "A History of a London Thief's Life in the Nineteenth Century," was a prisoner's effort to reconstruct a composite portrait of a criminal compiled from numerous testimonies he collected in jail.[29]

Irish rural areas presented a greater challenge for research. Investigators claimed to have found a destabilized society, fluctuating between mendicancy and menial labor and lacking any substantial middle to serve as ballast. Only a few landlords resided on their Irish estates. Unlike in England, tradesmen and affluent farmers were scarce. Clergy of both denominations and landlords (when in residence) were deeply divided over political issues or at odds with the working population. "In an inquiry about a population in which many of the ordinary distinctions of society are commonly merged in the same individual, and in an inquiry amongst a people the various classes of whom had long been at variance with each other, it became a matter of fearful moment to determine respecting whom the inquiry should be made, and from whom testimony could be received, which would not merely be impartial, but which would be admitted by all to be so."[30] Field investigators were ordered to conduct interviews in the presence of a group of witnesses, comprising a microcosm of the parish community. Each "grade in society," religious persuasion, and political party would be represented. Only statements that were not challenged by the entire group as improbable were to be given any weight. Those tiny representative assemblies of rural communities numbered from four to more than twenty individuals. A few women, usually widows and beggars, were present as well. In several groups, employers sat side by side with one or two of their employees and squires with their servants.

The process of official inquiry, therefore, reassured and reenacted local hierarchies. It also sanctioned laborers' leadership and organizations, endowing workers' associations with a tincture of official recognition by allowing them, for instance, to select their own representation and by seeking their approval of the inquiry. Rather than insisting on individuation, state investigations often acknowledged (or even enforced) the collectivity of workers and the integrity of local communities.

In the Field

Entering the factory, descending into a mineshaft, or facing the stench of an ill-drained street became essential to investigators' claims to have penetrated and exposed previously concealed sites. It gave them presence and rendered them visible. Walking into the slum or the foundry, encountering the poor, if only for a brief moment and under controlled circumstances, became by the early nineteenth century, independent of any formal inquiry, a public ritual performed by philanthropists and reformers. For social investigators who were not granted access to the factories, a key moment of observation was the shift change when laborers were leaving the gate en mass. Gaskell, for example, recommended standing at twelve o'clock at the cotton mill exit for a view of what he described as the most hideous group of men, women, and children: pale, flat-footed, short, slender, ungraceful, bow-legged, thinning hair for men, lower voices (caused by exaggerated sexual drive) for women. At this instant, working people could be stared at, compared, and assessed in the aggregate by an invisible onlooker. Visiting the poor, a custom rooted in religious practices, expanded into philanthropic tourism to prisons, special schools, and workhouses. The curious traveler of some social standing could stop in one of the model factories of the Ashworth family in Lancashire. Prince Albert associated the monarchy with these practices under the influence of Lord Ashley, who wrote him in June 1842, "the people of this country, who are sincerely attached to Monarchy as a principle, will love it still more in the person of a Queen, who feels and expresses a real interest in their welfare."[31]

As a mode of investigation, the less trumpeted visits of government officials—ostensibly a tool to guarantee the authenticity of the investigator's experience and the veracity of his report—were easy to manipulate. Once in town, government agents were followed by the watchful eyes of laborers and masters alike. There was ample evidence of the diligence with which proprietors prepared mills for official inspections, ordering the floors cleaned, removing the sick, sending children to wash and wear their Sunday clothes.[32] John Hope, M.P. for Okehampton and a member of the Sadler Committee on child labor, was unsatisfied with what he heard in the Westminster's committee room and decided to tour factories by himself. In late April 1832, he wrote to Lord Morpeth (both were opposed to the proposed legislation for curtailing work hours) that when visiting James Browne's factory he found only a few children and a very clean, well-regulated establishment. A worker later testified that Hope's visit to his mill was preceded by two weeks of preparations to guarantee that the visitor from London would be exposed to "the most positive picture of life in a factory."[33] Factory inspectors would later develop tactics to assure that their visits would come as a surprise. Factory commissioner-turned-inspector Leonard Horner told a select committee of the Commons that he had been often surprised how speedily the news of his visit spread in the nearest mills. One of his subordinates had just begun his visit to the first mill in the locality when a boy with "breathless haste" burst in crying, "The inspector is in the town."[34]

Attempts to limit government's access to sequestered spaces were common to the two distinct targets of early Victorian social investigation: old institutions that had been catered to mostly by the county or the parish (prisons, asylums, workhouses) and those erected by the forces of modernity, namely, factories. Proprietors of mills and wardens of prisons were wary of interventions from London and guarded their property or sinecure with similar zeal. In the summer of 1845, prison inspector Frederick Hill complained to London that a new governor at the county prison at Morpeth, Northumbria, "politely but decidedly" refused to allow him to question prisoners in private. The warden argued that the law did not warrant such a privilege, which would give the prisoners an opportunity to make false accusations against him. Home Secretary Graham asked the visiting justices of the prison to interfere, but they also turned down his request, as did the Court of Session in Newcastle-on-Tyne.[35]

There was little in the experience of the British state bureaucracy that prepared it for this undertaking. The English poor-law investigation commenced with an experimental small-scale study in order to verify whether the scheme of inquiry was in fact workable. Self-doubt was evident in the Irish Poor Law Commission's request to the readers of its official report to practically ignore the material garnered in the large towns of Ireland. This segment represented one of their earlier efforts before the system of inquiry matured. In a rare moment of bureaucratic modesty, the commissioners admitted that their instructions to assistant commissioners were too vague and general, and the manner of questioning and recording thus rendered that portion of the inquiry significantly less valuable than the rest. Irish poor-law commissioners decided, nevertheless, to publish material they considered inferior so they would not risk the accusation that evidence was "suppressed or mutilated."[36]

Only a few, if any, in Whitehall had any immediate knowledge of the new issues under national consideration, ranging from poverty in Ireland, child labor in the factories of Lancashire, or mining safety in Wales. The freshness of the task was reflected in the somewhat chaotic manner in which earlier commissions conducted their affairs. Similarly, there was no readily available cadre of experts with which to man commissions and inspectorates. (This resulted in great overlap in the personnel of these inquiries. Edward Tufnell, for example, partook in four different royal commissions.) The records of the Home Office reveal how difficult it was to fill the new government positions with capable individuals. An extreme example was that of factory superintendent James Webster, whom the Home Office reprimanded for inaccurate registration, ignoring violations of the law, and his offensive demeanor towards mill owners. On one occasion, standing at the gate of a factory in Ironbridge, he reportedly told the manager that he intended to enter the place in order to catch a bird for his dinner. It was also very difficult to convince him to conduct inspection away from his residence in picturesque Bath. His behavior did not improve after his superiors removed him to another district. It turned out that Webster was in the habit of receiving goods from factories he inspected, flannel from one mill, carpeting from another, woolen goods and calico shirting from a third and a fourth. He borrowed money from mill owners and managers and, even worse, was arrested twice for debt.[37]

There was constant wrangling over compensation for extra labor performed by the lower rungs of commissions and inspectorates. Plaintive requests for remuneration (beyond expenses or salaries) occupy much of the archival material left behind by royal commissions and testify to the absence of bureaucratic precedent and the meandering character of this institution of inquiry. The Irish poorlaw assistant commissioners, for example, were recruited for a few months but in some cases were asked to stay on for more than two years. One aspect of the professionalization of those bodies was the enhanced awareness of the lines separating duty from special effort and the rather detailed accounts of extra assignments these minor officials kept. Like many of the laborers they interviewed, low-level investigators felt that they were grossly underpaid and ill treated, although this affinity did not necessarily generate much empathy toward their interviewees.

In the field, improvisation was the rule. Factory commissioner Edward Tufnell, reporting from Lancashire, devised a new shorthand method. "Questions relating to the chief points of inquiry were prepared previous to the examination, and numbered. I then formed a list of all such words as were constantly occurring, such as 'factory,' 'children,' 'machinery,' 'cotton,' etc., and denoted each by a single stroke of the pen."[38] Also in Lancashire, John Cowell commissioned a special weighing instrument that could simultaneously measure the height and weight of children. One commissioner handled the scale, positioning the child with his own hands; a second supervised the clerk who recorded data; and a third, the medical commissioner, evaluated special cases. "Thus the results have a character of authenticity which does not often belong to statistical facts," Cowell proudly informed London. Employment of Children subcommissioner Scriven could not haul a scale into the pit and therefore decided to study the strength of the children by the circumference of their chests and height. He also developed his own four-pronged measurement table: very muscular, muscular, at par, below par. Alfred Power reporting to the Factory Commission from Leicester decided to refrain from questioning children under oath, claiming that this was an unfamiliar ceremony that could only terrorize them.[39]

The investigators' sense of independence rested, at times, on their allegiance to political mentors rather than adherence to a bureaucratic ethos. Factory com-

missioner James Stuart found the recommendations of the central board, especially the proposal to limit child labor to eight hours to enable shifts or "relays,"
unacceptable. He accused the three senior commissioners of ignoring the results
of his investigation in Scotland. Whatever was the content of the dispute between
the field commissioner and the central board, it assumed the language of contending standpoints. "The report of the factory commissioners is no more the report of the twelve persons appointed to see things with their own eyes, and to report their observations on them, than of any twelve gentlemen whom one may
by chance meet in St. Paul's church-yard. It is the report of three gentlemen residing in London, who for aught that appears in the report, never visited a cotton factory, nor a flax-factory, in their lives.[40]

The correspondence only became more venomous when Stuart accused the
board of deliberately omitting parts of the evidence he had sent from the final
report because it did not concur with their prefabricated conclusions. He duly
published his acrimonious exchange with London in the press. The ensuing public embarrassment—M.P.s already raised questions in the Commons—did not
prevent his later appointment as a factory inspector. In Manchester, Cowell was
also alarmed by the board's relay plan, so utterly removed from his own personal
views and the opinions he gathered locally. But his greatest humiliation was to
discover in the last days of June 1833 that, unbeknownst to him and while he continued to conduct his inquiries at full speed, the investigation had been terminated. There was no purpose to his labor. His colleague, Commissioner Tufnell,
took the commission's seal and left for London without giving him prior notice
or paying his bills. Abandoned in Lancashire, Cowell remonstrated to the central
board in a long string of letters suffused with indignation and self-pity.[41]

Investigators were disposed to immerse themselves in local causes and interests. In time, this became a more pronounced feature of the permanent inspectorates. As a mine inspector for the Glasgow area, Tremenheere was confronted
in early 1845 for his participation in local debates over the establishment of a police force for Lanarkshire and the alteration of the law on withholding wages
from laborers. In his defense he explained, "The only excuse I have to offer . . . is
the anxiety I felt on behalf of the population whose condition I had been engaged in investigating."[42] Two years earlier, John Heathcote, a superintendent
working in Manchester under Inspector Horner, was dismissed from his position
for writing an anonymous letter to a local M.P., signed "an overlooker," in which
he objected to various clauses of a pending factory bill. In another incident, the
Home Office censured Superintendent Trimmer after he sent an open letter to

the *Stockport Advertizer* in which he reflected on a magistrate's decision against a proprietor for employing children on Good Friday.[43]

Commissioners relished the opportunity of reporting on the harshness of their field visits. The Employment of Children report indicated that the cold season and the conditions were so taxing "that nearly all of [the subcommissioners] incurred serious indisposition." One agent was forced to give up his assignment and another could not recover throughout his tenure. A third suffered from unusual fatigue. "Nor will this amount of illness occasion surprise to any one who knows the toilsome nature of the duty of inspecting mines."[44] From Kirkaldy, a factory commissioner reported, "All of us, owing to the necessity of speaking loud in the working-rooms . . . and owing to the flax-dust floating in the rooms, have become hoarse. Sir David Barry and I have had our lungs sensibly affected."[45] These side remarks embedded in official reports indicate that social investigators did not necessarily conceive of their efforts in terms of disembodied, abstract observation. Returning from a sanitary inspection in 1843, Chadwick wrote to a friend: "Dr. Playfair has been knocked up by it and has been seriously ill. Mr. Smith has had a little dysentery. Sir Henry de la Bache was obliged in Bristol to stand at the end of alleys and vomit whilst Dr. Playfair was investigating overflowing privies. Sir Henry was obliged to give it up."[46] Itinerant officials' private ordeals echoed the plight they discovered. Sometimes the sights and sounds of human misery proved too painful to observe and register. "The state which females are in after pulling like horses through these holes . . . is painful in the extreme to witness," imparted an Employment of Children subcommissioner. This social investigator, it seems, did not deploy a "disciplining gaze" so much as a sentimental teary eye.[47] Mine visits provided a means to simulate the miners' experience or recreate their vantage point. Rather than merely interviewing witnesses, several government agents turned to their own impressions and feelings.

Subcommissioner Scriven, reporting from the West Riding, also realized that his arrival in the region was well known but little understood. He consequently decided not to conduct interviews in the cabins at the pits' mouth, as he had planned, but instead acquired the apparel of a miner—a flannel dress, clogs, and kneecaps—and descended into the pits himself. He felt that taking the depositions of children on the spot was the only viable method to arrive at their true condition. "And now that I have surmounted the dangers common to all whose duties or avocations require to do so," he wrote in his report, "I have reason to congratulate myself upon my resolve, because I feel that I have become more familiarized with their habits, practices, wants, and sufferings, can more faithfully describe them, and better stand the test of any future examination that may be considered necessary, than would have been otherwise possible."[48] Government officials anticipated they would be reviewed or questioned by parliamentary inquiry or the press. This awareness prompted a certain caution and even defensiveness.

However, John Roby Leifchild, another subcommissioner, resisted the temptation to employ himself as a measuring device. "My sensations during the descent and ascent of the upcast shafts enabled me to appreciate the complaints of the witnesses in reference to them," he wrote. Yet, "I am unwilling to record the unfavorable impressions produced upon me during my descent into, and perambulations through these Cimmerian regions, inasmuch as it is possible that more might be due to novelty than I could be aware of."[49] In his lingering doubt over the capacity of any subjective bodily experience to represent reality, Liefchild was more in tune with the cultivated aloofness of Chadwick and other senior commissioners than with the ethos of his own emerging class of fact collectors. Similarly, the subcommissioner remarked that the curious indifference of some young miners regarding the excruciating nature of pit labor should be qualified by the fact that they lived a sequestered life and had no standard against which to gauge their toil. His disclaimers notwithstanding, Leifchild's understated commentary testified quite clearly as to the nature of his experience in the bottom of the mine. Standardized scientific procedure could possibly claim the mantle of objective measuring apparatus, but, as the Employment of Children Commission demonstrated, the investigator's subjectivity (rather than partiality) was an important element of inquiry and reporting.

For related reasons, each field team in the Irish poor-law inquiry was comprised of an Englishman and an Irishman. Coupling investigators in this way acknowledged that Irish society was irreconcilably divided into "politico-religious parties" and that personal divestment from bias, or the even appearance of impartiality, was all but impossible. Nevertheless, leaving the investigation to foreigners ignorant of Irish social constructions, habits, and "the peculiar idioms of [their] language" would alienate prospective witnesses. A partnership was the "only mode of combining the national knowledge possessed by the one, with the impartiality almost certain by the other."[50] Thus, a standard of complete impartiality was relinquished for the hope that opposing biases (or perspectives) would compensate for each other. The affinity between investigators and Irish society arrived at an ironic conclusion when several of the Irish assistant-commissioners complained at the completion of their tasks that their English counterparts received better pay for the same extra work.[51]

Strangers in the Mine

Chadwick famously remarked on the 1842 *Report on the Sanitary Condition of the Labouring Population of Great Britain* that its findings "have been received with surprise by persons of the wealthier classes living in the immediate vicinity, to whom the facts were as strange as if they related to foreigners or the natives of unknown country."[52] The act of inquiry sought to ameliorate this alleged abdication of responsibility manifested in ignorance, another version of the "two nations" metaphor made famous by Benjamin Disraeli. Social discovery was conditioned on this ignorance. It presupposed that the weak populations were lost, abandoned, unknown, and therefore in need of retrieval and representation. The 1840s rendition of the social discovery idiom featured tantalizing evocations of images unbelievable ("stranger than fiction") yet true, making the near at once familiar and foreign. The mine investigation exemplified the status of the royal commissioner as a discoverer and an intermediary. No other inquiry generated so eerie and yet grand a sense of estrangement, documenting the subterranean world of the pits and in the process unearthing what was considered literally a distinct human race endowed with centaurlike bodies, half stunted, half colossal. Conversely, the investigator-as-intermediary represented government to its provinces, sometimes imparting knowledge rather then collecting information. Subcommissioners, for instance, were asked to inform miners about the importance of childhood to the growth and maturity of the human body.[53]

Thomas Southwood Smith, a known physician and a senior commissioner in the Employment of Children inquiry, intermediated between the sites of social malady and a group of statesmen and literary celebrities. In 1838, he took the Marquess of Normanby, secretary of state for the Home Office, on a tour of two of the most notorious Victorian slums, East London's Whitechapel and Bethnal Green. Southwood Smith cherished in particular his friendship with Charles Dickens, to whom he sent a few of his reports, including the instructions for the Employment of Children Commission. (Chadwick too courted the novelist but never received much attention.) In 1842, Dickens requested the doctor's help. "Can you tell me of your own knowledge, or through the information of any of the Mining Sub-Commissioners, what is the next best bleak and barren part? And can you, furthermore, while I am in those regions, help me down a mine?" Southwood Smith offered a few localities and, in addition, referred him to subcommissioner Dr. Charles Barham, who was "thoroughly acquainted with every nook in Cornwall and known to every mine."[54]

Communicating with miners and factory laborers was a different assignment altogether. While official investigations facilitated negotiations and compromises among the powerful, accumulating information depended on vertical negotiations between investigators and their local interlocutors. Their collaboration was essential. At stake was not just policy but also the proper representation of child laborers, miners, poorhouse inmates, and prisoners, as well as their habits, environments, and opinions. Government officials were often expected to observe the poorer population and to reproduce its "voice." In an implicit transaction of knowledge, working and nonworking men, women, and children gave testimony but at the same time were measured and enumerated.

The much-desired cooperation faced obstacles large and minute. To give one example—while conducting a public health inquiry in Dundee and Edinburgh, Hector Gavin, the English sanitary pioneer, complained that it was unfortunate that the survey was chiefly carried out by visiting Englishmen "to whom Scottish women will not readily confess the existence of diarrhea."[55] It was therefore not enough that government attempted, sometimes unsuccessfully, to protect the laboring witnesses from retributions. (For instance, six of the laborers who testified before Sadler's committee were sacked.)[56] Officials were to acquire the minimal language skills that would allow them to converse with locals. On these grounds, the Employment of Children investigation in Wales had to be delayed. "No information collected under this Commission being considered satisfactory unless derived, in part at least, from a personal examination of the Children and Young Persons themselves."[57] At times, some affinity had to be established between the population and the investigators, as in the decision to pair Irish and English agents. Conducting an inquiry in the company of a small group that represented (or mirrored) local society was familiar to other investigative endeavors. Dr. Mitchel inspected Shropshire's collieries escorted by the ground-bailiff, two charter masters (i.e., work contractors), and "a labouring collier."[58]

Language frequently was as much a barrier between government officials and their interlocutors as the asylum or factory walls. Blue book descriptions of mining procedures, for example, were peppered with technical as well as colloquial terms ordinarily employed by pitmen and owners alike. The reader, as the investigator, had to acquaint himself with that vocabulary. (Commissioners incorporated local terminology and dialect into their accounts as a mark of authenticity or as a tool of discovery and estrangement.) Peculiarities of language were proof of utter seclusion, a metaphor for the otherworldliness of the pit. The British took a seemingly benign and humorous approach toward the poor man's language, associating it, as other forms of eccentricity, with national distinctiveness. As a re-

viewer of *Oliver Twist* opined, the lower classes' "hitherto unknown tongue . . . in
the present phasis of society and politics, seems likely to become the idiom of England."[59] In the case of the urban demimonde and countryside vagabonds, however, linguistic creativity was an attribute of a separate culture that thrived sub-
versively on the margins of civilized society. Inaccessible slang and other distinct
features of speech were conceived to be a mask donned to conceal zones of illegitimacy and criminality from the outside world. Henry Mayhew most fully articulated this notion in his famous reports on the life in the lower regions of society in the metropolis but similar ideas guided official inquiries as well.

The notorious 1847 Commission into the State of Education in Wales (led by
three Englishmen who relied on fieldwork conducted by Welsh assistant-commissioners) went a step further, making the basis of its recommendations the
eradication of the indigenous language whose lingering use it blamed for the degraded state of Welsh society. Following the Rebecca riots (1839 – 43) against toll-
gates and workhouses and the Chartist agitation, the commissioners regarded the
Welsh language a hindrance for social mobility and education. Wales had to be
anglicized. "His language keeps [the Welsh] under the hatches, being one in
which he can neither acquire nor communicate the necessary information."[60]

Language could function as a hidden place for proprietors. Recalling mill
owners' resistance to factory legislation, Inspector Horner reminisced: "They
spoke with the confidence of superior knowledge and experience; used technical
terms, unintelligible, and, therefore, having a somewhat mystical import to those
they were addressing; and the legislators, with a very natural timidity and caution, did not venture to disregard altogether remonstrances so strongly made."[61]
Language barriers were minor in comparison with the visceral reluctance of the
poor to answer questions about their condition. Poor-law officials were advised
that while interviewing paupers, pen and paper or other formalities should be
avoided so not to induce suspicion. Tact, experience, and probably more than one
exchange were imperative. The investigator (as the later detective) engaged in
interpretive work or mind reading, gazing at his interlocutors awry. "Incidental
remarks, casual, and unsought conversations will frequently discover more than
twenty formal examinations." It was essential to overcome the "habitual suspicion of the lower orders of whatever appears done with a design would at once
lock up their lips, or induce them to pervert the truth under the notion that their
confessions would be turned against them."[62] Investigators were told to prepare
themselves to encounter silent, sullen types, angry characters, and numerous sto-
rytellers who fabricate tales for their own protection.

Royal commissioners, however, had to resort for the most part to their notebooks if not to the more domineering trappings of official authority. Informants' distrust was a challenge even during the Employment of Children inquiry, which ignited an incredible uproar in favor of miners and reproduced with great fidelity the unmodulated voices of working children and women. While Leifchild was touring the Northumberland and North of Durham collieries, a jury validated a work contract that had been signed by a minor. Miners were subsequently quite hostile toward the stranger sent by government to ask questions concerning their work and earnings and who, oddly enough, bothered to go into rarely frequented pits and towns, recording their words. "It was in vain that I went in the evenings from house to house, explained the objects of my mission, read to them my instructions, and combated their objections; vague suspicion still lurked in their minds."[63] Leifchild found it almost impossible to interview young laborers while they were in constant motion in the pits. It was as difficult to converse with them outside, for they were not inclined to spend much time answering questions. Their speech also seemed an obstacle. It was loaded with "numerous mining technicalities, northern provincialism, peculiar intonations and accents, and rapid and indistinct utterances."[64] Intensity and nuance of expression were hard to follow. Lack of linguistic richness, he claimed, compelled informants to translate superlatives or extreme anguish into homely expressions. Thus, "sore tired" would mean extreme fatigue, and a boy claiming that he was "hurt in his arm" had fractured the limb. This linguistic stoicism needed to be translated into more exact or familiar terms; similarly, another agent alluded to the height of London's St. Paul Cathedral to indicate the depth of a mine.

Other interviewees wanted to ask Leifchild questions rather than respond to his. "For a stranger to read the mind of a pitman," he concluded, "a circuitous approach and no small tact are requisite."[65] Based on his own account, it seems that the pitmen, in fact, were eager to converse with the official emissary, but on their own terms. Their answers were "so intermingled with extraneous remarks, explanatory of their opinions upon politics and public and private affairs . . . that it was essential that a large portion of it should be 'laid out' by a process analogous to their own 'separation.'"[66] The subcommissioner did not have much patience or esteem for the owners or local professional men either. In an environment that was hostile and partisan, Leifchild saw no reason to concern himself much with his informants' objections to his mission. At the same time, he made a great effort "not merely to allow but to create opportunities for the representation of the views of opponents."[67] A managed provocation of antagonistic views corresponded with the ethos of the national "condition of England" debate and with the notion of descriptive political representation.

Class suspicion, a psychological barricade, prompted much commentary among social observers. During the early 1830s debates over the new policies of information, G. R. Porter of the Board of Trade predicted that reliable statistical returns concerning "domestic employment and the condition of the people" would be all but impossible to obtain, for the "avenues for this kind of knowledge are guarded with jealousy."[68] Distrust of government and misconceptions of its aims would prompt individuals and groups to keep the world in ignorance, he maintained. Beyond lower-class wariness, a persistent mistrust informed the relationship between inspectors and proprietors and the relations among the proprietors themselves. Investigators were told to disarm and penetrate this shield, but they also exploited it. Inspector Horner reported to have had two venues to crosscheck information. Jealousy and competition among the masters would lead them to divulge information against another mill owner who habitually kept his factory working behind the regular closing time. Lack of solidarity among the workers offered similar opportunities to obtain or verify evidence. Those who did not work overtime, he alleged, usually would tell on those who did.[69] Serving as a commissioner of the education in Wales investigation, Jelinger C. Symons resorted to a rather crude method to overcome witnesses' hesitations. He promised a pence to Welsh children who would answer his questions in the most prompt and correct manner and even claimed that the children's desire for the penny assured that they would answer right or wrong and therefore guarantee the truthfulness of his overview. Symons thus brought the exchange relations between investigator and the investigated directly to the marketplace.

Cross Investigations

During the 1830s and 1840s, royal commissions faced charges of infringing upon recognizable modes—parliamentary or judicial—of open inquiry. J. Toumlin Smith's *Government by Commissions: Illegal and Pernicious* (1849) articulated the persistent conviction that government was vying to control information and eliminate traditional institutions. This and similar critiques presupposed that a proper procedure should include the possibility of crossexamination and that the investigator must assume a position of aloof neutrality, akin to that of a judge, among the adversaries in the field of investigation. In fact, many officials conceived of their duties precisely in these terms. The understanding of the official inquest as an inherently judicial procedure only accentuated issues of representation. When Symons arrived in the south of Scotland as an assistant commissioner of the handloom weaver investigation, he encountered considerable interest in the subject of inquiry. "Feeling confident that the truth has nothing to fear from publicity, I determined to hold open courts of inquiry in each of the larger towns of weaving villages."[70] The mock court was usually presided over by the provost or the local chief magistrate. Symons summoned employers directly. The weavers' representation was mostly left to their own choosing. At the beginning of his tour he allowed, as other commissioners in Scotland had, the witnesses to be "cross-questioned" by the other party. However, the specter of incessant interruptions and frequent altercations moved Symons to abandon this course of action. After the first day or two, he prohibited any interruption to the procedure. Witnesses were still allowed to refer to the testimony of former witnesses. Despite elaborate efforts to stage a court of inquiry, Symons ultimately claimed that he garnered the most valuable information about the actual condition of the "weaving body" from his surprise visits to their houses and workshops.

Assistant commissioner J. D. Harding, who conducted the handloom weavers investigation in eastern Scotland, questioned the manufacturers or their agents and only then approached the weavers, thus providing them the right of response rather than the privilege of speaking first. After it became apparent that witnesses were reluctant to express their views in public, he administrated the oath. In the smaller towns and villages, he resorted to another procedure, selecting witnesses himself on the spot and at very short notice. In contrast, William Augustus Miles, an assistant commissioner working in the southwest of England, decided to avoid the public ritual since, "by assembling persons representing all the interests concerned in this subject at the same time and place, a great deal of irritation was produced, and very little information obtained."[71] He consequently held separate meetings for different parties.

As a single investigator in the commission on the bleaching industry, Tremenheere commenced his research with summoning groups of about ten laborers to Bolton. "Since they were, as it were, plaintiffs in the inquiry, I thought it not more than right and proper that I should hear their case first."[72] Tremenheere asked one of the laborers to represent their views and tell him their story in "plain words" and then corroborated the statement by asking the others to concur. He also made a point of visiting bleach works that the laborers requested him to inspect. Tremenheere then had the testimony of the workers printed and given to J. H. Ainsworth, who headed the committee of the masters. "I do not think that I could have adopted any fairer course to both parties; and I may say, in my own justification, that during the examination of those working men, I did not put a single leading question to them, but endeavoured to draw out of them as well as I could, what they meant to say. Of course, I put down what they did mean to say in better language than they could have used themselves; but my belief is that I only communicated to the public the substance of their own observation and complaints."[73]

Tremenheere received from the masters their own list of works to examine. He ultimately called on twenty-seven plants selected from both sides' lists. Reported in the local newspapers, his visits generated much excitement from all sides. There was a certain randomness to his work, which he thought was beneficial. "I took the evidence very much as it came, and I thought that by taking people whom I had never seen before . . . I was justified in assuming that the story I had heard from the committee-men was true."[74] Tremenheere reflected on the course of action he had taken as a royal commissioner during a select committee hearing. The committee responded quite sympathetically to allegations made by owners against his behavior in the field. (This was the Commons' own way of reviewing or repeating investigation, another form of cross-examination.) A parade of disgruntled manufacturers marched into the committee room to argue that Tremenheere was too eager to find fault in the mills and too vulnerable to workers' manipulations, which the employers painstakingly described.

Counterinvestigations

In the new urban landscape and inside factories, all sides seemed vigilant. Employers watched their operatives and recorded their performance in much-hated logs. Inspectors scrutinized factory owners' compliance with the new legislation, and proprietors bemoaned their humiliation at the hands of government. Home Office inspectors, easily discernible as strangers constantly in transit, were carefully observed wherever they went but became truly indignant when their superiors in London insisted they fill out daily reports on their activities and whereabouts.[75] Mine inspector Joseph Dickinson was incensed. "I cannot divest myself of the idea that calling upon me at this late period of my service to send a weekly diary seems to imply mistrust," he protested to home secretary Sir George Grey. He reminded Grey that he had been "a convenient inspector" to handle delicate missions such as inquiring into mine accidents in times of social turmoil and that he was in frequent communication with London and lived in the middle of his district "with many eyes upon me."[76] Proprietors also claimed to feel violated by legislation that forced them to present their register books for inspection and threatened to punish them as criminals should they fail to do so. In response to the self-reporting duties, a pro-employers pamphlet declared, "This . . . is a novelty in British legislation—to compel a man to provide a registry of his own offences, upon which to procure convictions against himself contrary to every principle of British Law; and we question the right of Parliament to enact such a regulation and, I ask, are we, as Englishmen, bound to obey it?"[77]

Registers, ledgers, and record books were perhaps the most overbearing form of surveillance, not because of their discreet observational powers but for their ability to preserve memory, without which power was meaningless. (Practices of registration were arguably the most panopticonlike element of the entire factory system, for their threat did not rely on any single, continuous human agency.) In the case of inspectors' diaries, the demand for methodical self-reporting undermined one's sense of autonomy and stood in contrast to the Victorian conception of diaries as realms of privacy. It certainly undermined the gentlemanly ethos that rested on trust—trust fully demonstrated by the absence of monitoring. In the factory, the subjugation of the register to official scrutiny also challenged proprietors' autonomy. It was particularly poignant because the industrial regime as a whole rested on record books of all sorts for its economy and its discipline. In James Leach's anonymously published and aptly named *Facts from the Factories* (1844), the laborers found a way to exact their revenge on the punitive system that prescribed excessive fines for every minor infraction, such as coming to work a few minutes late. They set fire to the register book, the factory's archive. As Leach narrated the incident, a weaver was passing by the counter when he saw the dreaded "bate book" lying unattended. He seized the book, and after the operatives staged a "court martial" in which the book was found to contain forty pounds of fines, the sentence was "to disgorge the plunder."[78] Leach further detailed with undisguised joy how the book's demise instigated a moment of true panic among the factory managers. The master seemed struck as though he lost his dearest friend.

Laborers in industrial regions were in the habit of accumulating information about faulty production in factories, the lavish lifestyle of proprietors, and violations of the Factory Act. In the late 1830s, unemployed operatives in Glasgow formed a shadow inspectorate. While these investigators were prohibited from entering the mills, they still claimed to have better means to get to the truth than government officials did. The short time committeemen interviewed the parents of child laborers, examined the books of church organizations and other registers (to verify the age of the workers), and spoke to the adult operatives who were the actual employers of children and exercised greater control over them than their own parents or the masters.

With Sir William Erle's Royal Commission on the Organization and Rules of Trade Unions (1867–69), the laborers had their own (albeit nonelected) representation among the commissioners, author and jurist Frederic Harrison. He maintained close ties with the trade union movement. His minority report would become the basis for the 1871 Trade Union Act. A proposal to appoint a workingman for the commission was rejected, although union delegates were accepted as formal observers of the proceedings. In the late 1860s, unions engaged in extensive work of investigation and publication, collecting evidence to refute employers' claims and preparing witnesses. Concerns over the trade unions inquiry prompted efforts to further organize the movement, leading to the first Trade Union Congress in Manchester (1868) and later the creation of the Parliamentary Committee (1871). Invigorated politically by the extension of the franchise (1867) trade unions (as well as friendly societies) elaborated mechanisms to monitor and lobby royal commissions and parliamentary committees.[79]

Masters too initiated counterinvestigations to rebuke unfavorable government reports. In December 1850, a group of workers at Jarrow Pit in the north of England sent a memorial to the Home Office soliciting an inquiry into the safety of the colliery. The consequent visit by the mine inspector, Mathias Dunn, exposed serious faults. Alas, the manager of the pit, T. W. Jobling, decided to launch a study of his own. He requested three "coal viewers" to examine the pits and report on the method of ventilation and precautions taken against explosions. As expected, the investigation cleared the manager. He subsequently demanded that the Home Office present to him the original memorial, for he suspected that signatures were either forged or made by miners not employed by him.[80]

On occasion, the ministry or Parliament launched an official investigation in direct response to working-class demands. A delegation of the short time committees of Yorkshire thus arrived in London in October 1842 to urge Sir Robert Peel and several key members of his new Tory cabinet to adopt factory legislation that would reduce the workday for young men to ten hours and radically curtail female labor. The laborers' representatives portrayed the factory system as a world turned upside down in which children and women (factory labor rendered the latter ignorant of their domestic duties) assumed the role of providers. Creating a mass of idle, uneducated, and emasculated men endangered the safety of the state, the short time delegates warned. They conceded that the legislature had discussed the ten-hours question endlessly. Enough information had surfaced to substantiate their cause. Contradicting themselves, they requested that government initiate an inquiry under the pretext, "We have no facts to enable us to deal with one of the most perplexing and important of the questions which press upon our attention."[81] This delegation's journey to London indicated that working-class leadership appropriated a few of the prevalent political idioms (including gender and family ideologies), most importantly, the rhetorical association of reform with the idea and practices of social investigation.

Solicitations for investigation were often phrased as pleas for state paternalism. Such was a request sent in 1850 from a mining district in north Wales. The miners sought official intervention against the oppressive "truck system" and chose to address their highly deferential application to the queen. In a somewhat less humble tone, the frame knitters of Leicester asked to include their trade in the ongoing inquiry into the plight of the handloom weavers. The knitters promised that once their request was granted, they were "prepared to offer a mass of incontestable evidence which will evince that a state of physical suffering and perhaps of moral degradation is now endured and prevailing which ought not to exist in the nineteenth century in a country which boasts and justly boasts of its superior wealth and intelligence." The Handloom Weavers Commission and the Framework Knitters Commission were instigated in response to requests from laborers in these industries. The royal commissioner appointed in 1844 in response to a petition of 25,000 knitters saw it as his "paramount duty" to conduct the inquiry so the knitters would have "the fullest opportunity of making their condition known, at the least possible sacrifice to them of time or labour."[82]

Spectacle

Despite numerous displays of individual resistance, only rarely did commissioners encounter organized opposition during their investigation. The New Poor Law inquiry gained notoriety in working-class lore chiefly because of the policy it inaugurated. The same is true of the commission on education in Wales, which Welsh society initially welcomed. However, its report, known as "the treachery of blue books," with its condescending views of Welsh society and the Welsh language spurred a fury that never fully subsided in Welsh national consciousness. Reportedly, at the funeral of one of the assistant commissioners who died a few years after the report's publication, one attendee spat on his coffin and cried, "Here is buried a traitor to his country."[83] The strongest class-based challenge to official inquiry was leveled against the 1833 Factory Commission at the very beginning of the royal commissions era. Animosity began with a heated parliamentary debate that resulted in a single-vote margin in favor of the commission and culminated in Lancashire and Yorkshire with the full arsenal of oppositional politics, including the threat of violence. Fearful of the fate of the Factory Bill, the short time committees called for demonstrations wherever the officials appeared. A broadsheet warned commissioners more explicitly: "Have you all made your wills?"[84] In Manchester, on May 4, 1833, child laborers, boys and girls, led a procession, chanting rhymes in favor of Sadler's Factory Bill. The crowd marched through St. Peter's Field, thus evoking memories of the infamous 1819 Peterloo massacre. The local short time committee declined the commissioners' offer to appoint its representatives for a formal interview. In a move that was probably meant to alarm London as to the possibility of violence (and so undermine their employees), Manchester mill owners appointed Colonel Show, the military commander of the district, as their negotiator with the factory commission. In Leeds, Commissioners Drinkwater and Power entered into pamphlet warfare with Sadler, who, following the Reform Act (1832), had lost his seat in Parliament but still sought to represent the factory movement. Sadler contended that royal commissions deviated from accepted rules of holding public hearings. This commission refused to conduct interviews in the presence of a reporter or a stenographer, or to open the procedure to the public at large, and insisted that there was no obligation to publish the entire exchange between them and their witnesses. While government was determined to expose even the smallest inaccuracies in the testimonies of operatives, he argued, the masters' testimonies were exempt from similar scrutiny.[85]

Sadler questioned royal commissions' ability to conduct a proper investigation in the first place, for, as he claimed, they could not summon witnesses and compel testimony. When the commissioners reminded him that judges also took notes in shorthand, he replied that those were meant to help the judge's memory or for occasional reference but their accuracy was guaranteed by the attendance of the press and the public in the courtroom. "I confess that I have heard of no judges who follow the course which you prescribe, but those, perhaps, of the Inquisition."[86] He poked fun at the principle of "on the spot" investigation. The commission did not have to leave London for a spring tour at all. It was sufficient to examine mortality figures and other records where the victims of the factory system "being dead yet speak."[87] Moreover, the commissioners arrived in the manufacturing district in the wrong season. It was the winter that exposed the laboring children to the harshest conditions. Sadler also challenged the commissioners' personal qualifications. Social investigation, he claimed, demanded talents, habits, and experience quite different from those required by legal inquiries. (Drinkwater was a legal counsel at the Home Office.)

In rebuttal, the two commissioners disputed Sadler's claim to represent the views of the laborers.[88] Assuming a tone as indignant as their opponent's, Power and Drinkwater accused the former M.P. of malicious attacks on their good names. They consented to allow one or two representatives of the short time com-

mittees (and a similar delegation on behalf of the masters) to attend the interviewing room while the other side testified. These delegates could take notes in
order to assist them to follow the evidence, or even suggest topics of inquiry, under the condition that nothing would be made public until the investigation concluded. However, since the commissioners did not provide assurances that they
would permit full access at every single stage of the proceeding, the offer was
summarily rejected. The two commissioners argued that they were not authorized to hold an open court, and, even if they were, such a course would have hindered any investigation, especially in light of the notoriously raucous public style
of a few of the Ten Hours Bill's advocates. Contrary to the short time committees' stance, the laborers, they claimed, actually cooperated with their inquiry.[89]

Concluding their interviews in Leeds, Power and Drinkwater's ordeal was not
over. The West Riding of Yorkshire was the heart of the Factory Movement and
the seat of its firebrand mentor, Richard Oastler, also known as the "factory
king." Once the commissioners tried to leave Leeds, a comic game of hide-and-
seek began. Stating that they were continuing on to Huddersfield, the commissioners left town followed by a horseman. In Bradford, where they were next
spotted, they faced two large demonstrations and, according to one report, were
driven away from a factory by children. The commissioners then asked to travel
to Keighley but altered course to Wakefield where they changed horses for Don-
caster, still followed by a short time agent. A few days later, Oastler described the
episode in vivid detail to a cheering crowd in Huddersfield. At two in the morning, the king's commissioners and "King Richard's" emissary, the story went,
found themselves warming by the same fire in a public house. The movement's
man resisted the bid to push him away from the fireplace and sarcastically remarked, "I'll tell you what, gentlemen, we have been a long time in getting to
Keighley; it is quite a new road, we ought to have gone the old road."[90] In Huddersfield a reported fifteen thousand people participated in a night vigil that featured the burning in effigy of the three unfortunate district commissioners and
a local M.P. As constructed by Oastler, this was a story of an eye-level dual—the
king's men encountering the "commissioners" of a mock king.

Oastler's parody completes an intricate set of reenactments or masquerades,
including effigy burning, parody, countersurveillance, laborers' own ventures
into methodical social inquiry, and conversely, the investigators' moments of
cross-dressing on their way down to the bottom of the pit. These diverse performances were differently motivated and yet all retain a measure of ambiguity.
Even the most sympathetic act of mimicry, propelled by compassion, as the phil-
anthropist's wish to view the world from the workingman's point of view—

Madeley lith: 3, Wellington St. Strand.

Richard Oastler
12 Coffee Gallay Fleet Prison Dec: 9 1840.

The firebrand agitator Richard Oastler was a Tory radical and a mentor of the Factory Movement, which advocated the ten-hour workday and strong restrictions on child labor. Oastler attempted to manipulate several 1830s official social investigations in order to publicize the plight of factory workers in Yorkshire. He is shown here in Fleet Street Prison, where he was put in 1840 for debt incurred to his former employer. In jail, Oastler continued to circulate his views by publishing the *Fleet Papers*, weekly pamphlets denouncing the emerging liberal marketplace and the evils of the factory system. (Lithograph by [G. E.] Madeley, signed by Richard Oastler, December 9, 1840) standing (literally) in his shoes—replaces and silences. Conversely, defiant acts of impersonation were likely to further entrench power and its modalities. Parodying and mimicking government emissaries, working-class organizations implicated themselves in the state. Regardless of the identity of actors and the content of ritual, these masquerades were stranded between communication and its occlusion. Viewed in a larger setting, however, they comprised one type of expression in a richer domain typified by exchange.

In 1843, the American *Brooklyn Eagle* asserted that no government on earth had made greater efforts to ascertain the condition of the working classes than the British. "They are forever instituting commissions of inquiry, collecting statistics, and making luminous reports; but, unfortunately, their exertions do not ordinarily extend beyond those points. They are apt to suppose that they have performed their whole duty in ascertaining and exposing the injustice inflicted by law and custom upon the laborious poor; and hence, while vast amounts of philanthropy are displayed *on paper,* to the public gaze, the suffering masses plod on in sullen despair."[91]

The British government learned well the lessons of the French Revolution, the article continued. It was not enough to intimidate the people with the gallows. The "public gaze" was therefore not a form of surveillance and control but a cunning technique of governance that substituted real philanthropy with a mirage on the printed page. The American journalist's insight notwithstanding, it appears that the routines of documenting society were more efficacious than merely soothing the public mind. These practices were constitutive of the social equilibrium, or class system, that reigned in Britain by the end of the nineteenth century. Inquiry and inspection affixed or confirmed gradations of social standing, class, gender, and age. Investigative practices thus complemented the taxonomic work that was performed by the knowledge featured in the reports. Bear in mind, however, that the legislative process itself produced and enhanced social categories or taxonomies that were not necessarily rooted in either prior investigation or science. The Factory Act of 1833 inscribed into law the distinction between "young persons" (ages thirteen to eighteen) and children (nine to thirteen), but this typology was chiefly the result of political maneuvering.

Ultimately, the Victorian passion to police the lower classes was coextensive with, not predicated on, the fact-finding ceremonies of official social inquiries. The poor-law investigation, which was a paradigm for inquiries to come, generated two quite distinct tools to measure social veracity. The first was the infamous workhouse test that separated the deserving from the undeserving poor. It first gauged the integrity of the individual pauper and then "rehabilitated" her. The second was the massive social survey by a royal commission in which the panoptic ambition was only one motive and one motif. In the field of social investigation, actors, changing vantage points, observed and conversed, reenacted and mimicked. This is not to postulate parity between investigators and the investigated as much as to point to the possibility of reciprocity and the open-ended quality of the encounter. In particular, the precarious position of the field investigator permitted this mutuality and play.

Unlike Foucault's supposition that post-Enlightenment societies are those of the panopticon and not of the spectacle, it appears that with public investigations the visibility of the Victorian state and the visibility of the populace were indivisible, concurrent, and often spectacular. Besides, the shift from the field of investigation to the sphere of published texts further undermines the "gazing eye" trope in favor of describing investigative fieldwork in terms of the "astute ear." This ear was not merely an organ of surveillance or a metaphor for the supposed attentiveness of the state but a recording tool that enabled the transcription and archiving of testimonies and other utterances by investigators and their interlocutors. Admittedly, in times of perceived domestic threat, government pressured its local agents to become actual spies. To give an example, in the summer of 1839, factory inspector James Stuart was secretly asked to provide the Home Office with his occasional opinion of the "state of feeling among the working classes." His superintendents attended working-class meetings and recorded their proceedings. His supervisors also questioned him about the state of the harvest, the condition of the handloom weavers, and other domains that were outside his formal jurisdiction. However, an 1841 select committee investigated what was widely deemed improper use of public officials. Stuart claimed during the hearings, somewhat apologetically, that after complying with London's instructions for a while, he wrote the secretary of state that he saw no need to continue the practice. These sporadic assignments (which were largely discontinued after 1841) only exemplified how weak was the British government's surveillance mechanism in comparison with continental regimes.[92]

Facts Speak for Themselves

Blue books constituted complex microcosms in which were assembled disparate types of information, taxonomies, ideas, and voices, cloaked in the formalities of bureaucratic traditions. The entire process of investigation was geared toward their preparation. These modular tomes ordinarily opened with a shorter compendium that summarized the course of investigation, categorized evidence, and prescribed policy measures. Accompanied by substantial appendices, major reports often provided historical overviews as well, thus welding, sometimes tenuously, background and foreground. In these constructions, historical survey led to a synoptic view of contemporary circumstances and then leaped to future policy. Reports were calculated to satisfy the demand for hard, "authentic" facts but were also produced with an eye to the reading habits and other cultural sensibilities of the potential recipient. Officials toiled to render blue books accessible to larger audiences beyond elected representatives and government officials. In several instances, royal commission reports, occasionally in abridged forms, became popular reading material. Other official accounts, spread over thousands of pages, were practically impossible to read in full, instead offering the interested few an index or the possibility of endless rummaging. Their sheer size and impenetrability could signify official authority or, conversely, governmental excess.

Examining blue books' trajectory takes us from various scenes of writing and compilation into printing, dissemination, and consumption. Moving through these sequences in the large chain of inquiry, this survey complements the discussion about the conduct of investigative fieldwork. It addresses in particular the creation and meaning of the polyphony or heterogeneity that was a strong attribute of nineteenth-century social reporting. Diversity of style, evidence, and voices prevailed within and among specific documents. This was in part a product of blue books' multiple functions as books, records, and especially archives. Another diversity-producing catalyst was the range of authors, personal and institutional, involved in the making of each document.

Social reports' heterogeneity also emanated from their representational assignments and their capacity to reproduce *voice*. First, the demand to represent "public opinion" presupposed a multiplicity of views, an approach that corresponded to the discursive rules of the hegemonic (in the Gramscian sense) "condition of England" debate, which was constructed as an exchange requiring many debaters. As significantly, detail and heterogeneity were primary techniques to depict (or to elicit) social reality in the text. The printed text verified the truthfulness and the representational efficacy of the evidence presented. The most important principle of confirmation was "authenticity," a yardstick that was applied, at least rhetorically, even when specific evidence (for instance, statistics) did not lend itself to simple authentication. A more complicated assignment was to demonstrate that beyond its veracity the knowledge procured was indeed representative, in other words, that it either encompassed the field of inquiry or portrayed, from a recognizably disinterested vantage, what was the most typical of the subject matter. In the early decades of the nineteenth century, social reporters provided as synoptic coverage of the field of inquiry as they could, in accordance with the wish to capture all opinions and vantage points. Conversely, there were representational tasks that demanded a modicum of homogeneity in the official report, for example, the ambition to portray a unified government approach or action. As we noticed earlier, beyond matters of content, the printing template of blue books and the appearance of a serial publishing project conveyed the uniformity and authority of the state.

In the Victorian empirical culture, facts were also endowed with voice, and their evidentiary might allowed them to "speak for themselves." Connecting facts with the power of articulation received many official and vernacular renditions. The following discussion explores environments that equipped facts with speaking capacity and the tactics the working poor employed to voice themselves through facts. This chapter argues that blue books' multivalency and the state's insistence on the validity of its findings produced an inherently fragile text that could be easily plundered and reused for purposes unintended by Parliament and government, confirming that print statism was a medium fraught with risks for the state.

Scenes of Writing

The making of blue books was a process that took place in the field and in the metropolis, and featured many individuals and groups. The four factory inspectors, Leonard Horner, James Stuart, Robert Saunders, and George Howell, furnished one example of such collective exertion. During their biannual meetings (beginning in 1836), they read aloud their accounts of their respective tours of inspection. They maintained that reading these documents in each other's company rather than trading manuscripts drew immediate reactions, enabled on-the-spot joint decisions, and assured the equal standing of the four senior officials (and probably also the cohesiveness of their common voice). This routine enabled them to craft a general report and sometimes inspired alterations in their individual reports as well.[1]

For royal commissions of inquiry, prepublication work was an expensive and protracted undertaking that added months if not years to the commission's labor. Just the proofs for the English Poor Law Commission's enormous report cost over a thousand pounds. It took André Bisset, an assistant secretary to the commission's central board, a full year to arrange a digest of the circulars that included no less than five thousand folio pages. By the beginning of 1834, the commission employed fourteen people "transcribing reports of the commissioners and appendix and correcting the press for the total sum of £390.3.10."[2] As was evident in early commissions' fieldwork, lack of institutional experience left much to individual initiative. Irish poor-law assistant commissioner F. J. Flood was busy for nine months with the legal segment of his account on Irish vagrancy, for which he performed extra work such as translating the Dutch poor law and arranging statistical tables.[3] Alas, his diligently compiled report did not conform to a new format decided upon by the central board. The document had to be severely "remodeled." The two-tier structure of royal commissions, with its own measure of friction and class animosity, affected the process of composing a report. At times, assistant commissioners had to cede control over their accounts or other written utterances to their seniors. In the case of the Factory Commission, for instance, the pressure to dispatch immediate accounts to London was so great that John Cowell, working in Lancashire, found to his surprise that early drafts of the commission's final report featured short comments he had scribbled on the margins of the transcribed evidence.

In 1840, two factory superintendents accused their supervisor Inspector Stuart of introducing misleading changes into their accounts. A former superintendent, William John Wood, testified before a select committee that entries in his weekly ledgers were altered or erased in the official "report book." In one incident, Stuart changed Wood's account on a mill inspection from "five children under 13 do not go to school" to "five children under 13 have not gone regularly to school." "Certificate of school wanting for children under the age of 13" was replaced by "Schools established by the company, and the certificates to be regularly produced." "The master drunk, and incapable of showing me any books or certificates of age, and evidently has not attended to the Factory Act" was erased leaving only "a very small mill."[4] One point of contention with Stuart was whether Wood's inspection accounts should reflect the condition of the factory when he entered the premises or when he left. Stuart preferred the latter. Presumably, the inspection itself prompted mill owners to address minor offenses, and there was no need for further publicity. Stuart's reports evidently prettified the reality of compliance with the Factory Act in Scotland, and yet they could, possibly, qualify as truthful. John Beal, another superintendent, claimed that instead of framing his accounts around evidence (e.g., certificates of age, certificates of school attendance), Stuart took for granted promises made by proprietors and their managers to rectify violations. Beal read aloud from his own visiting books, showing case after case of abuses, big and small. His was a rather gossipy journal, recording impressions outside the scope of the law—a drunken overseer, masters who tried to avoid inspection, rumors concerning violation, and other such triflings.[5]

Wood and Beal's allegations so infuriated Stuart that he burst into such an indignant speech that the committee room was cleared and his words were stricken from the minutes. He later defended himself, asserting that the law did not compel him to follow his subordinates' records to the letter. These were merely aides, private documents, for his review. He invoked another matter of privacy, a directive from the Home Office to distinguish between information that referred directly to the Factory Act and knowledge deemed private, such as exact work methods, number of employees, and other details of industrial intelligence. The inspector, he claimed, had full discretion in this regard. "To insert in my report all the information which I had received from the superintendents would have entirely frustrated all the objects for which they had been enjoined to secrecy."[6]

This dispute demonstrated how routines of recording information employed during inspections ensnared proprietors and inspectors. As with other aspects of authorship under government patronage, confusion lingered over the status, indeed the very purpose, of particular texts. Because the lines separating private and public were ambiguous, a senior inspector could construe routine daily reports as private diaries. Interestingly, Ashley's committee jettisoned (at least implicitly) Stuart's distinction in its own publication. An appendix to the committee's report included a facsimile reproduction of the handwritten superintendents' abstracts and the alterations introduced by Stuart.

Corporate Authorship

Authors of official documents had a stake in their publication and vast circulation (see chapter 1). Mine inspector Hugh Tremenheere kept a mailing list of between seven and eight hundred recipients (mostly proprietors and managers of collieries and iron works) but also asked for two hundred copies for unspecified personal distribution. Occasionally, he sent proofs of his reports to "the most intelligent persons in each district, to guard against the chance of any important errors."[7] Edwin Chadwick also circulated early drafts and proofs in anticipation and solicitation of response. Officials vied for the publicity and the prestige that print culture bestowed on authors. Years after his bureaucratic prime, Chadwick asked Lord Russell to assist him with his promotion in the Order of the Bath and cited among his numerous achievements that his "published Reports have had, as shewn before a Committee of the House of Lords, an extent of sale and circulation unprecedented with that class of public documents."[8] In the Home Office records, there are many letters from officials imploring government to publish their reports as soon as possible. For instance, in the summer of 1854, mine inspector Herbert Mackworth asked the Home Secretary to issue a special report he had prepared on mine safety. "If the Reports of the Inspectors of Coal Mines are to be published I beg to request that this Report may not be omitted, as it contains the particulars of the precautions which ought to be adopted in all coal mines and the coal proprietors in my district have frequently applied to me for it."[9] It was important for Mackworth to show there was a local demand for his blue book.

As authors, commissioners did not stand to benefit materially from their literary products. However, as new types of personal expertise emerged, questions arose regarding their right to capitalize on the knowledge or skills they acquired in their formal capacity. Like Horner, several inspectors published unofficial tracts on social questions. However, the Home Office was less generous with lesser officials. In 1844, to give one example, factory subinspector R. Baker asked for permission to write the statistical chapter for a privately published book on the worsted trade. He requested that the unpublished statistical table he had submitted to the home secretary two years earlier be returned to him for use in the chapter, claiming the chart was prepared as voluntary extra work. The Home Office refused, saying that the secretary could not sanction the use of any information obtained through inspection. Such publication might foment distrust between proprietors and inspectors.[10]

Another aspect of authorship was the level of autonomy exercised by officials as writers. Senior members of royal commissions had remarkable discretion over the content of their reports, but the Home Office scrutinized and sometimes censored inspectors' blue books. A manuscript of an 1855 factory inspectors' account included a passage in which Horner defended his conduct against Manchester mill owners' accusations that he was vindictive. The factory inspectors also protested the masters' resistance to implementing an act that prescribed fencing off dangerous machines. Concerned about an open rift between his inspectors and mill owners, Secretary Sir George Grey preferred to eliminate this passage. It was essential for the value and authority of their report, he wrote the inspectors, "that they should be carefully and impartially written and should not contain anything approaching to personal disputes."[11] Horner was unwilling to yield his right of response. "I considered that in narrating events, which had occurred over the last half year, that had the most direct and important bearing upon my part and future official proceedings, I was acting in perfect conformity to the spirit and even to the letter of the section of the act under which the inspectors make their reports."[12]

The secretary eventually conceded that he could not enforce his will on inspectors but warned that if objections were raised in Parliament, he would not be able to defend the report. In another incident, Inspector Stuart was asked to eliminate an account of a discussion with the secretary of the Short Time Committee for the Eastern District about the fate of boy who had been dismissed from his factory job after giving evidence in an overwork case. Stuart expressed his hope that the committee would do its utmost to procure a position for the boy. The Home Secretary maintained that including the episode in the official document might imply that Stuart was too intimate with the laborers' organization.[13]

Factory inspectors' reports were sporadically criticized for their belligerent, partisan tone. The ministry also made recurrent demands for stylistic and content uniformity in the publications of the inspectorates. With only partial success, the Home Office endeavored to secure an enclosed system of information, delineating between what should appear in an internal exchange (the state's realm of privacy) and what was proper to present in a uniform public report. It also limited inspectors' access to the press in their local dealings and to politicians outside the department. In one case, the Home Office dismissed for "inexcusable breach of confidence" a superintendent who leaked a confidential letter from his superiors to an M.P. sympathetic to the short time cause who then read it in the Commons.[14]

Cabinets of Curiosities

The early 1830s tug of war between the Factory Commission and Michael Thomas Sadler's parliamentary report over child-labor policy sharpened the contrast between two archetypes or genres of official texts. Select committee reports usually abided by a strict formula. They incorporated material obtained outside the committee room—official records, letters, and petitions—but mostly consisted of endless transcriptions of interviews in question-and-answer form. Interviews allowed parliamentarians to register their views in the official record, which they often did unabashedly and at great length. There was some attempt, chiefly by the printer Hansard, to make the information more accessible. He suggested adding annotations in the margin and appending indexes at the end. A reader would therefore scan the entire sequence of an exchange whose veracity was assured by the presence of a stenographer and the completeness of the transcript. (Typically, when M.P.s wished to criticize royal commissioner Hugh Tremenheere's report on the bleaching works, they charged that he neglected to incorporate the questions he addressed to his interviewees and thus failed to report fully on his field conversations.)[15]

If select committee reports reproduced the temporal continuum of the inquiry, the royal commissions' claim to represent the region, social institution, or population under investigation also rested on the reproduction or simulation of space. This was accomplished by transporting narratives, illustrations, commissioners' journals, and interviews from the sites of inquiry and inserting them into official texts. The print archive replicated the field as well as the process of the investigation. Large appendices of royal commission reports often accommodated reams of miscellaneous factual matter, congested cabinets of curiosities. The commissioners of the Scottish poor-law inquiry explained the size of their report as a matter of fairness. "The course, which we have followed, may perhaps appear to have extended the Evidence to an unreasonable bulk, but it has this advantage, that we cannot be accused of partiality or unfairness in having selected any particular parishes or individuals for examination; and upon a subject of such importance as the Scottish Poor Laws, the principles and administration of which have been so much canvassed, it was desirable to satisfy the public mind that we had taken the utmost pains to inform ourselves on the subject from every source from which information could be derived."[16]

Fulfilling the democratic credo to open the governing process to public observation, official reports told the story of their own making. As political scientist Yaron Ezrahi recently argued, in a modern democracy, "seeing and witnessing . . . are inseparable from the attempts to define politics as a realm of plain observable facts which are accessible to all the citizens conceived as spectators."[17] In state-sponsored research, in particular, the demand for rendering the political process transparent coalesced with common scientific and judicial practices. Importantly, the medium of witnessing was print culture and the citizen/spectator was, in fact, a reader. The public could not attend the Factory Commission's interviewing room but was able to obtain the commission's report. As a reader, the Victorian subject was thus expected to master unprocessed information and to "judge for himself." The nineteenth-century discourse of public opinion rhetorically trivialized the division between readers and lawmakers to generate what an observer designated a "community of knowledge, as well as community of discussion."[18] Ever since the Commons regulated the printing and selling of parliamentary documents, the public's access to information was ostensibly equal to that of lawmakers.

It was not only the ethos of public opinion that likened citizens to legislatures. The chain of representation itself required that commissioned officials—government representatives—report back to legislative bodies, institutions that were by their own right representative and required to report back. At the end of the line of reporting stood the citizenry or the public (as well as, symbolically, the monarch), the ultimate recipient of these epistolary documents, which were, indeed, signed, sealed, and delivered.[19] The report as a genre was thus always implicitly incomplete and in search of addressees. Either walking the proverbial corridors of power in Whitehall, inhabiting committee rooms in Westminster, or reading in the comfort of their domestic spaces—officials as well as other implied readers of state reports were expected to make law, make a decision, or render judgment. The report was not produced for a reader but for an author of sorts, an author of opinion.

Ponderous appendices were ostensibly published to allow consumers to review the recommendations in conjunction with the evidence, in other words, to facilitate an unmediated encounter between facts that speak for themselves and readers who judge for themselves. Leaving facts to speak their own truth, to fend for themselves, evinced their power of persuasion. Paradoxically, it was also a symptom of the relative weakness of institutional science. There was no strong expert culture to mitigate between facts and (reading) publics as would emerge in the twentieth century. The national debate was intense precisely because of the absence of an accepted discursive authority.

Sometimes, the order of publication was reversed. Interim reports were circulated before any recommendation was made, an indication that generating knowledge was itself a cardinal purpose of these procedures. A few select committees never reached any decision and yet made public their evidence. The handloom-weavers commission presented the reports of the assistant commissioners to Parliament as they became available and issued its own report almost two years after the first of these accounts was made public. Similarly, when excerpts from field reports of the English poor-law assistant commissioners were published, one commentator questioned the legality of this practice. The document certainly publicized the limitations of the old poor-law apparatus, but its preparation only delayed the completion of the final report and thus seemed to defeat the commission's stated goal to provide evidence and recommendations for new legislation.[20]

Cut and Paste

Documents that were prized for the unmediated access they allowed to the field experience—a quality that relied on the facelessness of their compilers and the transparency of the texts themselves—often had unique personal imprints. Government was communicating through individual authors. Few public figures understood as well as Chadwick did the importance of print culture to the political process. Chadwick distinguished himself early on in questioning witnesses for the poor-law inquiry, prompting the chief commissioner, Nassau Senior, to compare him to a French cook who can concoct a delicacy out of shoe laces. Chadwick contributed to the popularity of the commission's interim report by exhibiting the most interesting cases in a lucid manner. He famously never missed an opportunity to peddle his penmanship.[21] But even lesser officials left a modest trace on the documents they composed. During the Irish poor-law investigation, assistant commissioners were regarded simply as recording devices whose accounts were "to bring the reader more immediately in contact with the witness."[22] Nonetheless, each team of investigators contrived a slightly different tactic for imparting information or narrating stories. One technique was to recount discrete episodes or "case studies" in full. Another called for weaving short quotations into a general statement on the affairs of the parish.

Labourers marry earlier than farmers. John Walsh, tradesman, says, "The poorer they are the earlier they marry;" but the parish priest denies this. Others say that early marriages are discountenanced by the general feeling; "under 20 is a won-der." There are few applications to the parish priest. The early marriages are to gratify passion and to serve themselves, and enable them to live better, as they thinking [*sic*] there will be more compassion for them if they are married.

Michael Millins says, "He knows men of 60 who never married, and they are not a halfpennyworth better off than those who have families. If that man is sick, who will attend to him without payment, or who will wash or cook for him?"[23]

This passage effectively recreates a speaking (not to say chattering) community. That there are clear disagreements about the details of everyday life does not detract from the impression that everybody speaks and everybody has been allowed a voice. In fact, the occasional dispute endows the text with a greater measure of realism because the speakers appear to be in dialogue with each other. This exchange simulated (or fabricated) daily local encounters, here generated by the investigative practices adopted by the Irish Poor Law Commission. In every parish, assistant commissioners conducted interviews with a group of locals who represented different rungs in the social ladder. Beyond recalling their own experience, the speakers peppered their conversation with stories about others. Investigators thus tapped into local discourse, whether comprised of opinion, memory, or sheer gossip. The priest who told the Irish poor-law assistant commissioners that forty women in his parish were seduced by men of a superior class might have had at his disposal reliable means to gather this bit of information. But the report also featured farmers talking about their neighbors, merchants telling stories regarding clients, and others who recalled rumors about destitute individuals and how the local poor grappled with deprivation. The anecdotal nature of such evidence did not preclude a systematic presentation in clear imitation of the aesthetics of statistics, with careful editing and, in some cases, tabular forms to arrange responses to written or oral questions. In early Victorian official reports, readers found statistical tables and testimonies, used side by side as competing or complementing tools to gauge society.

The editorial digestive process often meant breaking witnesses' responses and testimonials into short, incisive utterances or morselized narratives. When information had to be condensed for the purpose of a summary report or an abridged document, the job could be done simply with the help of scissors. Chadwick's personal files on the Factory Commission inquiry contain a few pages on which he pasted short clippings from previously printed material (an indication that the first phase of preparing a report was the printing of the handwritten evidence). He divided the cuttings into clusters under headings such as "Factory Women as Wives," "Morals—Bad," "Morals—Improved or Favourable," and "Diseases Pe-

culiarly Favoured by Cotton Factory Labour."[24] Garnering and registering
knowledge in concise narratives commenced in the field. Inspector Horner's record of a single infraction of the Factory Act, as taken from his inspection journal, was narrated as a story when initially entered in his report book.

> In going through the mill with Mr. Platt, I saw a very young child piecing to Wm.
> Fielden. The child appeared to me about eight years old, certainly not more than
> nine; it had its jacket off, and there was cotton on its clothes, so that it had been
> working for some time. It was a boy, Bradshaw Fielden, the brother of the spinner;
> there was no certificate; Mr. Platt said that it was contrary to his knowledge and
> orders, he sent for Thomas Goddard, his messenger, who declared that it was not
> only contrary to his directions, but that he had turned that child several times out
> of the mill. I called the parties before me in the counting-house; swore Mr. Platt
> to his having given repeated orders to his people that the law was to be strictly
> obeyed; swore Thomas Goddard to the above statement made by him, and there-
> upon I adjudged Fielden to pay a fine of 20S.[25]

Attention to detail was closely related to the judicial nature of the procedure.
(At the same time, as a model case, supposedly confirming the orderly day-to-day
application of the Factory Act, the details call attention to what appears to be
missing. Why didn't he question the Fielden brothers? Did they offer any defense? Was the proprietor complicit in employing under-aged children after all?)
In the retelling of such episodes, social reality is ingrained in the fine points of
the story, dryly conveyed. Concreteness of scene, actors, and action endows anecdotes with a palpable, even tactile quality.

Another approach to the social anecdote's power to engender reality highlights its structure rather than content. In literary critic Joel Fineman's view, the
anecdote, the minutest of narratives, has a complete, irreducible, or indigestible
form. As such, it has the capacity to interrupt engulfing texts that are also framed
as narratives (with beginning, middle, and end) by calling into question their
flow and comprehensiveness. Anecdotes thus do not necessarily describe reality
as much as point or gesture toward it, as they indicate that there is an "outside"
or exteriority to the text. The particular miniature narrative that interests Fineman is the historical anecdote, the *petite histoire* that enables the telling of history but resists the totalizing (and ahistorical) ambition of the *grand recit.* "The
anecdote produces the effect of the real, the occurrence of contingency, by establishing an event as an event within and yet without the framing context of
historical successivity, i.e., it does so only in so far as its narration both comprises
and refracts the narration it reports."[26] Official reports were not arranged as

mammoth narratives but were schematized—similarly to the teleological historical master narratives of old—as substantial bodies of knowledge (some of which was historical) that lead to particular conclusions. Like the historical narrative, the anecdote allows the narration of society (as in a case history) but undermines society-as-narrative or, in other words, the understanding of social life as a single story. The capacity of vignettes to refuse or at least resist enclosure was enhanced in social reportage by their separation from the rest of the text by actual or implicit quotation marks. As we shall see, authors of social reports employed diverse methods to emphasize rather than to efface those textual stitches. A truncated page composed of short narratives was also characteristic of the daily newspaper.

Anecdotes were certainly not the only representational technique available to capture social reality. The emphasis on eye witnessing as the portal to the social real (coupled with the "environmentalist" drive in social reportage) encouraged social observers to evaluate individuals and groups by their immediate surroundings. As Joseph Childers noticed about the 1842 sanitary report, "Working metonymically, focusing on connections, [Chadwick] and his sub-commissioners fix on the artifacts of lower class life: attire, cottages, work-shops, dungheaps, cellars."[27] Even if metonymy became the prevailing trope for realistic representation in social reportage and in Victorian fiction, the anecdotal narration of the experience of the poor and the investigative process strongly qualified that propensity (and the ocular emphasis in general) and introduced manifest temporality to social reporting. Metonymic displacements "flattened" the portrait of society by offering spatial instead of temporal associations. The poor could be conceived by and through their habitat and bodily extensions. In Horner's mundane anecdote, the child—"it"—is recognized as an object of scrutiny by the cotton on his clothes. In contrast, the anecdote endows the text with a dimension of time. Besides, royal commissions and other state-sponsored inquiries were not devised merely to draw dense pictures by words or numbers of the unrepresented in their physical setting. Conversation, mostly by method of interviews, and the concomitant seldom-missed opportunity to narrate stories and to give testimony dominated government and parliamentary reports.

Bureaucratic Poetics

The first report of the Employment of Children Commission (Mines) displays a panoply of composing and editing techniques. In the words of the *Spectator*, this account portrays horrifying human ordeals befitting "fictions of tales of dis-

tant lands."[28] Its authors selected excerpts from field depositions and pasted a
collage of quotations and observations classified according to the fourteen themes
of the investigation. The result is a three-tiered text featuring the testimony of
young miners and their families, presented in a smaller font and frequently in
phonetic English (to generate voice and accent); observations and remarks made
by individual subcommissioners; and the unified, anonymous, but commanding
voice of the senior commissioners. Field notes are reproduced with all their jit-
tery mishaps. For instance, Subcommissioner William Rayner Wood transcribed
or paraphrased his conversation with a child laborer: "No. 71. Banniester Lund,
6 years old:—Does not like t'pit; had rather be at t'top; work is hard; is not ill
tired; has not enough to eat; could eat more if he had it."[29] Wood is not quoting
as much as ventriloqizing the little miner. This utterance is short, shorthanded,
and factual, yet endowed with a poetic pace derived from repeated *ts*—tired, top,
pit, eat. It ends with the wonderfully suggestive "could eat more if he had it"
and is peppered with mine talk. Wood retains his narrative voice even as he assumes his interlocutor's voice. In doing so, he points to his own immersion in the
field of inquiry and, concurrently, to his distance from it.

The text moves telescopically and rather swiftly from statements by fragile,
overworked children to general overviews of entire regions. Squeezed in the middle, the subcommissioner is an observer and a witness. He delineates the scene of
suffering or confesses his own impressions and feelings. The testimonials were
too shocking even to gratify the Victorian taste for moral outrage. Such is the
story of Betty Harris from a coal pit at Little Bolton: "I have a belt around my
waist, and a chain passing between my legs, and I go on my hands and feet." A
sketch of a barely clad young woman harnessed to a trolley and pulling her load
in a steep, dark tunnel accompanies the text. The female "drawer" continues: "I
have drawn till I had the skin off me. The belt and chain is worse when we are
in a family way. My feller (husband) has beaten me many a time for not being
ready." Subcommissioner Jelinger Symons depicts children attending door-traps
in narrow tunnels, sitting alone for as long as twelve hours a day, waiting for the
carriage to pass. One child begs the passersby for a bit of candle wax so as not to
be left in the dark. "I found that the poor child had scooped out a hole in a great
stone, and, having obtained a wick, had manufactured a rude sort of lamp; and
that he kept it going as well as he could by begging contributions of melted tal-
low from the candles of any Samaritan passers by. To be in the dark, in fact,
seemed to be the great grievance with all of them."[30]

Symons's colleague Scriven, who took a partially dressed young girl to a public house for an interview, also employs the dark/light opposition. He reports of be-

ing chased by her alarmed collier who "became evidently mortified that these deeds of darkness should be brought to light." The girl testifies, "I run 24 corves a-day; I cannot come up till I have done them all. I had rather set cards or anything else than work in the pit." The investigator then completes the scene: "She stood shivering before me from cold. The rag that hung about her waist was once called a shirt, which is as black as the coal she thrusts, and saturated with water, the drippings of the roof and shaft."[31]

The mines report in its various guises perfected a particularly gory genre of social reporting that interjected charged language and sexual voyeurism in an effort to represent the physical and mental suffering of dependent populations. Government thus participated in the production of what might be termed Victorian pulp nonfiction. The report told provocative stories in a truncated way in which the rough seams between specific narratives were kept by employing different fonts, quotation marks, and faulty language. The rugged, seemingly uncontrolled form denoting the veracity of the evidence converged with poignant content—all packaged in the cheap blue paper cover supplied by cost-minded parliamentary printers. A certain crudeness of the text was mirrored in unprecedented sharp utterances by government officials. At one point, Symons exclaimed, "any sight more disgustingly indecent or revolting can scarcely be imagined than these girls at work—no brothel can beat it."[32]

This report also derived its power from controversial illustrations, which commissioners reportedly inserted to catch the attention of "busy members of Parliament and learned lords who might not have waded through a lengthy 'blue book' to find the facts which these pictures showed at a glance."[33] Assistant commissioner John L. Kennedy wrote: "I found reason to believe that no *words* I could use would convey to others, impressions, similar to those, which ocular inspection had given to myself. To aid the conception (for it can only be *aided* in endeavouring to convey the impressions received by the sense of smell as well as of sight in examining the place of work), I have had recourse to my friend Mr. Horner, to whose kindness I am indebted for the sketches which appear in the pages of this Report."[34]

The text seems to gravitate toward these illustrations, to caption but ultimately supplant them, providing detail and movement that were absent in the rather schematic sketches.

No. 2 shows the position in which the colliers are obliged to work in the thin seams. This sketch was taken from a collier at work in Mr. Roscoe's mine near Rochdale. He was quite naked, and had a broad scar on his shoulder, which he told me was

the mark of a kick he had received in a fight. It will be observed that the position
is much more constrained than in the preceding case. Indeed, had I not seen it, I
could not have believed that a man could have worked with so much effect in so
little space. The mine in which this man was working was not more than from 18
to 20 inches in thickness. His chest was brought down so as almost to rest on the
thigh, and the head bent down almost the knee; but even in this double-up position it was curious to see the precision and smartness with which he dealt his
blows.[35]

Consistently exalting the significance of visual perception, Employment of
Children investigators produced a text with a strong ocular property. The detailed
(and, significantly, illustrated) narrative offered a receding gaze, which allowed
the reader to peek into the field of inquiry within as well as between the lines.
However, the textual simulation of the investigator's presence at the scene was
predicated on the unbridgeable gap between field experience and its representation. The text might be translucent but not entirely transparent. The reader
needed occasionally to be reminded of that, for instance, by calling attention to
other sensorial experiences that could not be recreated in the text, or to the reporter's own sense of awe and amazement. If he had not been there, he would
not have believed it himself. Estrangement functioned as a means of persuasion,
and the suspenseful play between belief and disbelief sustained a hierarchy of
experience and distance between the investigator and the reader. As importantly,
it epitomized the lingering self-doubt concerning the limits of representation
which haunted the Victorian culture of the social fact.

This "tunnel vision" was not the only way the text undermined its own ocular emphasis. The shock induced by the mine visit was not exclusively prompted
by the sights that reached the eye in barely lit shafts but by what was harder to
see in a subterranean world. The inability of the casual glance to identify the
sex of miners was certainly a cause for concern. A caption to one illustration
described a drawer of a heavy, tublike container. A woman (Subcommissioner
Kennedy supplemented the picture) was dressed in flannel shirt and trousers
and wore a small cap on her head, as did the male miners. Coal blackened everyone's faces. The best (perhaps the only) method to determine her sex was—
metonymy again—the deteriorating necklace and earrings she wore.[36] Symons
contended that while visiting a mine in Yorkshire he found a group naked to
the waist and could distinguish the girls only by their breasts. Occasional difficulty in making this distinction "caused a good deal of laughing and joking."[37]
(In another mine, he found clothed women working side by side with stark

and away they run with prodigious celerity to the shaft, pushing the load with their heads and hands.   (Fig. 3.)

Fig. 3.

The command they hold over it at every curve and angle, considering the pace, the unevenness of the floors and rails, and the mud, water, and stones, is truly astonishing.   The younger Children thrust in pairs" (S. S. Scriven, Esq., Report, §§ 49—52: App. Pt. II., p. 65, 66).

John Marsden, aged eight and a half, Wike-lane Pit: " I hurry a ' dozen and twelve ' corves a day, [that is 20 to the dozen]; my brother Lawrence helps me, and we have to hurry the corves about 200 yards" (S. S. Scriven, Esq., Evidence, No. 42: App. Pt. II, p. 113, l. 14).—Joseph Hellewel, aged ten years, Weigh Pit: "I hurry about 40 corves a-day; they weigh each

Fig. 4.

The 1842 report of the Royal Commission on the Employment of Children sensationalized child and female labor in the mines. The bottom illustration represents young miners Ann Ambler and Will Dyson drawn up from the pit partially clad and cross-lapped. The top sketch depicts another young "hurrier" harnessed to a loaded corf with a chain passing between his legs. The report alleged that these children were remarkably muscular but their height and genital development were "stunted and defective."

naked men.) Several accompanying illustrations of miners were likewise ambiguous about their subjects' gender, including the images that depicted barely
clothed or even naked men and women at work.

In a few accounts, assistant commissioners elucidated their private opinion
about policy issues. For the most part these views amounted to outright support
for state intervention in the social field—for instance, Wood's enthusiastic call
for a centralized educational system.[38] These junior officials could not resist stylistic embellishment, usually by way of a celebratory flourish. Thus James
Mitchell described the pastoral scenery around the lead mines of Durham,
Northumberland, and Cumberland. "Weardale will be held by many to be the
most beautiful of them all. It gradually contracts into narrower spaces, and the
hills become loftier on proceeding westward from the low country."[39] Although
this prose also engaged an idiom of discovery, it was different from the shedding
of metaphoric light on the darkness of mines in Wales or Lancashire. The author dwelled on the lead country's romantic seclusion from the forces of modernity. He was especially struck by the inhabitants' unique language, which, "away
from the tide of human intercourse," still featured words that likely had never
been spoken elsewhere.

The printed products of the Employment of Children investigation combined
therefore a variety of literary genres and devices, including the sublime (as in
the awe-striking danger of the mine shaft), the humanitarian language of bodily pain, metonymic associations, schoolbook didacticism, and provincial lyricism
of origin and seclusion. As investigators digressed from their official purposes,
randomly turning their gaze sideways, so did their reports. The mines report was,
among other things, a textbook on the methods and machinery of mining and
miners' lives. Its ethnographic subject matter was sometimes as incidental as a
slip of the bureaucrat's pen. In one instance, Assistant Commissioner Scriven expressed concern about North Staffordshire miners' dangerous games. "By the
way of amusement," he noted, "the men would sometimes inflate the mouth
with a sufficient quantity [of oil] to produce a stream, by constricting the lips and
setting fire to it as from a grand burner, to the great glee of others who looked
on."[40]

A small item in Scriven's report from the Staffordshire potteries reveals the
disposition to exhibit literal objects. Sarah Limer, a ten-year-old painter at an
earthenware factory at Shelton, maintained that she attended a Catholic Sunday
school and could read and write. The subcommissioner remarked, "This child,
like many others, professes to write, but has no idea of holding a pen," a statement which he corroborated with a facsimile of her signature, a scribble that bore

no resemblance to her name.[41] It is not entirely clear why the assistant commissioner thought it proper to add ocular proof to demonstrate that a little girl's claim was groundless. The reproduced mock signature (therefore twice forged) testified to its own meaningless or, conversely, spoke—as facts indeed can sometimes speak for themselves—to the possibility that the subcommissioner's contention was erroneous—the child was illiterate, but she had a signature and could hold a pen. It was also ironic that the only signature that was faithfully replicated in this otherwise signature-congested document was that of a ten year old who could not write properly.

Discourse in the Social Report

The Employment of Children Commission report was, in many respects, one of a kind, an exception among early Victorian blue books and yet a foundational document in the genre of social reporting. It certainly generated more stir than other state-authored social reports of its era, mostly because it violated conventions of public exchange by depicting female nudity. Curiously, the same state that was strongly challenged in the Stockdale versus Hansard case for its damnation of a book of anatomy as a lurid work of pornography published a document that provided readers similar forms of titillation. Several features of this particular document are reminiscent of the properties that Mikhail Bakhtin admired in the works of nineteenth-century novelists or, even more famously, in the writing of Rabelais. Among them are a concurrent unfolding of diverse literary styles, multivocality of utterances and accents (which in the Employment of Children report are sometimes offered in phonetic dialect), the emergence of unsettling characters, and the "grotesque realism" (whose most explicit renditions in the report are the descriptions of overworked laborers' deformed bodies and the image of miners spitting fire for their amusement). There is a particular dialogical character to the manner in which the writing subjects, the commissioners (as well as the commission), double themselves in the text by conjuring up a sedate official persona and another self, the self of an other who inhabits the "field" away from office or home. While Foucault asserted that "all discourses endowed with the author function possess . . . plurality of self," the social report is remarkably fecund in generating authorial identities.[42] The field persona is an observer as well as a sufferer.

Subcommissioners sometimes employed a hybridized style, blending their voices with those of their interlocutors. (The tendency of social investigators—and later sociologists or anthropologists—to quote themselves, usually by referring to field notes, facilitates an inner dialogue that undermines the unity of the writing subject.) The report seems to exemplify the uncertain position (which was social but also discursive) of intermediaries, the investigator-authors who traveled between society and its outskirts. The notion of a multiplicity of languages, or heteroglossia, seems particularly pertinent for this discussion, for it corresponds to the multivalency of the initial field encounters between investigators and the investigated populations. Bakhtin associated the modern dialogic novel with the emergence of a new type of consciousness that enlisted the other to shape a complex, textured understanding of self.

In contrast, the emphasis on a single voice in the printed works of commissions, committees, and especially inspectorates points to the monological tendencies of official discourse. Moreover, the novelistic heteroglossia is often associated with a transgressive capacity that signified the decline of a single authoritative language, official genres, or central power. This aspect does not seem applicable to state-sanctioned social reportage. By issuing the Employment of Children Commission report government might have co-opted a multifaceted, risky, indeed heteroglotic form for its own purposes, but blue books were an aspect of a larger project to affirm the power of the central government. The official report signified asymmetrical power relations. Polyphony of the sort practiced in fact collectors' field notes may also be construed as a screen erected to occlude rather than to dialogue with others—to replace or speak for others. There was a hierarchy among the various speakers in the social report. Rather than dramatizing and accentuating social heterogeneity, the text may be rehearsing or simulating the shift from chaos to order, from moral outrage to rationality. It depicts a countersociety that should be exposed to the scrutiny and the regulatory power of the state.

One way of avoiding the difficulties inherent in any attempt to detect or theorize agency and voice in the text is to accept the text's fundamental muteness and to follow instead the ways historical readers *actualized* these documents to voice themselves. At the conclusion of this chapter, we therefore return to power relations outside the text where the exchange between lawmakers, government officials, mill owners, vicars, physicians, managers, miners, piecers, and hand-loom weavers took place.

Blue Books Dispatched

A few documents that detail the dispersion of royal commissions' reports have survived in the Public Record Office. The abridged Irish poor-law report was

shipped to a bookseller in London, a Mr. Fellows on Ludgate Street, for its further allocation. Out of 2,600 copies of "selections," 650 were sold for less than a
pound each, and 264 were given away according to the commissioners' requests.
Among these, 148 were sent to country newspapers in England and Scotland, 32
went to London newspapers, 32 went to magazines for reviews, and most of the
rest were given to the secretary of the English Poor Law Commission and to one
of its commissioners, Nassau Senior, for distribution. Prime Minister Earl Grey
received twelve copies. The king's copy was bound with Morocco joints and silk
"insides." Another special copy, somewhat less ostentatious, was prepared for the
king's sister-in-law, the Duchess of Kent (Queen Victoria's mother). Government
placed nearly a hundred advertisements for the report in newspapers and periodicals at the cost of one hundred pounds.[43] Of the 3,280 copies of the Rural Constabulary Commission report (1839), most were sent to local authorities: petty
commissions (1,392), watch committees (196), lords lieutenant (59), and Lancashire magistrates (35). Large numbers (1,105) were given to "individuals directed by the Commissioners," probably those who cooperated with the investigation or could assist in the cause of reform, and 140 copies were left for the
personal use of the commissioners. Another 210 went to newspapers.[44] In both
cases, the press was coaxed. Newspapers and review journals were the main vehicle for publicity, and commissioners did not wait for editors' requests.

Admittedly, the Irish poor-law and the constabulary reports had a rather modest circulation. Officials peddled other documents more vigorously. During one
of the recurrent parliamentary debates on printing, the Comptroller McCulloch
of the Stationery Office gave as an example of public waste the ten thousand gratuitous copies of the Committee of Privy Council on Education report, which included 680 pages on every school visited by an inspector. "Very many schoolmasters have their names blazoned abroad in I do not know how many different
forms, and the names of hundreds of the children at school are printed also, with
an endless mass of minute and trifling details."[45] The committee's secretary,
Ralph R. W. Lingen, responded, "the persons who have promoted the various
schools . . . are extremely anxious to see what is said of them by the Government
inspectors."[46] The committee was established to allocate grants in aid to voluntary contributions for building schools. The only privilege government retained
was that of inspection, and so reports were essential to that collaboration.

Despite the comptroller's sarcasm, the committee insisted on continuing the
gratis circulation of its reports, emphasizing that it did not wish to advertise its
activities to the public at large as much as to communicate with managers and
teachers of the schools under inspection. Unlike Joseph Hume, who thought that

official documents would reach their proper readers if a fee was charged, Lingen, Chadwick, and other bureaucrats maintained that reports would reach their destination only if they were sent directly to a preselected group. Lingen argued that recipients did not pass on the documents to booksellers. Hundreds of applications for them arrived in his office each year, far exceeding the supply. Twenty-five hundred copies were sent to certified teachers and to other correspondents, mostly clergymen. All wanted to keep a copy in their homes rather than share it with others. Lingen claimed that if reports were shared, they would not be as carefully read, and he had indications that recipients actually read the documents in their entirety. Naturally, they were concerned with their specific districts, but from his daily correspondence, he found recurrent references to reports of other inspectors and remarks that indicated a broader interest.[47]

In the case of the Committee of Privy Council on Education report, a circular system of communication developed in which reports' addressees were the individuals who gave information in the first place. Even frugal Hume used to send free copies of select committees' blue books to all witnesses who came to Westminster. They were entitled, he believed, to a copy of their own evidence as well as to the report.[48] The Irish poor-law commissioners argued that there was a great interest among those who responded to their queries and questionnaires to see the commission's report in print. Through distribution of reports, officials sustained networks of informants and local interlocutors. Witnesses' desire to receive and read official reports to which they contributed, especially their own testimony, may seem self evident or even trivial, but it was symptomatic of the exchange relations between London and the provinces, between government, local authorities, proprietors, and the working populations. Official documents—concrete objects—permeated the exchange between government and its citizens. This gesture was meaningful not only because an object changed hands but also because the act of reporting itself implied acknowledgment, gratitude, and respect.

For the Board of Health, dispersion of information was justified primarily in terms of public instruction. Chadwick maintained that the Board was ordered by the "highest authorities" that it must "conciliate public opinion." Otherwise, it had very little direct power. In 1852 Chadwick claimed that a distribution of a paper on the removal of sewer manure to farmland had already persuaded five towns to espouse the proposed scheme. An additional five or six towns were getting closer to adopting new sewage systems, and several others ceased building "bad works." "If we get this system in complete operation in a few towns, it will be worth, I apprehend, not only the whole expense of the printing ten times over but the whole expense of the Commission."[49] Chadwick sent the material to the officers of the local boards, some of whom were unpaid and otherwise would not purchase them. The local boards, in turn, lent copies to farmers. Chadwick asked the Stationery Office whether it would permit Charles Knight to print copies for commercial circulation as he had twenty years earlier for the poor-law report. The Board of Health, in particular, stubbornly circumvented printing regulations, but other commissioners and inspectors were often caught cutting bureaucratic corners to expedite the publication of their accounts. The secretary of the Commission on Municipal Corporations inserted into his official correspondence advertisements for the sale of the commission's report by, once again, publisher Knight. The Home Office ordered the secretary to provide a full explanation.[50]

Blue Books Intercepted

For those who were neither close to particular investigations nor beneficiaries of commissioners' largesse or habitual purchasers of parliamentary reports, the press was the main source on official inquiries. Newspapers and journals functioned as large-pored filters for official discourse, publishing long unedited segments from (or furnishing numerous details about) government and parliamentary investigations, hearings, periodical reports, and returns. Like other informational genres, midcentury newspapers were often in the habit of reproducing rather than digesting authentic facts. In addition, periodicals such as the *Edinburgh Review* and the *Quarterly Review*—Whig and Tory publications— offered extensive commentary on blue books, often in conjunction with other factual publications or even literary productions. Official literature was thus subjected to the comparative gaze or at least forced into a direct if fictitious exchange. For instance, the *Quarterly Review* examined the Factory Commission report together with seven other texts, including Sadler's report, John Fielden's pro-short-time *The Curse of the Factory System* (1836), Charles Wing's politically similar *The Evils of the Factory System* (1836), as well as James Phillips Kay's differently motivated *The Moral and Physical Condition of the Working Classes Employed in the Cotton Manufacture in Manchester* (1832).[51]

Other documents fared worse, steered away from the intended destinations set by Chadwick and others. The Society for the Abolition of Slavery throughout the British Dominions rearranged and republished the printed reports of two 1832 select committees—one in the Lords, the other in the Commons—that had deliberated over the fate of slavery. These committees issued bulky reports of their proceedings but did not append conclusions or recommendations. The Commons committee examined whether slaves could maintain themselves once emancipated (see chapter 6 for the 1860s American rendition of the same theme) and whether the danger of rebellion was greater if freedom was granted or refused. The inquiry, led by members friendly to the cause of abolition, was limited mostly to the island of Jamaica. Published evidence occupied 655 pages and was made available to the public despite planters' protests.

In the *Analysis* (of the Commons report) and the *Abstract* (of the 1,400-page Lords report), the society's editors excerpted the evidence, eliminated the question-and-answer format, and provided a running critique and interpretation through extensive use of lengthy footnotes. A few remarks in the text itself evaluated witnesses' integrity, but the edited testimonies generally were left without explicit commentary. The footnotes extended the text by offering information from the society's publications (its own archive) to substantiate or refute details given in the testimony or to respond to M.P.s' queries when witnesses hesitated or claimed they did not know enough to answer. The footnotes were especially comprehensive in dealing with pro-planter testimony. They highlighted inconsistencies and demonstrated how the witnesses unwittingly imparted facts that confirmed pro-abolition witnesses' description of plantation life. The deployment of corrective remarks disguised the manipulation of the text and sustained a semblance of a debate between the information given during the hearings and the positions (or facts) expressed by the society in footnote form. The society ultimately completed the parliamentary volumes by answering the initial questions: once emancipated the slaves could maintain themselves, and the danger of a rebellion was much greater with slavery still in place.

Besides the *Abstract* and the *Analysis,* two other antislavery documents presented abridged versions of the Lords hearings, employing a distinct tone and different editing techniques. Published anonymously, these documents attacked not just the proslavery stance but also the committee of the Lords, exposing the personal interests its members had in slavery. "Legion," the signatory of these publications, closely interpreted the exchange in the committee room. Long passages quoted in full from the actual transcripts, rather than paraphrased testimonies decorated with scholarly styled footnotes, dominated these tracts. The analysis followed witnesses' and peers' rhetorical patterns. Witnesses' reactions to tough questions, their pauses, hesitations, evasions, and minute discrepancies, were as important to the determination of veracity as the information they offered. "Legion" judged specific testimonies by their bearers' access to actual plantations and claimed that the testimony of (mostly antislavery) clergymen should be preferred to that of casual visitors or state officials who lived on the island but did not frequent the sequestered plantation world. He thus stretched the argument of the plantation as a different planet to bolster evidence close to his views. The plantation, as one witness asserted, was a "sealed book."[52]

Strong anti-aristocratic and anti–High Church sentiments pervaded these documents. Witnesses were seemingly cross-examined by "Legion" or more precisely indicted by their own words. The analytical method deployed in this rendition of the official transcripts forcefully resembled courtroom tactics. Early on (and counterintuitively), he designated the planters as the plaintiffs on whose shoulders lay the burden of proof in what he constructed as a virtual civil case. The authority of the institution, the House of Lords, was cunningly employed to undermine it. These abolitionist "reports" of the Lords proceedings implicitly assumed the accuracy of the original text, down to its minutest details. It was the completeness of the initial record that allowed "Legion" to perform his elaborate maneuvers.[53]

The furor over the publication of the *Report on the State of Education in Wales* (1847) also exemplified the vulnerability of published official accounts to hostile scrutiny. Based on careful reading of the report, a contemporary observer maintained that a few assistant commissioners did not have full command of Welsh, even though the commission had hired these locals because of their supposed command of the language. One of them obviously mistranslated children's responses to English, and another marked wrong the right answer in an arithmetic test. In a pamphlet *Artegall, or Remarks on the Reports of the Commissioners of Enquiry into the State of Education in Wales* (1848), Jane Williams attacked the chief commissioner's mastery of English grammar. "Until Commissioner Symons attains a more creditable knowledge of etymology and syntax, we would earnestly recommend him to abstain from the use of metaphors and from all figures of speech."[54] Such attention to trifling linguistic infelicities was a way to give the commission that denigrated the Welsh for their supposed ignorance of the English language a taste of their own venom. The report's publication prompted an avalanche of counterdocuments. Many of the commission's informants rose against the report, and some protested the representation of their views. The published minutia of the inquiry enhanced the possibilities of contestation about the commission's modes of operation, the evidence garnered, and the commissioners' speaking and writing skills.

Misrepresentation

Were blue books accessible (or familiar) to those weaker segments of the population who were often the subject of investigation? Certainly the better informed among the lower classes, once termed the working-class "aristocracy," had such access, and trade-union leaders vigilantly scrutinized the outpouring of government publications. During the sanitary campaign of the 1840s, for example, laborers' meetings organized by middle-class reformers featured lectures on topics of city hygiene. In such gatherings in the lower-class neighborhoods of London, the chair of the Metropolitan Improvement Society read excerpts from the government sanitary report. According to the *Morning Chronicle*, "the attention they gave to them was intense—not a person left the room until the discourse was concluded."[55] Documents such as the Factory Commission's report ultimately encouraged rather than deterred union leaders to partake in public adjudication of factual accounts and the debate over representation and misrepresentation of working-class subjects. Moreover, this particular report buttressed workers' belief that ultimately facts did speak for them. It served as an illustration for the ostensible power of social reality to articulate itself through an official account regardless of its compilers' intent. The commission prescribed policies that were evidently incongruent with the laborers' aims. Nevertheless, the evidence presented on the plight of the factory children vindicated the veracity of Sadler's report and supported the operatives' depiction of the factory system. In the language of the *Quarterly Review*, "Though the scheme of the Commission had partial success, inasmuch as it gave ministers a temporary power to overwhelm the ten-hours bill, yet their huge folio contained within itself an anti-dote to the poison."[56] It was true that the heart of the dispute between Sadler and the Whig ministry was not facts but policy. Yet, the "antidote" also could be found in other episodes when facts proved more elusive. It was a product of textual analysis and, as we shall see, textual thievery.

Mine inspector Tremenheere occasionally asked the Home Office for extra copies of his annual reports for dissemination among the workingmen. As M.P.s sought to improve the image of the legislature by giving away parliamentary papers, the inspector argued that leaders of the mining population (including the editor of the *Miners Advocate*) changed their views about the state's role in their districts as a direct result of examining his reports.[57] There are other indications that miners were interested in blue books, including a November 1852 application from a Newcastle-on-Tyne colliery for a select committee report on explosions in mines.[58] In another telling incident, coal miners demanded that Tremenheere alter an erroneous account he had published in a periodic report about their strike. The Leeds District Branch of the Coal Miners' Association declared that the inspector's description of the circumstances that led to the strike and lockout contradicted the facts and confirmed, without examination, the masters' version of the events. "We feel that we are misrepresented by the Commissioner whose duty it is to give a fair and impartial report of all things he is set over to watch, he has seriously prejudiced our cause before the public."[59]

Tremenheere countered that he based his account on "authentic documents" but promised to inquire into the alleged inaccuracies and to include corrections, if necessary, in his next periodic report. "I regret that the Miners . . . should see reason to state that my Report . . . is not fair and impartial. I beg that they may be assured that in this as in all my Reports, I have been guided both in what I have inserted and what I have omitted, by a desire to promote, according to the best of my judgment, the true and permanent interests of the working miners."[60] The miners pointed to various publications they authorized during the strike as proof that they were not "the unreasoning and unreasonable people they are usually represented . . . That their case and the facts of the strike contentions should be correctly reported to Government (seeing that an official was ordered to be present at all public meetings) will be clear."[61] This episode documents two chains of representation that involved, on the one hand, government and its commissioners and, on the other hand, miners and their delegations. Much of the dialogue between these two systems was conducted through an exchange of printed reports. The miners saw in the periodic report of the mine inspectors an essential part of their representation in Parliament and before the public and duly asked to rectify the alleged inaccuracies. This case also featured a state official who was convinced that he was representing miners by acting for them and by depicting their conditions in his published accounts.

Tremenheere was confident about the course of action he had taken in the mine districts and believed that his reports would either appease the restless minds of miners, among whom he found "ignorance on various subjects affecting their interest and society in general," or move owners to introduce serious improvements. Urging the Home Office to institute an inspection of the ventilation modes in all mines, he explained that such initiative would "produce a greater sense of moral responsibility among the employers."[62] Competition (or "jealousies") prevented one owner from knowing about safety measures installed in mines next to his. As for the laborers, inspection would lead "them to feel that they were not as they have hitherto considered themselves, quite neglected by the Government." The colliery population, he claimed, entered periodically into an "awkward state of mind." During such cycles, the miners were under the grand delusion that they held the entire industry in their hands. He was utterly convinced that next to their education there was nothing better to shake their beliefs and instill "sounder opinion" among them than an inspection. In Tremenheere's view, the interlocking function of inspection and reporting was to address two local problems of vision that were psychological rather than retinal. Owners were blinded by their animosity toward each other. Seclusion and ignorance planted in the miners' minds dangerous notions of false power. The solution was to liberate the two sides from their respective isolation by allowing them a comprehensive view of their situation, a touch of the social real. The presence of inspectors and, significantly, their reports on the scene had a direct sobering and therapeutic effect.

To illustrate the success of his methods, Tremenheere claimed he had received letters from "persons in the confidence of the working classes, expressing the satisfaction at my Reports, and anticipating good results from them to themselves and their children."[63] Chadwick also encouraged (albeit indirectly) working-class organizations to embrace his reports. In late 1843 and early 1844, he mailed dozens of his supplementary report on town burial to top clergymen, medical men, politicians, industrialists, writers, (e.g., Thomas Carlyle), and editors (e.g., Macvey Napier) and requested them to publicize his work further. More importantly, he asked individuals with good working-class contacts to encourage workers to petition both houses of Parliament and the queen in support of the measures proposed in the report. In this correspondence, Chadwick repeatedly claimed that his report represented the true view of the lower classes.[64]

Telling Truth to Government

The short-time movement that opposed the factory commission in 1833 eventually used in its pamphlets, handbills, and broadsides evidence from the commission's reports. It was Richard Oastler's standard tactic. For example, he published a pamphlet entitled *Intemperance and Vice: The Effects of Long Hours and Bad System; from the Report of Dr. Francis Bisset Hawkins, One of the Medical Officers of the Factory Commission, 1833.*[65] In a similar fashion, he appropriated and then redirected the early 1830s treatises about the working classes in Manchester and the industrial system written by W. R. Greg, James Philips Kay, and other ideological foes. Oastler capitalized on the supposed authenticity of the material reproduced in the official record. Its archival quality made it brittle. Breaking pieces of evidence and repositioning them outside their original context was premised on the printed text's inherent rigidity compared with the flexibility or fluidity of oral discourse. The interruptible property of printed texts was best illustrated, albeit in a different manner, by a nongovernment publication—the periodic reports of the Society for the Suppression of Mendicity in London. As the society conceded, its annual accounts had two distinct readerships: first, members of the organization and other interested citizens who read the front pages and, second, crooks, writers of bogus begging letters who were mainly interested in the list of potential victims appended to each report in the form of a roster of contributors.[66] Social investigations were a means to elicit, collect, and sometimes even pluck information from unsuspecting subjects. Voluminous printed accounts invited reciprocal behavior.

The 1833 clash between Oastler and the Factory Commission was rich with defiant, carnivalesque gestures. Workingmen lampooned official representatives (ostensibly of the king himself), celebrating their own potentate (King Richard) and engaging in a mock investigation of an investigation. Another clash between Oastler and a royal commission lacked perhaps this open-space theatricality but featured the same artful, eye-level maneuvering, this time over the record of Oastler's testimony. In late 1839, he sent two angry letters to Russell at the Home Office demanding that he be furnished with a copy of the evidence he had given to assistant commissioner Richard Muggeridge of the Handloom Weavers Commission.[67] Oastler wrote that in response to the official's solicitation, he agreed to testify in a public meeting of weavers and employers in Huddersfield. This was a rather subdued performance for the vociferous orator. Somewhat unexpectedly, he heeded the assistant commissioner's request not to excite the people. At the conclusion of his testimony, however, he suggested that he would be asked about other controversial issues, such as the poor law, the factory system, and, the most volatile topic, the right of the people to arm themselves. Muggeridge offered to interview him about these matters in private. Once again, Oastler consented on the condition that he would receive a precise and full copy of the entire conversation. Muggeridge accepted but stipulated that the transcript would not be published before the commission's report. The assistant commissioner had already been embarrassed publicly and had even found himself in trouble with his superiors when a copy of a testimony he had sent to another witness appeared in the *London Times*.

Talking to the government official in his hotel room, Oastler stated his blunt views on a number of points. To remove any future doubt, he read over Muggeridge's notes, initialed them, and later even sent a letter to the assistant commissioner confirming the transcript's veracity. Muggeridge, in fact, solicited the letter so as not to appear as a spy who clandestinely recorded private utterances. Oastler diffused his concerns, remarking that he "rejoiced at this opportunity of telling the Government all the truth."[68] In this narration Oastler was at his most shrewd self, informing the Home Secretary how tears came to Muggeridge's eyes when the official described a visit he had made to a weavers' village. The assistant commis-

sioner, Oastler claimed, thanked him profusely for his testimony, but despite recurrent requests, he had never received the coveted copy. Muggeridge shrugged
him off by saying that he had already transferred the evidence to London.

Oastler's initial request was rejected, rather obliquely, "because no proceedings were taken, or are at present intended to be taken upon that evidence."[69] His
second letter assumed his recognizable caustic style, accusing government of dis-
honesty, fraud, breach of contract, and robbing him of his own testimony. Evidently, the Home Office's reluctance was due to content of the testimony that
verged on incitement to rebellion. Talking to Muggeridge, Oastler had challenged the new poor law, calling it "treason." It was the duty of every man to resist the orders of poor-law officials, he asserted, declaring that if someone would
hold his wife hostage for parish relief, he would kill that man. He attacked the
employment of the army and the police to suppress the people and, to add impetus to his words, showed Muggeridge a dagger of the kind sold in Huddersfield shops. Muggeridge proposed that Oastler send one such weapon to Lord Russell and even gave him money for that purpose. (Oastler probably recounted that
episode to demonstrate that despite Muggeridge's desire not be seen as a spy, the
assistant commissioner was a provocateur.) "Why withhold from me the words
in which I have stated these things to the Government? Why refuse me that
which is mine?"[70]

Why did Oastler need a copy of a testimony whose content he remembered
quite well? His correspondence with the Home Office was clearly defiant. Did he
wish to provoke government to put him on trial over what he said in a formal interview with a royal commissioner? Or, conversely, did he hope to protect himself from prosecution? After all, he was helping government conduct an investigation. One way or another, he certainly wanted to publish these words as coming
directly from the official record, to have the opportunity to quote himself from
a royal commission's transcript. Since Muggeridge told him explicitly that his testimony was very important, Oastler maintained that, "If any information which
I could give were '*important*' to the Government, it must have been equally so to
the people, and the reason was then strong why I should not be *cheated* out of the
copy."[71] The request obviously confused the Home Office. An official scribbled
on Oastler's letter that his words were indeed inciting and dangerous but that a
greater harm might be incurred if Muggeridge would not follow through on his
promise.

Of the several methods of appropriating state publications that we have examined, the first focused on reframing a report. Thus, the Society for the Aboli-

tion of Slavery republished both houses' accounts on the West Indies slavery in a heavily edited form surrounded by discursive footnotes that dragged the text in a different direction. Reviewing government documents in the context of different social reports, literary descriptions, and other texts—as was the practice in the periodical press—also reframed or recontextualized government documents, although often in a more politically benign manner. It was more common simply to chip off bits of authentic evidence and redeploy them. These takeovers are inherently different from tactics of direct contestation, such as criticism of investigative procedures, challenge of specific evidence (as well as other issues of accuracy and truthfulness), or attack on policy recommendations. Appropriation implies an agreement between the aggressor and the victim over the fundamental veracity of the print archive as a repository of facts—however defined.

A second form of appropriation was the attempt to commandeer reports (or particular evidence) for the purpose of self-representation, or in Oastler's case, by quoting oneself from the printed page and therefore speaking of one's own opinion as a "fact." (The social investigator also quotes himself from the handwritten page of his field journals and thus articulates himself as a fact.) We should also consider less aggressive acts of appropriation such as the miners' occasional embrace of Tremenheere's reports as their own. This particular gesture was politically ambiguous and could be emblematic of relinquished agency. Nevertheless, it allowed miners to select which documents represented them and which did not, and also to partake in making government reports more "representative." A call to remedy misrepresentation has a different resonance than a mere challenge to the truthfulness or accuracy of government-disseminated information. Such a demand presupposes that it is incumbent upon the state to facilitate this particular form of representation.

The same semantic and material properties of information in blue books that were guaranteed by the power of the state, the prestige of the monarch, and, as importantly, the conventions of committing authentic facts to print—also rendered the report an easier target for looting. Paradoxically, at the conclusion of the investigative sequence, when the scenes and the subjects of inquiry were finally objectified—captured in a book—the attributes of the report as a printed text sustained by the "order of books" resulted in a loss of control by the text's individual and institutional authors. Unlike de Certeau's idea of "reading as poaching," these particular acts of theft were decisive and preconceived. Admittedly, these were rather modest gestures of resistance or opposition. In Oastler's case—one steals what one already has (or steals from a thief) but of course quoting oneself from the royal commission's record endowed the individual with a different voice. Quotation marks are a means to extract text out of context, to displace it and consequently to allow its continual movement, or in Jacques Derrida's words, "put between quotation marks [the iterable sign] can break with every given context, engendering an infinity of new contexts in a manner which is absolutely illimitable."[72] This perpetual movement was also an aspect of the nineteenth-century traffic in social facts. Most importantly, the authentic fact in the social report, separated by quotation marks of many kinds (in the Employment of Children Commission report these were different fonts) is already out of context and coexists in some friction with the rest of the text (as in the case of Sarah Limer's signature). Blue books' susceptibility to appropriation—as well as to the modes of interrogation and interpretation to which all texts are vulnerable—was an essential feature of print statism and the exchange relations between government and its reading subjects.

CHAPTER SIX

Can Freedmen Be Citizens?

"The nation is suddenly called to preside at the birth of a race. Such a crisis—
'a nation born in a day'—devolves upon rulers and people grave responsibilities."[1] These dramatic lines, proclaiming another "primal scene" in American
history, opened a petition submitted by the Boston Emancipation League to Congress in late 1862. The league proposed the creation of an emancipation bureau
to accumulate information about and devise policies for the newly freed slaves,
many of whom had already congregated behind Union lines. In March 1863, following the emancipation proclamation, Secretary of War Edwin Stanton appointed Robert Dale Owen, Samuel Gridley Howe, and James McKaye to serve
as the American Freedmen's Inquiry Commission to investigate "the condition
of the [emancipated] colored population . . . and to report what measures will
best contribute to their protection and improvement . . . and, also how they can
be most carefully employed . . . for the suppression of the rebellion."[2]

By this phase of the war, government was facing a true emergency—the
pressing need to manage the mushrooming refugee camps, to find some employment for former slaves, and to guarantee their well-being. Even though the
end of the war was not yet in sight, a debate on the nature of future racial
arrangements was already brewing. The Emancipation Proclamation (and later
the Thirteenth Amendment) sealed the fate of slavery but not that of the former
slave. While bondage as a social institution was doomed, the future status of
southern freedmen and free blacks everywhere remained unclear. Should they
be equal members of society? Could they become full citizens? For contemporaries it was evident that the answers to these questions would have consequences
far beyond the American South. The parameters of public debate were reshaped
to address these and other issues that emanated from the war. For one, government that previously had been silent on the question of slavery targeted the former Confederate states with new fact-finding tools. The circumstances of the
Civil War generated a substantial economy of information on the South and

freedmen distinct from previous abolitionist efforts to garner facts about slaves and plantations.

The American Freedmen's Inquiry Commission (AFIC) has been long recognized as the author of "a blueprint for radical reconstruction."[3] The commission's political influence was admittedly modest, but its reports were the first to articulate principles and propose programs that foreshadowed most of the innovations of later years, including the creation of a Freedmen's Bureau, full citizenship for African Americans, an irrevocable prohibition of slavery, and the enlistment of 300,000 black soldiers. As importantly, the AFIC was the first federal body to officially interview slaves and former slaves. By giving voice to those who had been barred from public testimony, the commission baptized them as participants in public exchange or even as citizens, in the most expansive sense of the term.

The birth of a race and of a nation as a question of knowledge and a subject of state-sponsored investigation is the focus of this chapter. The AFIC's work was symptomatic (and symbolic) of a particular historical moment when the slaves moved away from their masters' gaze to become instead a domain of knowledge and activity for the state. In addition to policy recommendations, the three members of the commission endeavored to provide a synoptic view of the history, present condition, and future of blacks in the United States, triggering a long and ambiguous history of federal attempts to address the predicament of race. At that juncture, northern attention was turning its focus from the master's whip and the slave's lacerated back to the "Negro-subject" himself—his aptitude, character, and ability to participate in the market and the polity. The following discussion explores the commission's fieldwork in search of black subjectivity, its selection of evidence, the subsequent reports, and their conceptual foundation. The relationship between social knowledge and the state is also examined. The appointment of the three-member panel appears to signify the proclivity of the modern state to enlist knowledge or science to define, create, or capture a new group of subjects as under its care and supervision. However, this model, which is often associated with the early works of Foucault, does not account for the peculiarities of our historical episode. As we shall see, science, mostly in the form of racial doctrines including refined racial typologies, was introduced into the project as an argument against protracted government intervention. It was an expression of strong ambivalence toward the state. Correspondingly, the commission warned against zealotry on the part of government and philanthropists in Howe's famous words: "The white man has tried taking care of the Negro, by slavery, by apprenticeship, by colonization, and has failed disastrously in all; now let the Negro try to take care of himself."[4]

The exigencies of war originated new forms of social imagination; most significantly, perhaps, they encouraged Americans to think of themselves as a society. In the case of the AFIC, the scale of the project prompted Owen, Howe, and McKaye to express their respective views concerning the nature of American democracy and to situate the United States among a host of European and New World nations that grappled with slavery and its aftermath. This panel's reports challenged the prevailing notion that by the superiority of its timeless institutions the United States escaped the social and political turmoil that befell the rest of the world, especially Europe, a position often labeled "American exceptionalism." In contrast to the ahistorical character of the exceptionalist stance, the AFIC offered a decidedly historicist view of U.S. society. It held that institutions and human nature are produced under particular sociopolitical circumstances and are, therefore, changeable and changing, hence, the birth of a new nation and of a new black subjectivity.

How could the commission substantiate its principles and recommendations by empirical research? Indeed, in the course of their investigation the three commissioners faced obstacles directly tied to the magnitude of the issues under consideration, the size of the terrain, and the lack of institutional experience. Yet, there were even greater problems of knowledge that overwhelmed this and similar attempts to study the freedmen. First was the subject of the inquiry itself. What can we know about four million people in the midst of a momentous transition? What would qualify as an adequate body of knowledge on freedmen? The abolitionist Edward Pierce, who at the time supervised the educational experiment in the Sea Islands of South Carolina, conceded that before granting former slaves full freedom and political rights their ability to sustain themselves should be gauged. However, he argued: "*The slave is unknown to all, even to himself, while the bondage lasts* . . . Not even Tocqueville or Olmsted, much less the master, can measure the capacities and possibilities of the slave, until the slave himself is transmuted to a man."[5] Herein lies the paradox: an a priori demonstration of the slave's full potential to be a member of society was deemed concurrently imperative and unattainable. The demand for empirical observation (originating with the freedmen's "friends," the abolitionists) was by itself bound to cast doubts on the former slaves' competence. To complicate matters, unlike other social problems such as slums, child labor, and asylums, the institution of slavery had not produced any widely accepted group of experts or types of expertise. Intertwined with the lack of experts was the predicament of discourse: What was the proper conceptual apparatus to investigate African American freedmen and free men, and what was the proper language to describe their condition and their past? The

Fleeing from Thomas "Stonewall" Jackson's army during the Second Bull Run Campaign, fugitive African Americans ford the Rappahannock River. During the early years of the Civil War, slaves fled in great numbers beyond Union lines, raising enormous logistical problems for the federal government. (Rappahannock, Virginia, August 1862, Timothy H. O'Sullivan, photographer, Library of Congress)

commission was asked to study a practical organizational question. It viewed the trajectory from unfree to free labor as the essence of the freedmen question. However, the panel was soon tempted to search for knowledge about, to imagine, and to theorize racial difference. Howe in particular seemed almost tantalized by the explanatory might of racialism. Social discourse organized around labor relations and racial discourse based on supposedly natural traits competed throughout the larger public debate over the destiny of the former slaves.

Imagining the State

During the war and Reconstruction, the federal state was also an object of imagination and invention. By creating the AFIC, the administration emulated, or, imagined itself to be, a Europeanlike state. There was little precedent for such an enterprise in the United States. The Sanitary Commission, born at the outset of the Civil War as a semiofficial body (also labeled a commission of inquiry) to oversee civilian efforts at maintaining the well-being of Union soldiers, did not sit squarely with the administration. Lincoln famously referred to it as "the fifth wheel on my wagon." Like the Sanitary Commission, which was modeled on the experience of Britain and France during the Crimean War (1854–56), the AFIC's roots in European bureaucratic culture could be traced to the precedent set by these two powers when they decided to set their slaves free. The British Parliament investigated slavery from the 1780s to the 1830s, as did the Broglie Commission in France (1840–43), of which Alexis de Tocqueville was a member. Both U.S. projects were supported by a coterie of northeastern reformers for whom the Massachusetts senator Charles Sumner functioned as a nonofficial representative in Congress. The Civil War allowed the cause of science—which had lost a great friend and much clout when John Quincy Adams left the White House more than thirty years earlier—to gain a degree of power, albeit limited and temporary, in national affairs. The National Academy of Science began operating in 1863 as an advisory board, and Sumner toyed with the idea of founding an academy for literature and an academy for the social sciences.[6]

Instituting the commission, the administration wished to give an aura of scientific impartiality to its attempt to master a charged debate. In this regard, the cabinet needed knowledge to sway public opinion, and government supplanted abolitionists in authoring emancipationist propaganda. (Incessant efforts to control the news typified the administration's wartime information policy.) Howe, a friend of Sumner, had argued earlier in the war, "We must be able to furnish . . . as early as possible as general and *reliable coup d'oeil* of the actual condition of those who are actually out of the house of bondage, their wants and their *capacities*. We must collect facts and use them as ammunition."[7] Sumner subsequently employed the panel's work to push Lincoln's administration further on the road toward emancipation. The Massachusetts senator was deeply involved in establishing the commission, selecting its personnel, and delineating its course of action.

He and Stanton staffed the panel with friends of the administration who also had some experience in social welfare and in authoring or publishing propaganda. Born in Glasgow, Robert Dale Owen (1801–77) was the son of the utopian reformer Robert Owen of the New Lanark fame. In the 1820s and 1830s, he championed the Owenite New Harmony colony in Indiana, labor unions, and women's rights. He later cultivated a conventional political career in the Democratic Party, serving in Congress (1843–47), where he was a vocal advocate for "manifest destiny." But when the Civil War broke out, Owen harnessed himself to the cause of the Union. He produced a string of pamphlets in which he developed the legal argument for emancipation, maintaining that international law invested government with the power to seize enemy property. Owen's colleague, Samuel Gridley Howe (1801–76) was a physician, a founder of institutions for the blind and the deaf, and a member of a diligent Boston-based reform clique. In the 1840s, he chaired the Boston vigilance committee and later supported the antislavery campaign in Kansas, including John Brown's escapades. Howe would remain vague as to his prior knowledge of Brown's plans for an armed action in Virginia, and following the raid on Harper's Ferry (1859), he was forced to flee to Canada. Least prominent among the three, Col. James McKaye (1805–88) was a New York land developer who sponsored the Loyal Publication Society that circulated pro-Union tracts during the war.

The commissioners ardently supported emancipation, yet none of them was associated with the radical Garrisonian camp within the antislavery movement. This was not merely a matter of nuance. Several notable abolitionists, who by 1863 acquired direct experience working with freedmen, were clearly shunned.[8] Of the commissioners, Owen had the most ambiguous personal history regarding blacks. Although he was a spirited emancipationist when the war began, it did not escape abolitionist memory that in the late 1840s he had been responsible for phrasing the exclusionary clause in Indiana's constitution that barred blacks from settling in the state.

In the Field

Authorized to conduct investigations wherever they deemed necessary "in order to obtain on the spot . . . authentic information," the commissioners were awarded the assistance of a secretary and a stenographer, limited access to government documents, a per diem of eight dollars a day, and the equivalent of the expenses of a colonel in the cavalry. During the first few months, the commissioners visited the seaboard states, often separating to comb a larger terrain, from Baltimore and Washington to Fortress Monroe and Port Royal. Later, after the submission of the interim report, the panel traversed the western department, inspecting camps and interviewing local politicians, army officers, black soldiers, journalists, and charity workers. Despite their long contact with slaves, masters were not considered credible for testimony except in those rare cases when their remarks might advance the commission's views. A slave owner from Nashville told the AFIC that her seven slaves were "devotedly attached to me; but still, there is the desire for freedom, which you know is very desirable to all."[9]

In the field, a stenographer recorded evidence with all the trappings of an official undertaking. Slave interviews epitomized the commission's double mission, documenting the past—slavery and its atrocities—and acquiring information to justify future racial policies. In South Carolina, Solomon Bradley, a twenty-seven-year-old soldier, recounted an incident in which a woman was brutally flogged and then tortured with hot wax merely because she had burned the edges of her owner's breakfast waffles. Robert Smalls, a pilot who, at the outbreak of hostilities, had run a steamer called the *Planter* out of Charleston Harbor (and during Reconstruction would become a U.S. congressman), volunteered information on a particularly foul form of collective punishment: slaves were put in stocks above each other and left to defecate.[10]

The black family and uncertainty over its resilience, demise, or complete absence was another theme in these interviews. Many of the questions scrutinized females' sexual appetite: "Have not colored women a good deal of sexual passion? . . . What proportion of the young women do not have sexual intercourse before marriage?"[11] The commissioners wanted to know the condition under which marital (or mock-marital) relations could be sustained or terminated, how family names were assigned, what labels such as *family* or *parent* meant, and how obedient children were to their elders. Even when the topic of conversation turned to the organization of the workday on the plantation, interviewers probed the possibility of domesticity under harsh conditions. They asked Harry McMillan, a field hand, whether during labor food was consumed in a family setting. The interviewers also solicited responses to a range of black stereotypes. Do "colored people" tell the truth? Do they keep their promises? Stature of manhood was also assessed. "Suppose a boy is struck by another boy what does he do?" McMillan replied: "I would tell my boy to strike back and defend himself." He further maintained that government should give each family four or five acres of land. Freedmen would rather own land than work for wages.

Owen conducted surprise visits to African American dwellings in Louisville, Kentucky. After calling on a slave woman, he wrote, "I found her in a room tidily kept and herself decently dressed."[12] In Kentucky the commissioners met William H. Howard, a former slave who had been allowed to hire away his labor. Howard purchased himself and later his future wife, whom he sent to Oberlin College. The commissioners remarked: "This man's house was exceedingly pretty; it was well furnished, and had a piano." Similarly, in Canada, Howe was careful to meet his informants in their native surrounding—their shops, farms, and private homes. Following a core tactic of Victorian social reportage, he ventured to establish a continuum between "decencies of life" manifested in the domestic space and human character, thus evaluating his subjects metonymically through their meticulously observed domestic environment. He was later satisfied to report, "Cooking, eating, and sleeping, are not done in the same room . . . [The rooms] are tidily furnished." Traveling in the American South, the commissioners sporadically recorded fragments of black culture: "Under such a slave system as this," they wrote, "the iron enters deep into the soul. Popular songs are the expression of the inner life: and the Negro songs of South Carolina are . . . plaintive, despondent and religious."[13] To extend its reach the panel dispatched two lengthy questionnaires. One, containing forty-two questions on the condition of the contrabands' (as the slaves that escaped to the Union lines were labeled) camps and the performance of black soldiers, they dispatched to army officers and treasury agents. The other survey canvassed clergymen and local surgeons on the free blacks in the North.[14] A Philadelphian, Benjamin P. Hunt, lent Owen his enormous collection of books and foreign reports on all aspects of slavery. Howe collected statistical charts and received substantial assistance from the Boston physician and statistician Edward Jarvis. In its New York City Second Avenue headquarters, the commission received letters from office seekers, businessmen who promoted fantastical schemes to exploit the newly available workforce, and many others who simply wanted to voice an opinion.

The AFIC customarily operated on the fine line between private enterprise and public duty, expert advocacy and political engagement. Its correspondence indicated how novel and peculiar for American public culture was such an official inquiry by "experts." It also exposed minor divisions of opinion and friction among the members of the commission. As early as May it appeared that the panel's work was susceptible to long delays, in part because the three commissioners had overriding obligations. Writing from Norfolk, Virginia, Howe claimed, "The more we see and reflect the more important and difficult our task appears."[15] One unforeseen problem lay with the army's ill treatment of former slaves, which undermined the cause of emancipation and the commission's own proposals. After extensive fieldwork the commission was able to complete by late June 1863 a preliminary report in which it advocated a division of the Confederate seaboard states into three departments, each controlled by a superintendent, and each further divided into smaller units of about five thousand freedmen. Former slaves would work, under supervision, on abandoned plantations in order to prepare themselves for freedom.

After the publication of the first report, the AFIC's funds were running out and the administration's attention seemed to slip away. Howe even suggested working for another three months without pay. The commissioners received an additional grant from Stanton but, nonetheless, by early 1864, a greater tone of desperation was creeping into their letters. They reminded Sumner that the French commission spent three years studying the issue of emancipating a quarter of a million slaves during a time of peace. McKaye, traveling on his own resources, conducted the last field trip of the commission. By then the commissioners felt that they had lost some of Secretary Stanton's support, a dissonance that would become clearer when the commissioners contemplated publishing their findings. To their great chagrin, McKaye and Howe had to publish their supplementary reports on field trips they carried out in Canada and Louisiana, respectively, without federal support. Owen submitted a final report in May 1864.

Estrangement

In view of this immense effort, it is rather surprising how little fresh information was incorporated into the two official reports. Owen wrote a lengthy historical survey of slavery in the western hemisphere that was rich in statistical and discursive data culled from British parliamentary documents and similar sources. The segment on U.S. slavery and its aftermath was, however, rather sparse in comparison. In their respective reports, the commissioners duly emphasized their fieldwork. Howe, for example, inserted an on-the-spot diary entry of a full day's journey to the refugees' communities. But this type of firsthand knowledge only exemplified how contingent was their experience upon the specific routes they took. Rather comically, some of Howe's most revealing anecdotes were recorded in hotel lobbies where he watched a multiracial staff interact. Field interviews yielded abundant details that revealed, for example, the vulnerability of the contrabands to abuse. Yet, in 1863–64 the specific conditions of former slaves were hard to capture and subject to rapid change. The elaborate questionnaires, in particular, produced a clutter of prejudice and confusion, contradictory responses that were practically useless.

For additional evidence on slavery, Owen turned to a foreigner's testimony, the just-published account by the English actress Fanny Kemble on her residence on a Georgia plantation in the late 1830s. The U.S. press deemed Kemble's observations particularly credible due to the author's reliance on her actual daily diary. Moreover, she was a bystander who had arrived in the South incidentally (due to marriage), remaining for a substantial span of time on a sizable (700 slaves) plantation. Kemble enjoyed unique access, especially to the lives of female slaves. A reviewer in the *Atlantic Monthly* remarked that defenders of slavery could not dismiss her account as a collection of haphazardly garnered facts representing the worst of slavery as had been the fate of other famous accounts about slavery, like Frederick Law Olmsted's 1850s travelogues, Theodore Weld's *American Slavery As It Is* (1839), or even Harriet Beecher Stowe's *Uncle Tom's Cabin*. A few southern apologists cleverly rejected the latter as a conceivably true and yet utterly unrepresentative story. "Indeed," the reviewer recalled, "the most cruel and necessary incidents, the hunting with blood-hounds, the branding, the maiming, the roasting, the whipping of pregnant women, could not be kept from knowledge. They blazed into print. But the public, hundreds of miles away, while it sighed and shuddered a little, resolved that such atrocities were exceptional. 'Twas a shocking pity, to be sure! Poor Things! Women, too! Tut, tut!"[16] The coexistence of public thirst for such sensational narratives and public skepticism toward the representational value of those anecdotes concerned the panel. The AFIC toiled hard, with meager results, to break away from the anecdotal mode.

Furthermore, in his final report Owen ignored thirty years or more of abolitionist and proslavery publicity. In this phase of the conflict, perhaps as a corollary of the "birth of a nation," the South was conceived to be in need of complete rediscovery. As the *Philadelphia Dial* declared: "To thousands of people in the North, the interior of the southern states is as much a terra incognita as the interior of unexplored Africa. We are learning, just now, its social features in a rapid rate."[17] A *New York Times* reporter enthused following McKaye's visit to the Sea Islands, "Facts were revealed by the investigation respecting these people—concerning their mode of life, their habits of thought, and the strong under-current of their former unhappy existence—of which I was entirely ignorant."[18] The *Times'* melodramatic report reiterated facts exceedingly familiar to readers of old abolitionist literature.

The condition of war, when society was in incredible flux, hindered investigation. Typically, the commissioners considered it expedient to register all freedmen, including "a description of the person, so as to insure identification, if possible, throughout life . . . It should be stated to each . . . that he must not alter [his name] hereafter . . . He should be made to understand that *aliases* are not permitted among freemen."[19] This proposal betrayed a sense of frustration leading them to conflate freedom with social control. In Canada, Howe found that one feature of racial freedom was to remain outside any systematic observation. It was almost impossible to acquire pertinent statistics because the Canadian government did not recognize the category of color, and official records failed to note racial distinctions except for on prison returns. Howe had to spend long hours perusing town records so he could assess the volume of taxes paid by different racial groups.

The transient quality of the field of inquiry—the impracticality of a fixed, exhaustive overview of slavery's aftermath—prompted the commissioners to focus on discrete case studies whether at home or abroad. One location that suggested itself for such scrutiny was the Sea Islands, of which a few accounts already reached the public. The emancipation of slaves in Jamaica and other corners of the Caribbean offered other possibilities. However, the commission had to sacrifice early plans to visit the West Indies for lack of time and support. Specific choices for comparison had ideological strings attached. For instance, interposing the abolition of Russian serfdom (1861) into the American debate implied that labor relations rather than race were at issue. There were similar features to both national undertakings, such as the reported thirst of freedmen for education and the respective efforts to create intermediary vehicles to train individuals for participation in society (military service and wage work for former slaves in America, new municipal institutions in Russia). In a banquet for Russian naval officers, Mayor Frederick Lincoln Jr. of Boston remarked that America and Russia were both progressive nations embracing the liberal cause of elevating the "great mass of the people." The irony of the United States following in the footsteps of a czarist regime escaped neither abolitionists nor friends of the Confederacy.[20]

Looking sideways to the experience of other nations and continents was common in numerous pamphlets and tracts that circulated during the war and Reconstruction to halt the course of black emancipation. Favorite among these was the attempt to brand the West Indies departure from slavery a failure. Other comparisons included various "mongrel" populations south of the United States or in Asia, in an effort to demonstrate that racial hybridity spelled degradation and lowliness. From either political perspective, the proclivity of Americans to indulge in comparisons with ancient and modern nations was not new. To the contrary, it had been at the core of the U.S. sense of difference founded on a blend of self-confidence and insecurity. Visiting Union and Confederate states at the beginning of the war, the English journalist William Howard Russell remarked, "The nation is like a growing lad who is constantly testing his powers in competition with his elders."[21]

An often alluded-to point of reference, more directed at the dangers of the future, was the caste system in India. Mary Putnam, to give a different example, conjured in her anonymously published, antislavery *Record of an Obscure Man* (1861) an imaginary African hinterland—republics and kingdoms of great sophistication and achievements—remarkably different from the African coast. At the same time, she problematized the very possibility of cross-cultural evaluation, incorporating into her text old travelers' accounts in which England, France, and parts of the United States were depicted as filthy dens of barbarity. Making Africa strangely familiar while estranging Europe and white America demonstrated the power of the comparative effort to alter judgments by shaking established cognitive anchors.[22]

By introducing the unexpected into a routine political debate, comparisons of the kind suggested by Putnam operated as a rhetorical contrivance that could be especially effective in a society accustomed to perceiving itself comparatively by borrowing from the experience, history, and political idioms of other nations. In nineteenth-century literature, estrangement was a strategy to concurrently conjure and critique social reality. A famous example is Charles Dickens's portrayal at the beginning of *Hard Times* of the radically industrialized Coketown as a man-made jungle populated with mechanical elephants and serpent-billowing smokestacks, a jungle that mass-produced subjectivity-deprived, identical human beings. Dickens's depiction was commensurable with his profound doubt about the feasibility (let alone desirability) of straightforward factual accounts of human society. *Hard Times* after all is a frontal attack on the cult of the fact. Taken to the extreme, the novelist warned, the cult of facts would lead to "a board of fact composed of commissioners of fact, who will force the people to be a people of fact, and of nothing but fact."[23] Western explorers' employment of techniques of estrangement (see chapter 3) also betrayed a strong desire to transcend mere description (or mirroring efforts) and with it implied skepticism about the power of inventories of facts to represent the truth of the West.

Historian Carlo Ginzburg (following the formalist Victor Shklovsky) recently called attention to the subversive might of estrangement as a device for dismantling customary forms of perception in, for instance, history writing or the arts. Exposing the strange, unfamiliar features of the ordinary in order to launch a social critique (e.g., Stoics describing sexual intercourse as a repulsive convulsion of muscles) is one model of the estrangement effect. Another form relies on preserving undiluted appearances against the taint and intrusion of superimposed intellectual notions. Marcel Proust's memory of his grandmother presenting objects in the order of their perception rather than according to their causal relations is a fine example. All Proustian prose is thick with estrangement of this sort. In contrast to Ginzburg's view, estrangement can perform diverse political work. It may problematize fixed notions, but, alternatively, it has the capacity of normalizing an idea or a principle of difference by demonstrating its previously undetected relations to what is familiar and safe. (The example of Coketown and other attempts to link industrialized Britain to equatorial Africa is double-edged, concurrently promoting anticapitalism and racialism.)

Statistical representation, which endowed the comparative imagination with a new medium, also possesses an incredible capacity for estrangement. In the early decades of the nineteenth century, it fascinated not just reformers but also enthusiasts who made the accumulation of figures a weekend pastime. Numbers could describe the familiar world in surprising and playful new ways: How many people cross London Bridge every day? How many umbrellas are owned in New York as against Boston? If we position all inhabitants of Philadelphia in a line next to each other, how many times will the line circle the globe?

Statistics can also estrange ordinary phenomena by offering unforeseen sequences not terribly different from those offered by Proust's memorable grandmother. Arranging the world by numbers, by volume, or by size establishes new affinities that transcend causal relations. To give an example from a segment of the commission's final report, Owen puts at three million the number of slaves that died while crossing the Atlantic. He reminds the reader that three million was the population of the thirteen colonies on the eve of the 1776 Revolution. He also computes—rather speculates—that the number of Africans who were taken as slaves was thirty-one million, which happened to be the size of the U.S. population in the mid-1860s. Contingent similarity (or identity) of size thus becomes meaningful by facilitating a new kinship, which Owen then presented to American readers in the language of numbers so they could imagine an affinity with the victims of slavery.[24]

Army Life

Attempts to find secluded settings and populations of African Americans for purposes of laboratorylike study began in the antebellum period. For example, Francis Lieber, an early political scientist, sent circular forms to prison wardens on the obviously questionable assumption that in confinement blacks and whites were subjected to equal treatment and, therefore, could be more accurately compared. (In contrast, southern apologists employed prison statistics to demonstrate the alleged degraded state of blacks in the North.) During the war, the military provided the setting for racial study and comparison. Army commanders recorded racial differences in camp life as well as under the pressure of battle. One general informed the commission that in an emergency, blacks, who had been accustomed to congregate against master or overseer, ran toward each other while white soldiers tended to disperse "each to himself and God for us all."[25]

Writing for the *Atlantic Monthly* on his command of black troops, Col. Thomas W. Higginson remarked that friends and foes subjected his First South

Carolina regiment to "microscopic scrutiny." The officers were surprised at how the smallest incidents in camp would come back to them "magnified and distorted" through letters of inquiry from all parts of the country. It was quite clear that the faintest sign of a coming breakdown—mutiny, mass desertion, riot—would bring an end to their experiment. Higginson's magazine articles were suffused with estrangement trickery, for the reformer-turned-officer was a keen social investigator. As he testified, "I was colonel by day and an observer of Negro life by night."[26] In the manner of Shakespeare's Henry V (or Higginson's contemporary, the British statesman and voyeur William Gladstone), he walked around camp incognito not only to check the sentinels but also to study his troops. Higginson acknowledged a barrier to whites' ability to know blacks, a mask that needed to be cunningly removed. He admired his soldiers' courage and discipline but condescendingly found them innocent, intuitive, and primitive. "A simple and lovable people, whose graces seem to come by nature, and whose vices by training."[27] Surrounded by former slaves in the unfamiliar nature of the South, he was perpetually transported elsewhere, to the Middle East, the Pacific Islands, and other exotic localities. "In all pleasant weather the outer 'fly' is open, and men pass and repass, a chattering throng. I think of Emerson's Saadi, 'as thou sittest at the door, on the desert's yellow floor,'—for these bare sand-plains, gray above, are always yellow when upturned, and there seems a tinge of Orientalism in all our life."[28]

Black music allowed peering "inside," into the soldiers' souls. They could endure everything, he noted, by the "other world trust," which was the spirit of their songs. They were excited when being watched singing and yet might sing the same song repeatedly in all circumstances and places. "Their philosophising is often the highest form of mysticism; and our dear surgeon declares that they are all natural transcendentalists."[29] They were evangelizing their own chaplain, he noted sardonically. Crossing the boundaries between white and black acquired an erotic flavor when he admitted to enjoying watching his soldiers bathing. To his "gymnasium-trained" eyes, their physiques appeared magnificent. "Such splendid muscular development, set off by that smooth coating of adipose tissue which makes them, like the South-Sea Islanders, appear even more muscular than they are."[30]

The remarkable power of single anecdotes to generate evidence on an entire race is also apparent in Edward Pierce's commentary on the circumstances in the Sea Islands. He reported that soldiers in Colonel Higginson's regiment gave him seven hundred dollars out of their salaries to send to their wives—ostensibly a propitious sign of strong family commitment. Black soldiers appeared capable of engaging in civic duties because early in the northern occupation of Hilton Head, they initiated a collection to pay for candles for their evening meetings. They reportedly felt that they should not expect the government to supply them. An object of careful watching, a whole case study to himself, was Harry, whom Pierce referred to as "my faithful guide and attendant." Harry (most likely, Harry McMillan who was also interviewed at length by the AFIC) was an entrepreneur in the making; a model for black resourcefulness. With his own money and a loan, Harry purchased a small farm of 313 acres at a tax sale (a sale of land confiscated by the federal government, which was often purchased by blacks). "The instinct for land," Pierce summarizes, "is one of the most conservative elements of our nature; and a people who have it in any fair degree will never be nomads or vagabonds."[31]

Case Studies

Curiously, the commission's choices for case studies followed the plot of Harriet Beecher Stowe's famous novel *Uncle Tom's Cabin*. Perhaps inadvertent, it was still symbolically potent because the novel had done more than any other text to mold American culture's conception of the geography and iconography of slavery. Howe followed the mulatto George Harris to a community of runaway slaves in modern Ontario, and Colonel McKaye went after Uncle Tom himself down to Louisiana. McKaye argued that the valley of the lower Mississippi was the most useful site for observation, for, unlike in any other Confederate region, former masters and slaves stayed put throughout the war. He titled his report "The Mastership and its Fruits: The Emancipated Slave Face to Face with His Old Master." This mutual glance enabled McKaye to retell the horrors of slavery while warning that, if given a chance, the master would regain hold of his bondsmen. In a somber letter to Sumner, McKaye was more explicit: "Nothing is more preposterous than to suppose that the hideous spirit of slavery is dead in the rebel states . . . Give it the opportunity and under another name and form it will take good care to perpetuate its power."[32]

The singularity of Louisiana only enhanced its appeal as a field of study. The free black population was well educated, intelligent, and orderly. Its presence and the bands of runaway slaves that roamed the treacherous Mississippi swamps altered the character of slavery in the region. These circumstances, he maintained, encouraged slaves to contemplate freedom and their masters to resort to the rod. The commission's final report made much of Louisiana tax returns, which revealed free blacks to have had more property, on average, than citizens in the

North, regardless of color. Black property ownership lent support to the contention borrowed from the ideology of the American Revolution, "It would be . . . a thing . . . repugnant to our system of government that four and a half million of the governed . . . should remain permanently taxed and not represented."[33] As for the incredible stories about swamp-dwelling fugitives (one Mississippi maroon was reported to have lived on top of a large cypress for three years), their unique experience demonstrated their resourcefulness and supported a prevalent notion that blacks possessed unique knowledge, unavailable to whites, of the southern terrain. This expertise supposedly made them particularly suitable to serve as spies and pathfinders for the Union.

Louisiana thus provided multiple opportunities for the exercise of the comparative imagination along lines of class and race. There were masters and slaves but also a prosperous free black community and a deprived, uneducated group of whites. McKaye was all too happy to label them "white trash." Their backwardness undermined notions of racial superiority and could deflect attention from the racial element of Reconstruction, since whites too were victims of slavery. He could argue that his most radical plan, dismantling Louisiana's feudal system by dividing huge plantations, would benefit both racial groups. The difference between poor whites and former slaves was most evident in their opposing attitudes toward education. By the testimony of military officers, the emancipated blacks were hungry for instruction, while low-class whites were universally indifferent to self-improvement. The ethnic fabric of whites in Louisiana, a region marked by traces of a foreign culture and foreign blood, enabled McKaye to establish the French aristocracy of the *ancien regime* as the historical counterpart to the local master class. (The report's allusion to "fruits" in its title, and the juxtaposition of slaves and masters also implied biological relations.)

Owen too employed the device of bashing "white trash." In an essay for the *New York Times*, he questioned whether poor whites could handle political power any better than blacks. Owen told an anecdote involving an ignorant and lazy white man he had met in Nashville. "Is it in favor of such insolent swaggers that we are to disfranchise the humble, quiet, hard-working Negro,"[34] he asked. Such scorn toward impoverished southern whites echoed the northern bias against Irish immigrants. The presence of a white "third man" in either region helped Owen and his colleagues to suggest a social geometry that mitigated the binary opposition between blacks and whites in favor of a more nuanced socioracial system in which whites and blacks as well as another race—the mulattoes—occupied differing positions. Howe even implied that skin color was sometimes dictated by one's position on the social ladder. "If you ring your bell," he recalled of his hotel experience in Canada, "the nimble mulatto . . . does not soil his dainty fingers by bringing the coal which you ask for, but sends a stalwart fireman, a traditionary white man, but so black and begrimed by coal, that in the South he might need free papers to prove his lineage." In Canada (as in Boston), Irish immigrants were constantly compared to runaway slaves. Colonel Stephenson of St. Catherine's told Howe that blacks acquired furniture while the Irish would not. The Irish beg for money; blacks rely on themselves. Some of the anti-Irish prejudice actually originated with his black informants. Mrs. Brown, a "colored" woman told him that, "They live like pigs, and worse than pigs. The colored people can't live, like the Irish, on potatoes and salt."[35]

Howe attributed to his case study great demonstrative value. The black community in Canada-West (modern Ontario) represented the social mixture (in terms of their relation to slavery) and the racial composition of blacks in America. In other words, it consisted of former slaves, children of slaves, and the descendants of freemen, but also, he wrote, "They are in about the same proportion of pure Africans, half-breeds, quarter-breeds, octoroons, and of others in whom the dark shade grows fainter and fainter, until it lingers in the finger nails alone."[36] Howe rejected the notion that the prosperous fugitives were an elite among slaves. They earned a living, respected women, sent their children to school, and improved in manners and morals not because they were "picked men," he posited, but because they were free men. Their remoteness from the regions and the experience of slavery, he believed, also offered some guarantee for the truthfulness of the evidence they provided. Their success was particularly useful in his attack of the philanthropic ideal of guided freedom, either through apprenticeship or through schemes of colonization. The runaway community in Canada compared favorably with the Liberian experiment. In Canada, the exiles arrived penniless and without aid to a cold and not entirely sympathetic place; as for Liberia, great expense was involved in sending people across the ocean to a hospitable climate and in supporting them for six months or more. Yet, the immigrants in Canada did stupendously well and those in Africa virtually failed under the protective shield of white benevolence.

It was a historicist conception of society that Howe and his colleagues adopted (a position rooted in a long abolitionist tradition). The slave and the master were predominantly products of time-specific power relations. While accepting many preconceived notions about the freedmen's alleged vices, the official report construed these behavior patterns as a result of slavery rather than of an inherently lacking moral sense. This principle figured prominently in press accounts of the preliminary report. The *New York Herald*, for example, highlighted the panel's point that slaves, having no property of their own, could not be expected to respect others' property. Needing to shield themselves from masters' despotism, they lied to avoid punishment. Unable to form marital relations by law, they were sexually "incontinent." Based on the opinion of "intelligent superintendents," the AFIC determined that these deficiencies could be easily eradicated by an appeal to the slaves' "self-respect" and by acknowledging their new rights. A similar argument was leveled in the *Final Report* against Tocqueville's view that the republic was trapped in a racial vicious circle: whites would not abandon their prejudice as long as blacks could not improve their lot, but as long as whites held these opinions blacks could not advance. The commission responded: "The whites have changed, and are still rapidly changing, their opinion of the Negro. And the Negro, in his new condition as freedman, is himself, to some extent, a changed being."[37]

Despite this hopefulness, the commissioners could witness from their New York offices the violence of the July 1863 draft riots. Howe's account also had a pessimistic streak. Equal rights in Canada did not eliminate bigotry. Whites there were as hateful as their neighbors south of the border, maybe more so. He remarked pointedly, "As long as the colored people form a very small proportion of the population, and are dependent, they receive protection and favors; but when they increase, and compete with the laboring class for a living, and especially when they begin to aspire to social equality, they cease to be 'interesting Negroes' and become 'niggers.'"[38] Howe became somewhat suspicious when his white interlocutors kept boasting that Canadian law provided equal protection and that public offices were as open to refugees as to others. The reiteration of these statements only demonstrated that a simple principle of justice was not taken for granted. One form of prejudice was keeping blacks off juries. Another was the segregation of schools, occasionally encouraged by the immigrants themselves. Prophetically, Howe predicted that schools would be the site of struggle over the caste system in the United States.

Seeking to address the gap between constitutional equality as a guarantee of American freedom and a civil society where prejudice runs rampant, Howe turned to racial theory. While blacks were evidently a strong and vital race, observed Howe, the mulattoes were merely a breed: morally solid but physically weak, prone to a host of ailments, somewhat emasculated, and infertile. "Breeds are produced, modified, and may be made to disappear, by social agencies . . . Different kinds of colored men are demanded and the supply meets the demand. Slender, light-built quadroons, or octoroons are wanted for domestic purposes; dark and heavier men for the field. Black women are wanted for their strength and fruitfulness; yellow ones for their beauty and comparative barrenness."[39] Under slavery, production and reproduction intersected. In the plantation, commercial interests disturbed natural laws and violated domesticity. (He also maintained that a disproportionate male to female ratio, as among the runaway slaves, encouraged amalgamation.)

Nevertheless, Howe speculated that in the social body, much as in the human body, there is a "recuperative principle" that "brings men back to the normal condition of the race." Under freedom, members of the same race would obey their "natural affinity," which tends to purify the "national blood," and marry among themselves. Under freedom and obeying the laws of nature, the refugees in Canada and the blacks in the northern United States would follow their inherent preferences to migrate below certain "thermal lines" back to the South. The mulatto would eventually disappear, predicted Howe, unwittingly echoing a similar projection (or expectation) about another race on the continent—the allegorical "vanishing Indian." The report's highly flawed statistical table purported to show that while in the South mortality rates were uniform across the racial divide, in the North, blacks had lower life expectancy than whites. By pointing to the mulatto's supposedly weak constitution, the official report explained the unthinkable: in freedom the African race had fared worse than in the slave states.[40] Howe used his brand of racism to fend off fears about future floods of cheap labor from the South as well as northern anxieties about miscegenation. He was, therefore, using one prejudice to overcome another. An 1863 pamphlet urging the Republican Party to embrace the cause of racial amalgamation introduced the term *miscegenation* to public discourse. The publication turned out to be a hoax perpetrated by two proslavery journalists.

Can They be Citizens?

Howe's theories informed the commission's vision of future racial harmony, a vision that historian George Fredrickson has labeled "the most authoritative and complete presentation" of what he termed "romantic racialism."[41] The panel maintained that while sexual intercourse would be naturally inhibited, social intercourse should abound. In fact, blacks should be encouraged not to congregate in separate communities but to intermingle with whites. Howe maintained that the proportion of blacks among whites should not exceed 5 to 7 percent if antagonism was to be avoided. This would "weaken the feeling which regards them as a separate and alien race."[42] Racial hostility would diminish without state intervention. Social amalgamation would give birth not to a new breed but to an improved national character combining the masculine and feminine traits of the two races.

Always the equivocator, Howe provided two explanations—one racial, the other social—for many of the traits he identified among the refugees. To combat the prejudice that former slaves shied away from hard work, he introduced examples of blacks' impressive commercial success. He conceded that, as he had personally observed, Irish immigrants ordinarily performed heavy menial work. He therefore proposed that the former slaves learned the way of the world and preferred to avoid hard labor as most people would. Alternatively, the mulatto's frail "physical organization" and lack of "animal vigor" rendered him less capable of menial work. In a like manner, Howe explained blacks' alleged propensity for "cheerfulness" as a disposition for infantile mirth, which was either the product of cultural modification initiated by the master class, which preferred slaves to live in some protracted state of childhood, or a property of the black mind rooted in physical constitution. He nevertheless noted that in Canada the race appeared to have a more sober apparition; blacks also looked older to him.[43]

Howe conceived of ingenious ways to measure racial differences—most notably to distinguish "pure" blacks and mulattoes, a distinction that had preoccupied his thinking since the summer of 1863. He tried to inquire with insurance companies in New York whether they insured slaves, assuming they might have maintained a rate scale for different racial types or at least kept records of mortality and death risks that would substantiate his speculations.[44] He corresponded over the fate of emancipated slaves in Indian tribes affiliated with the Confederacy—another opportunity for appraising and refining racial hierarchy. Howe appropriated many of his racial views from the Harvard naturalist Louis Agassiz, who warned against amalgamation, deeming it immoral and a recipe for national degeneration. Agassiz supported emancipation but opined that once the moral taint of slavery was removed, science (represented by the physiologist and the ethnographer) would enjoy free rein in determining policy towards blacks. Freedmen should be assured legal equality, but social and especially political equality would be checked.

Howe demurred. With an almost indignant tone, he responded to Agassiz that the manifest rights of blacks included "entire freedom, equal rights and privileges, and open competition for social distinctions" regardless of the consequences, "though heavens fall."[45] There was a pervasive tension throughout Howe's work between reverence for scientific theories and his convictions that there was only one just solution for the freedmen question. In a private letter written while on tour in Canada, he spoke somewhat dismissively of his mission to study the capacity of blacks. "You know, our people demand proofs that two and two make four in Africa as well as in Europe."[46]

Commissioners raised pragmatic justifications for granting full citizenship to former slaves. A point that Owen (and other observers) repeatedly hammered was that the enfranchisement of African Americans would ensure forever the defeat of the Confederacy and the loyalty of the reconstructed South. Only a third of the white population of the South was unreservedly loyal. This argument was increasingly dominant in the late 1860s when renewed southern participation in the electoral body threatened to jeopardize political causes dear to the citizens of the North, such as the payment of the war-incurred national debt. Black franchise became even more expedient in view of lingering anti-Union sentiments in the South. The AFIC also found itself in agreement with Tocqueville, who had predicted a rebellion if the slaves were emancipated but not granted full equality. "We cannot expect, in a democratic republic, to maintain domestic tranquility, if we deprive millions of their civil rights."[47]

Most characteristically, the commission sought positive signs that former slaves could indeed be upright members of society and the polity. The freedmen satisfied the test of modern, middle-class subjectivity by their inclination to marry and engage in domesticity as well as by their desire for education. The AFIC's reports attested to former slaves' marketplace ability. In St. Louis during the worst years of the war, only 2 out of 10,000 residents who applied for public assistance were black, and both were severely debilitated. Other exemplary cases of black self-reliance were of two Louisville, Kentucky, women who supported their master by renting out their labor. Their stories of grappling simultaneously with slavery and capitalism were particularly moving. However, despite the strong demand to examine the former slaves' market compatibility, the commissioners harbored certain suspicions toward the market. Owen and McKaye in particular inserted into their reports enthusiastic passages for the rights of workers. McKaye wrote, "It is the producing class . . . that under every form of civil government is most in danger of being made the victim of the leisure, capital, and opportunities of the non-producing class."[48] The commission demanded to abolish the practice of supplying freedmen working for government with goods instead of paying their wages in full. The slaves' earning capacity was understood to be primarily a mark of personal autonomy complemented by a rich civic culture, manifested, for instance, in church organizations. Bonding citizenship with independence and community resonated better with old republican ideals than with an outright celebration of market forces.

In contrast, for Edward Pierce in the Sea Islands the marketplace assured "harmony of interests among people of diverse origins and condition."[49] Unexpectedly, Pierce regarded consumerism and some degree of luxury to be an indication of masculinity. Consumption would guarantee the freedmen's dedication to labor once "four million people would become purchasers." The instincts and motives that were the economy's engine—love of life, desire to be well clad and nourished, and attachment to family—would overcome residual reluctance to work. The market could also ameliorate bigotry. "Your Irishman, who now works as a daylaborer, honestly thinks that he hates the Negro; but when the war is over, he will have no objection to going South and selling him groceries and houseful implements at fifty per cent advance on New York prices, or to hiring him to raise cotton for twenty-five or fifty cent a day. Our prejudices, under any reasonable adjustment of the social system, readily accommodate themselves to our interests, even without much aid from the moral sentiments."[50] This prediction was another testament to the widespread wish that "natural" forces instead of prolonged intervention would settle the freedmen question.

One of the strongest arguments in favor of full citizenship pointed to a conception of manhood outside the marketplace—the masculinity of the black soldier. Rather than justifying citizenship in terms of deservedness—always the moral asset of the weak—the AFIC would have the black soldiers virtually seize it, as though by partaking in the Union's military effort they simulated a grand slave revolt. "The history of the world furnishes no example of an enslaved race which won its freedom without exertion of its own," declared the commission, "and in such warfare it is fitting that the African race seeks its own social salvation."[51] Military service, the report quoted Higginson as saying, was the greatest school for freedom. The panel supported organizing and drilling military laborers into pseudo brigades with uniforms and badges around their hats labeled United States Service. "It tends to inspire with self-reliance, and it affords them protection." They noted, entirely oblivious to the irony, that the law in the form of military rule assumed for the black man the authority of his erstwhile master, but "he submits to it cheerfully and without sense of degradation."[52]

Owen maintained that there were no arguments against enfranchising African Americans that could not be made against the principle of universal suffrage itself. If Mary Putnam and Higginson suggested that because of a well-shielded cultural interiority there were limitations to whites' ability to know the slaves, Owen argued that the slave's tendency to hide his true opinion would be his protection against political manipulation. "Slavery had rendered him wary and suspicious. The habit of the slave is, while assenting to whatever his master says, secretly to hold to his own opinion . . . I do not think the freedmen will be found a ready tool for the political demagogue."[53] Supporting evidence could be found in the commission's record. Asked whether masters knew everything there was to know about their slaves, Robert Smalls replied "No, sir; one life they show their masters and another life they don't show."[54] The notion that the impenetrable space of black culture and black selves guaranteed their independence in the political arena typified the problematic at the foundation of the commission's research: a certain failure in the ultimate effort to study and, therefore, to unmask the black man was necessary to demonstrate his ability to be an equal member in the polity.

Other observers, too, reevaluated the former slaves' supposed deficiencies to be assets in the polity. If freedmen where deemed too inexperienced and uneducated for the vote, E. P. Whipple wrote, "We live in an era, in a strange condition in which it is the instincts of the ignorant that guaranty a republican government in the South rather than the intelligence of the educated classes."[55] While proslavery demagoguery could manipulate the uneducated Irish Catholic, he would never support the bigoted Know-Nothings since their animosity targeted him. Similarly, the black man could fall for abolition but would never support his former master when he attempted to deprive him of his rights. The master was most likely to control the votes of poor whites. Whipple continued that the U.S. system was invested in the idea that voting was the best way to qualify a man to vote. The franchise was at the foundation of all other social benefits, including education. Lastly, Owen's support for bestowing full citizenship on the freedmen had, in a way, the same rationale that led him to write the exclusionary clause against blacks in Indiana in the 1840s. Back then, Owen had proposed a referendum on enfranchising blacks in the state, but once the proposal failed he sided with exclusion. Since they could not be full citizens and the bias against them was endemic, it would be in blacks' best interest not to be there, he reasoned. Blacks and whites could live together if, and only if, political equality was maintained.

Publication

In June 1863, when the commission concluded its first report, it sought the attention of decision makers in Washington. Owen wrote to Sumner that he and his colleagues regarded it "to be of vital importance" that they would present the report to Stanton in person and read it aloud. They requested to schedule the presentation, which they assumed would take two hours, when the secretary would have time to reflect on the issues. (In previous centuries, especially in the preprint era, reading aloud to a ruler from a work dedicated to him signified or performed the text's "publication."[56]) Beyond persuading Washington officials, the commissioners were keen on circulating a printed version of the report for general consumption, and some of the commission's friends outside the administration were as eager to read it. Francis W. Bird reminded Sumner that other, less extensive studies on the condition of the freedmen had disappeared forever in the Department of War's files without ever being read by Stanton.[57] But the full circulation of the commission's report had to wait for the completion of its entire mission in the early summer of the following year.

On the Senate floor, Sumner enthusiastically supported the proposed publication of three thousand copies. "I have no hesitation in saying that it is one of the most able contributions to this question that has ever appeared in our country, or in any other country."[58] The ensuing debate assumed the form (or the façade) of a heated discussion on the role of government in procuring information through such unprecedented inquiry. Several Democrats challenged the commission's status as an official body and even its legality. Senator Edgar Cowan (Pennsylvania) associated the publication with wasteful endeavors that were perhaps tolerable in peacetime but not when the country was at war.

> [Cowan questioned] under what law these commissioners were appointed, and by what authority they have gone to all this pains to make this elaborate report, and whether, if it be such a valuable report as is here supposed, it cannot be put before the country in some other way than by the expenditure of the public money. In this age of publication, when every table in every house is loaded with information of all kinds and on all subjects, when the whole country is flooded with newspapers desirous and anxious to obtain that particular species of information which would interest the people, I should think there was machinery enough in existence which would gratuitously give to the people all they desire to know on this subject.[59]

Senator Hendricks, a Democrat from Indiana, defined the report as "facts and arguments [that] a certain set of gentlemen, irresponsible so far as the law is concerned, have seen fit to present in some communication which they have made to the War Department." The AFIC should pursue the channels of private enterprise to publish its report.[60] California senator John Conness remarked wryly that it was unfortunate that there was no document pertaining to the "poor, miserable Negro" that congressmen would not attack as either illegal or unconstitutional. The president had the right to investigate the administration of public affairs under his jurisdiction. "He speaks through the commission that he has appointed."[61] Ultimately, eight senators voted against the publication of the report, but twenty-four approved. Implying there were hidden motives behind the attacks on the report, Senator Benjamin Wade testified that if he were a friend of slavery, he would make every possible effort to suppress its publication. "I know of no document in the English language that sets forth the deformities of that institution in practice more vividly than does this document."[62]

Slavery Again: Counter Exceptionalism

The *Final Report* (which Owen later reproduced in book form, titled *Wrong of Slavery*) was crafted with the verve and poignancy of a political pamphlet. When the commission submitted its report, the presidential elections were looming. Thus, in the middle section , Owen inserted a passionate defense of the constitutionality of the Emancipation Proclamation. It is in the first section, however, that Owen showed his prowess as a writer, providing a comprehensive historical survey of slavery in the western hemisphere which features an argument that develops shrewdly and in unexpected ways. Owen decided to abandon anecdotal literary constructions, which had been the mainstay of antislavery propaganda, in favor of statistical analysis, which, he claimed, provided "a force of evidence against which sophistry strives in vain,—which compels conviction, except when the mind is closed against all proof by the hermetic influence of the prejudice."[63]

By offering statistical reasoning, Owen chose the weapon of his political foes. Before the war, statistical analysis was predominantly a proslavery tool deployed to refute the abolitionist depiction of the South by, for instance, comparing the physical condition of slaves favorably with that of poor laborers in the North or in Britain. (The southern journalist J. D. B. De Bow was a pioneer of statistics-based social research.) However, despite his professed preference, Owen's text relinquished neither the power of the inciting narrative nor the anecdotal stirring personal observations of slaves and bystanders. He interposed his statistical evidence—mostly on the enormous death toll that befell slaves—with two primary stories or histories. First, he wrote a grand narrative of slavery in the western hemisphere, beginning only a few years after Columbus's landing, and second, he described the slaves' journey from the moment of their capture in the African hinterland through their voyage across the Atlantic. His account positions U.S. slavery in a global political economy founded on the systematic abuse of labor. Calculating the death toll of slavery on the basis of scant information often required obscure sources, acrobatic adjustments, and heavy speculations (all of which are detailed in Owen's book). Nevertheless, he argued that three centuries of slavery victimized 31 million Africans, half of whom were transported over the ocean. The rest were fatally wounded in battle, deliberately slaughtered, or abandoned as unfit merchandise. Another three million died and were thrown overboard. Suffering extended beyond the slaves, a point he demonstrated by computing the high death rate of sailors exposed to epidemics and the unsanitary nightmare aboard slave ships. Mortality calculations had an immediate resonance during the bloodiest of American wars, and Owen exploited this war-brewed sensibility. Even if the slave merchants prettified their mortality records, he explained, these were still staggering figures when one considered that a battle is regarded to be particularly bloody when 10 percent of the combatants were killed or wounded. The loss at Gettysburg did not reach such a high rate.

But what happened to those who arrived in the New World? Owen turned his arithmetic from mortality to population growth, and after additional calculations arrived at the conclusion that in 1860 there were a mere 11,562,540 descendants of slaves in the western hemisphere—a number that showed a population decline in continents that knew little of war, famine, or plagues. Slavery "produced a retrogression of numbers at a ratio which, had it spread over the habitable earth, would have extinguished, in a few centuries, all human existence."[64] However, that was not the case in the United States. Only a half-million slaves had reached the country's shores, but by 1860 their descendants numbered 4,435,709. One group increased ninefold; the other diminished by a half of its original size. Owen cunningly led the reader toward the proslavery (and exceptionalist) argument that southern masters created a uniquely nurturing environment for their slaves, with the ultimate intention of undermining that very premise. In order to establish a connection between a population increase and comfort of life, one had to look into the "interior of slave-life"—the motives and circumstances of the population increase. Fanny Kemble's journal provided these insights and some of the details for Owen and Howe's contention that the plantations functioned as breeding farms. Masters encouraged procreation through intricate incentives and cruel intimidation. (Besides, nations suffering great calamity, like Ireland during the famine, experienced population growth as well.)

Here, Owen's approach to vital statistics is congruous with his pioneering advocacy of birth control. In *Moral Physiology* (1830), Owen promoted a rational limitation on procreation (by means of coitus interruptus) as a way to assure personal, familial, and social welfare. He was among the first to argue that the liberation of women relied on a smaller family. His historical survey addressed the excessive childbearing coupled with hard work that contributed to female slaves' ill health and great suffering. Ultimately, the failure of the American slave system found its utmost expression in the war itself. The rebellion shattered the illusion of success—population growth for slaves, political control for their masters. Owen completes the circle by demonstrating that in the United States, slavery ultimately produced an enormous mortality rate. Stating that the half million war fatalities were also victims of slavery, he suggested another affinity between slaves and the white Union soldiers who were dying in the battlefields and army hospitals as Owen was composing his treatise. By so formulating the story of slavery, Owen engaged in the ultimate act of triumph—the victor writes the history (in this case, the prehistory) of the vanquished.

Psychic Phenomena

The periodical and daily press excerpted and reviewed the five reports that Owen, Howe, and McKaye composed. The abolitionist camp was mostly enthusiastic. Lewis Tappan and Wendell Phillips wrote Owen letters commending his efforts. The commission's reports were read on the other side of the Atlantic as well. J. M. Ludlow, writing in *Good Words,* viewed the preliminary report as a pioneering step in the creation of a new apparatus of knowledge on slavery: "Where formerly [slavery] could only be outlined or lightly sketched from a few points of view, it may now be photographed in its minutest features, and from every point."[65] However, Owen's past political activities, especially his radical youth, provided ammunition for those who wanted to taint the commission's proposals as manifestations of subversive utopianism. A review in the *New York Herald* argued that the attempt to organize the blacks in "departments of labor" under the freedmen's association was "an imitation of the Fourierite phalanxes, whose fate is so well known to all our readers."[66] Was the AFIC an indication of a radical "Owenite" moment in federal affairs? According to a postwar rumor, had it not been for John Wilkes Booth's intervention, Lincoln would have probably appointed Owen to head the Freedmen's Bureau. It would have been interesting to see at the helm of the freedmen administration the person who in the late 1820s advocated "state guardianship," which would have placed two-year-olds in special boarding schools. But by the 1860s, Owen's radicalism—always tempered by a strong strand of authoritarianism, Benthamite planism, and condescension toward the downtrodden—was further diluted by years of involvement in Democratic party politics, increasing aloofness toward working-class issues, and an intensifying religiosity that stood in stark opposition to his freethinking youth.

Perhaps the most curious intellectual legacy Owen brought with him to the AFIC was his newly found interest in spiritualism. While Owen's Civil War pamphlets were circulating, a few of his spiritualist articles (prepared before the war) appeared with exotic titles such as "The Convulsionists of St. Médard," "The Electric Girl of La Perrière," and "Why the Putkammer Castle was Destroyed." His *Footfalls on the Boundary of Another World* (1860) did much to legitimize the immensely popular spiritualist movement. It was the first book on spiritualism accepted by a respectable publisher, Lippincott, the same Philadelphia firm that would later publish the *Wrong of Slavery*. (In the 1850s it was also responsible for the execution of Schoolcraft's project on the American Indian tribes.) Since 1848, spiritualism had swept the country, embraced by radicals of all stripes, including abolitionists and feminists. Owen was not part of this particular radical movement. He conceived his 1860 book to be a Baconian enterprise, setting himself "to collect together solid, reliable building-stones which may serve some future architect."[67] Both *Footfall* and *Wrong of Slavery* were expressions of a belief in facts (especially historical facts) and the merit of their aggregation.

Spiritualists regarded former slaves as prospective mediums and recognized an affinity between the freedmen's religious beliefs and theirs. Owen's own appreciation of black religious enthusiasm did not escape critics' ire but was a marginal issue in his report. More importantly, researching psychic phenomena may have prepared him to address what had become a dominant theme in 1860s freedmen studies—black mentality and other dimensions of the black psyche. Owen's interest in sleep and dreams and Howe's expertise in idiocy, lunacy, and deafness configured, to some degree, their respective journeys into the South, Canada, and black subjectivity. This aspect of investigation became paramount because of the peculiar problems of knowledge that haunted the freedmen's question. Four million men and women emerged from a collapsed society, as it was forcefully argued, profoundly damaged and with an alleged propensity to lie, cheat, steal, and replace sexual partners. Arguments about their capabilities and potential had to enter into a realm of motivation that preceded moral faculties.

Contemporary writers commented incessantly on the need to improve blacks' self-respect. This thrust was arguably a precursor of today's self-esteem movement. The AFIC's recommendations contain the notion of a role model manifested in its proposal to appoint in black regiments commanders with whom the soldiers could identify. Howe claimed to discern strong imitative faculties among freed slaves. There was much talk about instincts and desires in freedmen's lives. Black melancholy and soulfulness were often alluded to as well. The commission

proposed that military officers would exploit the freedmen's powerful religiosity
to instill in them devotion to the cause of their fight. Insight into their alleged
mental predilections was therefore a useful tool (replacing the master's rod) to
modify black people's behavior during the transition from slavery.

Another angle to the exploration of the black mind was tied to ideas of interiority or selfhood and worked in the opposite way. It demonstrated that black
subjectivity—regardless of content—was whole (or autonomous) and would
guarantee for the newly freed their survival in a free society. Here, the notion of
an enclosed, at times impenetrable, self paralleled the demand that blacks would
construct private spheres for themselves by establishing fixed sexual relations
and by creating physical spaces that would nurture family life. It was repeatedly
alleged that southern whites—rich and poor—failed to facilitate and protect the
private sphere. The imprint of a psychological approach was also evident in the
discussion about the opinions and prejudices of whites. Some came to understand
that racial bias would not succumb to reason, and therefore parading facts before
the reading public in the tradition of the Enlightenment would not do. Howe
thought that public policy should assume bias as a given. Prejudice was an in-
escapable effect of national and ethnic differences, a protective discourse akin to
gossip. "Peoples have their way of gossiping, just as individuals have; and a favorite one is that of criticizing their neighbors, and talking national scandal."[68]

The war environment was not conducive to a grand, slow-moving investigative enterprise of the kind that Owen, Howe, and McKaye had initially devised,
although many of their ideas would be incorporated into the Freedmen's Bureau
or implemented at a later stage when radical Republicans seized Reconstruction
from President Johnson. Their difficulties were not rooted in a lack of information. Rather, their project represented a single attempt to bring a modicum of order to an avalanche of facts and figures. Its reports ultimately revealed a deeper
wish in the midst of war to grapple with the country's shaken sense of itself, its
social and political regime, its past transgressions and present crisis. Owen, Howe,
and McKaye authored a remarkably progressive program in contemporary terms,
but mostly they wanted to normalize the freedmen's question and remove its disruptive edges. The commission insisted, for instance, that the contraband crisis
was one of numerous social evils that were inevitable consequences of war.

The desire to master a rapidly changing world may explain why Howe and
his colleagues appropriated and refined rather familiar racial theories that were
arguably incidental to the commission's actual recommendations. The AFIC provided one of the most comprehensive attacks on slavery as a global system of la-

bor abuse, but its relapse into racial reasoning betrayed the commissioners' doubts about the capacity of their critique of labor exploitation to address the issue of caste in the United States. Ultimately, the predominance of racial doctrine, especially in Howe's account, accentuated the ambiguity of social knowledge as an instrument for defining a group of people concurrently as others and as potential equals. At one point, it led to the absurd conclusion that African Americans' (or at least mulattoes') social inclusion was somehow conditioned on their eventual disappearance.

As for the question of U.S. citizenship, the commission (and other freedmen's advocates) offered diverse views and demonstrations of blacks' political subjectivity. At times, it was conceived entirely through notions of market competency (individualism, self-sufficiency, and domesticity); in other contexts it was grafted on the masculine agency of the soldier. In addition, the freedmen's prospective ability to partake in the polity was on occasion associated—paradoxically—not so much with individual autonomy as with black collectivity and the experience of slavery itself. Another important dimension of the commissioners' conceptual apparatus was the way it vacillated between idioms of labor and race. Class and racial categories competed, at other times served to enhance each other, and otherwise were consistently gendered. Abolitionists had often pointed to the sexual exploitation of the plantation. The commission understood this exploitation in terms of labor. At the same time, the productive/reproductive slippage was employed to uphold a false continuum between the sexual/procreative abuse of black women on southern plantations and racial amalgamation in a future free society. Thus the sins of the plantation were projected onto the prospects of the free.

Beyond the AFIC's work and similar efforts, the demand for the franchise originated with the black leadership and the freedmen themselves, who, in numerous gatherings and conventions, forcefully expressed their wish to become voting citizens. John P. Sampson argued in a North Carolina meeting that voting was a right, not merely a privilege, and without it "liberty is mockery." Depriving blacks of suffrage, "you affirm our incapacity to form an intelligent judgment . . . and . . . lead us to undervalue ourselves."[69] A national convention of black soldiers and sailors, to give another example, declared that "in sustaining the Union with the musket, [we] have won [our] right to the ballot." The veterans emphasized that they preferred the vote to any form of government assistance. Only the franchise would "lift us from the lap of hate and scorn" and "place us on the footing of full citizenship, where we ought to be."[70]

PART III

TOTEM ENVY

In August 1845, the ethnographer Henry Rowe Schoolcraft was invited by a young lawyer, Lewis Henry Morgan, to address a gathering of the New Order of the Iroquois, a fraternal organization of young white men convened for their annual meeting in Aurora, New York. By the light of the campfire, Schoolcraft declared, "No people can bear a true nationality, which does not exfoliate, as it were, from its bosom, something that expresses the peculiarities of its own soil and climate . . . And where," he insisted, "can a more suitable element . . . be found, than is furnished by the history and institutions of the free, bold, wild, independent native hunter race?"[1] Besides listening to literary expositions, Morgan and his friends in the New Order of the Iroquois dedicated much of their time together to Indian pageantry. These precursors of the modern men's movement painted their faces, wore native costumes, called each other by Iroquois names, and lit the "council's fire." Their most important initiation rite, duly labeled "Indianiation," was the Iroquois ceremony of adopting captive warriors. Much attention and care were given to structuring the fraternal society according to the organization of the original Iroquois League, whose remnants were now living on small reservations scattered throughout Canada and western New York.

By 1850, the United States had completed its westward territorial march to the Pacific Ocean. A new sense of national mission, celebrated as a "manifest destiny," sanctioned this rapid, aggressive movement. Many eastern tribes had been already removed and relocated west of the Mississippi. The Indian frontier, now wholly entrapped in U.S. territory, was relatively quiet, if only—as we know—for a limited time. Americans commonly assumed that the native inhabitants of the continent or their ways of life were vanishing and doomed for extinction, a prediction voiced at times as a great concern and, at other times, as a policy prescription. Just as the American Indian was expected to disappear, a new fascination with Indian artifacts, history, mythology, and customs emerged. These materials were to be salvaged in order to generate a new and epic national culture, distinct from that of England and other European countries. Walt Whitman, for example, maintained in 1846, "Have we no memories of the race, the like of which never was seen on any other part of the earth—whose existence was freedom—whose language sonorous beauty? . . . Are *these* not the proper subject for the bard or the novelist?"[2]

During the summer of 1845, the state of New York employed Schoolcraft to conduct a census of the Iroquois reservations, to which he added a study of their history and culture. He also published a private edition of this report under the title *Notes on the Iroquois* (1847). Two years later, Congress appointed him to supervise a comprehensive research project concerning all Indian tribes in the United States, including those in the just acquired territories of the West. This survey resulted in six monumental volumes issued annually under the initial title *Inquiries respecting the History, Present Condition, and Future Prospects, of the Indian Tribes of the United States* (1851–57). Also, in 1851, the young Lewis Morgan completed his own study *League of the Iroquois,* after years of gathering ethnographic materials for scholarly papers and collecting aboriginal artifacts for the New York State Cabinet in Albany. Morgan would become one of the leading figures of American ethnology, widely acknowledged as a pioneer in the fields of structuralist and evolutionary anthropology. He introduced kinship as an object of scientific inspection. Morgan's later work, especially *Ancient Society* (1877) inspired other discoverers of "society," namely, Marx and Engels, and consequently had a far-reaching influence on communist archeology.

Schoolcraft's and Morgan's projects during the 1840s and the 1850s featured an expanded role for the state in circulating knowledge about the Indian population for the purpose of policy making, state building, and commemoration. Indian research, moreover, took place during an important debate regarding the future of the aboriginal inhabitants of America, their character and prospects, a dispute that featured an intriguing permutation of the problematic of double representation—the relationship between political representation and scholarly or artistic depictions of social groups that were excluded from the polity. Concurrently, anthropology became a beneficiary of federal patronage of science through expeditions and explorations. By the second half of the 1840s, when the newly established Smithsonian Institution was poised to lead the national scientific community, its secretary, Joseph Henry, launched the *Smithsonian Contribution to Knowledge* series with Ephraim G. Squier and Edwin H. Davis's archaeological essay on the *Ancient Monuments of the Mississippi Valley* (1848).

The following two chapters examine Schoolcraft's and Morgan's respective enterprises by addressing the following questions: Why did the federal and state governments lend their support to these projects? How was ethnographic knowledge accumulated, presented, and validated (whether by specific techniques of representation or on the basis of the author's unique experience and expertise)? What role was assumed by these ventures in the actual relationship between the aboriginal tribes and U.S. society? What was the degree of Indian complicity in, collaboration with, or resistance to those inquiries? Finally, the discussion situates Schoolcraft's and Morgan's studies, as we began, in a discourse in which national and personal identities assumed an Indian face. In this regard, mid-nineteenth-century explorations of the Indian subject featured more complex exchange relations between investigators and the investigated than most other inquiries we have examined in this book. Racial masquerade was emblematic of the "removal policy" to the west, as was the desire to move Indians to the past.

Reenactment or role playing had two interrelated consequences. First, the elaboration of a familial alliance between the "red man" and the "white man" was mediated by various historical constructs that arranged the relationships between Indians and whites in temporal, sequential terms. Second, Morgan's "discovery" of society in the Iroquois reservation of western New York centered on familial institutions as the kernel of the human bond. Morgan would eventually apply his insight into Iroquois kinship (with important modifications) to the entire human society, past and present, in a somewhat expansionist fashion—from the concrete family to "the family of man." Important aspects of his ethnology would later become essential to the modern imagination of the social sphere, especially the perception of society as a multifaceted and yet inherently, or even inescapably, rational and functional total mechanism, a view he developed by gazing at an aboriginal "counter-society" and then back to his own. In addition, Morgan's work marks the transformation of ethnology itself from a frontier experience (or a missionary tactic) to a decidedly middle-class science. The focus of many of these projects on western New York enables a detailed examination of a specific locus of investigation. Among the Indian tribes, the Iroquois were particularly close to American society, further along than many other nations on the road to the coveted "civilization." They were also conceived of as having unique historical relations with the U.S. federal state, especially because of their own confederate organization. Interestingly, Schoolcraft, Morgan, Squier, and the Smithsonian's Henry were all natives of rural New York.

Grouping the literature on Indian tribes, much of which was dedicated to ethnography and archeology, together with what is ordinarily understood under the rubric of social reportage (e.g., investigations of slums, child labor, prisons, and asylums) merits further explanation. This classification may not seem as peculiar if we consider that facts about the Indians' physical and moral condition as well as about their civilization and history were tools of policy making. Before the Civil War, the native population was the only group for whom the federal government was directly responsible. Presumably independent nations—signing treaties with the United States and, at times, waging war against it—they were also dependent wards of the state and subjected to external impositions. State paternalism was most tangibly manifested in the bureaucracy of officials (superintendents, agents, and sub-agents) appointed to dispense provisions and cash grants (annuities) to Indian tribes and to oversee efforts at educating them. The most potent symbolic expression of this dependency was the convention—adopted by Indians and their white interlocutors—of referring to the will of the federal government in the person of the president, designated the "Great Father in Washington."

In the antebellum mind, native peoples occupied a precarious position between nature and human society. Their unsettled and unsettling presence generated a tremendously diverse market of knowledge: missionary annual reports that regarded the Indian as yet another domain of philanthropic attention, epic novels on the Indian subject (popular since the 1820s), philological dictionaries and other products of post-Enlightenment and mostly eastern salon anthropology, and expedition narratives that captured the Indian as an integral part of the studied terrain together with lizards, cacti, and rock formations. Typically, information was divided, as in Schoolcraft's national project, between the history, the present condition, and the future prospects of the native tribes.

Distinct discursive strategies governed each of these segments. While ethnology, archeology, and philology sought to capture a bygone or about-to-disappear Indian existence (and addressed the question of origin), the tribes' present condition was the subject of reformist literature that employed moral and vital statistics as well as other familiar modes of social reporting. The speculative or prescriptive "future prospects" were preoccupied with the possibility of acculturation. At the conclusion of the Civil War, the American Freedmen's Inquiry Commission asked whether former slaves could be citizens. Meanwhile, the Indian future was under slightly different interrogation: Can they be civilized? At the same time, the promise of citizenship was the logical conclusion of the civilizing process. This inquiry required not merely assessing educational policy and institutions but also adjudicating aptitude, in other words, scrutinizing the Indian subject's mental properties and stature of character.

The relationship between the Indian's glorious past and fragile present raised complex questions. The past/present/future typology threatened to fragment the Indian subject. It was a type of historicism that emphasized sharp discontinuities. Any attempt to delineate connecting paths required alternative historiosophical strategies. This approach stood in contrast to the self-conception of the antebellum United States as a society that had been born in perfection and thus escaped the forces of history. Discussions of the aboriginal subject were therefore never outside some temporal configuration that arranged not just sequences of events but also fundamentally distinct epochs and their relations. Thus Morgan's later work moved from actual history to "ethnological periods," and Schoolcraft's writings followed the trajectory of the Christian notion of moral history. In fact, the question of origin accompanied the Indian subject from the very beginning of the European presence in the Americas: Who were their ancestors? Did they come from a different continent? Do they belong to the same human grouping? Did they replace former civilizations or did they originate in them?

During the first half of the nineteenth century, the aboriginal was simultaneously removed along spatial and temporal axes. He was further distanced from U.S. society, which was also largely removed from its past as a frontier in which the Indian was an immediate presence rather than a subject of literature or scientific discourse, contemplation, and projection. In the 1840s, the literature on the past and the future of the Indian acquired a darker patina. The publication of Samuel Morton's *Crania*

Americana (1839), in which he presented the proto-racist, phrenology-inspired doctrine that would lead him to endorse polygenism rearranged the debate over the Indian along new and more polemical lines. Rooted in Enlightenment racial taxonomy, polygenism challenged the biblical narrative that traced a common origin for all humanity, arguing that indigenous peoples in America (and elsewhere) were of a different and inferior breed. Although many in the emerging scientific community (most importantly, Harvard professor Louis Agassiz) embraced this view and applied it to the freedmen question, polygenism met resistance. Many among Morton's opponents subscribed to no less racist positions but nonetheless could not accept, for diverse reasons, his direct challenge to the monogenist tradition. Both the staunch Democrat Schoolcraft and the Whig-turned-Republican Morgan framed their studies as resounding attacks against polygenism and its collateral pessimism concerning the future of American Indians and their ability to adapt to life in the modern world.

A consequence of this debate was a heightened sensitivity regarding the accurate portrayal of the Indian subject. Claims concerning misrepresentation abounded. "Misrepresentation" was a rather nebulous assertion that referred to factual errors due to faulty science or excessively sentimental treatment, especially in works of fiction. The term frequently denoted a moral failure, a misjudgment of the Indian, his virtues, and character. The intellectual "Indian wars" were largely waged among whites and involved nonaboriginals acting as "friends of the Indian," speaking for and representing the Indian in the worlds of science, art, and politics. The prospect of complete civilization and citizenship (or extinction), together with strenuous efforts to establish some affiliation between natives and antebellum white "natives," distinguished the literature on the Indian tribes from the kind of knowledge produced in the colonial context. (In the United States, empire is always closer to home.) Obviously, there were many similarities as well. As we shall see, U.S. anthropology attempted intermittently to delineate between American Indians and other indigenous societies but otherwise was committed to its inherent universalism. Moreover, Indian literature was susceptible to the fantasy and ambivalence that Homi Bhabha, among others, identifies as the subject of the colonial discourse: splitting, doubling, turning into its opposite, and projecting.

The federal executive was arguably the most important producer in this market of information on native tribes. The fate of the aboriginals as dependent or as enemy constituted a significant portion of the tiny administration's activities at the time and was the subject of numerous annual and special reports compiled by several federal agencies. Congress printed in great quantities government reports and narratives of expeditions, as well as additional documents that addressed native peoples— petitions, memorials, committee reports, and documents that originated in individual states. Since the 1820s, the annual reports of the Indian Office and later the Indian Bureau became a platform for the exposition of the removal policy. (The Indian Office was established in 1824 as part of the War Department and in 1849 was transferred to the newly created Department of the Interior.) The expulsion in the 1830s of the Cherokees and other "civilized nations"—the notorious "trail of tears"—entailed a fierce public controversy and intense production of pamphlets about the condition of those tribes.

Immediately after the Civil War, Congress launched an effort to reconstruct Indian policy. It also endeavored to study the circumstances of native tribes independent of the information it received from the federal executive, state governments, citizen groups, or the Indians themselves. The Doolittle Committee of 1865 examined the Sand Creek massacre of November 1864, but it also sought to respond to periodic complaints about corruption and mistreatment by the Indian administration. Senator James R. Doolittle and six other senators and congressmen, organized in three groups, conducted arduous field investigations that stretched from the prairies to the Pacific coast. In the process, they met with and recorded the words of many Indian chiefs. Since the early days of the republic, government had made a special effort to capture the voices of Indian leaders by transcribing speeches into official reports.[3]

Information concerning the material conditions of the Indian tribes and the relative success of their acculturation was comparable to the yield of social inquiries into the physical and moral condition of the poor. Unlike the lower echelon of society, however, native tribes' political representation was largely tied to their status as ostensibly independent entities. Washington, D.C., witnessed a hectic traffic of Indian delegations in town to negotiate treaties or present petitions. One such delegation of Pottawatomie leaders arrived in the Capitol in late 1845. The chiefs hired a former Indian official, Richard Smith Elliot, as a political advisor and press agent. The delegation made its presence conspicuous by carefully staging colorful appearances on Pennsylvania Avenue and other public spaces throughout the city and by regularly releasing information to the press corps on the course of the negotiations. Indians were invested in the flow of information about them, and they collaborated, albeit cautiously, in the effort to accumulate knowledge on their material condition, customs, and history.

CHAPTER SEVEN

Archives of Indian Knowledge

By the middle of the 1840s, Henry Schoolcraft was broke and desperately seeking sources of income. He supported his family by recycling ethnographical material in articles, books, and lecture tours, and even writing poetry based on native themes. Schoolcraft became a typical mid-nineteenth-century intellectual entrepreneur, persistently trying to interest publishers, learned societies, and, later, government, in his personal archive of Indian subject matter, which spawned many literary and scientific schemes. The scholarly interest in the Indian received an institutional foundation with the establishment in 1842 of the New York–based American Ethnological Society, headed by the doyen of American Ethnology, Albert Gallatin. The society would prove instrumental in Schoolcraft's lobbying efforts.

Schoolcraft's entire career following his appointment as an Indian agent on the Michigan frontier in the early 1820s did much to harness ethnography in the service of government. The following discussion focuses on the New York State and the U.S. Congress Indian studies, two projects in which the ambitions of an individual investigator coalesced with those of government. Both undertakings featured an interplay between two modes of the politics of representation: first, the idea that the management of a downtrodden population necessitated an inquiry into (and an elaborate depiction of) its physical and moral conditions; second, the radically different notion of representation by which government (either state or federal) had a particular responsibility to record, preserve, and display the remnants of Indian civilization.

Frontier Ethnology

Born in 1793 in Hamilton, New York and trained as a glassmaker, Schoolcraft traveled in 1818 down the Ohio River exploring the mineral resources of the Missouri and Arkansas regions. The following year, he returned as the geologist of the exploring expedition to the Northwest Territory under Lewis Cass, territorial governor of Michigan. In 1822, he arrived in Sault Ste. Marie, a frontier post, as an Indian agent to the tribes of Lake Superior. These rather modest appointments relied on the patronage of Secretary of War John C. Calhoun. Schoolcraft remained in government employment for the next two decades, later assuming the superintendency of Indian affairs in Michigan (1836) and gradually retreating from the frontier to Mackinac and finally Detroit. In Sault Ste. Marie, he married Jane Johnston, whose father, an Irish-born fur trader, was an important figure in the tiny frontier community. Jane's mother Susan was the daughter of Wabojeeg, a Powhatan Chief. The Johnstons' large household was equally conversant in Indian and western ways, and Schoolcraft's initiation into ethnography took place within the confines of his new family. The Johnstons were able to verify and expand information he garnered in numerous daily encounters with Indians who frequented the town and his agency. In his diary, Schoolcraft gratefully recounted how his mother-in-law instructed him about Indian ceremonies and usages. "I have in fact stumbled . . . on the only family in North America who could, in Indian lore, have acted as my guide, philosopher and friend."[1] In his first foray into ethnography, Schoolcraft also received guidance from a questionnaire written by Governor Cass. Cass was a leading proponent of fusing Indian policy with systematic accumulation of knowledge. He envisioned a "frontier ethnology" with which he sought to dismiss erroneous, mostly romantic (and in his view too charitable) views on the Indians' character, conditions, and prospects. Andrew Jackson's administration would endorse this line of investigation to elaborate the rationale for Indian removal. Cass regarded Indians as a "moral phenomenon" and rather bleakly judged them (primarily on the basis of linguistic analysis) to be lacking the capacity for improvement.

   Schoolcraft accepted Cass's work as an investigative template, embracing in the process his political views as well as the ambition to combat the ethnological establishment of the eastern seaboard by publicizing factual matter directly from the Indian frontier. For Cass, who in 1831 became Jackson's secretary of war, Schoolcraft was the model ethnologist, a government field agent whose position provided him "favorable opportunities for investigating the character and condition of these people, and [surveying] them with the eyes of a cautious and judicious observer."[2] According to the tradition exemplified in the life work of the statesman-ethnologist Gallatin, comparative philology was the main subject of inquiry. Schoolcraft's initial step was to study the Chippewa language, which he found quite complex and difficult to master. (At one point, he solicited government to withhold Chippewa treaty money in order that a dictionary of Chippewa could be completed for use in missionary work.)

Schoolcraft soon acquired national recognition as a field expert on Indian affairs. He corresponded with eastern scholars and publishers, entertained foreign dignitaries and writers visiting Michigan, and consequently was elected to American and foreign literary societies. As an informant on the frontier, he received much gratitude from luminaries such as the New York governor DeWitt Clinton and the philologist Peter Du Ponceau. His scientific reputation was bolstered by his claim to have discovered the source of the Mississippi (1832), which he fancifully named Lake Itasca (from the Latin *verITAS CAput*—or true head). Schoolcraft brought to his ethnological exertions a practical scientific training in the natural sciences and a collateral attachment to the aggregation of facts that originated in close observations.

At the turn of the 1830s, Schoolcraft shifted his focus from philology to history and mythology, ostensibly seeking to probe the Indians' "mental characteristics" and consequently to explain their somewhat puzzling reluctance to adopt Western civilization. "The whole mind is bowed down under these intellectual fetters, which circumscribe its volitions, and bind it, as effectually as the hooks of iron, which pierce a whirling Hindoo's flesh."[3] Rather than language, legends, and myth, stories of reincarnation, transformation, magic, and sorcery provided the deepest insight into the Indian character. He subsequently collected tales of the Chippewa, Ottawa, the Pottawatomie, and other local bands, an effort that led to the publication of his *Algic Researches* (1839). Throughout his career as Indian expert, Schoolcraft coupled a deep-seated identification with the aboriginal and an overtly condescending approach. He shared the perception of the native people as children who had lost their previous ("Hunter Stage") ability to govern themselves. These views were further fashioned by his religious conversion during one of the revivals that were common on the frontier during the early 1830s, the last decade of the Second Great Awakening. Once converted, the moral tone in his writing predominated.

Schoolcraft's preoccupation with legends and religious beliefs coincided with a new public taste for things Indian. *Algic Researches*' commercial success did not stem from any systematic effort to delve into the Indian mind but rather from the enthusiasm prompted by the discovery of an indigenous poetic style. The *Detroit Free Press* determined that the compilation was reminiscent of Greek mythology and had the originality of *Arabian Nights*. "Catlin may be called the red man's painter, Schoolcraft his poetical historian. They have each painted in

living colors the workings of the Indian mind, and painted nature in her unadorned simplicity."[4]

In 1841, with the advent of the first Whig administration, Schoolcraft lost his
government position under a cloud of scandal and accusations of wrongdoing.
Without federal employment, he decided to capitalize on his previous literary
success and moved away from the frontier to the intellectual milieu of New York
City. In response to a new archeological fad, he published in 1843 an article in
the *New York Commercial Advertiser* on a visit to the Grave Creek Indian mound
in Virginia where, reportedly, the first Indian inscriptions were discovered. Projects of such caliber could not secure his livelihood. The United States was still
reeling from the economic panic of 1837, and a trip to England did not yield the
expected revenue. Schoolcraft's personal affairs worsened further when his wife
died.

Schoolcraft developed a pattern of lobbying. He devised a grand plan for the
investigation of American ethnology, which he sent to the regents of the Smithsonian Institution. His design included a "Museum of Mankind," archaeological explorations, and a library of philology.[5] He proposed to utilize the State Department and the navy in securing antiquities from Polynesia, Asia, and Africa.
Ambitious schemes to establish ethnological museums abounded in the late
1840s. Lewis Morgan collected artifacts for a New York State cabinet. Ephraim
Squier envisaged a national museum that would house a large collection from
all over the world. Those enterprises were consistent with the universalistic
principles that guided the establishment of Smithsonian in 1846 and the zeit-
geist of the decade. America's national mission was conceived in vast, grandiose
terms that embraced the investigation and conquering of nature as well as the
inquiry into the natural history of "Man." A fine example of the popular reach
of such national desires can be found in the well-plowed pages of P. T. Barnum's
autobiography. That apostle of nineteenth-century popular culture recalled that
around 1849 he considered putting on an exhibition that "would excite universal attention." "This was nothing less than a 'Congress of Nations'—an assem-
blage of representatives of all the nations that could be reached by land or sea.
I meant to secure a man and a woman, as perfect as could be procured, from
every accessible people, civilized and barbarous, on the face of the globe. I had
actually contracted with an agent to go to Europe to make arrangements to secure 'specimens' for such a show."[6] This creation of an ethnographic Noah's Arc
never materialized. Barnum found other means to satisfy the public's racial curiosity.

Census Marshal

Schoolcraft marketed both his government projects as policy-making devices conceived around a census of Indian tribes: subjugating Indian affairs to the modern, fact-finding tools of political economy. As importantly, he maintained that state and federal authorities had a responsibility to assure faithful and comprehensive scholarly representation of the tribes' history and life. The statistical mission camouflaged the ethnographical nature of the New York project, for which the New York Historical Society served as a springboard. A society resolution called on the legislature to provide a census of the Indian population. George Folsom, a state senator and a member of the society, sponsored the campaign. In the spring of 1845, Schoolcraft became a census marshal for the Indian tribes of western New York. He would claim that this was the first time any American or European government commissioned a full census of a nation or tribe of Indians that addressed their material condition.[7] The state agreed to include research into history and antiquities. However, the Secretary of New York State N. S. Benton instructed him to conduct his study in as brief a time as possible and to exercise caution in his dealings with the Indians, for he was likely to encounter suspicion. "You will assure our red brethren that in taking this enumeration of them and making the inquiries into their present condition and situation the Legislature, the Governor of the State, or any of the officers have no other objects in view but their welfare and happiness."[8] Schoolcraft was to assure his Indian interlocutors that the census had nothing to do with the federal government or the Ogden Land Company, with which the Iroquois (especially the Seneca) were in constant dispute.

Schoolcraft spent more than two months in upstate and western New York, negotiating with the Indians to secure their cooperation and investigating oral traditions and archeological sites. He dedicated most of July to the Oneidas and the Onondagas, bringing along his nephew to assist him with the census. He proceeded to the Tuscarora reserve, where he completed the count in early August, then paused for more than a month on the various Seneca reservations delegating canvassing to a few assistants. The new scientific research tool promoted by Schoolcraft proved inadequate. State officials had originally designed the elaborate statistical tables for a white farm or urban society, and the categories employed were, in a large part, irrelevant to the material conditions and life of the Iroquois, as "advanced" as these tribes were. The Seneca (then the largest among the descendants of the Six Nations of the Iroquois), especially the residents of the Tonawanda reservation, were reluctant to cooperate with the canvassers, causing serious delays. Schoolcraft attributed this attitude to their unfamiliarity with statistics and confusion as to the benefits of enumeration.

> In truth, of all subjects upon which these people have been called on to think and act, during our proximity to them of two or three centuries, that of political economy is decidedly the most foreign and least known to them ... If I might judge, from the scope of remarks made both in and out of council, they regarded it as the introduction of a Saxon feature into their institutions, which, like the lever, by some process not apparent to them, was designed, in its ultimate effects, to uplift and overturn them ... Everywhere, the tribes exalted the question into one of national moment, Grave and dignified sachems assembled in formal councils, and indulged in long and fluent harangues to their people, as if the very foundations of their ancient confederacy were about to be overturned by an innovating spirit of political arithmetic and utilitarianism.[9]

Indeed, the census debacle seemed to expose the cultural gap between the investigator and the investigated more than any other method of observation and registration. The alien language of statistics precluded the exchange relations that were characteristic of other modes of sharing Indian knowledge, an aspect that might have contributed to the discord. However, notwithstanding Schoolcraft's patronizing sarcasm, rational and pragmatic motives were at the core of the Iroquois animosity. The tribes were then in the midst of a battle over the fate of two Seneca reservations. Their leaders suspected that the census was part of a sinister scheme to take over additional land or, equally threatening, a preliminary step to state taxation of their property. Thus they were particularly reluctant to tally their farm products and belongings. There was also an issue of pride at stake. Schoolcraft quoted one of the chiefs as claiming that they had little to exhibit, equating statistical representation with intrusive public scrutiny of private matters.

Like officially commissioned investigators on the other side of the Atlantic, Schoolcraft functioned as an intermediary, concurrently collecting and imparting information. A law that had been recently enacted granted the tribes the power to initiate suits in state courts and also provided that the chiefs should meet in council each year to elect a clerk and a treasurer by a plurality of votes. (Thus, in an attempt to overhaul the Iroquois system of self-government, majority rule was to replace traditional Indian requirements for unanimity.) The New York governor asked Schoolcraft to examine Indian attitudes on the subject. Schoolcraft apparently went a step further, trying to convince the Seneca that they should adopt the new system. Months later, several members of the tribe charged in a petition that Schoolcraft had threatened them that failure to embrace the new law in full and within the year would prevent them from ever benefiting from it.

Notes on the Iroquois

In many respects, the Iroquois were model tribes. Their numbers were actually increasing. Reproducing yet close to cultural extinction, they simultaneously confirmed and defied the "vanishing Indian" trope, a point that Schoolcraft took as a sign of their reversal of fortune. In his report to the state of New York, Schoolcraft was optimistic about the Iroquois future on the path towards civilization. "It is by the numbers of the several tribes of our North American stocks of red men, compared with their means of subsistence, and their capacity of producing the supply, that we are to judge of their advance or declension in the scale of civilization."[10] In the expanded, private (and, significantly, illustrated) edition of his official account, titled *Notes of the Iroquois,* he developed a chauvinistic theme, insinuating that the Iroquois's superior degree of manly democracy (in comparison with the indigenous civilizations of South and Central America) somehow reflected on the quality of the nation that subordinated and inherited them. "No nation of the widely spread red race of America," he wrote, "has displayed so high and heroic a love of liberty, united with the true art of government, and personal energy and stamina of character, as the Iroquois."[11] Their long resistance to European incursions and the durability of their institutions demonstrated Iroquois's aptitude "as an active, thinking race of men." During these years, Schoolcraft, among others, promoted the intensification of the native motif in the country's public life; toying, at one time, with the idea of replacing America with an aboriginal name, Alleghenia. In his report, Schoolcraft suggested the Iroquois past, especially its history of warfare, was so intermingled with that of the colonies that it should be acknowledged as a branch of U.S. history.

Despite the partial nature of his research, Schoolcraft saw great hope in the evidence on "moral statistics." Canvassers counted 350 church members of all denominations (although 3,081 still adhered to their native religion). Fourteen reservation schools enrolled nearly half the school-age children, while 870 individuals or more had signed the temperance pledge. Schoolcraft noted with satisfaction that for the most advanced group, hunting was, as in civilized communities, "*an amusement*, and not a means of reward."[12] The surveyors found a total of 371 farmers, 20 mechanics, 7 physicians, 17 teachers, 2 lawyers, and 151 semi-hunters. The remaining 400 adult males were largely unemployed but worked seasonally in farms, sawmills, or as unskilled laborers. Schoolcraft regarded these individuals together with the semihunters as a hindrance to the continued progress of the Iroquois and subsequently suggested their resettlement in the West. Otherwise, he urged the state to offer tribesmen full citizenship, arguing that nothing would benefit the Indian as much as his admission to the rights and immunities of citizens. He wrote against the annuities system. The periodic allocation of funds was an opportunity for reckless traders to exploit the Indians' weaknesses and encourage dangerous consumption of "showy but valueless articles."

Historical and ethnological material occupied the bulk of the Iroquois report. Schoolcraft provided historical sketches for each of the Six Nations, supplemented by Indian miscellany, from brief accounts of principles of government to pottery, archeology, language, and witchcraft—whatever he could find during short field trips, in his personal repository, or in books written by others. In the field and in the library, Schoolcraft was, as he fully admitted, a collector of facts; his cut-and-paste texts exhibited a multitude of retrieved Indian objects, whether a legend, an artifact, or a religious practice. What little he presented by way of relating these pieces to each other rested on drawing, or merely suggesting, broad-stroke comparisons and analogies with other native societies, ancient civilizations, or sometimes, biblical stories.

The concluding third of *Notes on the Iroquois* featured raw material, evidence, beginning with Schoolcraft's letter of appointment and instructions. This trace of official authority preceded excerpts from Schoolcraft's private journals under the title, "Extracts from a Rough Diary of Notes by the Way."[13] Entries had been recorded in an abrupt style while Schoolcraft surveyed archeological sites. In a manner reminiscent of western travelers' (or urban social investigators') reports, Schoolcraft reproduced many words in an abbreviated form, ostensibly lifted directly from the original handwritten notebook. The rest of the document featured transcripts of letters sent to Schoolcraft from local informants, among which was a communication from James Cusick, a Tuscarora, detailing his tribe's history. Schoolcraft added a passage borrowed from a book published by Cusick's brother some twenty years earlier. "As the work of a full blooded Indian, of the Tuscarora tribe, it is remarkable. In making these extracts, no correction of the style, or grammar is made, these being deemed a part of the evidence of the authenticity of the traditions recorded."[14] He also included reports sent by Lewis

Morgan and George S. Riley, two members of the Grand Order of the Iroquois, on a Seneca council meeting they had attended. Schoolcraft acknowledged the incompleteness of his research yet emphasized the authenticity of the material he had amassed. Typically, he offered gratuitous remarks about the pristine quality of the information. "Notes and sketches were taken down from the lips of both white and red men, wherever the matter itself and the trustworthiness of the individual appeared to justify them. Many of the ancient forts, barrows and general places of ancient sepulcher were visited, and of some of them accurate plans, diagrams or sketches made on the spot, or obtained from other hands."[15] These were preliminary findings for future usage, and he associated them with other New York state ventures to commemorate and preserve its history by, among other means, obtaining historical documents in Europe on New York's colonial past.

New York was not the only state that studied its aboriginal inhabitants. Following its neighbor, Massachusetts conducted in 1849 its own survey of its resident Indians. This modest effort was firmly rooted in the Victorian discourse of reform and registration rather than the ethnographical sensibility that propelled the New York project. Commissioners Francis W. Bird, Whiting Griswold, and Cyrus Weekers were appointed "to visit the several tribes . . . of Indians, remaining within this Commonwealth, to examine into their condition and circumstances, and report to the next Legislature what legislation . . . is necessary in order best to promote the improvement and interests of said Indians." The inquiry took place at a time when the Indian population was so minuscule (847 individuals) that in the appendix, the committee listed the name and age of every Indian man, woman, and child in Massachusetts, most of who were "half breeds" and heavily mixed with the African American population. The commission dispatched questionnaires but emphasized its fieldwork: "We have seen them in their dwellings and on their farms, in their school-houses and meeting-houses, have partaken of their hospitalities of bed and board, have become familiar with their private griefs and public grievances." Despite initial distrust, the commissioners reported that they received full cooperation.[16]

The report typified Massachusetts-style social reform, which was close in spirit to the British model. The committee recommended the integration of the aboriginals into white society, including the offer of citizenship. At the same time, it contemplated the appointment of a state Indian commissioner and various schemes to aid those who wished to stay within state guardianship, at least for a period of transition from dependency to citizenship. The report featured statistics on property, schools, and churches. Indians were asked about their relationship with the state and the prejudice they suffered from whites. This inquiry, much more than Schoolcraft's, endeavored to integrate the opinion of the Indians themselves, brought in their own words, into the policy-making process. A memorial by one of the small tribes was published verbatim. The commissioners alluded to the experience of other oppressed peoples. Foreshadowing the Civil War–era freedmen's debate, it maintained, "The history of all conquered and proscribed races and classes, illustrates the impossibility of elevating such races and classes, while under civil and political disabilities."[17] Drawing an implicit analogy between the experience of blacks and Indians, it quoted Frederick Douglass: "Take your heels off of our necks, and see if we do not rise."[18]

Duties and Obligations

In February 1846, Schoolcraft completed supervising the printing of *Notes on the Iroquois* in Albany and arranged to send copies to various societies, libraries, and political figures. Two weeks later, he arrived in Washington and began mustering support for a new enterprise. Based on his New York experience, he proposed to Indian Commissioner William Medill to conduct a general census of the U.S. Indian tribes. No other measure would better substantiate Indian policy. "It is idle to suppose that we can perform the functions of government towards [the Indian tribes], in the best manners, without an exact knowledge of the facts on which the exercise of such governmental power depends."[19] With western expansion, contacts with indigenous tribes and the need for legislation and policy making were bound to increase. The census component of Schoolcraft's plan had two related focal points: first, demography, or, more precisely, the ability of Indians to reproduce themselves in comparison with "European races"; second, the physical and moral condition of the Indian tribes. In a few years, he predicted, Indians would reside at the center of the Union and the question of their integration would become more acute.

Schoolcraft arranged for a member of the House Committee on Indian Affairs to introduce an amendment to the War Department appropriation bill providing for an Indian census. The amendment for $10,000 failed to survive a conference committee. The provision calling for a census was retained, but the appropriation itself was stricken out; the Indian administration was required to perform the task itself without external assistance. Schoolcraft intensified his lobbying campaign. He convinced a group of senators to send a letter to Secretary of War William Marcy on the importance of gathering materials relating to Indian history and languages. "These tribes are rapidly passing away, and much of what is most wanted, respecting them, will soon be out of reach. They are now concentrated, where these investigations can be conveniently made and the period is favorable for the inquiry," wrote the senators.[20] There was some tension (or, conversely, peculiar and rather strong causal relations) between the argument for the urgency of devising a new and comprehensive Indian policy to further the U.S. civilizing mission and the notion that ethnological knowledge should be recorded with the utmost speed because Indians were about to disappear. These seemingly incongruous purposes required recurrent explication and explanation. The origins and the characteristics of the tribes might not be as important as determining the right mode of governing them, Schoolcraft reasoned in another plea to Medill, but the means of accomplishing this purpose were rooted in this type of knowledge.[21]

Adding a sharper political angle to his campaign, Schoolcraft wrote directly to President James Polk asking, in so many words, for a government position in lieu of the one he had lost. He claimed the Whigs had punished him for defending Martin Van Buren's administration against a nasty press campaign that alleged injustice in the operation of the Indian bureaucracy.[22] Meanwhile, a petition drive led by key members of the American Ethnological Society produced an appeal that emphasized the imperfect state of knowledge on the Indian race and the importance of this material "to enable government to perform its high and sacred duties of protection and guardianship over the weak and still savage race placed by Providence under its care."[23] Secretary Medill joined the chorus, urging Congress to uphold the vision of a greater project that would include the history of the Indian, "explain their former, and account for their present condition; and afford some indication of their probable prospect in the future."[24] If in New York Schoolcraft was able to conduct ethnographical research only as a supplement to the census, Medill's letter legitimized the value of the historical and ethnological research to policy making. Congressional debates on the proposal featured the familiar exchange between those who argued that additional Indian research was necessary and others like Senator Thomas Hart Benton, who inveighed, "our papers [are already] teeming with all sorts of information that everybody had ever dreamed of." Nevertheless, on March 3, 1847, an amendment to the War Department appropriation bill provided $5,000 for the project. Schoolcraft was to run the survey and receive a salary of $1,600 a year.[25]

Government's moral responsibility to record ethnological knowledge was argued for on multiple grounds. Schoolcraft and his backers referred primarily to the federal duty to secure the well-being of the aboriginal inhabitants. But they also conceived of the documentation of Indian culture as an obligation government had toward the Indians apart from any policy consideration, and, moreover, a duty the country had to itself and to humanity. "It is a duty we owe to the nations of the world," wrote former secretary of war John Spencer, "to investigate the history, the language, the means of policy of the original inhabitants of this continent,—not merely, for their own sakes, but, as probably, shedding great light on the history of other nations."[26]

A similar range of motives propelled the persistent but ultimately failed drives to persuade Congress to purchase painter George Catlin's gallery of Indian portraits and curiosities. When Catlin returned from the West in 1837, he exhibited his collection in Washington, D.C., and worked hard to get Congress interested in procuring it. For the next fifteen years, there would be recurrent applications for congressional patronage while Catlin moved his elaborate collection to Europe, where it was presented to great effect, at least initially, in Paris, Versailles, and London. The collection included six hundred paintings covering forty-eight different tribes and featuring portraits, dresses, weaponry, and other artifacts, besides two tons of minerals and fossils hauled from the frontier. Catlin testified that he was guided by his vision of making his collection, "the nucleus of a *museum of mankind,* to contain eventually the records, resemblances, and manufactures of all the diminishing races of native tribes in various parts of the globe."[27] The collection was also peddled as a monument for the Indian race.

A repeated argument in all solicitations was that every major country in Europe had one national site of the type that the United States was woefully lacking. Italians interested in the history of Rome could visit the Vatican. The French artist in search of the Gauls found their remnants in the Louvre. For the English, the Tower of London was the repository of the Saxons' weapons and armor. America needed her own museum where artists might freely study this "bold race who once held possession of our country."[28] This endemic Europe-envy suffused public discourse in nineteenth-century America. In contrast, the plan implicitly expressed the wish to disengage from a European past by demonstrating a special bond between Americans and Indians, that was, in a self-contradictory manner, to follow the example of, for instance, the French and the Gauls.

To add a sense of urgency, it was reported that a year after Catlin visited their camps, the Mandan Indians were extinct, victims of smallpox. The library committee pleaded on behalf of future generations, "The intelligent American of fifty years hence will go in search of them wherever they may be found, but it will be a subject of grief and shame to him, if he must seek them in the galleries of some European capital."[29] By 1852, Catlin was incarcerated in an English prison for debt and was willing to reduce drastically the asking price of his collection. Prompted by a new campaign, a select committee asserted that in all countries but especially in a republic there was great responsibility on government to educate the people "in valor, wisdom, and virtue." Here the two educational missions of the federal government—informing the populace and civilizing the Indian—seemed to merge. If Barnum conceived of his museum as a grand, universal spectacle, the congressional committee insisted that for the future of the United State, it was important to make Washington, D.C., spectacular. Employing a recognizable republican hype, it declared: "How shall we better strengthen the bonds of union, than by rendering the Capital an object of pride and interest to the people of every State! How shall we impress mankind with the excellence of the republican system more easily and more effectually than by exhibiting to them the achievements of art and science in the classic seat of republican authority."[30]

Catlin's campaign did not share the utilitarian dimension of Schoolcraft's or the ethnographer's political acumen. Still, both projects vied for government patronage for a national gesture that rested on a theme current in nineteenth-century evangelical philanthropy and expressed by the twin concepts of "lost" and "found." The Indian soul would be saved by Christian compassion and civilization. Museums, galleries, and monumental publishing projects would preserve Indian culture. Another common denominator in Schoolcraft's and Catlin's (and Barnum's) visions of museumification was the immersion of the American national theme, represented here in the figure of the Indian, in an imperial mission whose limits transcended the actual boundaries of the United States.

Indian Census

Schoolcraft's Indian census and the ethnological survey relied heavily on statistical tables and questionnaires mailed to numerous current (and former) field agents, schoolteachers, missionaries, and other individuals knowledgeable about the Indians because of either lengthy contact or scholarly research. Local officials of the Indian Office were in charge of enumeration. Schoolcraft wanted the census to be so detailed as to list the names of the heads of every Indian family in the country. He planned to report periodically to Congress to assure continual public support, planting the seeds for enduring serial publication.[31]

Schoolcraft composed a comprehensive statistical schedule that included ninety-nine items for each Indian family and sixty-seven questions relating to tribal affairs. The statistical research recognized the Indian tribe and the extended Indian family, the band, as a social unit whose advancement should be measured in tandem. The charts specified thirteen male occupations. The quantity of household products such as knitted or woolen goods was a gauge for level of housewifery. Schoolcraft sought to list literary rates, to count teachers and students, and to follow the success of temperance societies. Another set of queries comprised a census of manufacturing and commercial intercourse, listing mills and machinery and the extent of the fur trade.

Schoolcraft's zeal yielded a ponderous document that seemed inadvertently to parody scholarly erudition. The hefty questionnaire included 347 items arranged in 28 topical divisions. The language section alone featured thirty-two questions and a vocabulary list of 350 words. Each of the queries in this mammoth compilation unleashed a lengthy string of minute questions. Schoolcraft's preoccupation with the Indian mind (besides the aboriginal family) was strongly evident. For instance, query number 189 solicited information concerning "Credulity and Susceptibility of Being Deceived."

> Are the Indians very prone to be deceived by professed dreamers, or the tricks of jugglers, or by phenomena of nature, of the principles and causes of which they are ignorant? Is not the surrounding air and forest, converted, to some extent, by this state of ignorance of natural laws, into a field of mystery, which often fills their minds with needless alarms? Are their priests shrewd enough to avail themselves of this credulity, either by observing this general defect of character, or by penetrating into the true causes of the phenomena? Do the fears and credulity of the Indians generally nourish habits of suspicion? Do they tend to form a character for concealment and cunning?[32]

He asked informants about dancing and amusements, sports, death and funerals, the "character of the race," oratorical competence, practices of cleanliness, family government, discipline of children, and the proportion of work divided between husbands and wives. "How is Order Preserved in the Limited Precincts of the Lodge?" inquired Schoolcraft, "Casual observers would judge there was but little. Inquire into this subject, and state what are the characteristic traits of living in the wigwam, or Indian house. How do the parents and children divide the space at night? How are wives, and females of every condition, protected in respective places, and guarded from intrusion?" Schoolcraft wanted to know what were the Indians' relations to property were, whether they had any notion of equity, and how such possessive rights were acquired and preserved over time and generations. He told his correspondents a story (most likely from his own tenure as an agent in Sault Ste. Marie). Years ago, the tale went, an Indian from the British dominions (Canada) applied to an American Indian agent for payment by the United States of a private debt contracted by a "North Briton," a resident in Hudson's Bay. "How did the mind operate in this case, and how does it operate generally, in tracing the claim of right and title in property, and of obligation in the affairs of debtor and creditor? Endeavor to trace the process of individuality in rights and property."[33] Although its enthusiastic application seems somehow at odds with Schoolcraft's previous work, political economy enhanced the impression of science at work. Mid-nineteenth-century statistical practices were as suffused with moralism as Schoolcraft's literary endeavors. Ultimately, in the effort to correct the misrepresentation of the Indian, Schoolcraft prepared his subject to be judged.

The last item in the questionnaire requested that prospective collaborators state whether they were acquainted with any substantial errors in popular accounts of "our Indian Tribes." (If the respondent was unknown, Schoolcraft demanded references.) Previous inquiries, he maintained, were made chiefly by casual visitors to the Indian country (many of them foreigners, he emphasized), "who have necessarily taken hasty and superficial glances at their mere external customs and ceremonies."[34] Circumspection should be applied whenever there appeared to be a clash of interest between the source of information and the Indians themselves. There was a great prejudice toward them, he warned, and preconceptions regarding their character. It was their due to be evaluated candidly by using the best sources, he maintained. Schoolcraft even provided a few examples of previous deceptions. An English popular writer had alleged that in 1837 the United States had borrowed money from a wealthy Indian chief to pay its annuities to his tribes. American policy had been challenged abroad because of such "ill-digested" or worthless information. Schoolcraft and the Indian office were also aware of potential resistance to the canvass. They ordered field agents not to alarm their aboriginal counterparts and appended minute details on the proper way to fill out the printed forms. He recommended that the time of the annual payments would afford a good opportunity for collecting much of the information.[35]

The long list of questions betrayed a certain sense of grandeur—personal, institutional and national—but the heft of the questionnaire threatened to submerge the entire project. It was printed, bound as a book, and sent first to several hundred selected individuals; later it was coupled with the first volume of the survey. This became, as we saw in the case of British royal commissions, a common procedure of bureaucratic print culture; another gesture toward transparency intended to incorporate the reader into the process of investigation and to demonstrate the project's quality, consistency, and impartiality. It was evident, however, that many of the questions presumed particular answers.

The national census of the Indian tribes failed more spectacularly than the earlier New York poll. Indian tribes were concerned that the census would eventuate unwanted change, including new efforts at their removal. A year and a half into Schoolcraft's tenure, many of the major tribes had reported no data at all, although Schoolcraft was by then inundated with ethnological material from other sources. It became, once again, quite impossible to squeeze Indian existence into the uncompromising rubrics of statistical tables designed to display information such as school attendance and farming equipment. The census faced the combined antagonism of distrustful chiefs and government agents who did not want to bother with a tedious task that promised no remuneration. Writing to Secretary of War Marcy in early 1849, Schoolcraft acknowledged that the fieldwork faced strong difficulties, "owing to the misapprehensions, and objections of some of the Indians, and Indian agents, and the inaptitude, unpreparedness, or incapacity of the latter generally."[36] For reasons of health and work, Schoolcraft could not embark on his own tour of inspection. Only in 1854 did he consider simplifying the schedules by dividing tribes into advanced, intermediate, and nomadic bands. He planned this as a first step toward a new census in the spring of next year, but that census never materialized as Congress and the Indian Office lost patience with the subject.

Even earlier, with the arrival of a Whig administration in 1849 and the relocation of the Indian Office to the new Department of the Interior, Schoolcraft found himself pulling political strings to defend his position. His colleague (and lodger) Smithsonian secretary Joseph Henry wrote to the secretary of the Interior on his behalf that the scientific world was expecting the United States to provide a full account on the race it dispossessed. "We would urge especially that the investigations be actively prosecuted at the present tim[e] while Mr [Schoolcraft] is in the vigour of physical and mental power."[37] Indeed, Schoolcraft's failing health would prove detrimental to the character of the entire operation. An illness during the summer and fall of 1849 left him unable to use his right hand. His health gradually and irreversibly deteriorated. By 1851, he rarely went to the Indian Office and became isolated from its affairs. A few years later, complete paralysis took over. He could not write anymore and had to rely on the services of others, especially his second wife, Mary Howard Schoolcraft. Schoolcraft made his last journey in 1856 and routinely declined all scholarly and social invitations.

During those years, the ballast of the project shifted from accumulating statistics and ethnological information to publishing, which, taking lawmakers' am-

uick Md.
May 1863

INFORMATION

RESPECTING THE

HISTORY CONDITION AND PROSPECTS

OF THE

INDIAN TRIBES of the UNITED STATES:

Collected and prepared under the

direction of the **BUREAU OF INDIAN AFFAIRS** per act of Congress

of March 3rd 1817.

BY HENRY R. SCHOOLCRAFT L.L.D.

Illustrated by

S. EASTMAN, CAPT. U. S. ARMY.

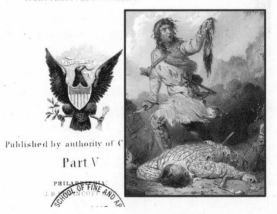

Published by authority of C

Part V

PHILADELPHIA
J. B. LIPPINCOTT

Detail from the title page of the fifth volume of Henry Rowe Schoolcraft's *Historical and Statistical Information Respecting the History Condition and Prospects of the Indian Tribes of the United States* (1851–57). The illustration above the title is a sketchy rendition of Seth Eastman's famous drawing (inset) of an Indian warrior scalping a white man, titled, "The Death Whoop," an engraving of which is featured in the second volume of the series.

bitions into consideration, he conceived as a serial project crowded with illustrations. In 1850, the department appointed Capt. Seth Eastman to make the engraved illustrations for the report. Schoolcraft wrote to Minnesota senator Henry Sibley that printing the account in the ordinary style of public documents was tantamount to doing injustice to the historical and ethnological research. It was a "national work" and ought to be presented in the same spirit. The document should not be confined to a single volume. In a letter to the social science pioneer Francis Lieber, Schoolcraft predicted that the material would fill at least fourteen quarto volumes of five hundred or more printed pages each.[38] In October 1850, Schoolcraft signed a contract with the publisher Lippincott, Grambo and Co., previously known for publishing Bibles. He would spend a few months each year in Philadelphia to oversee the printing. An edition of twelve hundred copies finally appeared in January 1851, at a cost of $8,661, more than half of which was paid to three lithography firms that mounted large operations employing, among other methods, the innovative technique of chromolithography. Another edition of six hundred copies of the first volume was printed for new members of Congress in 1852 as part of their book privileges.[39] Congress then stipulated that subsequent volumes would appear annually until the completion of the project.

Besides closely supervising the printing, which had become a demanding task, the former field expert had to spend most of his time editing the bulky volumes. Schoolcraft wanted to make his final installment a summary of the findings and write a defense for the federal Indian policy, for which he received the special permission to take two years rather than one. His application for a leave of absence to visit European archives was denied. All in all, Congress would spend $126,711.59 on the Indian survey. Only a third of that sum went to amassing information and to editing. The rest funded printing and publishing. This production made Lippincott's national reputation as a first-rate publisher and earned him a substantial sum of money. Schoolcraft's wife and son received a salary and travel allowances. In 1850, during his negotiations with Lippincott, he arranged for the reissue of his private work, beginning with *Personal Memoirs*. Alas, this and similar books that he republished with Lippincott proved to be commercial failures.[40]

Archives

The six volumes of *Inquiries respecting the History, Present Condition, and Future Prospects, of the Indian Tribes of the United States* were beautifully crafted quarto tomes with gilded fronts and covers embossed with an Indian motif. More than three hundred plates, mostly by Eastman, adorned the text, including eighty full-page illustrations of various aspects of aboriginal life such as buffalo hunting, wild-rice gathering, maple-sugar making, sports, and ceremonies. They rendered the production more exquisite and introduced an element of titillation. They included scenes of exotic religious practices and, possibly more inciting, depictions of half-naked females at work. Furthermore, the title page featured a detail from an iconic Eastman illustration (of which he produced a few versions) called the Death Whoop: a fierce warrior clasping in his raised hand the scalp of a slain white man who is lying on the ground. Opening an exuberant volume that documents Indian history, this image constituted another uncanny "bee in the book."

Copies were sent to foreign governments, learned societies, and literary celebrities. President Millard Fillmore, who received a presentation copy, complimented the execution of the first installment. Critics would juxtapose the volumes' lavish execution with their jumbled content, for the series ultimately consisted of roughly stitched-together old and new articles, about a tenth of which were produced by Schoolcraft himself. The remainder featured pieces written specifically for the project, excerpts from books, vocabulary lists, expedition narratives, tables, and some unedited replies to the questionnaire. Schoolcraft arranged the vast material according to the thematic subheadings of the questionnaire but otherwise did little. The text's disorder, which exceeded any contemporary standard for presenting authentic evidence in its undiluted form, testified not only to Schoolcraft's diminishing health but also to a measure of incompetence shared by him and the federal administration. In this case, publishing a report turned out to be easier than conducting field research. When, at the end of the decade, Schoolcraft's wife Mary Howard commissioned a private edition of the project, she quite properly chose to designate it *Archives of Indian Knowledge.* Once again, congested cabinets of curiosities spring to mind.

As an encyclopedic publication, Schoolcraft's tomes purported to cover every aspect of Indian life and research and thus relinquished the emphasis on new scholarship. Schoolcraft solicited contributions from a variety of experts and even published a posthumous piece on Indian skulls by his foe Samuel Morton. He also inserted an account of his own discovery of Lake Itasca, illustrated by a color engraving. In his expedition through the library, Schoolcraft retrieved accounts of the exploration of De Soto and Coronado, eighteenth-century travel sketches, and other such miscellany about the West. Fresher information included a study of Chippewa traditions by William Warren and George Gibb's account of Redick McKee's expedition through northwestern California. It took another century for a complete index to be prepared.[41]

Whenever possible, Schoolcraft made strong statements supporting his convictions about the unity of the human family. He forcefully endorsed manifest destiny as well as the federal treatment of the Indian tribes. This was a patriotic tract, and Schoolcraft reiterated his praise for the democratic inclinations of North American aboriginals as opposed to the feudalism he detected among the Incas and the Aztecs. His religiosity was also fully articulated. The decline of the Indian denoted his own moral failure, a fall from grace, and an attachment to misguided religious beliefs and rituals—all of which Schoolcraft explained by a curiously mechanical malfunctioning of the Indian mind. "If the Indian mind could be taken apart, as a piece of mechanism, it would be found to be an incongruous and unwieldy machine, which had many parts that did not match, and which, if likened to a watch, only ran by fits and starts, and never gave the true time."[42] The Indian was now facing a fateful dilemma. It was the white man's duty to offer the route toward civilization. It was the red man's burden to make the correct choice and to abandon his language, religion, hunting culture, and tribal identity. Ultimately, Schoolcraft's argument for the removal policy was reminiscent of the utilitarian workhouse test, Bentham's notion of less eligibility. While living in conditions of abundance, the Indian remained idle and attached to his misguided ways, leading to inevitable extinction. Moving the Indian away from the surplus of the bountiful regions would impose a regime of work and production and disengagement from the destructive life of hunting.[43]

Schoolcraft appropriated his model of regeneration directly from the biblical narrative of Exodus. It took the Hebrews forty years to return to the civilized state from which they had fallen—forty years of desert education outside human society. He advocated terminating the independent status of the tribes and subjecting the aboriginal to the same moral, economical, and religious system in which whites lived. With the Indians placed on isolated reservations where they could live according to American social codes, their transformation at the hands of educators and missionaries would be made easier. History as a morality tale was Schoolcraft's way of giving coherence to the disparate material he committed to print. Glowingly, he assumed the title of the Indian Historian to Congress and presented his official project as a work of history. That may have been prompted by Schoolcraft's responsiveness to popular taste, as historical narratives enjoyed commercial success at the time. His notion of history as a comprehensive, all-encompassing archive and, at the same time, a narrative with a moral rudder befitted the grandiosity of the national undertaking. The printed archive was the proper monument to the vanishing race as well as a legacy that Schoolcraft wanted to leave directly to the Indian tribes to whom he always felt obliged.

The publication ameliorated a deficiency in Indian life. In Schoolcraft's conception, the six volumes did not merely compensate for the lack of fully developed Indian historiography; they also literally brought the Indian to the stage of history. They made history.

Public response was mixed. Writers who praised him did so largely because of the report's material opulence. Schoolcraft's course of action, however, was alien to the sensibilities of the 1850s scholarly milieu. Personal and ideological animosities were also at play. The intellectual community's ambivalence was manifested in the shifting response on the pages of the *North American Review.* A short, one-page review in July 1851 celebrated the first installment.

> It is worth much more, in a national point of view, than is usually achieved by any single session of Congress, consumed in no matter how many speeches. It is, mechanically, a beautiful specimen of book making. The engravings are finely executed, and the letter press is from the hands of an editor, than whom there is no one in the country more competent to the task of grouping the facts and elucidating the mysteries of Indian tradition and history . . . The plan of this book is strictly national. It could only be achieved by a wealthy nation. To gather all the scattered proofs and traditions, in respect to the Indian races of America—to bring them together, in due relationship, for the future student—is to confer incalculable benefits upon science, history and art.[44]

The reviewer maintained that the publication's most important aspect was the inspiration it could provide for national art. This project thus assumed the function (otherwise associated with Catlin's gallery) of aestheticizing the Indian subject. Implicitly supporting Schoolcraft's editorial style, the reviewer argued that the project should have included all records on the subject "without mutilation," for no editor could know what part of a specific chronicle, tradition or artifact would invigorate art in the future, inspire the poet, painter, sculptor, or dramatist, for history's best use is art. "The errors and misconceptions of tradition are still portions of history, and are themselves not infrequently seized upon by genius." Even outlandish tales by early voyagers like the "Isles of Devils" were turned by the likes of Shakespeare into unsurpassed works of beauty. The reviewer further proposed that government should embrace another literary venture—a collection of all narratives ever written of discovery voyages to the New World. The publication of Henry Wadsworth Longfellow's *The Song of Hiawatha* (1855), which was clearly based on material collected by Schoolcraft for his federal project, seemed to demonstrate the artistic need for access to raw historical material.

"Transporting Water and Grass Seed, Valley of San Joaquin, California." This illustration from Schoolcraft's Indian volumes is typical of the nineteenth-century preoccupation with women's labor and the female naked body which also was evident in British social investigations. (Seth Eastman, after sketches by Edward Kern)

Two years later, Francis J. Bowen, the editor of the *North American Review*, attacked Schoolcraft's editorial incompetence, especially the printing of random and unreliable information. He quoted Alexander von Humboldt, who reportedly dismissed the work as a valueless compilation. Bowen called for public scrutiny of federal appropriations. He contrasted the enormous resources that had been invested in this "sumptuous" work with the government's parsimony in publishing Wilkes's exploring expedition reports and other scientific accounts such as the Coast Survey, which "appear[ed] in a dingy pamphlet the typography of which would be a disgrace to a penny newspaper."[45] For political reasons, Schoolcraft's project thrived at the expense of more valuable scholarly enterprises. In the wealth of information on the West's geology, geography, and discovery, the Indian himself was pushed aside, almost disappearing, sneered Bowen, repeating the cliché about writing the character Hamlet out of the play that bears his name. Bowen, it seems, was right. Schoolcraft's work did not so much commemorate the Indian as simulate his disappearance.

Coming at this phase, the criticism threatened to abort the project, which relied on annual appropriations. Schoolcraft believed that the polygenist camp was conspiring against him and that the archeologist Ephraim Squier stood behind a few hostile reviews. (Schoolcraft had criticized Squier's work in unflattering terms.[46]) One way or another, Schoolcraft was by then branded by many as a vestige of old amateurish ethnology. In January 1858, a particularly nasty review appeared in the *New York Herald*, attacking not just Schoolcraft but congressional excess as well. "Year after year massive quartos . . . fall like mud avalanches upon an unoffending public; provoking infinite mirth among those acquainted with aboriginal subjects at home, and astonishing scientific men abroad, by their crudity and incoherence. They are printed on costly paper, in luxurious type, and are full of sprawling outlines of beast and bird, smeared with bright yellow or dirty red, which for any scientific value they possess might be copied from the walls of a country schoolhouse; and the text is to match."[47]

The anonymous writer called Schoolcraft "a garrulous old man who should have been left to mumble his rubbish . . . under the porch of the corner grocery." A tone of bitterness and paranoia crept into Schoolcraft's correspondence during this period. In October 1853, he assured Indian commissioner George Manypenny that he had systematically organized the project according to a preconceived plan and that the material was untainted by the speculations and theories that had muddied public judgment of the Indian. They couldn't be expected to become political economists over night and manage their affairs. "There are persons in America who believe that our duties to the unenlightened aboriginal nations are overrated," he wrote about his polygenist foes. These individuals would not feel great sadness if the Indian race should soon perish.[48]

Property

In 1858, the ailing Schoolcraft appealed to Congress to compensate him for services rendered during his decade of work on Indian history. The following year, Schoolcraft's wife secured the passage of a private act under which Congress granted her and her husband an exclusive fourteen-year copyright for his Indian history. She had written to the Committee on Indian Affairs. "Congress determining to print no more of the "Indian History" consigns said plates, to the vandalism of rust, in the ghostly vaults of the capitol, with other . . . rubbish while to the author's deeply venerating wife, these souvenirs, would be inestimable, & cherished with all a woman's adhesiveness . . . and pride of a husband, who has spent a long life of dignified research in science, literature, & art & commands immortal fame as the only consecutive historian of the Red Race, known to the world's traditions."[49]

The copyright included the exclusive use of the engraved plates. Mary Howard then began arranging the publication of a commercial edition with which she hoped to recoup the family's fortunes. She recruited Spencer Fullerton Baird of the Smithsonian to help her find buyers for her husband's work in the scientific community at home and in Europe. There had been an earlier initiative to issue a private edition of the work. After the first volume was printed, the Schoolcrafts obtained permission to use the steel plates. In endorsing this project, Senator James Pearce, chairman of the library committee, wrote, "The only motive the Gov. had in ordering the publication was to preserve and diffuse the information it contained of a people fast fading away. A private edition would more completely effectuate this object by more widely diffusing this great national memorial."[50] Pearce claimed that the committee had always allowed such privileges to authors of "timely publications" under its supervision and that no special copyright was required. However, without copyright the Schoolcrafts had to spend more money and to charge fifteen dollars per volume. Mary Howard hoped, "Now that the book is no longer a 'Public Document' and the market cannot be overstocked by congressional *presentations*, of it, at home & abroad; we think it can be plausibly sold at $10 per volume."[51] Congress's unprecedented decision to concede by law to a private citizen an exclusive copyright of one of its formal publications showed the absence of a strict distinction between private and public ownership of official reports. Moreover, Lippincott, who was hired to execute the report, became in the early 1850s the Schoolcrafts' private publisher. He republished some of Schoolcraft's old writings and (quite reluctantly) the pro-slavery manuscript, *The Black Gauntlet: A Tale of Plantation Life in South Carolina* (1860) written by Mary Howard as a response to *Uncle Tom's Cabin.*

In another twist that exemplified the confusion over governmental and personal stakes in intellectual property, illustrator Seth Eastman claimed that Congress had wronged him and demanded proper compensation for his artwork. In a memorial prompted by Schoolcraft's copyright, Eastman argued that prior to his appointment as the project's artist he had contemplated a literary undertaking of his own, based on the knowledge of the Indian subject he had acquired in his leisure time.[52] He had made a great effort "perfecting himself in his art," acquiring material, and drawing sketches. He had in his possession sixty-seven paintings and sketches, which he eventually used for the six-volume enterprise. Government paid the engraver $325 for each of these plates, but Eastman received no compensation beyond his salary as an officer of the U.S. army. He now asked Congress to pay him for his property, which it had unduly granted to another person.

The congressional committee that examined the matter was sympathetic to Eastman's complaint. It recommended paying seventy-five dollars for the copyright of each of the sixty-seven pictures, a total of $5,025. The bill, however, never passed, and seven years later, the Senate Committee on Claims considered again compensating Eastman. This time, senators were less obliging. It was brought to the committee's attention that the illustrator's wife, Mary Eastman, published a book, *Chicora, and other Regions of the Conqueror and the Conquered* (1854) that featured twenty-one of Eastman's drawings; most, if not all of them, were identical to those in the official publication. As far as these twenty-one pictures were concerned, the committee argued, the Eastmans had already secured a priority of rights. As for the rest of the application, Eastman was employed by government and received a salary. He also had used, without pay, government-owned plates for his wife's book. The illustrator, the committee concluded, was not entitled to any special compensation.[53]

Ancient Monuments

In his oration before the Grand Order of the Iroquois, Schoolcraft commended his young listeners for banding together for the cause of scholarship. In Europe, he remarked, literary institutions depended on the benevolence of monarchs but republicans relied on the ability of individuals. Among the aboriginals, the to-

temic bond secured the tie between men and society. The union the Grand Order formed was just as noble, a totemic union of minds. "It is a band of brotherhood, but a brotherhood of letters . . . You aim at general objects and results, but
pursue them, through the theme and story of that proud and noble race of the
sons of the Forest, whose name, whose costume and whose principles of association you assume. Symbolically, you re-create the race."[54]

The following year, the brotherhood of science in America would have its own
totem and grand order in the form of the Smithsonian Institution. The institution soon decided to inaugurate its most prestigious publication forum, the *Smithsonian Contribution to Knowledge,* with a work on an Indian "theme and story,"
Ephraim G. Squier and Edwin H. Davis's *Ancient Monuments of the Mississippi
Valley* (1848). Like Schoolcraft, Squier, the monograph's primary author, regarded his archaeological work as a first step in a prospective national project.
The monograph did much to bolster the institution's standing as a leading scientific force.

Born in 1821 in Bethlehem, New York, Squier was editing a weekly newspaper in Chillicothe, Ohio, when in 1845 he and Davis, a local physician, began exploring archaeological sites in the region. The following year he became the
Clerk of the Ohio House of Representatives and, embarking on a political career
that would later lead to a short appointment (1849–50) as chargé d'affaires to
Guatemala. The two budding archeologists explored large artificial mounds, ostensibly shrines or burial sites whose ancient builders' ties to contemporary Indians was uncertain. In the early decades of the nineteenth century, there was
much debate over the identity of the mound builders. Their enigmatic origins
and mysterious disappearance stirred the taxonomic imagination of American
scholars and fiction writers. Were they survived by or destroyed by Indians? Were
they more advanced? Did they come from South America or had they migrated
there? Some thought that the answer to these and other questions could refute or
affirm Morton's controversial ideas. The most prevalent among the contending
views was that the mounds were constructed by a superior civilization. As an additional justification for his Indian removal policy, President Jackson employed
the speculative theory that inferior Indians had driven the more sophisticated
mound builders away.[55]

At the conclusion of two years of research, Squier was looking for public patronage for publishing their survey. In March 1847, he wrote Smithsonian secretary Joseph Henry, boasting that he and Davis might finally solve the "grand ethnological problem" presented by the mounds.[56] Squier had already described his
findings to Gallatin, who offered the support of the American Ethnological So-

ciety. Henry decided to adopt the project and to utilize this manuscript as a model for all future publications in terms of scientific protocol, stylistic uniformity, and production value. It was uncharacteristically risky of him to sponsor a monograph on such an incendiary topic. Yet he was keen on demonstrating that, despite his own training as a physicist, the new institution would address diverse scholarly interests. (The Smithsonian was charted to engage social research into topics such as penal reform in addition to natural science.) This account, moreover, presented an opportunity to display the might of science, not so much in resolving questions of origin as in properly representing the aboriginal subject matter in print. It was essential that Squier's finding would follow the acceptable scientific procedures that were the norm in the most admirable European institutions: peer review by an expert panel ostensibly unaware of the author's identity or affiliation. Through the Smithsonian series, Henry devised an apparatus of official publication very different from the unprincipled, haphazard patronage Congress bestowed on literary and scientific projects.

In a letter to Squier, Henry delineated a procedure for reviewing his monograph. The authors would apply to the Smithsonian for publication. The Smithsonian secretary then would refer the memoir to the Ethnological Society to determine whether it was an original contribution to knowledge. If the committee of the society replied in the affirmative, the memoir would be accepted for publication. Subsequently, Henry referred the study to the society for a blind examination and in response received Gallatin's endorsement for publication. As a gesture to scientific transparency, Henry published the entire exchange of letters between himself, Squier, and the Ethnological Society, as a preface to Squier's volume and later in the Smithsonian's annual reports. This approach became a template for the treatment of scholarly work.[57] Alas, the correspondence was heavily altered to fit the review process. The society was well acquainted with Squier and his work before the review began. Henry even dictated changes in the society's "independent" report, claiming, "I am obliged to be very cautious in conducting the first business of the Institution in order that I may not establish precedents which may embarrass my future operations."[58] He asked Squier to add to the preface (in fact, to fabricate) a mock application for the Smithsonian's assistance in making public his scholarship. In many respects, the first secretary of the Smithsonian was the moral compass of American science, but in his zeal to formalize the rituals of scientific publication, he falsified the record and presented a misleading account of the correspondence that had taken place. Employing this masquerade, the Smithsonian rendered the description of an indigenous past as a form of pure scientific endeavor (in the tradition of natural history), a process through which the Indian himself, once again, disappeared and the Smithsonian came to regulate and stratify the fraternal world of American science.

Squier was in charge of supervising the report's production. New York City artists made most of the engravings and woodcuts. From Washington, Henry followed the process carefully. He was preparing for a strictly uniform serial publication. Dictating the little details of the page outlay, he demanded, for instance, that Squier use only one column for the text's footnotes. "I am responsible for the style of the work," he insisted, "as this is the beginning of a series of volumes each [volume] of which must be on the same plan it is highly important that we start aright."[59] A few weeks before the monograph appeared, he wrote to Asa Gray, "I think it will make one of the most beautiful books ever published in this country."[60] In his view, only the Smithsonian could conduct a project of such quality.

In short, with the rise of the Smithsonian, the authoritative voices of the institution and science, in many ways mightier than that of the executive or Congress, were to overshadow the scholar's own authorial presence. Correspondingly, Henry censured Squier for the arrogant tone of his prose.[61] He also forbade him to add any theoretical speculation to the description of the mounds and their contents. Squier, a polygenist, was initially defiant but ultimately conformed to Henry's preferences.

The monograph's introduction carries a familiar assurance to the reader, "Care was exercised to note down, on the spot, every fact which it was thought might be of value . . . [n]o exertion was spared to ensure entire accuracy, and the compass, line, and rule were alone relied upon."[62] Otherwise, the preface was of a fresh character. It commenced with a short overview of previous literature on the mounds, at the conclusion of which the authors maintained that because of deficiencies in previous studies they had decided to start over, to jettison any preconceptions, and to devise a new plan of investigation. The main text was structured around visual representations (maps, woodcuts, engravings) of the mounds and the relics found in them, further enhancing the impression of a methodical survey focused on description and classification. Any direct mention of contemporary Indians was avoided. Three stock aboriginals occupied the front left corner of the frontispiece, which depicted "Ancient Works, Marietta, Ohio," but it seems that they were placed there for aesthetic reasons only, merely to frame the picture. The engraving of another famous site, Grace Creek Mound in western Virginia, which in the 1840s became a tourist attraction, depicted the mound in its modern condition: fenced and covered with trees, with a group of visitors enjoying a picnic at its base. Most of Squier and Davis's text was occupied by detailed description of artifacts and places. The run was modest (1,000 copies) and sumptuously bound in red morocco. It was categorically decided that only institutions would receive copies. As a work of science, the publication was distributed in exchange for the transactions of literary and scientific societies. Additional copies were given to all the colleges and principal libraries in the country.

Schoolcraft and Squier signified two modes of mid-nineteenth-century field-work-based scholarship that in one form or another required the assistance of organized science and the state. Squier and Davis's method of demonstrating the value and precision of their work was largely based on standardized procedures of research and publication as well as on strong markers of institutional authority. These conventions were sustained by a loosely defined scientific community and were devised to guarantee the veracity, importance, and originality of the information as well as the transparency of the process itself. Schoolcraft's techniques of verifying information rested on his proximity to the field of inquiry—his lengthy residence on the frontier and his familial ties with indigenous people—and to his association with the federal government. He also employed recognizable modes of representing authentic facts on the printed page. Schoolcraft and Squier shared an entrepreneurial zeal and were uneasy in their relationships with formal institutions. Schoolcraft's national project demonstrated federal inexperience, on the one hand, and the power of Congress in the dispensation of patronage to publishing ventures, on the other.

Why did Congress bother, for nearly a decade, to allocate substantial sums to what would become one of the costliest antebellum publication enterprises? This project was certainly an early attempt by the state to engage in a large-scale social survey (outside the census) based on detailed and rather intrusive statistical returns and canvassing performed by government officials. More importantly, Schoolcraft's work corresponded with political and national sentiment and with previously published exploration reports established an official history of the West. The federal government did not need scientific tools to devise a new policy, but Democratic administrations were interested in a strong endorsement of their existing policy. With this goal in mind, the ethnological material was as efficacious as statistics. This may also explain why, even after the exceedingly partial outcome of the poll became apparent to all, the project was not aborted. Schoolcraft's surveys thrived on party politics (although the support of Senator Charles Sumner—no friend of the Democratic Party—indicates a somewhat broader appeal.) In the midst of toiling over the first volume, Schoolcraft supported Lewis Cass's candidacy for the 1848 presidential election. He even wrote Cass's campaign biography. The ultimate failure of Schoolcraft's Indian census featured a tacit collaboration between native groups, who refused to be enumerated and be known to the federal government through detailed statistics (and thus exercised a measure of control over their representation), and federal field agents, who, for a variety of reasons, were strongly reluctant to conduct the survey and to impose the will of the Indian Office on their local interlocutors.

CHAPTER EIGHT

The Purloined Indian

The circumstances of Lewis Henry Morgan's research and writing seem incommensurable with Henry Schoolcraft's frontier experience and official patronage. Nevertheless, the social and national foundations of Schoolcraft's ethnology were present in Morgan's discovery of and attachment to the Indian subject. The book he published in 1851, after seven years of continuous yet mostly leisure-time research in western New York, was revolutionary. In *League of the Iroquois,* Morgan offered relatively little by way of Indian history. He also did not parade disconnected facts about native cultures and antiquities. Artifacts were described in conjunction with his observations on the social matrix of the Iroquois nations. His was a synchronic (rather than merely synoptic) look into the Iroquois league's political bodies, laws, family structures, religion, and culture, and how these elements operated in concert to enhance the particular political organization of the league. Ultimately, Morgan was as much a researcher of the Iroquois's political affairs or "state" as a social investigator. Like Schoolcraft, he was interested in the Indian mind. But Morgan regarded indigenous institutions and political arrangements as positive manifestations of mental capabilities. In the first of his ethnological monographs, Morgan inverted the paradigm, asking not how native ways impeded civilization but how this society, the Six Nations of the Iroquois, had remained viable for such a long time.

Morgan's book has been often considered (in fact, celebrated as) a prototype of structuralist anthropology. In it Morgan also made the initial steps toward the introduction of anthropology of kinship—which had not been an object of the ethnological gaze—by observing that the Iroquois family was structured differently from the western one. It expanded laterally—uncles were designated by specific terms as fathers, cousins were siblings, and so forth. He also learned that descent among the Iroquois was strictly matrilineal. These findings would lead to *Systems of Consanguinity and Affinity of the Human Family* published by the

Smithsonian in 1870 (on the basis of circulars sent through the State Department all over the globe). Marx and Engels enthusiastically embraced Morgan's later work, in which he delineated a course of human social evolution closely linked to material progress. Engels produced his treatise *The Origin of the Family, Private Property and the State in the Light of the Researches of Lewis H. Morgan* (1881) under the influence of Morgan's *Ancient Society* (1877). He went as far as declaring that Morgan's typology of the human family contributed to anthropology as much as Darwin's theory of evolution did to biology and Marx's theory of surplus value did to political economy.

In *League of the Iroquois*, Morgan also eschewed elaborate techniques to demonstrate the authenticity of the material he was presenting to his readers. Instead, in the preface he made two unusual gestures. First, he dedicated the book to his native informant: "To HÄ-SA-NO-AN'-DA (Ely S. Parker) A Seneca Indian, this work, the materials of which are the fruit of our joint researches, is inscribed: in acknowledgment of the obligations, and in testimony of the friendship of the author."[1] Second, as for the integrity of his evidence, Morgan (writing in third person) succinctly remarked, "Circumstances in early life, not necessary to be related, brought the author in frequent intercourse with the descendants of the Iroquois, and led to his adoption as a Seneca. This gave him favorable opportunities for studying minutely into their social organization, and the structure and principles of the ancient League."[2] The circumstances Morgan alluded to, rather vaguely, were his leadership in the New Order of the Iroquois, the "secret" fraternal organization of young aspiring professionals and businessmen in 1840s western New York.

This chapter focuses on Morgan's activities in the New Order of the Iroquois and his encounters with faux Indians, actual Indians, and ethnological information. It explores two mechanisms for the transmission of social knowledge: first, racial mimicry or masquerade, and second, the agency and representational work of the individual informant. Putting on "red face" was essential to the content of Morgan's ethnological work, to his sense of social discovery, as well as to the textual character of his reports. Racial cross-dressing was also emblematic of Indian-white relations in general and symptomatic (if atypical) of other social investigators' desire to cultivate some affinity with the investigated population. In comparison with Schoolcraft's project, it seems that the state receded from the scene of Morgan's investigations but, as will become patent, it never really disappeared. Like ethnographers and social investigators, Morgan served as an intermediary between government and the Indian.

The New Order

Morgan was born in 1818 to the wife of an affluent farmer near Aurora. After graduating from Union College, he returned home to study law, where he soon became involved in the Gordian Knot, a literary club that drew many of its members from the nearby Cayuga College. Whereas the early 1840s found Schoolcraft looking desperately for employment, the lingering depression following the panic of 1837 left Morgan with an abundance of free time. He was admitted to the bar but could not find a position. For a time he devoted himself to the temperance crusade, lecturing in nearby villages, but then immersed himself in the activities of his fraternal organization. Importantly, the Gordian Knot was a substitute for the type of social setting elsewhere offered by Freemasons and comparable associations. In the late 1820s, western New York had witnessed the emergence of the Anti-Mason Movement, instigated by the mysterious disappearance of William Morgan (not related to Lewis) who at the time of his alleged kidnap and murder (1826) was working on a manuscript aimed at exposing the secrets of Freemasonry.

Initially, members of the Gordian Knot wore white robes (in accordance with the Greek-revival vogue) and elaborate regalia and chose for their meetings the abandoned Masonic lodge in Aurora. Soon after, Morgan and his colleagues decided to "cut the knot" and to abandon the white robes in favor of an Indian theme.[3] In 1842, the new association was to be renamed the Cayugas (after the Indian nation that had occupied the region) but quickly assumed the identity of the entire Iroquois Confederacy, duly labeling itself, the Grand (or New) Order of the Iroquois (or the New Confederacy of the Iroquois). The society decided to replicate the internal organization of the Indian nations. An official plan was adopted, and the following summer the Grand Order of the Iroquois was formally established at a conference in Aurora attended by 150 delegates. For an aboriginal name, the organization selected We-yo-ha-yo-de-za-de Na-ho-de'-no-sau-nee, or "they who live in the home of the dwellers in the long house," in other words, those who replaced the Iroquois.

Morgan further elaborated the notion of substitution in an 1844 article he wrote for the *Knickerbocker.* The piece began with a quotation from the famed late eighteenth-century Iroquois orator Red Jacket: "Who then lives to mourn us? None. What Marks our Extermination? Nothing."[4] At the core of the article was a tale about a Cayuga Sachem, the historical figure Karistagia, or Steeltrap.

Ninety years earlier, the story goes, he had a prophetic vision occasioned by the first white visitors to the region. Steeltrap observed them come and go with an "anxious eye." Watching from the pastoral serenity of Cayuga Lake, the sachem, now in a state of slumber, was alarmed by the sight of the forest disappearing and the rising spire of a church surrounded by broad streets and cottages. He had a second detailed vision of a different spectacle, a restoration scene: a council house was once again located in its original grove, a council fire was lit, warriors were clad in the costumes of the ancient Cayugas, and bands of warriors brought a captive ready for the adoption ritual, a war dance.

Steeltrap consulted Delonoga (Copperhead), the aged prophet of the Cayugas, who construed the first part of the vision as foretelling of the rise of the "pale face" and the demise of the Indian, who would then be compelled to wander westward from his home. The symbol of the substitution was a bright star rising in the East while a dim star declined in the West. The prophet found promise in the second scene; it predicted the destruction of the new race and the return of the Indians to their forefathers' world. Morgan hinted here at the possibility that the new Indians were none other than the "braves" of the New Order of the Iroquois. The article concluded didactically with biographical details about Steeltrap and Copperhead, a short history of the Cayugas, and the original names of their clans or tribes. Morgan described the tortured existence and the desolation of the nation, which by 1800 had emigrated almost entirely to Ohio and Michigan (a small part joined the Senecas near Buffalo). Only two painted posts initially marked the graves of the sachem and the prophet. These were removed to make room for a "public convenience" and a road that passed over the graves, "a striking illustration of the truth, that we retain but little feeling or respect for the unfortunate Indian, and would fain disturb him, even in the silent resting place of the tomb."[5] During the same month in which Morgan published his vision, the fraternity adopted a song by the warrior George Glendinning, whose chorus declared:

> Then raise on high the battle cry
> We scorn the white man's laws;
> We form a band, called throughout the land
> Grand Order of the Iroquois.[6]

Members of the order decided to establish branches wherever they would go. Morgan reported that at its height the order numbered four hundred individuals. The league's annual conventions, rich with pageantry and initiation rites performed in the woods at midnight, were held in Aurora and usually attended by literary celebrities such as Schoolcraft and Alfred B. Street. Morgan was probably the group's most enthusiastic leader and served as its grand chief between 1844 and 1846. In late 1844, he settled in Rochester, where he practiced law and established a chapter of the order. That year he began writing reports on his Iroquois research, which he read during New Order meetings and eventually published in the *American Review* as "Letters on the Iroquois" (1847). Soliciting historian George Bancroft's patronage, Lewis described his society in some detail.

> We are all young men and the primary object of our confederacy is to rescue and preserve all that remains of the Six Nations—their manners, customs and organization, their history, mythology, and literature . . . We also aim to create and encourage a kinder feeling towards the Red-Man founded upon a true knowledge of the virtues . . . of his character. Our confederation is literary and social and entirely secret from the world . . . In our organization we have followed the old Confederacy in all respects and have studied it out in order to perfect the same. We think it is now firmly planted and can near an Indian order that will be an honor to the Republic and has a tendency in the said to do justice to the Red Man.[7]

In the quest to find patrons among the elders of American ethnology and the literary world, the Grand Order sought the cooperation of Lewis Cass, Washington Irving, William Cullen Bryant, and even John Quincy Adams. Morgan framed his essays on the Iroquois as letters to Albert Gallatin. He also met with the Onondaga chief Abram La Fort and with Joshua V. H. Clark, who was then working on the history of Onondaga County. The New Confederacy bestowed honorary membership on both.

The playfulness of Indian pageantry coalesced with the ponderous sincerity of a scholarly and reform association. These two missions were perhaps best manifested in Morgan's idea that performing Indian rites and methodically building the order according to the authentic structure of the Indian confederacy constituted doing justice to their memory. At the same time, the Indian motif was grafted onto what was fundamentally a fraternal society modeled on Freemasonry. In a letter to a new chapter of the Grand Order, Morgan specified that the Indian customs assumed the role that uniforms had for Masons or voluntary fire companies (another form of mid-nineteenth-century fraternal association). "They seem to lend dignity and interest to the organization, and in my way of viewing the subject, an Indian costume is indispensable and one of the most interesting departments of the order. Have the whole equipage, dress, bow, tomahawk, and head dress of feathers, the bow next to the coat goes the furthermost."[8] For their initiation rite, members performed the ceremony of war captives in full regalia.

The Warriors met for the initiation of W. Hurd. The Council fire in the Valley of the Shistus. Soon after it was lit up, the boundaries of the sacred ground being intruded upon by a pale face, he was sent howling through the forest, causing the rocky banks of fair Cayuga to re-echo with his yells. By the presence of mind of one of the Braves the initiation then followed. He was led to the sacred spot by Shenandoah. After having gone through the regular ceremonies some of the bold and daring warriors sallied forth bringing back with them the produce of the White mans cornfield which was roasted by the glowing coals of the Council fire and served as nutritive aliment to the empty abdomens of our Warriors. After having chanted the war songs and danced the war dance each warrior returned to his wigwam to enjoy the exquisites of somnolency.[9]

The Grand Order's desire to duplicate the original Iroquois ways presented a problem of knowledge. The founders were familiar with the names of the Six Nations but not much more. Morgan was born and raised in the land of the Iroquois, but by the time he was a child the Cayugas were all but gone. It was Morgan's proximity to the actual Iroquois nations that prompted him to assume an Indian face. As it was for social investigators in urban settings, the proverbial other was both near and unknown.

Morgan began combing history books for details, though these sources proved grossly inaccurate. While he had already acquired some information from Indian acquaintances, his friendship with Seneca interpreter Ely Parker produced a few of the most important breakthroughs. Morgan met Parker in 1845, and the young Seneca (sixteen years old at the time) introduced him to his grandfather Jemmy Johnson, the most revered living authority on Iroquois culture, especially on the spiritual beliefs of the early nineteenth-century Iroquois religious innovator Handsome Lake. In his initial interviews with Johnson, other Seneca elders, and members of the Parker family, Morgan was particularly interested in learning Seneca words that he could use for the New Order's communications. He sought information on the structure of the league so that the order could employ authentic titles for its office holders. Every "tribe" had a sachem, a head warrior, a prophet in charge of the initiates, as well as modern functionaries: a secretary, a treasurer, and a librarian—offices that were also adorned with Seneca monikers. In the 1845 meeting, the New Order added the functions of Leader of the War Songs and Keeper of the Wardrobe.

The supposedly secretive interior of the New Order (in imitation of Freemasonry conventions but, as importantly, a sequestered peer environment in which adolescents could become men) was thus to be sustained by the probe into the "secrets" of the ancient Iroquois. In their performances and initial forays into ethnology, the New Order exercised three modes of Indian representation. First, they impersonated natives and simulated aboriginal society through rituals, attire, implements, bodily practices, and the organization of their fraternity. Second, amassing and committing information to writing, they functioned as a receptacle of Iroquois memory. In the preamble of their constitution, the New Confederacy defined itself as the "repository of all that remains of the Indians." Third, the young members embarked on advocacy and publicity in order to demonstrate to white society the intrinsic value of aboriginal civilization.

Ultimately, Morgan would engage in a fourth form of representation, by speaking and negotiating on the Iroquois's behalf. Acquiring, presenting, and representing Indian knowledge also constituted an act of judgment. As he explained his emerging ethnological plan: "We study other and ancient races as much through their institutions and governments as in their political transactions. How then shall a just estimate of the Iroquois be formed if we confine ourselves to their exploits upon the warpath and in council."[10] For that purpose, he defined five categories of investigation: government (alliances, councils, decision making), people (social condition, manners and customs, arts, games, dress), laws (property, descent, marriage, punishments, captivity and adoption, hostility), religious systems, and historical events. Morgan's was not the only effort at Iroquois scholarship to emerge out of the New Order experience. Other members presented papers during monthly and annual meetings, and some of Morgan's findings were the result of collective exertions. Clark was to write about cemeteries in the Onondaga country. Isaac Hurd, to give another example, devised a set of rules for interviewing informants. It "is imposed upon the inquirer to make his questions simple, yet comprehensive, brief, yet embracing all the important points necessary to be known. It will not do to ask questions, and then answer them, as best suit the fancy of the investigator, for in that case the facts which he supposed he had likely obtained, are not facts, but a specious decoction of his own brain."[11] This elementary advice was a step up from the confused state of ethnological conversation between white visitors and Indian hosts. The former usually asked questions that the respondent could satisfy by a simple yes or no. Rarely would the Indian informant bother to go beyond a direct, monosyllabic reply.[12]

In September 1845, three chiefs of the New Order visited the Tonawanda reservation to witness the Condolence Council. The council convened to raise new sachems to replace deceased ones. This presented an invaluable opportunity to study first hand the political framework of the Six Nations and the process of leader selection that was still a functioning ritual. The ceremony featured the roll call of the Iroquois supreme chiefs, the fifty sachems that comprised the highest council of the league. Chatting with a few Indian acquaintances, Morgan was able to complete the sachem list. The roll documented the dispersion of sachemships along nations and clans and was the key to the structure of the entire league. Upon his return to Rochester, he boasted to Schoolcraft, "I think the Old Confederacy or the mere shadow of it which is left, is opened to the New." Now he was so "crammed with matter pertaining to the Iroquois that I intend for my own relief to sit down immediately and write a series of essays upon the government and institutions of the Iroquois for publication."[13]

The Condolence Council, Morgan's portal into Iroquois society, had been the league's most important mnemonic device, its living archive. The council's ceremonies had been expanded during the colonial period into a complex drama in which, for over a century, British and French governors, their agents, and other European actors performed side by side with native leaders. In modern versions participants divided into two moieties, mourners and condolers, or the "clear-minded," and the sequence of rituals had a strong reciprocal character. Expressions of grief interlaced with recurrent attempts to lift the spirit, wipe tears, open ears, and clear throats. In addition to the eulogy or the roll call of the fifty founders, the rites featured the Requickening Address, recitation of Iroquois laws, presentation of new chiefs, songs, a feast, and Rubbing Antlers, the celebration dance.[14] The ultimate purpose of these rites was regeneration. Through moments of acting out mourning, consolation, and rebirth, the council restored society to its old functioning form.

In his correspondence with Schoolcraft, Morgan offered another rationale for publishing his findings. It was the best way to put the other New Order "nations" in possession of knowledge. Indeed, as new information arrived, the New Confederacy modified itself accordingly. It therefore decided to drop the Tuscarora Nation because as relative newcomers to the original league (they joined in the 1720s) they did not partake in the sachem structure. The relationship between the new and the old leagues seemed even closer when Morgan, Charles Talbot Porter, and Thomas Darling arrived in the Tonawanda reservation in the fall of 1847 for their adoption into the Seneca Nation. For ten days, the visitors witnessed games and dances staged in their honor and at night listened to Seneca elders reminiscing about Iroquois tradition and historical events. Each morning, Morgan made sure to record the information in his notebook. The adoption ceremony took place in the council house where Jemmy Johnson, the religious instructor, bestowed Seneca names on the young guests, identified the specific tribes that they now joined, and explained the reasons for their adoptions. Two chiefs escorted each neophyte, holding his arms and chanting. The audience responded enthusiastically. After three rounds, the simple ritual ended. The evening concluded with a formal dance and a feast paid for by the guests. Morgan was adopted into the Hawk clan and received the Indian name of Ta-ya-do-wuh'-kuh meaning the one who is lying across the bridge, or the bond between Indians and whites.

Red Face

Like many modern scholars who have explored his ethnological project, Morgan acknowledged the importance of the Grand Order in igniting his initial interest in ethnology. However, he dismissed the society's activities as adolescent play, a temporary phase that led serendipitously to important discoveries but was otherwise immaterial. Nevertheless, the experience of the New Order was more than merely an accidental venue for Morgan's ethnology. In the second half of the 1840s, he conducted only half a dozen short field trips. Much of the information he gathered came from informants. Most importantly, Morgan asked different questions than other ethnologists because he wanted to sustain the New Order as a miniature replica of the Iroquois League. His interest gravitated towards issues of organization and function. His insights into the political structure of the Iroquois and its familial arrangement were due in no small part to Grand Order's weekend pursuits. This, rather than his later adoption, was ultimately the foundation of his insiderness.

Playing Indian is a recurrent theme in American history, a practice that has served diverse social and political purposes. While Morgan and his friends were masquerading in the western part of the state, bands of tenant farmers in upstate New York followed the tradition of the Boston Tea Party and disguised themselves in mock Indian attire to protest the leasehold tenure. In the mid-1840s, the antirent movement turned to violence when "Indians" prevented the auction of farmland and attacked agents, sheriffs, and uncooperative neighbors. The New York State Assembly decided to prohibit by law the use of the Indian disguise.[15] However, the New Order of the Iroquois masquerade seems to have originated from a somewhat different social environment, the rise of a new urban middle class and, with it, the male culture of fraternal organizations. Their initiation rites were an essential practice of nineteenth-century bourgeois masculinity. As described by historian Mark Carnes, young men were leaving protected private spheres—increasingly dominated by their mothers—and seeking experiences that would permit them to enter the world of adult men. Beyond initiating adolescents through elaborate rituals, these fraternities facilitated communities and equipped their younger members with social contacts important for their future success in the marketplace.

The New Iroquois's passion for transforming into Indians in a historically correct fashion meant that this particular rite was to be emplotted as a story of captivity, surrender, and implied torture. (Concocted rituals of capture and torment resolved by adoption were the staple initiation ceremonies of most fraternal organizations.) The fantasy of being taken over and then saved by aboriginals was particularly potent in American culture, as confirmed by the numerous permutations and longevity of the Pocahontas stories. It was a known custom among the Iroquois to decimate enemy nations by adoption, although most enemy warriors were tortured and killed. Those who consented to adoption were virtually reborn; their old identity obliterated. Adoption severed all preceding ties, including birthrights, marriage, and children. It was symbolically the moment of crossing over, of surrender and remaking.

Torture and rebirth were common motifs in other culture's initiation rites, where male adolescents on the verge of adulthood are often consigned to liminal groups that reside outside the confines of society. According to one interpretation, reenacted torture was an instrument to shatter the bonds between mother and son or an expression of a desire to undermine the exclusive female hold on reproduction; here, by the "birthing" of men by other men (usually older men) through, for instance, mock adoptions and the forging of new identities.[16] In the case of the Grand Order, the figure of the Indian assumed the role of the patriarch. We have already encountered traces of this fantasy on the national level in the wish to recognize Indians as ancestral figures replacing other symbolic parents, moving attention from the British mother country to the masculine native. Morgan and his friends were thus acting out the desire to assume an indigenous (and therefore non-European, exceptionalist) national identity. Schoolcraft's national vision rested on an imagined or, rather, entirely fabricated kinship with an authentic past based on a shared scenery and nature, a vision of utilizing aboriginal history for forging new nationalism. In the Grand Order's identification with the Iroquois, there were hints of animosity against the young men's own American fathers or forefathers—evidenced in Karistagia's dream of avenging the intrusion on Iroquois land—as well as traces of what Freud termed "family romance," the child's fantasy of replacing his parents with a more noble pair. This private wish had a larger resonance in the cultural landscape of the early republic, when Americans first formalized and practiced the cult of the "founding fathers," revering them as specimens of human perfection. Could it be then, that the United States was supplementing the pantheon of its progenitors with another set of mythic ancestors like Red Jacket, Copperhead, and the venerated fathers of the Iroquois League?

What singled Morgan's group out from other nineteenth-century fraternal bodies borrowing the Indian theme was its emphasis on the accuracy of the emulation and insistence on maintaining actual relations with a group of Indian nations. This aspect also distinguished the New Iroquois from the later anthropological tradition of close observation. The history of anthropology is crowded with explorers who "went native" and practiced what Bronislaw Malinowski would formulate as the practices of participant-observation. But in this particular episode, in what may be modern anthropology's moment of birth, racial masquerading was not merely a cunning technique to obtain information. It worked the other way around. First, Morgan and his friends became "Indians." Then, they assumed the mantle of ethnographers. Ethnology, as much as playing Indians, was the substance of their rite of passage.

This understanding of the Grand Order's activities foregrounds the impersonation of Indians over the specific content of the fraternity's rituals. The most relevant historical context of playing Indians might be not the burgeoning fraternal organizations but the growth of yet another transgression of racial boundaries. In the 1840s, minstrelsy or black face became a popular art form and thrived from northeastern cities to the California gold mines. Donning the black mask allowed white performers to appropriate black music and dance while simultaneously negotiating racial curiosity and hostility. These performances gave license to the articulation of disruptive social notions about class, gender, and sexuality. As minstrelsy, red-face pageantry had the double consequences of transporting cultural knowledge and forms and, at the same time, reconfiguring the relationship between original performers and their surrogates. Indian masquerade resulted in the adoption of games, attire, dances, ceremonies, names, and ultimately ethnological knowledge. One crucial aspect of that traffic—and relations between whites and Indians in general—was the symbolic dissolution of the bonds between contemporaneous Indians and their ancestors or ancestral memory.

Gender ambiguity further complicated the widening split between the Indian and the historic Indian. While the latter was manly and ancestral, he was also an aesthetic being, as clearly demonstrated by the spectacular drawings in Schoolcraft's six-volume project and other treatments of the native theme in books, paintings, and sculptures. The Indian was an object of beauty, whose otherness could substitute for gender differences. The persona that was assumed by Indian pageantry was strongly female if only by virtue of its performativity. It certainly needed a host of accouterments: facial and bodily paint, headwear, dresses, feathers, and similar adornments.

The benign nature of the Grand Order's games, the strong empathy that Morgan and his friends expressed towards the Senecas, and the Senecas' cooperation with their ethnological project only masked the ambiguous character of the young whites' gesture. They commandeered aboriginal otherness for transgressive pleasure, for their rites of passage, and to craft an exceptionalist native identity. (This rendition of antebellum nativism rested on Indian heritage.) As in Schoolcraft's and Ephraim Squier's projects, in the Grand Order's insistence on the historicity of the objects of their emulation, the Indian (or the glorious Indian of yesterday) vanished. This disappearance rested on the assumption that the aboriginal would entirely assimilate. We should not regard Indians as merely our fellow men, opined Morgan; they should become part of American society. He consequently recommended that their common tribal property be divided among them. Private property was the first step towards making them citizens of the state. "When this time arrives," he concluded, "they will cease to be Indians, except in name."[17] The Jacksonian treatment of aboriginals as dependent children has received scholarly attention, but it is highly significant that the Indians, in fact, occupied alternating positions as ancestors and descendants. This oscillation continued to dominate the relationship between aboriginal and white societies well into the twentieth century. Whatever roots this ambivalence toward the Indian had in private desire, it also affected the way national policy was devised and justified.

As a story of mimicry and exchange, the Grand Order's masquerade shares a few intriguing affinities with Edgar Allan Poe's "The Purloined Letter" (1844). (Jacques Lacan famously employed this story to explicate his notion of the "mirror-stage" in which the child recognizes himself completely through his image in a mirror or in his mother's eyes. Lacan's concept inspired Franz Fanon's views of racial identification in *Black Skin, White Masks* (1952) as well as many later readings of racial and gender cross-dressing). Poe's is a tale of the double theft of a compromising private letter, at the center of which is a technique of obtaining or retrieving an object. The aggressor assumes the vantage point of his victim. In the first scene, it is the minister who boldly purloins the queen's compromising letter in her own chamber and in the presence of the unsuspecting king; in the second scene, the nimble detective Dupin appropriates the letter (now hidden in the minister's domicile) under the nose of the obtuse police. In "The Purloined Letter," the effort to recognize oneself in the other (or to see oneself from the mirror reflection's point of view) was premised on a physiognomic technique of mimicry.

Poe's story encapsulates important themes in antebellum culture: its fascination with hoaxes, deceptions, and crime (including crimes of identity by confidence men, a term coined in the period), the increasing desire for social critique, and most importantly, the attempt to grapple with the immense fluidity of positions and identities offered by the new marketplace. In some important respects, the "Dream of Karistagia" was itself a version of "The Purloined Letter" (and in a different manner, the Iroquois's own Condolence Council), not just as a story of double appropriation but because the second scene (deceptively) restored and addressed the primary scene. The dream triggered a succession of further substitutions. Grand Order braves reenacted tribal society, initiated each other into a mock-Indian peer group, and then were adopted (in fact, only a few leaders were) by the genuine Seneca. But there was also an opposite way in which the New Order of the Iroquois embraced the old. Both leagues adopted each other as children and fathers in an apparent, yet misleading symmetry. Similar mirroring episodes were evident on the national scene. In the nineteenth century, Indian tribes were first removed from white society so they could (paradoxically) better resemble it. Some argued that only from outside the boundaries of U.S. society could this civilizing mimetic process succeed. Native peoples relocated to the West and then the United States placed itself in the West as well, in ways real and symbolic.

Names of the Fathers

Morgan's formal adoption, and what he considered his intimate knowledge of the Iroquois, seemed to relieve him from the conventions of reports written by the fact collectors of the earlier period. *League of the Iroquois* is unencumbered by the obsession with the authenticity of objects or veracity of facts; these were assured by the social intercourse that surrounded the text. It seemed that the document stood in equipoise to its scene of research rather than collapsed into it. The book is not an account of red-face (or other field experiences) but its after-the-fact conclusion. This property of the monograph, juxtaposed to Schoolcraft's *Notes on the Iroquois* published only five years earlier, may serve as the basis for one story of the coming of age of anthropology itself. (If *Notes* appeared to be stuck in the mirror stage and, as the rest of Schoolcraft's oeuvre, exemplified a somewhat retentive aggregation of field objects ostensibly reproduced in great fidelity, *League* transgressed the mirror by identifying the work of culture and attempting to capture, rather than merely reflect, it in a theoretical framework. This is the trajectory from ethnography to ethnology, or—drawing further from the Lacanian well—from the imaginary to the symbolic.) Morgan established a theoretical contrivance that, in later decades and with important alterations, he would apply universally. In this new ethnological mode, facts were separated from artifacts. Like Schoolcraft, Morgan collected Indian material culture, in his case, for New York State. New York initiated its own version of state building and cultural production, launching projects to document the state's history, geology, and native past. However, working for the state cabinet accentuated the difference between ethnographical texts functioning as museums and actual museums—another venue for Indian representation.

Morgan dedicated the first part of *League of the Iroquois* to discussing political institutions. In the second, he surveyed cultural aspects such as faith, religion, burial customs, moral sentiment, festivals, and marital relations, while the third section featured material culture and matters that pertained to language, geography, and place names. Morgan wrapped his ethnological findings in reformist passages, beginning with a preface on the book's purpose in inspiring kinder feelings toward the Indian and concluding with a chapter on the future of the aboriginal.[18]

He asserted that Iroquois historical resistance to European incursions indicated strength, at the roots of which he saw the conscious building of social and political institutions. The "founders of the League" were aware of the impairing effects of divisions into small, contending hunting bands. By instituting a federation, they sought to establish an empire that would control surrounding nations and protect the Iroquois from incessant war. As a modular concept, the League of the Iroquois had the potential of further expansion.[19] Was Morgan then falling victim to the trickery of mirrors? Unwittingly, perhaps, he recognized in the Iroquois a distant image of the United States, imperial ambitions and sagacious founding fathers included. Publishing his book just a year after the contentious Compromise of 1850, Morgan was particularly attentive to the formidable stability of Iroquois society.

At this point, Morgan arrived at the crux of his ethnological discovery. The league, he posited, was merely an elaboration of the family organization that sutured the entire Six Nations together in "one common, indissoluble brotherhood."[20] Later in his scholarly career, Morgan would refine his views of familial configuration and descent, but as early as this monograph he conceived of (or, in fact, invented) kinship as the primary structural principle of society. At the same time, he realized that family designations could divert from western norms. In the Iroquois, the scope of the nuclear or "biological" family was drastically extended by means of language. His work implicitly acknowledged the arbitrary nature of human kinship and by implication the importance of mock kinship. Familylike social commitments mitigated between affiliations of blood and large political organizations, between society and the state. This was the social mortar (the totemic link) offered in the antebellum United States by fraternal organizations, as well as by literary, religious, and reform associations.

The Iroquois social bond was achieved by a particular pattern of kinship and descent that supported tribal society and then braided tribes into discreet nations. Kinship-tribes (distinct from the political nations) were never made up of descendants of the same father, for the father and his son were never of the same tribe. The building blocks of that regime were eight tribes with which the founders of the league "sought to interweave the race into one political family."[21] The tribes (Wolf, Turtle, Beaver, Bear, Deer, Snipe, Heron, and Hawk) were divided among the five nations and maintained fraternal ties. The Mohawk of the Wolf tribe acknowledged the Seneca of the Wolf tribe as his sibling. Cross-relationship among tribes of the same name were stronger than fellowship among tribes of the same nation. This hybridity of the Iroquois social identity that prescribed "national" and "tribal" affiliations—western concepts superimposed on native societies—was responsible for the ability of the entire structure to hold firmly together. (Morgan's finding may be of some interest to observers of identity politics debates today, especially in light of the racial hybridity sanctioned by the census of 2000.) If any of the five nations wanted to break off the alliance, it would have broken the cord of tribal brotherhood, the sinews of the Iroquois society.

Iroquois could marry into any tribe except their own. Matrilineal descent was a guarantee to preserve the individuality and the unity of the tribe. A man could not take a sachemship with him into a different tribe. He could not leave the title or for that matter any other sort of property, including his tomahawk and other war implements, to any of his sons. Morgan argued that the purpose of that convention was "the perpetual disinheritance of the son" in order to maintain the purity of bloodline.[22] Tribal affiliation transferred through the mother, not through her husband who, in a previous state of society when the mother plausibly had multiple sexual partners, was not necessarily the father of her children. No distinction was made between the lineal and collateral lines. The maternal grandmother and her sisters were equally mothers; the children of a mother's sisters were brothers and sisters; the children of a sister were nephews and nieces, and the grandchildren of a sister were grandchildren. Out of the tribe, the paternal grandfather and his brothers were equally grandfathers, the father and his brothers equally fathers, and so forth. In his later work on consanguinity, Morgan called this the "classificatory family" rather than the western "descriptive family" (comprised of biological fathers, mothers, and siblings) and attempted to identify similar structures among other so-called primitive societies, proclaiming that family structure attested to a society's location on the road to civilization.

It is somewhat ironic that Morgan, who engaged in masculine Indian role-playing, would find out that among the Iroquois the relationship between father and son was disjointed. At the same time, it was clear to him that this society was conceived by men and for men, and that the matrilineal line was a way to retain the identity (and "names") of the original tribal chieftains. Every facet of Iroquois culture—religion, dances, ceremonies, artifacts, and architecture—was put in place for the specific reason of sustaining the sociopolitical edifice. Functionalist at heart, Morgan regarded these operations as enhancements of social intercourse. He construed the elaborate Indian dances, for example, as a means to allow controlled encounters between the sexes but also as a device to ignite a national spirit. Similarly, the council fires were sites of political decision-making, but in addition functioned as a public sphere where the Iroquois came together literally and symbolically.

What Morgan discovered in Iroquois society was not actual fathers or borrowed fathers but what Lacan called (somewhat opaquely) the "name of the father," that is, the entire symbolic order of society that separates the child from his mother and assures social cohesion. Morgan was fascinated by actual Indian names. They bestowed identity, either by the totemic principle by which affiliation was determined through a shared symbol, a fetish, or by the custom of naming individuals figuratively and renaming them whenever their social status changed. (Indian place names were probably one of the earliest indications for the American child of the presence of the cultural other.) Morgan took an Indian name early on and received another one upon his adoption. At the age of twenty, before leaving Aurora for college, he inexplicably adopted a middle name, Henry. (Schoolcraft also assumed different native names, and for almost a year in the early 1840s, he went by Colcraft.) Such trifling acts of personal transformation or self-making were emblematic of the emerging marketplace-bound and anxiety-ridden mass society.

It has been suggested that the presence in western New York of utopian communities and other forms of radicalism inspired Morgan's insight into Iroquois kinship. Between the 1820s and the 1850s, the region was a fertile ground for religious and social experimentation. Early in this period, a wave of evangelical enthusiasm earned western New York the label "the burned-over district." In the 1840s, religious inventiveness was supplemented by the proliferation of political radicalism, from the women's movement (whose first conference was held in 1848 in Seneca Falls) to socialism (Millerite communities of property and Fourierist socialist phalanxes), spiritualism, and abolitionism. Mormon families, Millerite communities, and free-love communes, all practiced unconventional economical and sexual arrangements. Their example may have contributed to Morgan's ability to discern differing social structures.[23] However, the split between father and son was not necessarily a characteristic of utopian communities but rather a facet of the modern middle class and its model or myth of the self-made (and therefore parentless) man. Morgan's own biography exemplifies the rupture between the world of the father (who was a farmer on the old western New York frontier) and his son. The farmer's son became a lawyer, whose livelihood depended on the whims of the market. Any reading of *League of the Iroquois* should, therefore, consider the role of western New York in forging a new American middle class. During the rapid commercialization that followed the opening of the Erie Canal in 1825, communities in that region experienced, probably earlier than other parts of the country, the remaking of domesticity along the separation of spheres and its removal from the market place. Correspondingly, there is in Morgan's ethnological work an immense appreciation of the familial institution in all of its permutations and extensions, and yet a certain awareness of the family's fragility or insufficiency; hence, the importance he associated with transfamilial arrangements.

In the Long House

Morgan aestheticized Iroquois society in a manner distinct from that of his ethnological predecessors. The Iroquois political system was itself an artifact that his analysis rendered a complete, coherent, and perfectly rational apparatus. His effort to decipher the principles underscoring Iroquois stability can also be read as a manifestation of the period's fascination with the working of elaborate mechanical devices, as evident in Schoolcraft's writing on the Indian mind and in several of P. T. Barnum's enterprises. Associating the Iroquois regime with an artifact also rested on the symbolic self-designation of the Iroquois as dwellers of the longhouse. In this metaphor, craftsmanship, government, and domesticity merged. "In their own figurative enunciation of the idea, the chiefs served as braces in the Long House—an apt expression of the place they occupied in their political structure."[24] In antebellum parlance, the house trope often denoted the American Union as well.

Morgan had a keen interest in material culture. He regarded Iroquois craftsmanship as an expression of intellectual ability. However, in a manner that would so profoundly impress Engels, he insisted that material objects were expressions of social organization. (Conversely, the interest in material culture was no more than a variant on the metonymic employment of physical environment to define and judge individuals and communities, as was customary in urban social inquiries.) "The fabrics of a people unlock their social history. They speak a language which is silent, but yet more eloquent than the written page." This capacity for articulation was especially apparent in the Iroquois techniques of memory keeping. In the absence of written language, they registered treaties and laws by weaving wampum belts. With the help of an interpreter the belt could "tell" about an exact law or a transaction. The notion of the speaking artifact or the artifact as a memory aid reappeared in Morgan's commentary on material culture. He considered his collection for the New York State Museum "a memento of the red race ... [who would be] ... enabled to speak for itself through these silent memorials."[25] The eloquence of those articles was predicated on their placement in a museum in Albany. Morgan subscribed to the principle that it was government's duty to accumulate relics of aboriginal culture. "We stand with them in many interesting relations," he wrote, repeating Schoolcraft's words in a letter to the Regents of the State University of New York in yet another attempt to define those links.[26] New York had committed itself to gather historical material following Governor John Young's visit to the historical and antiquarian museum in Hartford, Connecticut.[27] Morgan collaborated in this effort, first sending plans of five archaeological sites together with about fifty ethnographic articles. Finding archeological relics was common in antebellum western New York, where farmers stumbled upon aboriginal objects almost daily.

In 1848 and 1849, when the state cabinet was expanding, Morgan proposed to gather "a full exhibition of the manufactures of the Indian tribes still remaining within our State."[28] The regents granted him $215 to supervise the project. His official assignment brought him again to the Tonawanda reservation. While in Albany arranging the collection and finalizing the report, he introduced into the state legislature a bill for the support and education of Indian students at the State Normal School at Albany, thus reaffirming the Janus face of American ethnology: reforming the Indian while preserving his legacy. His account for the regents' third annual report was accompanied by richly colored engraving prepared by Richard H. Pease of Albany. Pease also engraved two plates of Indian subjects which Morgan used for his *League of the Iroquois* published early the following year. In the fall of 1850, Morgan traveled to the Six Nation Reserve on the Grand River in Ontario, where he obtained and purchased objects such as a shell breastplate, a carved can, silver beads, a wampum belt, and a fine burden trap. Unlike other collectors of Indian relics (and in line with social investigators), he was interested in a comprehensive collection of daily implements rather than spectacular ceremonial gear, large weapons, or artifacts that belonged to departed Indian dignitaries.[29]

Informants

In April 1844, Lewis Morgan visited Albany to peruse Indian treaties. Scanning the shelves of a local bookstore in search of information on the Cayuga, he ran into a young Seneca from the Tonawanda reservation, Ely Parker. Educated in a Baptist missionary school and the Yates Academy, Parker (Hä-sa-no-an'-da, "Leading Name") was serving as an interpreter and advisor to the Seneca chiefs in their dealings with authorities in Albany and Washington. In Washington, young Parker became a celebrity. He fraternized with President James Polk at the White House, small-talked with Daniel Webster and Henry Clay, and later bragged about riding around the city in Mrs. Polk's carriage. By his mid-twenties, Parker was formally elevated to the Grand Sachem of the Seneca and thus was the de facto leader of the Six Nations. Trained throughout this period as a lawyer and as an engineer, he worked in the 1850s for the New York state canal before moving west. In Galena, Illinois, he befriended a former army captain by the name of Ulysses S. Grant who was then a clerk in his father's store. When the Civil War began, Parker attempted to enlist. Rejected at first, he tried again and eventually joined Grant's headquarters as his military secretary. Parker witnessed the most famous battles of Grant's campaign. The conditions of Robert E. Lee's surrender were recorded in his handwriting, and he was inside the courthouse at Appomattox on April 9, 1865, as a member of Grant's staff. Parker left the army with the rank of an honorary (brevet) brigadier-general. After Grant entered the White House in 1869, Parker became Commissioner of Indian Affairs, the first Indian to hold this position.

But before all of that, in the mid 1840s, Parker was Morgan's informant. In fact, the entire Parker family assisted Morgan and his colleagues in their research. They helped him in ways similar to the introduction to the native world that the Johnstons gave to Schoolcraft in Sault Ste. Marie in another bicultural family setting. The Parkers were among the small number of Christians (Baptists) on the reservation, where most other Senecas still resisted the invasion of the white man's religion. Ely's siblings posed for illustrations for Morgan's book. Levi, an older brother, was depicted in the book's frontispiece (in an engraving probably made from a daguerreotype) wearing a traditional garment. Dressed in attire that Morgan obtained in 1849 for the state museum, Caroline was also a subject of an engraving. (Morgan's relationship with Parker's sister was close and flirtatious.) It was in discussions with Ely's parents, William and Elisabeth, that Morgan first became acquainted with the structure and the domestic uses of the longhouse. Morgan borrowed additional material for his book directly from Ely and his brother Nicholson's essays on Iroquois customs.

In the fall of 1848, Morgan wrote to Ely Parker and requested that he record in full Johnson's speech to the annual council. He also wanted to know exactly how Indian objects were crafted and what were their correct designations. "What is the name of these earthen dishes? Give me the names both of the earthen and the brass. I have also a calumet, a long one about two feet. The stock is wood, and covered with a case of beadwork. It is from the west. Give me its name."[30] Morgan hoped that Parker would help him come up with a ringing, one-word appellation for the state's Indian collection. The Parkers acquired or made most of the objects. They were also recipients of much of the funds Albany had allotted for putting together the collection. When visiting the reservation the following year, Morgan purchased many items but also received gifts, such as a pipe from William Parker for which he reciprocated with a German silver tobacco bag. Morgan later exhibited the curiosities in his office, where Rochester women were invited to observe the trove of Indian domestic artifacts. In June 1850, Morgan received an additional $250, and he promptly shipped to the state capital a model of an Iroquois house made by William Parker and a canoe.[31]

Cooperation with ethnologists had a practical rationale. Throughout the 1840s and 1850s, the Senecas were fighting the treaty of 1838, which guaranteed the sale of the Tonawanda and Buffalo Creek reservations to the Ogden Land Company. That agreement was obtained by an obvious deceit; several chiefs were bribed, and others were not consulted. In order to revoke the treaty—it took two decades to circumvent it—the Seneca requested and received help from many white organizations and individuals. With the Senecas' blessing, the Grand Order initiated a petition drive and dispatched Morgan to Washington to lobby for their cause—another form, innocuous as it may be, of supplanting the Indian. Because of the urgency of protecting the Indians from the incursions of the Ogden Land Company, the Indians' public image became an acute concern. In the early 1840s, the Quakers who controlled other Seneca reservations, helped broker a compromise that the Tonawanda band rejected because it sacrificed their reservation and Buffalo Creek to save two others. In December 1848, at the urging of the Society of Friends, the Senecas at Cattaraugus and Allegheny abolished the old forms of government and adopted a new republican regime, calling themselves "the Seneca Nation of Indians."[32]

Importantly, Morgan's exposition of the Iroquois political tradition took place soon after their government was put into disrepute and was in jeopardy. Another incident exemplified the increased dependence of the Tonawandas on Morgan and his friends. During the condolence ceremony in the fall of 1845, the Iroquois asked their guests to induce a white man selling whiskey to leave the reservation. The Indians would not chase him away themselves. The attending members of the New Order bought the jug and poured it out. Shortly after, they were called again. This time they drew up a warrant authorizing them to pour the whiskey into the creek. According to the testimony of Charles Talbot Porter—Morgan's brother-in-law and brother warrior in the Grand Order—once Morgan was known as a leading "friend of the Indians," the Seneca were willing to extend their support for his studies. "Everything was communicated to him with a cordial frankness and fullness that prevented him from falling into errors, which are inevitable when information is given with reserve or perhaps with intentional inaccuracy."[33]

During this campaign, Parker wrote Schoolcraft a formal letter to solicit expert advice, which he intended to incorporate into the public drive. First, he asked whether, according to the information at Schoolcraft's disposal, the two remaining Seneca reservations had enough fertile land to support the inhabitants of the Tonawanda and Buffalo Creek. Second, he wanted to know whether in his census Schoolcraft had discovered that Indians governed themselves entirely by the principle of consensus. "Tell us, if you please, whether the Indian ever recognized the majority principle, whether in fact they knew any thing about *majorities* and *minorities* before the principle was introduced by the whites."[34]

Schoolcraft confirmed that if Tonawanda and Buffalo Creek were lost, the remaining land would not be sufficient for the entire nation. He also maintained that according to Iroquois customs, decisions crucial to the future of a particular Iroquois faction must be made unanimously. Therefore, the treaty of 1838, which had not won unanimous consent, had not been properly ratified.[35] This exchange reversed the course of the original racial masquerade and brought ethnological expertise full circle. Parker was now speaking from Schoolcraft's throat, the ethnologist was instructing his Seneca informant of his tribe's political protocol. This circulation of ethnological material was made complete by the fact that despite his intimate knowledge of the Seneca and the access he had to the Iroquois elders, Parker was also quite familiar with, and sometimes consulted in, various printed accounts on the Iroquois and their history written by whites such as De-Witt Clinton. Similarly, Ely Parker was reportedly very proud of Morgan's *League of the Iroquois* and used it to present himself. He even gave a copy to Secretary of State Daniel Webster when the latter accompanied President Millard Fillmore on a visit to western New York.

Pale Face

It should come as no surprise that Parker decided to join the New Order of the Iroquois so that he could secure the accuracy of its pseudo-Iroquois rituals. According to a Rochester paper, he was spotted one August 1846 day in Aurora, sporting full Indian attire, dancing in a torch parade of the New Order. The white "warriors" wore fringed leggings, headdresses, and frock coats and brandished tomahawks.[36] In a few of its features, Parker's trajectory into white society was the mirror image of Morgan's path into Indian culture. In 1847, the same year that Morgan and two of his friends asked to be adopted by the Seneca, Parker became a member of the Batavia Lodge Number 88 of the Free and Accepted Masons. He later joined other Masonic lodges and was one of the founders of Miners Lodge, Number 273 in Galena where he became the first Worshipful Master in 1858. The Freemasons cherished the Indian sachem and conferred on him various official and ceremonial duties. In a Chicago banquet, Parker described the Masonic fraternity as his sanctuary. "Where shall I go when the last of my race shall have gone forever? Where shall I find home and sympathy when our last council fire is extinguished? I said, I will knock at the door of Masonry and see if the white race will recognize me as they did my ancestors when we were strong and the white man weak. I knocked at the door of the Blue Lodge and found brotherhood around the altar."[37]

Parker's presence in white society had great symbolic power. In Appomattox, when Grant introduced his staff to Lee, the confederate general was, according to one account, perplexed. He suspected that in order to humiliate him Grant had brought with him a black officer. Immediately realizing his mistake, Lee did not lose his composure. He extended his hand and said, "I am glad to see one real American here," to which Parker replied, "We are all Americans."[38] Whether such a conversation ever took place or not, Parker's Indian origin assigned him moral authority to heal the fratricidal wounds, both as the ultimate ancestral American and as the remnant of the first victims of (by implication, fraternal) bloodshed on U.S. soil. His first biographer, his great nephew Arthur Parker, re-marked, "It was in the handwriting of an Iroquois sachem, and an *Indian* that the two warring factions of the white race were finally united."[39] In later decades, Parker would be active in the Grand Army of the Republic, a politically powerful organization of Union war veterans and another form of fraternal as-sociation in the nineteenth-century United States. The Civil War invested the at-tachment of the Iroquois to their federated political arrangement with even greater significance, which Parker elaborated on in his oratory.

Parker was proficient in two languages and a resident of two cultures. How-ever, his assumption of a doubled identity was a permanent fixture—in many ways an extension of his parents' home that required reiteration—not merely a youthful initiation rite. Increasingly, he found himself experiencing his Indian self through white means. His most cherished Indian relic, which he wore in offi-cial portraits throughout his life, was a medal George Washington gave to his great-great-uncle, Red Jacket, in 1792. (Morgan probably purchased the medal from Jemmy Johnson for the State Museum but instead of sending it to Albany gave it to Parker, who reimbursed him.[40]) In Washington as a youth, Parker vis-ited Mount Vernon with a friend and then went to George Washington's church in Alexandria. They sat in the first president's pew and imagined themselves rev-olutionary war generals. Later in life, he lived among whites and only rarely un-derwent what his white friends described in terms of cultural relapse.[41]

Red Jacket had been famous as a spokesperson for the Indian cause in Wash-ington and Albany. Likewise, many of the services that Parker extended to the Iroquois were in the realm of representation in places of power and in the pub-lic arena in general. Being an informant to several ethnologists launched a ca-reer as a dispenser of knowledge about Indian life and culture. This exchange of information was woven, as a token, into his negotiations with the outside world. Parker was not a political leader as much as a "voice" for the Six Nations and, al-ternatively, a "representative man," a living monument to Indian aptitude and Indian sorrows. Like the English miners who were attentive (and sensitive) to the manner in which they were depicted in official government reports, Parker protested in July 1853 to Commissioner Manypenny about a statement made by New York subagent Stephen Osborne. In one of his reports, the official Osborne claimed that slowly but surely the Tonawanda Senecas were "retrograding." Parker wanted government to know that the despite their harassment by the Og-den Land Company the Seneca were making progress.

Parker capitalized on the cultural fascination with Indian eloquence, and his voice was suffused with indignation. Throughout his public career, he lamented the fate of the Indian nations at the hands of the white man. These sentiments were even more pronounced in his private correspondence and diary. When he visited the Capitol in 1846, the picture of the pilgrims' landing prompted him into thinking about the injustices his people had suffered. "[The pilgrims] are represented as in a starving condition, and being about to land, an Indian has come forward offering them provision of his bounty. Who now of the descendants of those illustrious pilgrims will give one morsel to the dying and starving Indian."[42]

Rage for the fate of his ancestors was intermixed with personal frustration. Despite his meteoric career, he was barred at important junctures of his life. Trained as a lawyer, as a noncitizen he could not join the bar. At the beginning of the Civil War, Secretary of War William H. Seward told him, and he remembered those words for many years, that it was not his struggle. (His eventual military career as well as the enlistment of three hundred other Iroquois was—not unlike the enlistment of blacks—a basis for the claim that their place among whites was fully earned.) At the apex of his tenure as Indian Commissioner, he was trapped by his foes among the missionaries who had supervisory power over Indian affairs. They accused him of upholding corrupt administrative practices. Merely two years after his appointment Parker had to leave his post, even though a congressional investigation cleared his name.

Parker's bitterness was dignified, wry, and subtle. When Schoolcraft requested ethnological material for his national project, Parker disguised sarcasm with flattery. "A few day ago I accidentally stumbled against your last edition of *Notes of the Iroquois* and picking it up I carefully pursued it, and founded that you had collected in your book more than I have or can expect to have in some time to come. I should very much dislike to send my collections, when so much is already before you."[43] Likewise, his journal description of Morgan's adoption was double-edged. "As I heard the long shrill whoops and looked upon the motley group of warriors who had stripped themselves for the dance, I could not avoid reflecting upon the changed condition of the Indian race. Once the savage yell and the painted band was the terror of the white man . . . As the dancers played their warlike antics before me, with pleasure I thought of the time when my fathers were strong, when their arms were felt over half the American continent, when with joy they danced around the captive bound for torture at the stake."[44]

In a way, his Indian persona, anger included, reflected white expectations. On September 26, 1891, the aging General Parker addressed veterans at Gettysburg. He centered his speech on the depiction on the battle's monument of the Delaware chief Tammany. "I believe," he said, without blinking, "that if ever

Ely Parker, the Seneca sachem turned Commissioner of Indian Affairs, intermediated in his youth between his Iroquois community in western New York and the white world. He assisted in the ethnographic research of Henry Schoolcraft and Lewis Morgan, who dedicated his pioneering *League of the Iroquois* (1851) to Parker. In this portrait (taken in Elvira, New York, c. 1855), Parker is donning the medal that George Washington gave his great-great-uncle, the Seneca orator Red Jacket, in 1792. (Western Reserve Historical Society, Cleveland, Ohio)

there was a good Indian he was one, and that, too, before he was a dead one."[45] Parker did not hesitate to enumerate in front of the veterans a long list of cruelties committed against the Indian, but he also drew an implicit affinity between Tammany's struggle for freedom against a treacherous enemy and the battle cry for freedom of the Union soldiers in Gettysburg. Thus, in a rather astute way he assured his listeners, whose compatriots and ancestors he castigated for abusing his forefathers, that their appropriation of the figure of Tammany was not entirely misplaced.

This episode demonstrates the multivalent quality of Parker's role in Victorian mnemonic culture as a living repository of indigenous culture and sentiment. Schoolcraft had remonstrated, speaking to the members of the Grand Order that, "there are no plate columns of marble [to commemorate the Indian]; no tablets of inscribed stone—no gates of rust-coated brass. But the MAN himself survives, in his generation. He is a WALKING STATUE before us. His looks and his gestures and his language remain. As he is himself, an attractive *monument* to be studied."[46] (Schoolcraft's remark on the Indian-as-statue collapsed the difference between the opposing modes of collective memory which Pierre Nora's recently defined as traditional "milieus of memory" as opposed to modern "sites of memory.") Parker would assume a double task in this regard as a personification of the "walking statue," the living ghost but also its spokesperson and investigator—an object and a subject. Later in life Parker was engaged in plans to commemorate the Seneca past in actual monuments and sites. In 1890, he led the campaign to build a monument, which he wanted to be in the shape of a tree, depicting Red Jacket in an oratorical pose, broken war implements, and the longhouse in ruins. He petitioned the state legislature of New York to set aside an ancient Seneca burial place located on the State Agricultural Farm near Geneva.[47]

Leaving the federal government in the early 1870s, Parker moved to New York City, where he assumed a modest position at the police department as an architect and later as a supply clerk. He was still an attraction, a pilgrimage site. Jacob Riis, the Danish reporter who became the most influential social investigator of New York slums, visited him frequently. Despite long silences, Riis was grateful for those meetings. He found Parker's affinity with his childhood heroes, Leather Stocking and company, to be irresistible. The imaginary world of the frontier, he admitted, was one of the forces that attracted him to the United States in the first place.[48]

Parker's sense of irony probably prevented him from completely falling for the mirror illusion. Whatever he offered by way of material assistance, he understood the ludicrousness in the white man's performance. However, he was deeply implicated in the substitution, as he too endeavored to speak for or represent the historical Indian by assuming his imminent disappearance. The subtext of his public career, as much of the state's involvement in supporting lavish ethnological ventures, was bringing the ancestral Indian to his proper burial. Only then could a new nation replace the old. The underscoring anxiety was arguably that if left unburied the dead would come to haunt us. We should also bear in mind that Parker supported a civilization policy when he was appointed Indian commissioner and much before. As commissioner, he advocated terminating the practice of negotiating treaties with the tribes. Parker believed that his task was not to preserve Indian tradition but to assure his people a fair treatment on the road to integration and commemoration.

The relationship between the aboriginal and the antebellum United States needed constant working and reworking through ethnology, physical anthropology, red face, museumification of the Indian past, literature, and visual depiction on state emblems, sculptures, and flags. In this historical process, ethnoknowledge became a currency, in part, because of its ability to change hands, its removability. It traveled from the Michigan frontier to New York City, from Rochester to Albany. It connected trifling local encounters with the nation's capitol. It built scientific institutions, monuments, and personal careers and, in the case of Parker, a confluence of loyalties and affiliations. Ethnoknowledge appeared as a commodity in the exchange relations (however unequal) between the two societies. For the Seneca, their involvement with ethnology was also a matter of necessity. They wanted to retain their land.

The intense efforts to establish or redefine the association between ancient Indian cultures and the modern United States—Schoolcraft's and Morgan's persistent search for similitude, resemblances, and reflections to justify or ease the substitution—were a surrogate for a lack of actual "descriptive" kinship. They were also a response to Morton and the American School's insistence on the impossibility of a shared biological ancestry. The absence of obvious blood kinship did not preclude the possibility that a palpable substance tied both communities together. In Schoolcraft's romanticism was an endorsement of an affiliation based on common climate and soil, which, in turn, associated American nature with American democracy. Schoolcraft's poetic style greatly influenced young Morgan. But Morgan's rationalist materialism would lead him to postulate that human intelligence creates its own synchronic social and material environment. Moreover, he maintained that similar structures—social, technological, and architectural—could be found across continents and oceans. Although this argument went beyond the natural features on the American terrain, it still upheld that social relations have decidedly spatial manifestations. The longhouse could be rebuilt wherever the Iroquois might go. Once they entered the building, they resided in some particular relations to each other. Similarly, the United States could be defined in universal terms and make its own expansion a sign of the superiority of its institution. As Morgan wrote in the early 1840s, America was a perfect idea that was just made more "geographically complete."[49] His research later in the century extended to embrace the human family in its entirety and tied together American expansionism and ethnology (or science in general) by making the latter an imitation of the former rather than simply its justification.

The Iroquois had attracted special attention much before the 1840s, in part because of their location close to the eastern seaboard and the longevity of their contacts with the white world. They are probably the most studied tribes in North America. Since the early days of the republic, the U.S. federal structure and the confederate design of the Iroquois were considered to have a special relation to each other. It has been hypothesized that the "founding fathers" followed the Iroquois example in constructing the political alliance among the American states. The latest permutations of this theory flourished during the Constitution's bicentennial. In September 1987, Cornell University hosted a conference on "The Iroquois Great Law of Peace and the United States Constitution." The discussion continued in a number of other academic venues, as well as in popular journals, newspapers, and radio shows. Senator Daniel K. Inouye, the chair of the Senate Committee on Indian Affairs, introduced a resolution to commemorate the Iroquois's early advice to the founding fathers and to affirm the "government to government relationship." "I think that as we celebrate the Constitution bicentennial, we should realize that our Constitution came into being, in many ways, because of Indian contributions. George Washington and Benjamin Franklin, in several papers, spoke with great admiration, great awe, over the skill with which the leaders of the Iroquois nations were able to maintain the sovereignty of each nation, but yet were able to form a confederacy and serve as a unit. This gave our Founding Fathers the idea of the federal-state relationship."[50]

Among the evidence that has been marshaled to demonstrate that the United States appropriated Iroquois federalism (a notion that Morgan—regardless of his red-face antics and Iroquois-face ethnology—surely would have found sacrilegious) has been a pamphlet, *Apocalypse de Chiokoyhikoy, Chiefs des Iroquois* (1777). Written in French and published by the Continental Congress, it used an Iroquois prophecy that emphasized the synthesis of European and Iroquois ways in North America.[51] These conjectures have been under dispute for a long time.

Most significantly, they seem to express a longing to establish a closer intimacy with the aboriginal peoples of America. The urge is still intensely enduring in various branches of the environmental movement, contemporary ("New Age") spirituality, and the sort of rituals current in the men's movement and other red-face expressions.

Conclusion

In the nineteenth century, the American and British states embraced two novel tasks, investigation and publication. Documenting society and nature, the two countries propped and configured domains of exchange in which state institutions collaborated and feuded with reform organizations, political parties, individual reformers, and the press over the production and circulation of knowledge and information. The state designated an audience (or multiple audiences) in need of information and another, overlapping, set of publics requiring representation. It then set forth to satisfy both wants. Conversely, the new medium represented and even came to define the subject and the boundaries of the state. Print statism thus functioned as a field of communication and as an archive. The procedures elaborated during the early part of the century for supporting print statism amounted to a profound transformation of the "public sphere" that was arguably more radical than the one Habermas associated with the endemic commercialization of the press at the conclusion of the century.

The nineteenth-century state inhabited diverse fields of knowledge, from the decennial census to the perpetual publication of laws. Enterprising state officials and lawmakers in Washington and London entertained even greater visions that included direct communication between the state and its citizens and the kind of mass political education that British blue books and the U.S. government's print products offered the lay reader. By the middle of the century, public arenas were characterized by a growing inequality among participants and increased efforts to standardize, ritualize, and often stage or mimic debate. Parties controlled political conversation (at least in the United States) and a new, popular, market-driven press was already in place, although not yet as dominant as it would become by the end of the century. However, the emergence of conventions for diffusing knowledge and conducting public exchange as well as the intrusion of the market did not stifle agency. As this book demonstrates, production of knowledge equipped British and American governments with great advantages and even power, but the vehicles and rules for making, diffusing, and consuming texts were unwieldy and, at times, proved inimical to the goals of the state. The traffic in facts, reports, and books had a reciprocal, indeed, dialogical quality—although a fully rational dialogue was not necessarily the prime modality of this commerce.

Within a wide range of informational tools, the grand inquiry occupied a unique place, for it anchored and reorganized the state's archive and reenacted and refined the state's investigative faculties. The large-scale investigation was a means to extend or exceed the boundaries of the state. Such projects were often called into being when traditional institutions and procedures of representational politics seemed inadequate. It is, therefore, not terribly surprising that many of the specific inquiries examined in parts 2 and 3 surpassed the limits of their declared goals or at least contained an excess of performance and reportage, betraying seemingly unbound documentary zeal. This proclivity was particularly noticeable during episodes of social and political tension, as, for instance, the case of royal commissions' investigations into child labor and poor law, or the American Freedmen Inquiry Commission's survey on the condition of former slaves. But the grand inquiry's ambitions reached beyond documentation. While conducting investigations, official emissaries endeavored to settle the very questions government had commissioned them to study and reflect upon in their reports and recommendations.

Thus, royal commissions in Britain created local assemblies and courts, delineated and sanctioned class distinctions, and acknowledged working-class organizations and leadership. The freedmen's investigation and other Civil War and Reconstruction inquiries (for instance, the congressional investigation that followed the postwar race riots in Memphis and New Orleans) had to negotiate and determine, via the investigative process, the social and political status of the newly emancipated slaves. Beyond justifying Indian removal policy, Schoolcraft's research took part in the civilization effort by rendering Indian culture an object worthy of museumification. This may be the reason why—unlike other social investigators—Schoolcraft did not bother with articulating native voice. The logic of the civilizing mission prescribed that the Indian was to vanish so a new person could appear. Paradoxically, the aboriginal was denied a voice so that he could be given a voice as a civilized individual and a citizen. Regardless of investigators' intentions, the inquiry was enmeshed in the field of investigation, altering it not only by making recommendations but also by staging events and by (literally) making noise. Public hearings, interviews, and inspections produced auditory exchanges, clamor, and, ultimately, voice. As a type of "orature," the official report begins with orality or aurality.

The entire sequence of inquiry comprised a chain of registration and substitution that intermeshed texts and performances. Schoolcraft's and Morgan's Indian projects provide extraordinary illustrations of the proximity of ritual and documentation. Despite strong claims of engaging in policy making—at least in Schoolcraft's ventures—both scholars were ultimately writing Indian history and making Indian culture historical. (Robert Dale Owen wrote a history of slavery—under federal auspices—to signify the ultimate destruction of the peculiar institution.) The two ethnographers exercised what Joseph Roach recently labeled "surrogation," an always partial, anxiety-saturated performance that reenacts and substitutes for vacant people and missing cultural forms. Surrogation ultimately constitutes a mode of memorization, centered, in Roach's language, on "effigies"—actors, celebrities, masks, and periodic masquerades—as tools of collective memory and reinvention.[1]

In the Iroquois, the two ethnologists found a society that already had been archived, in the sense that it was acutely aware of its own historicity. After all, Eli Parker, Morgan and Schoolcraft's chief informant was himself an investigator and chronicler of Iroquois society. It was thus fitting that Morgan's propitious moment of discovery—when he finally had a glimpse into Iroquois society—took place while he witnessed the Condolence Council rehearsing and memorizing the entire Iroquois structure. In the previous centuries, the Iroquois elaborated this ritual of substitution as a method of preserving Indian memory in the face of European incursions and the constant need to renegotiate their position with foreign powers. Morgan's New League of the Iroquois's antics, which were fashioned in accordance with what he learned at the condolences ceremony, were, in turn, a mnemonic device, a ritual of registration and memory keeping. These successive acts of surrogation (and subrogation) began with Iroquois rituals but were ultimately supplemented by printed texts, another form of effigy, as well as the state archive or the ethnological archive. The chain of substitution continues, for in the twentieth century Morgan's writings and the subsequent work of native and white scholars—invention and fiction included—were accepted by many latter-day performers of the Condolence Council as canonical texts. In this regard, the New Order was successful in archiving the Iroquois, although it was unable to completely civilize the Indian.[2]

Ambiguities of exchange, representation, and surrogation are as discernible today in early twenty-first-century attempts at public investigation. In late 2002, the U.S. Congress created the National Commission on Terrorist Attacks upon the United States, commonly known as the 9/11 Commission. In the absence of independent mechanisms of investigation such as the British royal commission of inquiry, the federal government assured the panel's public standing by populating the commission with an equal number of Republicans and Democrats. (Politicizing the inquiry in such a manner presumably assured that opposing biases would balance each other.) Congress accordingly delineated a rather convoluted process that allowed the president and the congressional leaders of the two parties to determine membership. The law prescribed that the board's mission would be to examine the course of events before and during the attack on the World Trade Center, to scrutinize government response, and subsequently to make policy recommendations. The commission had in the privileges of congressional inquest, including taking evidence under oath and the power of subpoena.

This obviously was not a "social" investigation. No community, class, or occupation was put under scrutiny or marked for extraparliamentary representation. Yet, the panel charged itself with a greater mission, which included a deep sense of responsibility to bereaved families and to the public at large. In its official web site the commission stated, "The Commissioners and staff are dedicated to working on behalf of the safety and security of the American people and the thousands of families who lost loved ones on September 11, 2001. The Commission strives to relate to family members and keep them apprised of the progress it makes during the course of its investigation into the attacks upon our Nation."[3] Indeed, this panel did more than any other official body to substantiate the public status of these families (who had lobbied hard to make sure that Washington would sanction an independent investigation). Together with other spectators, the victims' relatives endowed these sessions with the atmosphere of an open assembly. Audiences occasionally applauded, cheered, and hissed witnesses. The often-reiterated responsibility toward the 9/11 families and the public precipitated unforeseen events, such as the apology that former counterterrorism chief Richard A. Clarke offered the families. Clarke's gesture then prompted the expectation that other senior officials would follow with similar acts of contrition. In that particular stage of the inquiry, and for a brief moment, the process seemed to introduce to U.S. politics the type of public self-searching and therapeutics that over the last decade or so has been part of truth and conciliation commissions in South Africa and elsewhere.

Fact-finding rituals—public investigations—have the capacity to carve out public spaces for such an unscripted exchange between the state, the public, and commissioned individuals, including the introduction of practices and idioms borrowed from the experience of other societies. The potential for transactions of this kind is grounded less in the supposed impartiality of the commission or its relative independence from the political process than in the manner in which it imitates elected representative bodies. The 9/11 Commission, in particular, insisted on representing, in the sense of "acting for," the "American people." Appointing an investigative panel that operated within congressional practices, the federal government seemingly reproduced one of its investigative mechanisms, but, in turn, the commission surrogated the state including its representational duties, such as doing the people's work. Giving voice to the 9/11 families may also be considered a gesture of filling in for a state that was obviously reluctant to do so.

Most indicative of the commission's representational reach was its somewhat unusual decision to contract a trade publisher, W. W. Norton, to issue an authorized ten-dollar edition of its official report. Published in late July 2004, the 567-page report became an instant best seller. Norton's president Drake McFeely admitted being initially flabbergasted by the enthusiastic public reaction. Upon reflection, he remarked, "For $10, it's a quick impulse buy, to buy a piece of history, and then they start reading it and find out they have a lot to learn."[4]

Affordability and accessibility was one of the main criteria for choosing this venue for disseminating the report. Norton promised to give a copy of the report to each family of the 9/11 victims. The authorized edition supplemented the publication of the report on the Internet and the Government Printing Office's own official version. Meanwhile, in the tradition of intercepting and redirecting state papers, another private publisher, PublicAffairs Books, issued *The 9/11 Investigations*. This tome weaves highlights of the 9/11 commission's interim staff reports and the Joint House-Senate Inquiry report on the attack into a single narrative and reprints key witness testimony.[5] Sensing commercial opportunity, other publishers also offered their own versions of the 9/11 report.

The commission explained its decision to contract Norton as part of its duty to communicate with the "American people," which it appropriated as its public. Commission chairman and former New Jersey governor Thomas H. Kean explained, "Our mandate requires the Commission to report to the President and the Congress. Our report, ultimately, is for the American people. We want the public to read the Commission's findings, evaluate its recommendations, and engage in a dialogue on how to improve our nation's security."[6] Kean reportedly wanted the public to read the report before the "spin doctors" took over.[7] Another commissioner, Timothy J. Roemer, said he was reluctant at first but then embraced the idea of a trade publication because he "wanted to make sure that the American people had access to this product."[8] One observer argued that because the event under scrutiny was a "national trauma," government had to inform the people "as broadly and as quickly as possible."[9] The commission's spokesperson Al Felzenberg cited as precedents Kenneth Starr's report on the Monica Lewinsky scandal (1998) but also, curiously, the publication of the Pentagon Papers (1971) and the Nixon White House tapes (1974). The 1968 Kerner Commission on race riots issued a commercial edition of its report. Similarly, Random House published the Warren Commission's report on the assassination of President Kennedy shortly after its submission. The latter sold more than 1.5 million copies within a couple of months of its release.

The commission's strong wish to be read met with an equal public eagerness to peruse the report or at least to purchase it. Norton received the text already formatted and had four days to print and bind the book and deliver it to bookstores. On July 22, 2004, bookstores sold 150,000 copies, and Norton announced its intention to print another 200,000 copies beyond the initial run of 600,000. Once again, government (at least vicariously) was in the business of producing a best seller. Bookstore owners reported that the demand for the 9/11 Commission report was surpassed only by the enthusiasm that followed the publication of Bill Clinton's autobiography or the Harry Potter installments. Katie Foreman, a thirty-six-year-old graduate student from Washington, D.C., told the Associated Press she had followed the hearings online and in the newspaper but was glad she could obtain the report in book form. "This is one I'll read every page of . . . I'm shocked at how many warnings there were before the attacks. I want to get the full official record and read it for myself."[10]

Reporters employed every cliché in their lexicon to juxtapose the report's somewhat surprising popularity (after all the book market was already saturated with 9/11 material) with the proverbial tediousness of most official tomes. Interestingly, this was presented as a literary success. As are many government publications, the book was written by a committee. A group of seven to twelve, mostly staffers, sitting at the commission's offices in the U.S. General Services Administration Building spent many nights going through endless drafts of each chapter. At the same time, the press was eager to identify specific authors. The *San Francisco Chronicle*, for example, emphasized that Philip D. Zelikow, the commission's executive director, is an accomplished author. Zelikow and a senior advisor to the commission, historian Ernest R. May, had collaborated in writing a book about the White House during the Cuban missile crisis.

There were clear efforts to make the report more palatable to a large readership. The commission's spokesman said it outright: "It was a long, arduous process to get to the point where [the report] tells an engrossing story—of opportunities missed in some cases, of tremendous courage and foresight in some cases, filling in details that were not always known or dispelling misconceptions."[11] In a most telling move, the document's compilers decided to forgo a strict chronology in favor of a more enticing plot line. They swapped chapters 1 and 2 in the original draft because the opening chapter in the final version, which describes the story of each of the four planes that crashed, was deemed more dramatic. The chapter, titled "We have some planes," is then followed by historical background.

While several key practices associated with the political culture explored in this book have recently resurfaced in ways reminiscent of their original mid-nineteenth-century form, others appear to be on the verge of extinction. Since the early decades of the twentieth century, the production of policy-oriented social knowledge has been regularized within government and concurrently become a major field of academic production. Similarly, the state has refined and expanded its media presence. It has also continued directly to generate and disseminate knowledge, which over the last half-century is more efficiently arranged as transparent, bodiless "information." (Parkinson's warnings about the state printer's predisposition to devastate forests seem somewhat less urgent in the age of cyberspace.) There is perhaps less tolerance today for government propaganda that is packaged too recognizably or for instruction films and pamphlets of the kind that were popular in the 1950s. However, White House press conferences or USDA consumer recommendations, to give two examples, still have the capacity to grab great attention. Presidents still appoint special panels—hence the investigations into various aspects of the war in Iraq or the 2001 bipartisan Commission to Strengthen Social Security (CSSS) headed by the late senator Daniel Patrick Moynihan and Richard Parsons, CEO of AOL/Time Warner.

Nevertheless, the ambitious, large-scale, social investigation that endeavors to devise new institutions and policies is often derided as symptomatic of a much-maligned expansionist bureaucratic culture. Since the early 1980s, there has been great reluctance in Britain to appoint royal commissions of inquiry to grapple with major public issues. (The situation is somewhat different in Commonwealth countries such as Australia or New Zealand.) Prime Minister Margaret Thatcher suspected social experts of all sorts to be liberal sycophants of the welfare state, although in 1991 her conservative replacement John Major appointed the Runciman Commission on criminal justice. Later, Tony Blair appointed two commissions—one on care for the aged and the other on reforming the House of Lords. In the United States, the transformation was more complex and stretched from the Moynihan Report of 1965 and the adversarial reactions it prompted among the Left, to Hillary Rodham Clinton's health reform report of the early 1990s and the opportunity it gave conservatives to undermine the welfare state.

The health care investigation was one of the last classic, massive, civic fact-finding expeditions into the realm of social policy. The administration initiated a task force of public figures and experts who interviewed a host of other experts and "ordinary people" who, because of their personal experience, testified to the miseries inflicted by ill-run and wrongly motivated health-care institutions. There was also a row over the secrecy of the procedure. Some argued that the administration was working hard to circumvent the lawmaking process in Congress. Finally, the protracted investigation yielded a ponderous document, which signified by its sheer size and unreadability the excess of a supposedly unbridled bureaucracy. This ritual, and its discontents, would have been quite familiar to British factory commissioners of the mid-1830s.

In contrast to the fate of Clinton's Task Force on National Health Reform, it seems that the needs of the modern media privilege the traditional legislative inquest. This is certainly the case in the United States, where congressional hearings have been quite effective in publicizing, dramatizing, and representing social issues, from smoking to AIDS. This success has had much to do with the quasi-judicial and open-ended character of the proceedings (including the possibility of cross-examination), their remarkable visibility, and the opportunities they give individual lawmakers and witnesses to commandeer the exchange. It is this type of public performance that heralded the return of "representative men," like movie actors and pop singers who serve as spokespersons for particular illnesses (or rather their victims) or for other sufferers of deprivation or wrongdoing, or, conversely, those like the 1840s "factory cripple" William Dodd who are made celebrities on the foundation of their public testimony.

Other ideological constructs and customs that all but faded away after the nineteenth century reemerged in yet another indication of our postmodern condition. Thus, open advocacy for fragile groups has eclipsed the ostensibly neutral standing of science. In recent decades, numerous public experts have jettisoned their impartial posture in favor of open identification with particularly vulnerable groups, for example, victims of child abuse or rape. We have also witnessed the increased efficacy of personal narratives of suffering and overcoming and the general cultural fascination with ubiquitous public confessions. Another retro-phenomenon is the new legitimacy earned by virtue discourse in determining public policy, as shown by the renewed efforts over the last fifteen years to separate the deserving poor from the undeserving. In the case of one neoconservative, historian Gertrude Himmelfarb, such calculations are consciously and directly imported from the early Victorian moral imagination, especially Bentham's notion of "less eligibility" that once governed the notorious post-1834 workhouse policy.

Social problems are frequently grasped through the "authentic" experience of unique individuals rather than ordinary citizens John and Jane Doe who were constructs of drab statistical charts and bureaucratic lore. Likewise, presidents—starting with Ronald Reagan—have performed a Let-Us-Now-Praise-Famous-Men act in their annual State of the Union address (the modern, televised version of the early-nineteenth-century annual message) when they point to a select few heroes, usually seated next to the First Lady. The cultural propensity to focus on the life experiences of the few and, at the same time, the mixture of fascination and scorn toward experts and (unfeeling) science was characteristic of the nineteenth century. But in contrast to Dickens's views, the cult of facts, of social experts and expertise, is suspected today by some of harboring too strong an empathy toward the lower stratum of society.

By the end of the 1990s, another official report captured public attention and became a national best seller—special prosecutor Kenneth Starr's voyeuristic account of President Bill Clinton's sexual liaison with a woman in the White House. The published report was issued concurrently by three publishers and sold a million copies. Its emphasis on the details of Clinton's sexual escapades exposed Starr and his team to textual scrutiny and public ridicule, demonstrating, once again, the risks involved in crafting, publishing, and circulating an official report.

Abbreviations

BL   British Library
GHA   Gray Herbarium Archives, Harvard University, Cambridge, Mass.
HL   Huntington Library, San Marino, Calif.
HoL   Houghton Library, Harvard University, Cambridge, Mass.
JCBL   John Carter Brown Library, Providence, R.I.
LC   Library of Congress, Washington, D.C.
MHS   Massachusetts Historical Society, Boston
NARA   National Archives and Records Administration, Washington, D.C., and
            College Park, Md.
NYHS   New York Historical Society
PRO   Public Record Office, Kew
SA   Smithsonian Institution Archives, Washington, D.C.
UCL   University College, London

Introduction

1. Karl Marx, "The Eighteenth Brumaire of Louis Bonaparte," in Karl Marx and Frederick Engels, *Selected Works in One Volume* (London, 1970), 171. Edward Said employed this quotation from Marx to launch his *Orientalism* (New York, 1978).

2. Hanna Fenichel Pitkin, *The Concept of Representation* (Berkeley, 1967), 8–9.

3. Gwyneth Tyson Roberts, *The Language of Blue Books: The Perfect Instrument of Empire* (Cardiff, Wales, 1998), 217–18.

4. John Stuart Mill, *Utilitarianism, On Liberty, Considerations on Representative Government, Remarks on Bentham's Philosophy*, ed. J. M. Dent (London, 1993), 258–59.

5. "Letter to John Penn," in *Works of John Adams*, vol. 4 (Boston: Little, Brown, 1856), 205.

6. Melissa S. Williams, *Voice, Trust, and Memory: Marginalized Groups and the Failings of Liberal Representation* (Princeton, 1998), 27.

7. Benedict Anderson, *The Spectre of Comparisons: Nationalism, Southeast Asia and the World* (London, 1998), 42.

PART I • *Monuments in Print*

1. *Quarterly Review* 70 (June and Sept. 1842): 159.

2. J. C. Frémont, *The Expeditions of John Charles Frémont*, ed. Donald Jackson and Mary Lee Spence, vol. 1 (Urbana, Ill., 1973), 269–71.

3. Quoted in Edwin L. Sabin, *Kit Carson Days, 1809–1868*, vol. 1 (New York, 1935), 362.

4. Justin McCarthy, *Modern Leaders: Being a Series of Biographical Sketches* (New York, 1872), 194.

5. William Charvat, *The Profession of Authorship in America, 1800–1870* (Philadelphia, 1959), 49.

6. Geoffrey Nunberg, "Farewell to the Information Age," in *The Future of the Book*, ed. Geoffrey Nunberg (Berkeley, 1996), 120.

7. For orature, see Joseph Roach, *Cities of the Dead: Circum-Atlantic Performance* (New York, 1996), 11–12; Ngugi wa Thiong'o, *Penpoints, Gunpoints, and Dreams: Toward a Critical Theory of the Arts and the State in Africa* (Oxford, 1998), 103–28.

8. John Stuart Mill, *Writings on India*, ed. John M. Robson, Martin Moir, and Zawahir Moir, vol. 30 (London, 1963), 33.

Chapter One • Blue Books and the Market of Information

1. Nassau Senior to Lord Brougham, March 9, 1833, 44,843, Lord Brougham Papers, UCL. See also Senior to Brougham, December 16, 1832, 44,440.

2. Harriet Martineau, March 5, 1834, Harriet Martineau File, Society for the Diffusion of Useful Knowledge Papers, UCL.

3. *Third Report of the Controller of the Stationery Office*, 1890 (c 5993) 26, pp. 18, 19.

4. Lawrence Goldman, "Experts, Investigators, and the State in 1860: British Social Scientists through American Eyes," in *The State and Social Investigation*, ed. Michael J. Lacey and Mary O. Furner (Washington, D.C., 1993), 95.

5. *Hansard's Parliamentary Papers*, 3d ser., 123 (Dec. 7, 1852): 1069.

6. Since the mid-1830s, government's periodical reports and reports of royal commissions of inquiry were under the supervision of the Stationery Office. Although they were presented to the House of Commons in a printed form they were still labeled parliamentary papers. The designation *parliamentary papers* as an overarching label to describe all official publications was in use throughout the period under discussion.

7. In their appearance, blue books often resembled pamphlets. Official print ephemera could also be purchased in loose leaves.

8. *Cobbett's Weekly Political Register* 81 (July 6, 1833): 17–18.

9. *Cobbett's Weekly Political Register* 80 (Apr. 6, 1833): 22.

10. J. Toulmin Smith, *Government by Commissions Illegal and Pernicious* (London: S. Sweet, 1849), 168.

11. Ibid., 182–83.

12. In the nineteenth century, there were seven categories of printing for the House of Commons: votes, petitions, journals, returns, bills, command papers, and reports (select committees).

13. *Report from the Select Committee on the Printing Done for the House of Commons,* HC 1828 (520) 4, p. 7 fn. *Report from the Committee for Promulgation of the Statutes in Great Britain. Parliament, House of Commons Sessional Papers of the Eighteenth Century,* ed. Sheila Lambert, vol. 105 (Wilmington, Del., 1975), 5–7.

14. L. G. Graves, *Luke Graves Hansard: His Diary: A Case Study in the Reform of Patronage,* ed. P. and G. Ford (Oxford, 1962), xviii.

15. *Report from the Select Committee on Printing Done for the House,* HC 1828 (520) 4, p. 49.

16. There were other parliamentary printers. In the 1820s, Eyre and Strahan (later Eyre and Spottiswoode) printed the bills, journals, reports, and miscellaneous papers of the House of Lords and also had a patent for the separate business of printing acts of Parliament, forms of prayer, Bibles, and prayer books and were booksellers for the acts and prayers. Nichols printed the votes of the House of Commons and performed confidential night work. Hansard printed the Commons reports, returns, bills, and command papers.

17. *Second Report from the Committee on Public Documents,* HC 1833 (717) 12, pp. 6–7. *Second Report from the Select Committee on Printed Papers,* HC 1835 (392) 18, pp. xxix.

18. J. C. Trewin and E. M. King, *Printer to the House: The Story of Hansard* (London, 1952), 150. *First Report from the Select Committee on Public Documents,* HC 1833 (44) 12, p. 13.

19. *First Report from the Select Committee on Public Documents,* HC 1833 (44) 12, p. 3.

20. Ibid., 23.

21. Ibid., 6.

22. *Report from the Select Committee on Public Petition,* HC 1831–32 (639) 5, p. 3.

23. *Report from the Select Committee on the Printing Done for the House of Commons,* HC 1828 (520) 4. Also see *First Report from Select Committee on Publication of Printed Papers,* 1840 (130) 15, p. 6.

24. *The Poor Man's Guardian: A Weekly Paper for the People* (June 29, 1833): 205.

25. *Report from the Select Committee on the Printing Done for the House of Commons,* 1828 (520) 4, p. 8. Of 24,492 petitions presented from 1823 to 1831 not less than 10,685 were printed. Of 13,610 petitions referred in 1839 to the committee of petitions, only 1,133 were printed (from four-ninths to one thirteenth). *First Report from Select Committee on Publication of Printed Papers,* 1840 (130) 15, p. 10.

26. *Hansard's,* 3d ser., 31 (Feb. 18, 1836): 553.

27. *Journals of the House of Common* 90 (Aug. 13, 1835): 344. The selling of votes of the House had become the established practice after the revolution of 1688. *First Report from Select Committee on Publication of Printed Papers,* HC 1840 (130) 15, p. 5.

28. From an average of 973,053 annual copies in the three years preceding the decision to an average of 920,010 in the three years that followed it (a reduction of slightly less than 5 % in the number of copies between 1833–35 and 1836–38); *First Report from Select Committee on Publication of Printed Papers,* HC 1840 (130) 15, p. 8. In the 1830s, the largest run of any document was the private bill resolution (12,000 copies). Commissions' reports were printed in between 2,000 and 3,000 copies.

29. *Hansard's,* 3d ser., 32 (Mar. 24, 1836): 579–83. For Lord Lennox's complaint, see *Hansard's,* 3d ser., 103 (Mar. 15, 1849): 755.

30. Trewin and King, *Printer to the House,* 190. *Hansard: His Diary,* ed. Ford and Ford, 161.

31. Trewin and King, *Printer to the House*, 208–9. The publication in question was *Report from the Selected Committee on the System of Transportation*, 1837 (518) 19.

32. Joseph Redlich, *The Procedure of the House of Commons: A Study of its History and Present Form*, trans. A. Ernest Steinthal, vol. 2 (London, 1908), 49–50.

33. *Report from the Select Committee on Publication of Printed Papers*, HC 1837 (286) 13, p. 9.

34. *First Report from the Select Committee on Publication of Printed Papers*, HC 1840 (130) 15, p. 11.

35. *Hansard's*, 3d ser., 36 (Feb. 1, 1837): 73.

36. Ibid., 74.

37. *First Report from Select Committee on Publication of Printed Papers*, HC 1840 (130) 15, p. 11.

38. Edwin Chadwick to Florence Nightingale, August 28, 1860, Add. Mss., 45,770, f. 151, BL. Nightingale responded in the affirmative. Nightingale to Chadwick [copy], September 3, 1860, Add. Mss., 45,770, f. 159, BL.

39. Chadwick to Nightingale, February 19, 1858, Add. Mss., 45,770, f. 10, BL. See also Chadwick to Nightingale, August 2, 1858, Add. Mss., 45,770, f. 25, BL.

40. Smith, *Government by Commissions*, 172–73.

41. *Report from the Select Committee on Printing*, HC 1854–55 (447) 11, p. viii.

42. *Hansard's*, 3d ser., 122 (June 25, 1852): 1317; also, see *Hansard's*, 3d ser., 123 (Dec. 7, 1852): 1067.

43. *Letter (March 19, 1849) From the Board of Health on Printing Reports in the Octavo Form*, HC 1849 (293) 45, p. 3.

44. J. R. McCulloch, Comptroller of the Stationery Office, to Sir Charles E. Trevelyan, Treasury, March 26, 1849 in *Letter (March 19, 1849) From the Board of Health on Printing Reports in the Octavo Form*, HC 1849 (293) 45, p. 7.

45. *Hansard's*, 3d ser., 84 (Feb. 24, 1846): 14–15.

46. *Report from the Select Committee on Parliamentary Papers*, HC 1852–53 (720) 34, p. 163.

47. Edwin Chadwick to Lord Brougham, June 1849, 10,807, Brougham Papers.

48. *Hansard's*, 3d ser., 123 (Dec. 7, 1852): 1067.

49. *Report from the Select Committee on Parliamentary Papers*, HC 1852–53 (720) 34, p. 159.

50. Ibid.

51. This description is taken from Joseph Hume's testimony. *Report from the Select Committee on Parliamentary Papers*, HC 1852–53 (720) 34, p. 168. *[Six] Report[s] from the Select Committee on the Combination Law*, HC 1824 (51) 5.

52. *Report from the Select Committee on Parliamentary Papers*, HC 1852–53 (720) 34, p. 161.

53. *Hansard's*, 3d ser., 123 (Dec. 7, 1852): 1066.

54. Ibid., 1068, 1070.

55. *Report from the Select Committee on Parliamentary Papers*, HC 1852–53 (720) 34, p. iii.

56. *Hansard's*, 3d ser., 178 (Mar. 24, 1865): 215. A different printing project based on a selection of government papers (especially diplomatic documents) began in the 1850s under the

title *The British and Foreign State Papers*. These volumes were edited by the librarian of the foreign office, issued annually, and sold for about thirty shillings per volume.

57. Lord Stanley, "What Should We Do with Our Blue Books? Or, Parliament as the National School Master" (London: Savill and Edwards, Printers, 1854), 13.

58. *Report from the Select Committee on Printing*, HC 1854–55 (447) 11, p. 31.

59. It is not clear what report he had in mind, but see "Bill to Amend the Law as to Marriage with a Deceased Wife's Sister or Niece," HC 1854–55 (56) 4.

60. *Report from the Select Committee on Printing*, HC 1854–55 (447) 11, p. 32.

61. *Hansard's*, 2d ser., 18 (Mar. 6, 1828): 989. *Report from the Select Committee on Printing Done for the House*, HC 1828 (520) 4, p. 8.

62. "A plan for a new Police Gazette to replace the old Hue and Cry, 1827," HO 44/58, *PRO*. Government also published three gazettes (*London Gazette, Dublin Gazette*, and *Edinburgh Gazette*) that were used mainly for official and legal advertisements.

63. *Second Report from the Select Committee on Printing*, HC 1847–48 (710) 16, p. 4.

64. *First Report of the Select Committee on Printing*, HC 1847–48 (657) 16, p. 27. The first experiment in this direction was not to print the evidence of the third report of the Sanitary Commission. The Home Office decided to submit the appendix in manuscript form (p. 26).

65. *Report from the Select Committee on Printing*, HC 1854–55 (447) 11, p. 48. Printing the reports for the Sanitary Commission cost between £10,000 and £12,000. *Report from the Select Committee on Miscellaneous Expenditure*, HC 1847–48 (543) (543-II) 18, part 1, p. 50. The average cost of printing was about £3,000.

66. *Report from the Select Committee on Printing*, HC 1854–55 (447) 11, p. 46.

67. Benjamin Disraeli, *Sybil, or, the Two Nations* (1845; Ware, Hertfordshire, 1995), 196.

68. Anthony Trollope, *The Eustace Diamond* (1872; New York, 1998), 24.

69. *Hansard's*, 3d ser., 179 (June 1, 1865): 1144.

70. *Hansard's*, 3d ser., 178 (Mar. 24, 1865): 215.

71. *Hansard's*, 3d ser., 146 (July 17, 1857): 1690.

72. T. J. Ward, *The Factory Movement, 1830–1855* (London, 1962), 102; Lytton Strachey, *Eminent Victorians* (1918; New York, 1988), 101.

73. David Low, "The Book of the Month—(Heavyweight Section)"[caricature], *Evening Standard*, June 10, 1930.

74. The term was coined by Lord Derby in 1867. Trewin and King, *Printer to the House*, 241.

75. Quoted in F. Knight Hunt, *The Fourth Estate: Contributions Towards A History of Newspapers, and of the Liberty of the Press*, vol. 1 (London, 1850), 7.

76. Jürgen Habermas, *The Structural Transformation of the Public Sphere: An Inquiry into a Category of Bourgeois Society*, trans. Thomas Burger (1962; Cambridge, Mass., 1991), 66–67.

77. Cyril Northcote Parkinson, *The Law and the Profits* (London, 1960), 130.

Chapter Two • The Battle of the Books

1. For example, in 1849, Congress printed extra copies of the following documents: *Coast Survey*, 4,500; *Report on Commerce and Navigation*, 10,000; *Patent Office Report on Agriculture* (which was displayed by Stevens in the committee hearing), 100,000; *Patent Office Report on Machines*, 50,000; *King's Report on California*, 10,000; *Banks of the United States*, 5,000;

Foster and Whitney's Mineral Report, 10,000; *Proceedings Relative to the Death of General Taylor*, 30,000. *Report from the Select Committee on Parliamentary Papers*, HC 1852–53 (720) 34, p. 178. Beyond circulation by congressmen, the Library of Congress and the State Department were initially responsible for sending copies to designated colleges, learned societies, and state and territorial libraries. The responsibilities for educational distribution were transferred in 1858 to the Department of the Interior.

2. Ibid., 176. The witness estimated the federal expenditure on publication to be about £100,000 annually (at that time, about $600,000). J. R. McColluch gave a similar assessment about the expense of parliamentary printing in Britain, although Hansard's figure was substantially lower, £28,000. These general estimates may not be accurate. It is difficult to distinguish in the historical records between expenses for printing reports, and other stationery and printing appropriations. In the U.S. case, publication budgets often came from the contingency fund of both houses rather than from the printing budget. However, it is safe to assume that, relative to the size of its budget and the scope of its federal activity, the federal government spent proportionally much more than the British government on state printing.

3. *Report from the Select Committee on Parliamentary Papers*, HC 1852–53 (720) 34, p. 171.

4. The closest term to *parliamentary papers* in the United States was the similarly nebulous concept of *government publications*. A law approved in 1847 defined pamphlets or books that were published, procured, or purchased by Congress as "public documents." See Leroy Charles Merrit, *The United States Government As Publisher* (Chicago, 1943), 2.

5. There were attempts to persuade Congress to produce more documents for educational purposes by, for instance, distributing to schools public documents such as the president's annual message and the publications of the Smithsonian Institution. See "Memorial of Joseph L. Smith," March 24, 1856, RG 46, SEN 34A-H17, 34th Cong., 1st sess., NARA.

6. Culver H. Smith, *The Press, Politics, and Patronage: The American Government's Use of Newspapers, 1789–1875* (Athens, Ga., 1977), 72.

7. James L. Harrison, *100 GPO Years, 1861–1961* (Washington, D.C., 1961), 12.

8. Suzanne deLong, "What is in the United States Serial Set?" *Journal of Government Information* 23, no. 2 (1996): 123–35; and Richard J. McKinney, "An Overview of the U.S. Congressional Serial Set" (Washington, D.C., 2002). For the initial House of Representative order for serial publication, see House of Representatives, *Journal* (Dec. 8, 1813) 13th Cong., 2d sess., 166–67.

9. *Report on Public Printing*, Senate Doc. 99, 15th Cong., 2d sess., serial 15, p. 1.

10. *On Executive Patronage, Expenditures of Government… and Public Printing in Connection with Retrenchment*, Senate Doc. 399, 28th Cong., 1st sess., serial 437, p. 43.

11. *Report of the Superintendents of Public Printing*, House Misc. Doc. 110, 35th Cong., 1st sess., serial 963. *Report on an Investigation into Alleged Corruption in Public Printing*, House Report 648, 36th Cong., 1st sess., serial 1071. Smith, *The Press, Politics, and Patronage*, 226.

12. Harrison, *100 GPO Years*, 54.

13. Charles Sumner to William T. Bingham, December 31, 1860; Sumner to C. F. Smith, February 7, 10, 1860, Charles Sumner Papers, LC.

14. Sumner to Theodore Parker, Jan. 6, 1853 [copy], vol. 10, 262.5; Sumner to Parker, March 27, 1853 [copy], vol. 10, 263.5; Parker to Sumner, August 18, 18[53?] [copy], vol. 6, 261. Theodore Parker Papers, MHS.

15. George P. Button to [Hunt?], April 21, 1849, Letters to the Clerk of the House of Representatives, RG 233, HR 30C-B1, NARA.

16. *Congressional Globe* (Sept. 23, 1850): 1923. William L. Hickey, ed., *The Constitution of the United States of America* (Philadelphia, 1848).

17. *Congressional Globe* (Sept. 23, 1850): 1923.

18. Ibid.

19. *Report of the Commission of Patents for the Year 1858: Agriculture* (Washington, D.C.: James B. Steedman, 1859), or, House Exec. Doc. 105, 35th Cong., 2d sess., serial 1012, p. 239.

20. *Congressional Globe* (Mar. 7, 1850): 473−74.

21. Ibid., 475.

22. Ibid.

23. Harrison, *100 GPO Years*, 54. The 1875 report contained 536 text pages and 128 pages of woodcuts.

24. *Congressional Globe* (Jan. 17, 1850): 172.

25. Ibid., 173.

26. Ibid.

27. Ibid., 174.

28. *Congressional Globe* (Dec. 31, 1850): 139. By the second session of the fortieth Congress (1868), the cluster of executive documents known as the Annual Message of the President, reached almost 11,000 pages and cost approximately $110,000 to print. This was one of the most important federal documents issued, and three thousand copies were made with an abridgment printed in a massive 35,000 copies. The document was dispatched to specific newspapers in central areas ahead of time so to that they would be able to publish it on the day of its formal presentation to Congress. *Cost of Public Printing and Distribution of Public Documents*, Senate Report 247, 40th Cong., 3d sess., serial 1362, p. 3. The *New York Herald* employed express horse service to beat other newspapers in getting Jackson's annual message to New York in 1835.

29. *Congressional Globe* (Dec. 18, 1850): 77. The document under consideration was Senate Exec. Doc. 64, 31st Cong., 1st sess., serial 562.

30. *Congressional Globe* (Dec. 19, 1850): 96. Also see *Congressional Globe* (July 26, 1850): 1464.

31. *Congressional Globe* (Jan. 21, 1852): 332.

32. *Congressional Globe* (Jan. 17, 1850): 171.

33. Ibid., 171−72. Other congressmen also complained of spreading ink and fading illustrations.

34. *Congressional Globe* (Dec. 12, 1850): 35; *Congressional Globe* (Dec. 17, 1850): 66. Also see "Memorial of German-American Agriculturists and Citizens for Printing of the Agricultural Report of the Patent Office in the German Language," House Misc. Doc. 41, 37th Cong., 2d sess., serial 1141.

35. *Congressional Globe* (Dec. 12, 1850): 35; (Dec. 17, 1850): 66.

36. *Congressional Globe* (Dec. 17, 1850): 66.

37. Ibid., 67.

38. Ibid., 68.

39. Ibid.

40. "Memorial of Eugene Plunkett," December 21, 1852, 32d Cong., 2d sess., RG 46, SEN 32A-H17, NARA.

41. *Congressional Globe* (Dec. 23, 1852): 138.

42. Clarence E. Carter, "The United States and Documentary Historical Publication," *Mississippi Valley Historical Review* 25 (June 1938): 4—7. In early 1833, the Clerk of the House, Matthew St. Clair Clarke, was inundated with requests from libraries and colleges for copies of the twelve volumes of Sparks's *Diplomatic Correspondence of the American Revolution*, which according to a law past by the Twenty-second Congress were to be granted to all incorporated literary institutions in the country.

43. *United States Telegraph,* January 28, 1830. Also, see House of Representatives, *Journal,* 21st Cong., 1st sess., 350, 363, 368, 404, 419. "An Act Making Provision for a Subscription to a Compilation of Congressional Documents," H.R. 652 (Feb. 28, 1831) House of Representatives, *Bills and Resolutions,* 21st Cong., 2d Sess.

44. *Register of Debates in Congress,* vol. 1, preface (Washington, D.C., 1825).

45. *National Intelligencer,* January 24, 1843.

46. The distribution list of the *Documentary History of the American Revolution* included dignitaries (e.g., James Madison, John Quincy Adams, and Andrew Jackson), foreign ministers, government departments, lawmakers (3 copies each), justices, states, territories, and colleges. *Senate Record Book of the Distribution of Publications by Act or Resolution,* 33d Cong., RG 46, SEN 33d-B3, NARA.

47. John Spencer Bassett, *The Middle Group of American Historians* (New York, 1917), 241—43, 287—88.

48. *Report of Select Committee of House of Representatives, on Purchase and Publication of Madison Papers,* Senate Misc. Doc. 20, 30th Cong., 1st sess., serial 511.

49. "Petition of Elizabeth Hamilton for the Patronage of Congress to the Publication of Her Late Husband's Papers," Senate Doc. 52, 29th Cong., 1st sess., serial 473.

50. "Petition of Samuel L. Gouverneur," Senate Misc. Doc. 10, 30th Cong., 2d sess., serial 533, p. 2.

51. *Congressional Globe* (June 13, 1850): 1203—4.

52. *Congressional Globe* (Aug. 21, 1850): 1623.

53. Ibid., 1624.

54. *Congressional Globe* (Aug. 26, 1850): 1664.

55. Ibid., 1665.

56. Ibid.

57. Ibid., 1668.

58. See, e.g., A. B. Farlin to Thomas Campbell, Clerk of the House of Representatives, February 19, 1849, Letters to the Clerk of the House of Representatives, RG 233, HR 30C-B1, NARA.

59. William Morrison to Campbell, August 26, 1848 [copy], Letters to the Clerk of the House of Representatives, RG 233, HR 30C-B1, NARA.

60. Morrison to Thomas Stall, n.d. [copy], Letters to the Clerk of the House of Representatives, RG 233, HR 30C-B1, NARA.

61. Printed circular from Thomas J. Campbell, Clerk to the House of Representatives, Jan-

uary 15, 1849, Letters to the Clerk of the House of Representatives, RG 233, HR 30C-B1, NARA.

62. The most expensive item was the *American State Papers,* which cost $235.50. "Letter from the Clerk of the House of Representatives transmitting additional estimates of appropriations of the contingent expenses of the House of Representatives," 33d Cong., 1st sess., n.d., Letters to the Clerk of the House of Representatives, RG 233, HR 33C-C1.2, NARA.

63. *Congressional Globe* (Aug. 21, 1850): 1661.

64. *New York Herald,* January 17, 1858.

65. *Cost of Public Printing and Distribution of Public Documents,* Senate Committee Report 247, 40th Cong., 3d sess., serial 1362.

66. Ibid., 6.

67. Ibid.

68. In 1864, government printed 50,000 copies of the *Army Register of Volunteers* without any gratis allocation. It was poorly executed and failed to sell. However, the *Congressional Directory* cost less than sixteen cents a copy and large numbers were sold. A few senators and representatives bought hundreds of copies for their own distribution. *Cost of Public Printing and Distribution of Public Documents,* Senate Committee Report 247, 40th Cong., 3d sess., serial 1362, pp. 12–13.

69. *Congressional Globe* (Jan. 31, 1872): 723.

70. George Alfred Townsend, *Washington, Outside and Inside* (Hartford, Conn.: James Betts and Co., 1873), 239

71. Ibid., 250–51.

72. Ibid., 239.

73. Ibid., 251.

74. Ibid., 240.

75. *Congressional Globe* (July 13, 1870): 5528.

76. Ibid., 5528.

77. Ibid., 5624, 5645.

78. Townsend, *Washington, Outside and Inside,* 240–41.

79. Ibid.

80. Thomas H. Benton to John Charles Frémont, March 20, 1843, in *Expeditions of John Charles Frémont,* ed. Jackson and Spence, vol. 1, 164–65.

81. *Congressional Globe* (May 24, 1866): 2804. *The War of the Rebellion: A Compilation of the Official Records of the Union and Confederate Armies,* 70 vols. in 128 parts (Washington, D.C., 1880–1901). Carter, "The U.S. and Documentary Historical Publication," 16.

Chapter Three • The Bee in the Book

1. William Goetzmann, *New Lands, New Men* (New York, 1986), 178. This figure may be less impressive if one takes into consideration the limited scope of federal government activity before the Civil War.

2. Catherine Coffin Phillips, *Jessie Benton Frémont: A Woman Who Made History* (San Francisco, 1935), 69.

3. Charles Wilkes had his wife copy his narrative on the exploring expedition. One member of the scientific corps of the expedition, Horatio Hale, left his manuscript with his mother, novelist Sarah Josepha Hale, to proofread.

4. J. J. Abert to Frémont, April 26, 1843, *The Expeditions of John Charles Frémont*, ed. Donald Jackson and Mary Lee Spence, vol. 1 (Urbana, Ill., 1973), 342.

5. *The Journals and Miscellaneous Notebooks of Ralph Waldo Emerson*, vol. 10, ed. Ralph H. Orth and Alfred R. Ferguson (Cambridge, Mass., 1971), 431; Bernard De Voto, *The Year of Decision: 1846* (Boston, 1942), 40.

6. *Publication of Result of late Exploring Expedition of J. C. Frémont to California and Oregon*, Senate Committee Report 226, 30th Cong., 1st sess., serial 512, p. 3.

7. *Letter of J. C. Frémont to National Intelligencer on his last Expedition across Rocky Mountain, and Route for Railroad to Pacific*, Senate Misc. Doc. 67, 33d Cong., 1st sess., serial 705.

8. *Expeditions of Frémont*, ed. Jackson and Spence, 270. Frémont's biographer raises the possibility that the bumblebee anecdote was a fabrication inspired by the bee motif in William Cullen Bryant's *The Prairie* (1834) and in Washington Irving's *Tour on the Prairies* (1835). Tom Chaffin, *Pathfinder: John Charles Frémont and the Course of American Empire* (New York, 2002), 144–45.

9. *Notes of Military Reconnaissance from Fort Leavenworth in Missouri to Sand Diego, in California*, Exec. Doc. 41, 30th Cong., 1st sess., serial 517, p. 15.

10. Ibid., 419.

11. Thomas Hart Benton, *Thirty Years' View, or, A History of the Working of the American Government for Thirty Years*, vol. 2 (New York, 1861), 579.

12. "Letter of the Clerk of the House of Representatives U.S. . . . relative to the distribution of Frémont's Report," House Doc. 118, 29th Cong., 1st sess., serial 483. "Resolution to inquire into causes of delay in delivery of Frémont's Report, and the possibility that any officer or person in employ of Senate has withheld or disposed of documents in manner contrary to rules of Senate," Senate Doc. 486, 29th Cong., 1st sess., serial 478.

13. Asbury Dickins to E. Weber and Co., Letters on Frémont's Maps of California and Oregon, September 25, 1848, RG 46, Office of the Secretary of the Senate, Transcribed Copies of Outgoing Correspondence, 278, NARA. Also see Dickins to Weber, January 27, 1849, RG 46, Office of the Secretary of the Senate, Transcribed Copies of Outgoing Correspondence, 307, NARA.

14. Dickins to Alexander Dallas Bache, May 5, 1847, RG 46, Office of the Secretary of the Senate, Transcribed Copies of Outgoing Correspondence, NARA.

15. Dickins to Boyd Hamilton, June 27, 1851; Dickins to Sherman and Smith, April 4, 1851, RG 46, Office of the Secretary of the Senate, Transcribed Copies of Outgoing Correspondence, NARA.

16. Quoted in Anita M. Hibler, "The Publication of the Wilkes Reports, 1842–1877" (Ph.D. diss., George Washington University, 1989), 206.

17. William H. Dall, *Spencer Fullerton Baird: A Biography* (Philadelphia, 1915), 78.

18. *Brief Account of the Discoveries and Results of the United States Exploring Expedition* (from the *American Journal of Science and Arts*, vol. 44) (New Haven: B. L. Hamlen, 1843), 1. The findings of Napoleon's expeditions to Egypt were published in twenty-three sumptuous

and enormous volumes (measuring 107 cm. by 71 cm.), Commission des sciences et arts d'Egypte, *Description de l'Égypte, ou, Recueil de observations et des recherches qui ont été faites en Égypte pendant l'éxpédeition de l'armée française,* 23 vols. (Paris: Imprimerie impériale, 1809–28).

19. *Brief Account of the Discoveries and Results of the United States Exploring Expedition,* 4.

20. *Publication of Result of late Exploring Expedition of J. C. Frémont to California and Oregon,* Senate Committee Report 226, 30th Cong., 1st sess., serial 512, p. 3.

21. *On Causing to be Published additional Copies of Scientific Work of Exploring Expedition,* Senate Doc. 405, 29th Cong., 1st sess., serial 477, pp. 10–11. By the resolution of February 20, 1845, a copy was awarded to each state; two each to France, Britain, and Russia; one apiece to twenty-five other countries, one to each of the commanders of the three main vessels that participated in the journey, one to the Naval Lyceum in Brooklyn, and two to the Library of Congress.

22. *North American Review* 63 (July 1846): 100–101.

23. [Charles Davis], "The United States Exploring Expedition," *North American Review* 61 (July 1845): 106–107. *Southern Literary Messenger* 11 (May 1845): 310.

24. Instructions of James K. Paulding, Secretary of the Navy to Charles Wilkes, quoted in Daniel C. Haskell, *The United States Exploring Expedition, 1838–1842, and its Publications, 1844–1874* (New York, 1940), 34. For Gov. Isaac I. Stevens's expedition from St. Paul to Puget Sound, it was determined, "Each officer and scientific man of the expedition will keep a daily journal, noting everything worthy of observation of a general character. These journals will be deemed a part of the results of the expedition, will be turned over as a part of its archives, and will be made use of in preparing the report. This is not intended to preclude copies being taken and published by the writer, after the publication of the report and proceedings of the expedition." *Reports of the Explorations and Surveys, to Ascertain the Most Practicable and Economical Route for a Railroad from the Mississippi River to the Pacific Ocean,* vol. 1 (Washington. D.C.: A.O.P. Nicholson, Printer, 1855), 4.

25. *Report from the Library Committee on Exploring Expedition, Maps, Plates, Etc.,* House Report 160, 28th Cong., 2d sess., serial 468, p. 6. William F. Party, *Copyright Law and Practice* (Washington, D.C., 1994), 340.

26. The difference between this edition (published by Lea and Blanchard in 1845) and the original one was the size and type of paper, the substitution of forty-seven woodcuts for steel vignettes, and the exclusion of sixty-four plates. An English edition issued by Wittaker and Co. omitted the entire appendix on Wilkes's instructions to his officers, which had comprised one-fifth of the text but was deemed tedious by the British publisher.

27. Charles Wilkes, *Autobiography of Rear Admiral Charles Wilkes,* ed. William James Morgan et al. (Washington, D.C., 1978), 542.

28. Quoted in Hibler, "Publication of the Wilkes Reports," 154–56.

29. Augustus A. Gould, *United States Exploring Expedition,* vol. 12, *Mollusca and Shells* (Philadelphia: C. Sherman, Printer, 1852).

30. Dirk J. Struik, *Yankee Science in the Making* (Boston, 1948), 293.

31. Of the appropriations already spent, the largest expenditure was for engraving natural history plates ($41,189.13). Engraving charts and maps cost $24,810.85, engraving narratives and other plates $16,808.71, and printing the text $20,633.27. During those years, James Dana

received $16,200 for preparing four volumes for publication, Charles Pickering received $9,654.41, Louis Agassiz $5,916.66 (2 vols.), and Asa Gray $5,400.00 (2 vols.). *Report of the Library Committee on the Progress of the Publication of the Exploring Expedition*, Senate Committee Report 391, 35th Cong., 2d sess., serial 994, pp. 1–2.

32. *Congressional Globe* (Mar. 3, 1859): 1616–18.

33. *Congressional Globe* (Feb. 26, 1853): 880.

34. *U.S. Statutes at Large*, vol. 12, p. 368. "Collections of Exploring Expedition Directed to be Transferred to the Smithsonian Institution," House Doc. 117, 35th Cong., 1st sess., serial 958.

35. Robert V. Bruce, *The Launching of Modern American Science, 1846–1876* (New York, 1987), 209.

36. Quoted in Barbara Novak, *Nature and Culture: American Landscape and Painting, 1825–1875* (New York, 1980), 129.

37. *Congressional Globe* (Apr. 5, 1853): 312.

38. Ibid., 313.

39. Ibid., 313–14.

40. Ibid., 315.

41. John Russell Bartlett, *Personal Narrative of Explorations in Texas, New Mexico, California, Sonora, and Chihuahua*, vol. 1 (1854; Chicago, 1965), 399.

42. *National Intelligencer,* April 26, 1854.

43. *Washington Union*, April 27, 1854, *Mexican Boundary Commission*, Scrapbook, microfilm ed., p. 277, Bartlett Papers, JCBL.

44. *Washington Union* [April 1854], *Mexican Boundary Commission*, Scrapbook, clipping 2, microfilm ed., p. 277, Bartlett Papers.

45. Major Emory to General Robert B. Campbell, April 24, 1854, reprinted in the *Washington Union* [April 1854], *Mexican Boundary Commission*, Scrapbook, microfilm ed., p. 279, Bartlett Papers. The paper also published a letter from the Chief Clerk of the Interior Department, George C. Whiting, reporting that Bartlett had admitted that Pratt's illustrations were at his possession and that he used them for his private publication (p. 290).

46. *New York Quarterly Review* (July 1854): 3, *Mexican Boundary Commission*, Scrapbook, microfilm ed., p. 319, Bartlett Papers.

47. *New York Times,* June 16, 1854.

48. Ibid.

49. *Churchman,* n.d., *Mexican Boundary Commission*, Scrapbook, microfilm ed., p. 334, Bartlett Papers.

50. Republished in *Providence Daily Journal,* [July? 14, 1858?], Scrapbook, microfilm ed., p. 312, Bartlett Papers. William H. Emory, *Report on the United States and Mexican Boundary Survey,* 2 vols. in 3 (Washington, D.C.: A. O. P. Nicholson, 1857–1859). Congress decided to print 10,000 copies of the first volume of Emory's report, the narrative, and 3,000 of the botanical and zoological volume.

51. *Mexican Boundary Commission*, Scrapbook, microfilm ed., clipping 1, reel 11, p. 352, Bartlett Papers.

52. Ibid.

53. Robert V. Hine, *Bartlett's West: Drawing the Mexican Boundary* (New Haven, 1968), 87.

54. Fred E. Cannon to Jacob Thompson, October 8, 1858, box 2, binder 1, Requests for

copies of the *Report and Maps Relating the Pacific Railroad Route*, 1854–61, Records of the
Office of Explorations and Surveys, Department of the Interior, RG 48, NARA.

55. William Goetzmann, *Army Exploration in the American West, 1803–1863* (New Haven,
1959), 296.

56. Lt. John W. Gunnison, in charge of the middle route—38th and 39th parallel—and
other members of the expedition were killed by Utah Indians on October 26, 1853. George P.
Merrill, *The First One Hundred Years of American Geology* (New Haven, 1927), 315–16; *National Intelligencer,* March 14, 1807.

57. *Report of the Secretary of War on the Several Pacific Railroad Explorations,* House
Doc. 129, 33d Cong., 1st sess., serial 737.

58. *Explorations and Surveys for Pacific Railroad,* vol. 11, *Explorations, 1800–1857,* Senate
Exec. Doc. 78, 33d Cong., 2d sess., serial 768; House Exec. Doc. 91, 33d Cong., 2d sess., serial
801.

59. Edgar Conkling to Jefferson Davis, August 9, 1855, Requests for copies of the *Report
and Maps Relating to the Pacific Railroad Route,* 1854–61, Records of the Office of Explorations
and Surveys, Department of the Interior, RG 48, Entry 724, NARA.

60. Levi Jones to Jefferson Davis, August 7, 1855, Records of the Office of Explorations and
Surveys.

61. Dr. Christian Raub to the Secretary of War, November 6, 1858, binder 1, box 2; August
Harvey to Jefferson Davis, December 22, 1856, binder 2, box 2; Richard Rigely to Floyd,
Nicholsville, KY, January 25, 1858 and another letter in February 26, 1858; Henry B. Dawson,
December 31, White Plains, NY, 1857; Gibson to Floyd, May 27, 1858, binder 2, box 2, Records
of the Office of Explorations and Surveys.

62. David Wyrick to Abbot, July 21, 1858; Wyrick to [Acting] Secretary Drinkard, July 29,
1858; Drinkard to Wyrick, July 27, 1858. In a later request for documents, Wyrik wrote "I suppose there hardly another to be found who takes more pride in collecting and Reading Governmental Reports than I do—as well as preserving of them." Wyrik to Humphreys, January
9, 1859, binder 1, box 2, Records of the Office of Explorations and Surveys.

63. John H. Carpenter to the War Department, May 17, 1857, binder 1, box 2, Records of
the Office of Explorations and Surveys.

64. Gibson to Floyd, May 27, 1858, binder 1, box 2, Records of the Office of Explorations
and Surveys.

65. E. Franseen to Jefferson Davis, November 4, 1856, binder 2, box 2, Records of the Office
of Explorations and Surveys.

66. J. J. Ames, October 7, 1857, binder 2, box 2, Records of the Office of Explorations and
Surveys.

67. Samuel B. Cowdney, November 29, 1859, binder 2, box 2; Breven, n.d., binder 2, box 1,
Records of the Office of Explorations and Surveys.

68. George M. Fowle to Floyd, January 12, 1858, binder 2, box 2, Records of the Office of
Explorations and Surveys.

69. Thomas H. Howell to Floyd, January 20, 1858, binder 2, box 2, Records of the Office
of Explorations and Surveys.

70. W. J. Merton [and ?] April 27, 1858; David White to Floyd, June 25, 1857, binder 2, box
2, Records of the Office of Explorations and Surveys.

71. W. B. Maclay to Floyd, [March?] 25, 1858; Asa Gray to Lieut. Abbot, August 15, 1857; Spencer Baird to Humphreys, Jan 30, 1858, binder 2, box 2, Records of the Office of Explorations and Surveys.

72. William J. Loomis to the War Department, July 8, 1858, binder 2, box 2, Records of the Office of Explorations and Surveys.

73. John Fitch to Floyd, November 14, 1857, binder 2, box 2, Records of the Office of Explorations and Surveys.

74. J. W. to Floyd, Philadelphia, March 19, 1858, binder 2, box 2, Records of the Office of Explorations and Surveys.

75. Fred E. Cannon to Jacob Thompson, Geneva, N.Y., October 8, 1858, binder 1, box 2, Records of the Office of Explorations and Surveys.

76. John McKiernan to the Secretary of War, February 3, 1859, binder 1, box 2, Records of the Office of Explorations and Surveys.

77. Capt. W. C. Palmer to Humphreys, March 12, 1856, binder 1, box 2, Records of the Office of Explorations and Surveys.

78. A. Marschalk to [U.S. Representative] Jacob Thompson, Belton, Texas, November 20, 1858, binder 1, box 2, Records of the Office of Explorations and Surveys.

79. Alexander S. Taylor to Secretary Floyd, March 31, 1858, binder 1, box 2, Records of the Office of Explorations and Surveys.

80. The Polytechnic College of the State of Pennsylvania, September 30, 1858, binder 1, box 2, Records of the Office of Explorations and Surveys.

81. H. W. Wood to Secretary Floyd, April 27, 1858, binder 1, box 2, Records of the Office of Explorations and Surveys.

82. Stein to Floyd, February 24, 1858, binder 1, box 2, Records of the Office of Explorations and Surveys.

83. J. N. Hurd to the Secretary of War, September 23, 1858, binder 2, box 2, Records of the Office of Explorations and Surveys.

84. Augustus Addison Gould to Senator Benjamin Tappan, December 17, 1843, quoted in Haskell, *U.S. Exploring Expedition*, 74. In order to guarantee early publicity, Gould suggested issuing before full publication of the report "short Latin characters" of the new species and their names in one of the scientific journals or in a government pamphlet. He consequently published short notices in the *Proceedings* of the Boston Society for Natural History.

85. The British government published sporadically geological surveys on the British Isles. See, e.g., Sir Henry de la Beche, *Report on the Geology of Cornwall, Devon, and West Somerset* (London: HMSO, 1839). It included 624 pages, many woodcuts, and twelve plates. Also see *Memoirs of the Geological Survey of Great Britain and of the Museum of Economic Geology,* 2 vols. (London: HMSO, 1846).

86. George Alfred Townsend, *Washington, Outside and Inside* (Hartford, Conn.: James Betts and Co., 1873), 240—41.

PART II • *The Culture of the Social Fact*

1. *Appendix to First Report of the Royal Commission on Children's Employment (Mines); Reports and Evidence of Subcommissioners,* Part 2, HC 1842 (382) 17, p. 63.

Chapter Four • Scenes of Commission

1. Herman Finer, *Theory and Practice of Modern Government*, rev. ed. (New York, 1950), 47.

2. W. Cory, *A Guide to Modern English History*, vol. 2 (London, 1882), 366.

3. *Quarterly Review* 50 (Jan. 1834): 348 fn.

4. Also alluded to are the Poor Law Commission for England and Wales (1832–34) and two investigations that had meager effects on policy making, the Poor Law for Ireland Commission (1833–36) and the Rural Constabulary Force Commission (1836–39). Other investigations include the Handloom Weaver Commission (1837–41), Health of Town Commission (1843–48), Framework Knitters Commission (1844–45), and Bleaching Works Commission (1854–55).

5. Since the monarch did not enjoy the judicial prerogative to interrogate witnesses, it is hardly plausible that the crown could delegate such authority to a commission. Hugh M. Clokie and Joseph F. Robinson, *Royal Commissions of Inquiry: The Significance of Investigations in British Politics* (Stanford, 1937), 85–87. Only in 1921, with the Tribunals of Inquiry (Evidence) Act, were royal commissions given compulsory privileges.

6. *Daily Telegraph*, February 15, 1865, item 116, Sir Edwin Chadwick Papers, UCL.

7. The Poor Law Commission had eight commissioners and twenty-four subcommissioners. The Factory Commission had fifteen full commissioners but still adopted the office/field division. The Employment of Children Commission (Mines) was led by four commissioners who supervised twenty subcommissioners.

8. [Letter to the *Times* in 1831] in William John Fitzpatrick, *The Life, Times, and Correspondence of Dr. Doyle, Bishop of Kildare and Leighlin* (Boston, 1862), 319.

9. *Appendix to First Report of the Royal Commission on Children's Employment (Mines)*, Part 2, p. h12.

10. Irish Poor Law Commission, *The Miseries and Misfortunes of Ireland and the Irish People from the Evidence Taken by the Commissioners for Inquiring into the Condition of the Poorer Classes in Ireland* (London: John Reynolds, 1836), 8–11.

11. Sidney and Beatrice Webb, *Methods of Social Study* (London, 1932), 90.

12. G. Calvert Holland, "The Mortality, Sufferings and Diseases of Grinders," Part 1 (London: John Ollivier, 1841), 7.

13. *First Report of the Royal Commission on Children's Employment (Mines)*, HC 1842 (380) 15, p. 266. For the remark on Welsh stature, see p. 250.

14. Kirkman Finlay, "Letter to the Right Hon. Lord Ashley on the Cotton Factory System and the Ten Hour's Bill" (Glasgow: John Smith & Son. Printer, 1833), 9.

15. Peter Gaskell, *The Manufacturing Population of England* (1833; New York, 1972), 72.

16. "Letters from the Home Office to the Handloom Weavers Commission," HO 74/1, ff. 148–49, 155–58, 165–66, PRO. Also see, J. M. Collinge, ed. *Office Holders in Modern Britain*, vol. 9, *Officials of Royal Commissions of Inquiry 1815–1870* (London, 1984), 25–26.

17. *Appendix to First Report of the Royal Commission on Children's Employment (Mines)*, Part 2, p. H1.

18. Factory commissioner Rickards's expenses in Manchester (£86.14.0) included renting and fitting an office (carpentry); painting (for writing on the office door); bell-hanger's fees;

an oak table, candlesticks, fenders and fire irons, library table and other office furniture (chairs, carpets); coal, mounting a map of Lancashire; seal-engraver's fees, printer for circulars; "diaries" for mill owners; advertisement in Bolton, Manchester, Stockport, and Preston; and postage. George Rickards to the Treasury, May 22, 1834, T/3736, PRO.

19. "Final Account," March 18, 1837, T 1/4100, PRO. The Poor Law for England and Wales Commission cost only £6,565.17.2; the Factory Commission, £4,919.17.2; the Municipal Corporations in England and Wales Commission, £24,700. These were not the most expensive investigations. The Commission of Arbitration for Inquiring into Claims of Compensation for the Abolition of Slavery cost £140,722.12.11. *Return on Commissions of Inquiry,* HC 1842 (449) 26, p. 373. The Mine Commission cost £8,214.2.4. *Return on Commissions,* HC 1846 (187) 25, p. 318.

20. Irish Poor Law Commission, *Miseries and Misfortunes of Ireland,* 8.

21. *Factory Commission Report (1),* 76. Chadwick to Lord John Russell, July 2, 1866 [copy], item 1733, Chadwick Papers.

22. *Factory Commission Report (1),* 78.

23. Ibid., 77. John Cowell to the Central Board of the Factory Commission, May 3, 6, 9, 1833 [copies], item 41, Chadwick Papers.

24. *First Report of the Royal Commission on Children's Employment (Mines),* 267.

25. *Appendix to First Report of the Royal Commission on Children's Employment (Mines); Reports and Evidence of Subcommissioners,* Part I, HC 1842 (381) 16, p. 758 fn. For the miners' gathering at Bransley, see p. 262.

26. *First Report from the Select Committee on Bleaching and Dyeing Works* HC 1857 (151 Sess. 2) 11, p. 242.

27. *Report on the Poor Laws in Scotland,* ii.

28. Chadwick to Home Secretary Lord John Russell, August 1836 [copy], item 1733, Chadwick Papers. Also, see Irish Poor Law Commission, *Miseries and Misfortunes of Ireland,* 8.

29. Constabulary Commission Files, item 14, Chadwick Papers. See also "Practices of Habitual Depredators; as Disclosed in a London Prison," *Report from the Constabulary Force Commission,* HC 1839 (169) 19, pp. 205–15.

30. Irish Poor Law Commission, *Miseries and Misfortunes of Ireland,* 6.

31. Frank Prochaska, *Royal Bounty: The Making of a Welfare Monarchy* (New Haven, 1995), 80–81, 88. Gaskell, *Manufacturing Population of England,* 161–63.

32. *Report from the Select Committee on the Bill to Regulate the Labour of Children,* HC 1831–2 (706) 15, pp. 150, 152–53, 172, 183, 204, 287, 381, 420, 494–95.

33. Diana Davids Olien, *Morpeth: A Victorian Public Career* (Washington, D.C., 1983), 91; *Report from the Select Committee on the Bill to Regulate the Labour of Children,* HC 1831–32 (706) 15, pp. 150, 172, 420.

34. *First Report from the Select Committee on the Operation of the Factory Act,* HC 1840 (203) 10, pp. 63, 905–912.

35. Ibid. Frederic Hill to Home Secretary Sir James Graham, July 30, 1845; Hill to Under-Secretary H. Manners Sutton, October 28, 1845; Hill to [Under-Secretary Manners Sutton?], March 12, 1846, HO 1845/46, PRO.

36. Irish Poor Law Commission, *Miseries and Misfortunes of Ireland,* 12.

37. Under-Secretary Fox Maule to Webster, April 24, 1837; Maule to George Howell, May

18, 1837; Maule to Howell, June 3, 1837; Maule to Webster, July 9, 1839, Letters from the Home Office to Inspectors of Factories, Mines, and Colliers, HO 87/1, PRO.

38. *Factory Commission Report (1)*, 749.

39. John Cowell to the Central Board of the Factory Commission, May 21, 1833 and July 24, 1833 [copies], item 41, Chadwick Papers. Also, see "Correspondence and Accounts of the Factory Commission," September 10, 1833, T 1/3736, PRO. On Samuel Swain Scriven's methods, see *Appendix to First Report of the Royal Commission on Children's Employment (Mines)*, Part 2, p. 65. On Alfred Power's decision, see *Factory Commission Report (1)*, 531.

40. Stuart to Wilson, August 32, 1833, in *Evils of the Factory System Demonstrated by Parliamentary Evidence*, ed. Charles Wing (London: Saunders and Otley, 1837), 492.

41. John Cowell to the Central Board of the Factory Commission, June 24, 29, July 1, 3, 10, 1833 [copies], item 41, Chadwick Papers.

42. Tremenheere to the Home Office, February 3, 1845, HO 45/952, PRO.

43. On the Heathcote affair, see the correspondence between Heathcote, Horner, and the Home Office (Mar.–May 1843) in HO 45/423, PRO.

44. *First Report of the Royal Commission on Children's Employment (Mines)*, 2.

45. *Factory Commission Report (1)*, 10

46. Chadwick to Major George Graham [copy book], December 7, 1843, item 2818/1, Chadwick Papers.

47. *First Report of the Royal Commission on Children's Employment (Mines)*, 95.

48. *Appendix to First Report of the Royal Commission on Children's Employment (Mines)*, Part 2, 58.

49. Ibid., Part 1, 519.

50. Irish Poor Law Commission, *Miseries and Misfortunes of Ireland*, 9.

51. See petition from the Irish assistant commissioners, May 4, 1836, T 1/4100, PRO. Also, assistant commissioner Thomas Nuget Vaughan's correspondence with the Treasury, June 6, 16, 1836, T 1/4100, PRO.

52. Edwin Chadwick, *Report on the Sanitary Condition of the Labouring Population of Great Britain*, ed. M. W. Flinn (1842; Edinburgh, 1965), 397.

53. *First Report of the Royal Commission on Children's Employment (Mines)*, 268.

54. Mrs. Charles L. Lewes, *Dr. Southwood Smith: A Retrospect by His Granddaughter* (Edinburgh, 1898), 88.

55. Hector Gavin to Chadwick, December 21, 1853, item 797, Chadwick Papers.

56. For attempts to protect witnesses, see, e.g., *First Report from the Select Committee on the Operation of the Factory Act*, HC 1840 (203) 10, pp. 21–22, 141; *Second Report from the Select Committee on the Operation of the Factory Act*, HC 1840 (227) 10, p. 16.

57. *First Report of the Royal Commission on Children's Employment (Mines)*, 3. Also see request from the Home Office to the Treasury to remunerate superintendent Charles Brown for journeys to Holywell, where his presence was needed due to his knowledge of the Welsh language, April 3, 1838, T 1/3736, PRO.

58. *First Report of the Royal Commission on Children's Employment (Mines)*, 9.

59. *Quarterly Review* 64 (June 1839): 92.

60. *Report on the State of Education in Wales*, HC 1847 (870) 27, Part 1, 2.

61. Leonard Horner, *Employment of Children, in Factories and Other Works in the United*

Kingdom and in Some Foreign Countries (London: Longman, Orme, Brown, Green, and Longmans, 1840), 2.

62. "Memoranda of Instructions for Ascertaining the Causes of Pauperism," n.d., item 22, Chadwick Papers.

63. *Appendix to First Report of the Royal Commission on Children's Employment (Mines),* Part 1, 539.

64. Ibid., 514.

65. Ibid., 515.

66. Ibid.

67. Ibid., 520.

68. G. R. Porter to the Privy Council on Trade, August 14, 1832, reprinted in *First Report of the Select Committee on Public Documents,* HC 1833 (44) 12, pp. 15, 28.

69. *First Report from the Select Committee on the Operation of the Factory Act,* 5.

70. *Report of the Commissioners on Handloom Weavers: Assistant Commissioners' Reports,* HC 1839 (159) 42, p. 1.

71. *Report of the Royal Commission on Handloom Weavers,* HC 1840 (43-I) 23, p. 407.

72. *First Report from the Select Committee on Bleaching and Dyeing Works,* HC 1857 (151 Sess. 2) 11, p. 2.

73. Ibid., 3.

74. Ibid.

75. The demand for daily accounts came from Secretary Lord Russell, October 8, 1836, HO 87/1, PRO. Inspectors were to report to the Home Secretary quarterly. Superintendents were to give a detailed account of each day of employment to the inspectors.

76. Dickinson to Home Secretary Sir George Grey, June 8, 1863, HO 45/7006, PRO.

77. [A Lancashire Cotton Spinner], "Letter to the Right Hon. Lord Ashley on the Cotton Factory Question, and the Ten Hours' Factory Bill" (Manchester: Henry Smith, Printer, 1833), 7.

78. [James Leach], *Stubborn Facts from the Factories by A Manchester Operative* (London: John Ollivier, 1844), 17–18.

79. A. E. Musson, *The Congress of 1868: The Origins and Establishment of the Trades Union Congress* (1955; London, 1968); Simon Cordery, *British Friendly Societies, 1750–1914* (Houndmills, Basingstoke, Hampshire, 2003), 95.

80. T. W. Jobling to Secretary Grey, February 1, 1851, HO 45/3491, PRO.

81. "The Ten Hours' Factory Question: A Report Addressed to the Short Time Committees of the West Riding of Yorkshire" (London: John Ollivier, 1842), 32.

82. "Memorial from the Framework Knitters of Leicester to Home Secretary Lord John Russell," May 23, 1838, ff. 355–56, ff. 417–20, HO 44/31 PRO. Also see "Memorial from the Leigh Silk Weavers Committee to the Home Secretary," January 29, 1844, HO 45/657; "Petition from the inhabitants of Rhos Parish of Ruabon County of Denbigh in North Wales," December 16, 1850, enclosed in Richard Cobden to Secretary Grey, July 7, 1851, HO 45/3868, PRO. *Report of the Commissioner Appointed to Inquire into the Condition of the Framework Knitters,* HC 1845 (609) 15, p. 2.

83. Gwyneth Tyson Roberts, *The Language of Blue Books: The Perfect Instrument of Empire* (Cardiff, Wales, 1998), 103.

84. T. J. Ward, *The Factory Movement, 1830–1855* (London, 1962), 92.

85. John Cowell to the Central Board of the Factory Commission, May 3, 6, 9, 1833 [copies], item 41, Chadwick Papers.

86. Michael Thomas Sadler, "Protest Against the Secret Proceedings of the Factory Commission in Leeds" (Leeds: F. E. Bingley and Co., 1833), 7.

87. Sadler, "Protest Against the Secret Proceedings," 12.

88. John Elliot Drinkwater, "Letter to Michael Thos. Sadler" (Leeds: Printed for Baines and Newsome, 1833), 9.

89. John Elliot Drinkwater and Alfred Power, "Replies to Mr. M. T. Sadler's Protest against the Factory Commission" (Leeds, Printed for Baines and Newsome, 1833), 9, 11–12.

90. [William Cobbett's] *The Poor Man's Guardian: A Weekly Paper for the People* (June 29, 1833): 208–10.

91. *Brooklyn Eagle*, May 8, 1843, clipping, item 116, Chadwick Papers.

92. *Fifth Report from the Select Committee on the Operation of the Factory Act*, HC 1840 (227) 10, pp. 125–28. In 1838, Chadwick (then the secretary of the Poor Law inspectorate and a royal commissioner on rural police force) provided the Home Office with a confidential statement on trade union activities. See January 29, 1838, ff. 82–85, HO 44/31, PRO.

Chapter Five • Facts Speak for Themselves

1. "Factory Inspectors Half Yearly Meetings," January 16–18, 1836, ff. 48–50; January 18, 1836, f. 49, LAB 15/1, PRO. Also see July 6, 1838, f. 109.

2. "Expenses of the Poor Law Commission since September 4, 1835, Completed in May 26, 1835," T1/4100–102, PRO.

3. Flood to [Assistant Secretary of the Commission Hamilton Dowdall?], July 1836 [copy], enclosed in Dowdall to the Treasury, July 29, 1836, T 1/4100, PRO.

4. *Second Report from the Select Committee on the Operation of the Factory Act*, HC 1840 (227) 10, pp. 107–9.

5. Ibid., 15, 58, 76–80, 175.

6. Ibid., 92.

7. Hugh Seymour Tremenheere to G. Cornewall Lewis, October 23, 1848; Tremenheere to Lewis, July 5, 1850, HO 45/2366, PRO.

8. Chadwick to Lord Russell, July 2, 1866 [copy], item 1733, Sir Edwin Chadwick Papers, UCL.

9. Herbert Mackworth to Secretary Lord Palmerston, August 23, 1854, HO 45/5374, PRO.

10. Saunders to Under-Secretary Manners Sutton, September 3, 1844, HO 45/657(/8), PRO. Also see John James to R. Baker, August 21, 1844; Baker to Saunders, August 31, 1844; Home Office to Saunders, September 5, 1844, HO 87/1, PRO.

11. Under-Secretary H. Waddington to Horner, June 11, 1855, HO 87/3, PRO.

12. Horner to Waddington, June 13, 1855, HO 45/6249, PRO.

13. Under-Secretary Manners Sutton to Stuart, November 25, 1844, HO 45/1417, PRO.

14. Under-Secretary Maule to John Beal, July 18, 27, 30, October 13, 17, 31, 1840; Home Office to Horner, June 15, 1841, HO 45/1417, PRO,

15. *First Report from the Select Committee on Bleaching and Dyeing Works*, HC 1857 (151 Sess. 2) 11, p. 240.

16. *Report on the Poor Laws in Scotland,* ii.

17. Yaron Ezrahi, *The Descent of Icarus: Science and the Transformation of Contemporary Democracy* (Cambridge, Mass., 1990), 69.

18. Thomas Erskine May, *The Constitutional History of England since the Accession of George III, 1760–1860,* vol. 1 (New York, 1895), 409.

19. Reports of royal commissioners were officially delivered to the Home Office in manuscript form with the signatures and seals of the commissioners.

20. *Quarterly Review* 50 (Jan. 1834): 349.

21. Nassau Senior to Lord Brougham, January 4, 1833, 44, 437, Lord Brougham Papers, UCL.

22. Irish Poor Law Commission, *Miseries and Misfortunes of Ireland,* 11.

23. Parish of Carrick in County Tipperary, ibid., 265. For an analysis of the different linguistic choices of the three commissioners in the 1847 Education in Wales investigation, see Roberts, *The Language of Blue Books,* chap. 5.

24. Item 42, Chadwick Papers.

25. *Second Report from the Select Committee on the Operation of the Factory Act,* Appendix, 115.

26. Joel Fineman, "The History of the Anecdote: Fiction and Fiction," in *The New Historicism,* ed. H. Aram Veeser (New York, 1989), 61.

27. Joseph W. Childers, "Observation and Representation: Mr. Chadwick Writes the Poor," *Victorian Studies* 38 (Spring 1994): 411.

28. On the *Spectator*'s remarks in the context of the 1840s language of discovery, see Gertrude Himmelfarb, *The Idea of Poverty: England in the Early Industrial Age* (New York, 1983), 356–57.

29. *Appendix to First Report of the Royal Commission on Children's Employment (Mines): Reports and Evidence of Subcommissioners,* Part 2, HC 1842 (382) 17, p. H30.

30. *First Report of the Royal Commission on Children's Employment (Mines),* HC 1842 (380) 15, p. 161.

31. Ibid., 80.

32. Ibid., 24.

33. Lewes, *Southwood Smith,* 74.

34. *Appendix to First Report of the Royal Commission on Children's Employment (Mines),* Part 2, 156–57.

35. Ibid.

36. Ibid., 161.

37. *Appendix to First Report of the Royal Commission on Children's Employment (Mines),* Part 1, 182 (381) 16, p. 96.

38. *Appendix to First Report of the Royal Commission on Children's Employment (Mines),* Part 2, H12.

39. Ibid., 721.

40. *First Report of the Royal Commission on Children's Employment (Mines),* 137.

41. *Appendix to First Report of the Royal Commission on Children's Employment (Mines),* Part 2, p. c38.

42. Michel Foucault, "What is an Author," in *The Foucault Reader*, ed. Paul Rabinow (New York, 1984), 112.

43. "Distribution List of the Irish Poor Law Report," March 15, 1836, Treasury/Irish Poor Law Correspondence 1833–1839, T 1/4100, PRO. These figures, however, do not include the distributions of reports in Ireland.

44. "Distribution List of the Rural Constabulary Commission Report," item 7, doc. 6, Chadwick Papers. Five thousand copies of this particular report were sold.

45. *Report from the Select Committee on Printing*, HC 1854–55 (447) 11, pp. 4–5.

46. Ibid., 33.

47. Ibid., 34. The cost of 10,000 copies for 1851–52 (1,397 pages) was £1,211.10.11.

48. *Report from the Select Committee on Parliamentary Papers*, HC 1852–53 (720) 34, p. 173.

49. Chadwick to McCulloch, February 24, 1852 [copy], item 1296, Chadwick Papers.

50. C. Macaulay to Sir C. E. Trevelyan, December 11, 1852; Treasury Minute, December 14, 1852; Macaulay to Trevelyan, December 24, 1852; Treasury Minute, January 7, 1852, in *Report from the Select Committee on Printing*, HC 1854–55 (447) 11, p. 145.

51. *Quarterly Review* 57 (Dec. 1836): 396–443.

52. "Legion," *A letter from Legion to ... the Duke of Richmond ... on the Slavery Committee of the House of Lords: Containing an exposure of the character of the evidence on the colonial side produced before the Committee* (London: S. Bagster Printer [1833]), 13.

53. For an example of "interception" by pro-employer advocates, see William Rathbone Greg and Samuel Greg, "Analysis of the Evidence Taken Before the Factory Commissioners as Far as It Relates to the Population of Manchester and the Vicinity Engaged in the Cotton Trade" (Manchester, 1834).

54. Quoted in Roberts, *The Language of Blue Books*, 212.

55. *Morning Chronicle*, January 27, 1844.

56. *Quarterly Review* 57 (Dec. 1836): 413.

57. Tremenheere to Lewis, July 5, 1850, HO 45/2366, PRO.

58. Joseph Bell to Lord Walpole, November 23, 1852, HO 45/4206, PRO.

59. "Memorial from the Miners of Pontefract Lane Colliery in Leeds," September 27, 1859, HO 45/6782, PRO.

60. Tremenheere to Waddington, September 28, 1859, HO 45/6782, PRO. See also Secretary Lewis to the Pontefract Lane Colliery Miners, October 17, 1859, HO 6782, PRO.

61. John Holmes and the Delegates of the Miners of the Leeds and Wakefield Districts, "A Memorial to Secretary Lewis," September 14, 1859, HO 6782, PRO. Also see "Letter from a Meeting Held in Lofthouse Gate Near Wakefield at the Star Inn to Secretary Lewis," October 4, 1859; Henry Shaw, Elijah Stocks and the Delegates of the western portion of the Leeds Branch of the Coal Miners Association to Secretary Lewis, September 13, 1859, HO 6782, PRO.

62. Tremenheere to Secretary Grey, December 31, 1846, HO 45/1490, PRO.

63. Ibid.

64. See, e.g., Chadwick to James Simpson, December 25, 1843, January 4, 1844, April 25, 1844; Chadwick to Dr. Holland, January 6, 1844; Chadwick to Dr. Laycock, January 11, 1844 [copybook], item 2181/1, Chadwick Papers.

65. B. F. Hawkins, "Intemperance and Vice, the effects of long hours and a bad system from the report of Dr. Bissett Hawkins, one of the medical officers of the Factory Commission, 1833" (Bradford, 1835), *Richard Oastler's Collection: Short Times Tracts*, Goldsmith's Library of Economic Literature, University of London.

66. Society for the Suppression of Mendicity, *Fourth Annual Report* (London, 1822), 22.

67. Richard Oastler to Secretary Lord Russell, August 29 and September 14, 1839, and n.d., ff. 181–203, HO 44/33, PRO.

68. Ibid., f. 194.

69. Ibid., f. 181.

70. Ibid., f. 187.

71. Ibid., f. 185.

72. Jacques Derrida, "Signature Event Context," in *Limited Inc.*, trans. Samuel Weber and Jeffrey Mehlman (Evanston, Ill., 1988), 12.

Chapter Six • Can Freedmen Be Citizens?

1. "Memorial of the Emancipation League (Boston, Mass.) praying for an immediate establishment of a Bureau of Emancipation," Senate Misc. Document 10, 37th Cong., 3d sess., serial 1150, p. 1. The notion of a nation born in a day was probably taken from Isaiah 66:8.

2. United States War Dept., *The War of the Rebellion: A Compilation of the Official Records of the Union and Confederate Armies*, ser. 3, vol. 3 (Washington, D.C., 1899–1900), 73–74.

3. John G. Sproat, "Blue Print for Radical Reconstruction," *Journal of Southern History* 23 (February 1957): 25–44.

4. Samuel Gridley Howe, *The Refugees From Slavery in Canada West: Report to the Freedmen's Inquiry Commission* (Boston, 1864), 104.

5. Edward L. Pierce, "The Freedmen at Port Royal," *Atlantic Monthly* 13 (Sept. 1863): 301.

6. Charles Sumner to Francis Lieber, Washington, January 31, 1864, in *The Papers of Charles Sumner: Microfilm edition*, ed. Beverly Wilson Palmer, reel 64/294. Also, see Lieber to Sumner, New York, January 31, 1864, ibid., reel 77/642.

7. Howe to Francis W. Bird, Washington D.C., September 17, 1862, Samuel Gridley Howe Papers, HoL.

8. *Anti-Slavery Standard*, March 18, 1863, 2.

9. The commission was denied the absolute power to call for any official document they wished to examine for fear of interfering with "official business." Sumner to Howe, Washington, April 9, 1863, *The Papers of Charles Sumner*, reel 64/244. For the slave-owner testimony, see "Testimony of Mrs. DeMoville from Nashville Tennessee," November 23, 1863, quoted in Ira Berlin et al., *Freedom: A Documentary History of Emancipation, 1861–1867*, ser. 1, vol. 1, *The Destruction of Slavery* (Cambridge, 1985), 312.

10. The commission's forty-eight black interviewees were unrepresentative of the black population. Most of the witnesses came from the upper regions of the South, about half were runaways, and many others had been manumitted or had purchased their freedom. Only twelve women were included, although their testimony figured prominently in the commission's reports. For interview with Solomon Bradley, see *Records of the American Freedmen's Inquiry Commission*, testimony, file 3, in Letters Received by the Office of the Adju-

tant General, Main Series, 1861–1870, File 328-0 1863, microfilm M 619, reel 200, pp. 274–77, NARA.

11. Ibid., 278–91.

12. Robert Dale Owen, *The Wrong of Slavery: The Right of Emancipation* (Philadelphia: J. B. Lippincott and Co., 1864), 121.

13. Howe, *Refugees from Slavery*, 63. Howe visited St. Catherine's, Hamilton, London, Toronto, Chatham, Buxton, Windsor, Malden, and Colchester. American Freedmen's Inquiry Commission, *Preliminary Report*, Senate Exec. Doc. 53, 38th Cong., 1st sess., serial 1176, p. 86.

14. These two questionnaires indicate that during the summer of 1863, Howe decided to focus his inquiry on the supposed physical differences between blacks and mulattos and was interested in particular in fertility, demography, and diseases. The questionnaires are in the American Freedmen's Inquiry Commission Papers, HoL. Benjamin Hunt to the AFIC, Philadelphia, May 27, 1863, James McKaye Papers, LC. Owen, *Wrong of Slavery*, 214.

15. Howe to Sumner, Norfolk, Va., June 11, 1863, *The Papers of Charles Sumner*, reel 77/133.

16. *Atlantic Monthly* 70 (Aug. 1863): 260–63.

17. The *Philadelphia Dial*, quoted in the *National Anti-Slavery Standard*, July 18, 1863, in a report on the address in Philadelphia of a former southern female slave Oneda E. Dubois.

18. *New York Times*, June 13, 1863. The *Times* reporter H. J. Winser served as a clerk to McKaye during the visit.

19. American Freedmen's Inquiry Commission, *Preliminary Report*, 16. Also, see Howe to Sumner, Norfolk, Va., June 11, 1863, *The Papers of Charles Sumner*, reel 77/133.

20. J. Lang, "Results of the Serf Emancipation in Russia" (New York: Loyal Publication Society, No. 47, 1864). *Liberator*, June 17, 1864; *National Anti-Slavery Standard*, August 19, 1863.

21. William Howard Russell, *My Diary North and South*, ed. Eugene H. Berwanger (1863; Philadelphia, 1988), 37.

22. On the caste system, see Charles Sumner, "The Question of Caste: Lecture Delivered in the Music Hall Boston, October 21, 1869," in *The Works of Charles Sumner*, vol. 13 (Boston, 1870–83), 131–83. [Mary Putnam], *Record of an Obscure Man* (Boston: Ticknor and Fields, 1861), 171–91.

23. Charles Dickens, *Hard Times* (1854; New York, 1980), 16.

24. Carlo Ginzburg, "Making Things Strange: The Prehistory of a Literary Device," *Representations* 56 (Fall 1996): 17–19.

25. "Queries and answers respecting the colored convicts in the Sing-Sing state prison," August 19, 1833, Francis Lieber Papers, HL. For anti-emancipation propaganda, see, e.g., "Free Negroism; or, Results of Emancipation in the North, and the West Indies," Anti-Abolition Tracts—no. 2 (New York: Van Evrie, Horton and Company), reprinted in *Anti-Abolition Tracts and Anti-Black Stereotypes: General Statements of the "Negro Problem,"* ed. John David Smith, Part 1 (New York, 1993), 37. The general's remark was quoted in the *New York Herald*, August 15, 1863.

26. Thomas W. Higginson, "Leaves from an Officer's Journal [part I]," *Atlantic Monthly* 14 (Nov. 1864): 527

27. Thomas W. Higginson, "Leaves from an Officer's Journal [part II]," *Atlantic Monthly* 15 (Jan. 1865): 65.

28. Thomas W. Higginson, "Leaves from an Officer's Journal [part I]," *Atlantic Monthly* 14 (Nov. 1864): 528.

29. Ibid., 70.

30. Ibid.

31. Edward Pierce, "The Freedmen at Port Royal," *Atlantic Monthly* 12 (Sept. 1863): 309–11.

32. McKaye to Sumner, New York, January 20, 1864, *The Papers of Charles Sumner,* reel 30/244.

33. Owen, *Wrong of Slavery,* 198. James McKaye, "The Mastership and its Fruits: The Emancipated Slave Face to Face with his Old Master: A Supplemental Report" (New York: Loyal Publication Society, no. 58, 1864), 8. Free blacks in Louisiana had an average of $525 worth of property (by another account close to $700). The average property in the loyal states was only $484. These assessments refer to the 1860 census. American Freedmen's Inquiry Commission, *Final Report,* Senate Exec. Doc. 53, 38th Cong., 1st sess., serial 1176, p. 101.

34. Quoted in E. P. Whipple, "Reconstruction and Negro Suffrage," *Atlantic Monthly* 16 (Aug. 1865): 245.

35. Howe, *Refugees from Slavery,* 56, 63–64.

36. McKaye, "The Mastership and Its Fruits," 1.

37. *Preliminary Report,* 3. *New York Herald,* August 15, 1863. *Final Report,* 98–99.

38. Howe, *Refugees from Slavery,* 40.

39. Ibid., 18–20.

40. The slaves were also favorably contrasted to American Indians in their attitudes toward women. Evidence included the 1847 Constitution of Liberia, which featured provisions for women's property rights. Howe, *Refugees from Slavery,* 96. *Final Report,* 105.

41. George M. Fredrickson, *The Black Image in the White Mind: The Debate on Afro-American Character and Destiny, 1817–1914* (New York, 1971), 101–2, 124, 160–64.

42. *Final Report,* 103. Howe, *Refugees from Slavery,* 103. *Letters and Journals of Samuel Gridley Howe: The Servant of Humanity,* ed. Laura E. Richards, vol. 2 (Boston, 1909), 512.

43. Howe, *Refugees from Slavery,* 56, 99–100.

44. The Knickerbocker insured mostly "house slaves," mechanics, and steamboat sailors or operators. The company took detailed descriptions of the slaves' racial features, but its president could not discern any variance in death risks dependent on racial mixture. Frederick Law Olmsted to Howe, New York, August 13, 1863, American Freedmen's Inquiry Commission Papers.

45. Howe to Agassiz, August 18, 1863, in *Louis Agassiz: His Life and Correspondence,* ed. Elisabeth C. Agassiz, vol. 2 (Boston, 1886), 613–14.

46. Howe to Mary Peabody Mann, Toronto, September 6, 1863, Horace Mann Papers, MHS.

47. Owen, *Wrong of Slavery,* 201; *Final Report,* 99; Whipple, "Reconstruction and Negro Suffrage," 246.

48. McKaye, "The Mastership and Its Fruits," 35; *Final Report,* 25.

49. Pierce, "The Freedmen at Port Royal," 291.

50. Ibid., 311.

51. *Preliminary Report,* 22–23.

52. Ibid., 7, 10.

53. Owen, *Wrong of Slavery*, 201.

54. "Testimony taken by the Commission, Department of the South," *Records of the American Freedmen's Inquiry Commission*, Microfilm M 619, reel 200, p. 287, NARA.

55. Whipple, "Reconstruction and Negro Suffrage," 242–44.

56. Owen to Sumner, New York, June 29, 1863, *The Papers of Charles Sumner*, ed. Palmer, reel 28/647. Roger Chartier, *Forms and Meanings: Texts, Performances, and Audiences from Codex to Computer* (Philadelphia, 1995), 33.

57. Bird to Sumner, Boston, July 2, 1863, *The Papers of Charles Sumner*, reel 28/670.

58. *Congressional Globe* (June 27, 1864): 3285.

59. Ibid., 3286.

60. Ibid.

61. Ibid.

62. Ibid.

63. Owen, *Wrong of Slavery*, 62.

64. Ibid., 83.

65. For the abolitionist reaction, see Richard W. Leopold, *Robert Dale Owen: A Biography* (Cambridge, Mass., 1940), 364. J. M. Ludlow, "American Slavery: As It Now Stands Revealed to the World," *Good Words* (1863), 827.

66. *New York Herald*, August 8, 186[4?].

67. Robert Dale Owen, *Footfalls on the Boundary of Another World* (Philadelphia: J. B. Lippincott and Co., 1860), 5.

68. Howe, *Refugees from Slavery*, 38.

69. Quoted in Roberta Sue Alexander, *North Carolina Faces the Freedmen: Relations During Presidential Reconstruction, 1865–67* (Durham, 1985), 19.

70. Quoted in *Proceedings of the Black National and State Conventions, 1865–1900*, ed. P. Foner and G. Walker, vol. 1 (Philadelphia, 1986), 289–90.

PART III • *Totem Envy*

1. Henry Rowe Schoolcraft, "An Address Delivered before the Was-ah Ho-de-no-sen-ne, or New Confederacy of the Iroquois . . . at its Third Annual Council, August 14, 1845" (Rochester, N.Y.: Jerome and Brother Printers, 1846), 6.

2. Walt Whitman, *The Gathering of the Forces: Editorials, Essays, Literary and Dramatic Reviews and Other Material Written by Walt Whitman as Editor of the Brooklyn Daily Eagle in 1846 and 1847*, ed. Cleveland Rodgers and John Black, vol. 2 (New York, 1920), 136–37.

3. See, e.g., *Cherokees, Chickasaws, Choctaws, and Creeks: Speeches, Negotiations and Treaties with the United States*, Indian Affairs 92, 7th Cong., 1st Sess. ASP07; *Treaty with Florida Indians, with speeches*, Indian Affairs 198, 18th Cong., 1st sess., ASP08.

Chapter Seven • *Archives of Indian Knowledge*

1. Henry R. Schoolcraft, *Personal Memoirs of a Residence of Thirty Years with the Indian Tribes on the American Frontiers* (Philadelphia: Lippincott, Grambo and Co., 1851), 107–8.

2. [Lewis Cass], "Review of Travels in the Central Portions of the Mississippi Valley," *North American Review* 26 (Apr. 1828): 365–66.

3. Henry R. Schoolcraft, "Mythology, Superstitions and Languages of the North American Indians," *Literary and Theological* Review 2 (1835): 103.

4. Schoolcraft, *Personal Memoirs*, 652, 654; *Detroit Daily Advertiser,* April 17, 1839; *Detroit Free Press,* April 21, 1839.

5. Schoolcraft, *Plan for the Investigation of American Ethnology* (New York: NY Historical Society, 1847), reprinted in *Annual Report of the Board of Regents of the Smithsonian Institutions,* Part I (Washington, D.C.: Government Printing Office, 1886), 907–14.

6. P. T. Barnum, *Struggles and Triumphs, Or, Forty Years' Recollection of P. T. Barnum,* ed. Carl Bode (New York, 1981), 170–71.

7. New York State Senate Document 84, 68th sess., 1845; *Laws of the State of New York* (1845), 136. However, in 1788 the legislature of Virginia ordered the enumeration of the Powhatanic tribes. Henry R. Schoolcraft, *Notes on the Iroquois; or Contributions to American History, Antiquities, and General Ethnology* (Albany: Erastus H. Pease and Co., 1847), 5.

8. Schoolcraft, *Notes on the Iroquois,* 9–10. Also, N. S. Benton to Schoolcraft, June 25, 1845, June 25, 1845, Schoolcraft Papers, LC.

9. Schoolcraft, *Notes on the Iroquois,* 5–6.

10. Ibid., 1. He calculated the Iroquois's increasing population based on somewhat flimsy historical evidence. He found in the United States and Canada 6,942 Iroquois, out of whom 3,843 were in the state of New York (25–26).

11. Ibid., iii. The thirty-seven illustrations in the private edition were mostly of negligible value and included a portrait of Pocahontas and small woodcuts of artifacts and archeological sites.

12. Ibid., 12.

13. *Report of Mr. Schoolcraft, to the Secretary of State, Transmitting the Census Returns in Relation to the Indians,* New York Senate, Doc. 24, 1846, pp. 206–32.

14. Schoolcraft, *Notes on the Iroquois,* 475.

15. *Report of Mr. Schoolcraft,* 4–5.

16. *Report of the Commissioners Relating to the Condition of the Indians in Massachusetts,* Massachusetts House Report 46, February 1849, pp. 4–5.

17. Ibid., 48–49.

18. Ibid., 51.

19. Schoolcraft to Medill, February 24, 1846 [copy], Schoolcraft Papers.

20. Cass, Dickerson, and Dix to Marcy, July 21, 1846 [copy], Schoolcraft Papers. Also see Schoolcraft to William Medill, February 24, 1846, Schoolcraft Papers. Office of Indian Affairs Circular, September 1, 1846, Letters Received by the Western Superintendency, 1846–1848, Record Group 75, NARA.

21. Schoolcraft to Medill, July 28, 1846 [copy], Schoolcraft Papers.

22. *Memorandum for the President,* August 1846 [draft], Schoolcraft Papers.

23. *Report of the Committee of Indian Affairs on Albert Gallatin's Memorial on the Statistics of Indian Tribes to Accompany Bill H. R. No. 649,* House Report 53, 29th Cong., 2d sess., serial 501, p. 3.

24. "Medill's Report," February 1, 1847, in *Report of the Committee of Indian Affairs.*

25. *Statutes at Large,* 29th Cong. 2d sess., vol. 9 (1847), 204. Schoolcraft accepted the official position on March 19, 1847. Letter of Appointment, William L. Marcy [Secretary of War] to Schoolcraft, March 18, 1847, Schoolcraft Papers.

26. Enclosed in a letter from Schoolcraft to Marcy, August 2, 1846 [copy], Schoolcraft Papers.

27. *Memorial of George Catlin Praying Congress to Purchase His Collection of Indian Portraits and Curiosities,* in Senate Misc. 152, 30th Cong., 1st sess., serial 511, p. 3.

28. Ibid.

29. *Committee of the Library to Whom was Referred the Memorial of R. R. Gurley, Praying for the Purchase of Catlin's Collection of Paintings,* House Report 820, 30th Cong., 1st sess., serial 527, p. 2.

30. *Report of the Select Committee on the Expediency of Purchasing Mr. George Catlin's Collection of Indian Scenes and Portraits,* Senate Report 271, 32d Cong., 1st sess., serial 631, p. 2.

31. Schoolcraft to Medill, March 25, 1847, Office of Indian Affairs, Letter Received, Misc., Record Group 75, NARA.

32. Henry R. Schoolcraft, *Historical and Statistical Information Respecting the History, Present and Prospects of the Indian Tribes of the United States,* vol. 1 of 6 (Philadelphia: Lippincott, Grambo and Co., 1851), 548–49.

33. Ibid.

34. Ibid., 567.

35. "Circular to the Superintendents, Agents and Sub Agents of the Indian Department," May 1847, Schoolcraft Papers.

36. Schoolcraft to Marcy, February 1, 1849 [copy], Schoolcraft Papers, LC. In a May 1849 letter to Medill, Schoolcraft urged him to dispatch someone to the western agencies to induce the agents and subagents to fill up the forms. Schoolcraft to Medill, May 20, 1849 [copy], Schoolcraft Papers.

37. Joseph Henry to Secretary of the Interior Thomas Ewing, June 19, 1849 [copy], Schoolcraft Papers.

38. Schoolcraft to Lieber, March 22, 1851, Schoolcraft Papers, Rhees Collection, HL.

39. Schoolcraft to Indian Commissioner Luke Lea, December 10, 1852, Office of Indian Affairs, Letter Received, Misc., Record Group RU 75, NARA.

40. "Expenses of Collecting and Digesting Statistics of the Indian Tribes of the U.S.," *Abstract of Expenditures of the United States,* Record Group 213, vol. 5, p. 183, NARA. Henry R. Schoolcraft and Lippincott, "Memorandum of Agreement," December 6, 1850, Schoolcraft Papers.

41. Frances S. Nichols, *Index to Schoolcraft's "Indian Tribes of the Untied States,"* Bureau of American Ethnology, Bulletin 152 (Washington, D.C., 1954).

42. Schoolcraft, *Historical and Statistical Information,* 3:58.

43. Ibid., 1:367–68; 2:x-xi; 4:179, 461; 6:28–29.

44. "History of the Indian Tribes," *North American Review* 73 (July 1851): 243. Friends of Schoolcraft wrote several of these reviews. For example, see *Knickerbocker* 37 (May 1851): 458–59, and *Knickerbocker* 39 (June 1852): 553.

45. Francis J. Bowen, "Schoolcraft on the Indian Tribes," *North American Review* 77 (July 1853): 245, 247.

46. See, e.g., Schoolcraft to Spencer Fullerton Baird, March 25, 1851, Assistant Secretary Incoming Letters, 1850–1877, RU 52, SIA. George Robbins Gliddon to Ephraim George Squier, April 16, 1851, Ephraim George Squier Papers, LC.

47. *New York Herald,* January 17, 1858.

48. Schoolcraft to George Manypenny, October 1, 1853, Office Of Indian Affairs, Letter Received, Misc., RU 75, NARA.

49. Mary Howard Schoolcraft to the House of Representatives Committee of Indian Affairs, January 21, 1859, Committee Papers, RG 233, HR 35A-D8.7, NARA; Private Bill no. 9, 35th Cong., 2d sess; *Congressional Globe,* 35th Cong. 2d sess. (Jan. 21, 1859): 517.

50. George Manypenny to Schoolcraft, June 11, 1853, RU 75, Letters Received, Misc., NARA.

51. Mary Howard Schoolcraft to Spencer Fullerton Baird, November 12, 1859, Assistant Secretary Incoming, RU 52, SIA.

52. "Report [to accompany bill S. 308] on Seth Eastman's Memorial," Senate Committee Report 151, 36th Cong., 1st sess., serial 1039.

53. "The Committee on Claims on Seth Eastman's Memorial," Senate Committee Report 160, 39th Cong., 2d sess., serial 1279. In 1863, the Schoolcrafts proposed to publish the remainder of the material collected under the Act of 1847, but despite support in the Senate a $10,000 appropriations failed in the House. Judging by remarks made during the discussion, it appears that senators were in fact somewhat knowledgeable about the volumes' content. *Congressional Globe* (June 25, 1864): 3257–58.

54. Schoolcraft, "An address delivered before the New Confederacy of the Iroquois," 4–5.

55. Robert E. Beider, *Science Encounters the Indian, 1820–1880* (Norman, Okla., 1986), 112.

56. Squier to Henry, March 24, 1847 [draft], Squier Papers.

57. Henry to Squier, June 23, 1847; Henry to John Russell Bartlett, June 23, 1847, Squier Papers. On the alterations introduced to the original correspondence, see Gallatin to Henry, June 16, 1847, Albert Gallatin Papers, NYHS. An edited version of that letter was included in the published correspondence. See, e.g., Smithsonian Institution, *Annual Report* (1847), 186. Henry to Squier, April 28, 1847 [draft], Joseph Henry Papers, SIA.

58. Henry to Squier, June 23, 1847; Henry to John Russell Bartlett, June 23, 1847, Squier Papers.

59. Henry to Squier, April 18, 1848; also see Henry to Squier, April 14, 1848, Squier Papers.

60. Henry to Gray, May 23, 1848, Historic Letters, GHA.

61. Henry to Squier, August 18, 1848, Squier Papers.

62. Ephraim George Squier and E. H. Davis, "Ancient Monuments of the Mississippi Valley: Comprising the Results of Extensive Original Surveys and Explorations," *Smithsonian Contributions to Knowledge,* vol. 1 (Washington, D.C.: The Smithsonian Institution, 1848), xxxiv.

Chapter Eight • The Purloined Indian

1. Lewis H. Morgan, *League of the Ho-Dé-No-Sau-Nee or Iroquois* (Rochester: Sage and Brother, 1851), x.

2. Ibid., x–xi.

3. Lewis H. Morgan Diary Entry, October 19, 1859, printed in "How Morgan Came to Write *Systems of Consanguinity and Affinity*," ed. Leslie A. White, *Papers of the Michigan Academy of Science, Arts and Letters* 42 (1957), 260.

4. "Aquarius" [Lewis H. Morgan], "Vision of KAR-IS-TA-GI-A, a Sachem of Cayuga," *Knickerbocker* 24 (Sept. 1844): 238.

5. Ibid., 245.

6. Carl Resek, *Lewis Henry Morgan: American Scholar* (Chicago, 1960), 24.

7. Lewis H. Morgan to George Bancroft, August 16, 1844, George Bancroft Papers, MHS. The Oneidas were located at Utica; the Onandagas at Syracuse; the Cayugas, further divided into four tribes, were at Aurora, Auburn, Ithaca, and Owego; and the Seneca, also divided into four, were at Waterloo, Canandaigua, Rochester, and Lima.

8. "Proclamation of the Tek-a-ri-ho-ge-a Instituting and Confirming the Wolf Tribe of the Oneida Nation at Utica," in Elisabeth Tooker, *Lewis H. Morgan on Iroquois Material Culture* (Tucson, Ariz., 1994), 74.

9. Thomas R. Trautmann, *Lewis Henry Morgan and the Invention of Kinship* (Berkeley, 1987), 42–43.

10. Skenandoah [Lewis H. Morgan], "To the general Council Fire of the Confederacy at the Falls of the Genesee, 11 Gya-ong-wa [Oct.] 1845," in Robert E. Beider, *Science Encounters the Indian, 1820–1880* (Norman, Okla., 1986), 201.

11. Quoted in Beider, *Science Encounters the Indian*, 210. Also see Tooker, "Issac N. Hurd's Ethnographic Studies of the Iroquois: Their Significance and Ethnographic Value," *Ethnohistory* 27 (Fall 1980): 363–69.

12. Eli Parker to William C. Bryant, November 26, 1884, reprinted in Arthur Caswell Parker, *The Life of General Ely S. Parker: Last Grand Sachem of the Iroquois and General Grant's Military Secretary* (Buffalo, N.Y., 1919), 216.

13. Morgan to Schoolcraft, October 7, 1845, Schoolcraft Papers, LC.

14. William N. Fenton, *The Great Law and the Longhouse: A Political History of the Iroquois Confederacy* (Norman, Okla., 1998), 136–39.

15. David Maldwyn Ellis, *Landlords and Farmers in the Hudson-Mohawk region, 1790–1850* (Ithaca, N.Y., 1946), 242–50, 271–72. Also see David R. Roediger, *Wages of Whiteness: Race and the Making of the American Working Class* (London, 1991), 104.

16. Mark C. Carnes, *Secret Ritual and Manhood in Victorian America* (New Haven, 1989), 12–13.

17. Morgan, *League of the Iroquois*, 456.

18. The book was published in two different styles. A luxurious ($35) edition on tinted paper included twenty-two colored plates and illustrations that had been prepared for Morgan's reports for the New York State Board of Regents. These volumes had full gilt edge and were bound in blue leather boards decorated with a chief's headdress in gold. In the general edition ($15), maps, plates, and woodcuts were in black and white, and the volume was bound with either cloth or leather. William N. Fenton, Introduction to Morgan, *League of the Iroquois* (1962; New York, 1993), vi.

19. Morgan, *League of the Iroquois*, 57–48.

20. Ibid., 60.

21. Ibid., 79.

22. Ibid., 84.

23. Trautmann, *Lewis Henry Morgan and the Invention of Kinship*, 66.

24. Morgan, *League of the Iroquois*, 102.

25. Quoted in Fenton, Introduction to Morgan, *League of the Iroquois*, xiv.

26. Lewis Henry Morgan, "To the Honorable the Board of Regents of the University of the State of New York," November 13, 1848, *Second Annual Report of the Regents*, 85.

27. *Second Annual Report of the Regents of the University, on the Condition of the State Cabinet of Natural History with Catalogue of the Same*, New York Senate Doc. No. 20, 1848 (Albany: Charles Van Benthuysen, 1848), 10.

28. *Third Annual Report of the Regents of the University*, New York Senate Doc. No. 75, 1849 (Albany: Weed, Parsons, 1850), 10.

29. Tooker, *Lewis H. Morgan on Iroquois Material Culture*, xiv.

30. Morgan to Parker, Rochester, October 30, 1848, in Tooker, *Lewis H. Morgan on Iroquois Material Culture*, 53, 56.

31. Ibid., p. 75. *Third Annual Report of the Regents*, 15.

32. Society of Friends, *Documents and Official Reports Illustrating the Causes Which Led to the Revolution in the Government of the Seneca Indians, in the Year 1848* (Baltimore: William Wooddy and Son, 1857).

33. Charles Talbot Porter, "Personal Reminiscences," in Morgan, *League of the Iroquois*, ed. Herbert M. Lloyd, vol. 2 (New York, 1904), Appendix B, 156.

34. Parker to Schoolcraft, May 2, 1846, Schoolcraft Papers.

35. Schoolcraft to Parker, May 7, 1846, Schoolcraft Papers. Two years later Parker wrote Schoolcraft asking him to keep an eye on the Tonawanda case in Washington (Parker to Schoolcraft, Jan. 23, 1848, Schoolcraft Papers). In 1850, Parker tried to get Schoolcraft to find him a vacant Indian agency in the Midwest or the West (Parker to Schoolcraft, Feb. 25, 1850, Schoolcraft Papers).

36. *Ithaca Daily Chronicle*, August 17, 1846, quoted in William H. Armstrong, *Warrior in Two Camps, Ely S. Parker: Union General and Seneca Chief* (Syracuse, N.Y., 1978), 31.

37. *Masonic Chronicle* (Columbus, Oh.) 16 (Nov. 1896), quoted in Parker, *Life*, 97.

38. Ibid., 133.

39. Ibid., 141.

40. Tooker, *Lewis H. Morgan on the Iroquois Material Culture*, 303, fn 30.

41. These incidents usually involved heavy drinking. Parker, *Life*, 132–33.

42. Armstrong, *Warrior in Two Camps*, 33.

43. Parker to Schoolcraft, April 10, 1848, Schoolcraft Papers. However, Parker continued to send Schoolcraft ethnological material about Indian games, dances, and crime. Parker to Schoolcraft, May 8, 1848, Schoolcraft Papers.

44. Resek, *Lewis Henry Morgan*, 38.

45. "The Gettysburg Speech of Grant's Military Secretary," reprinted in Parker, *Life*, 183.

46. Schoolcraft, "An Address Delivered Before the New Confederacy of the Iroquois," 7. Emphasis in the original.

47. Parker, "Memorial To the State Legislature, New York, February 1, 1888," reprinted in Parker, *Life*, 212–13, 218–20.

48. Ibid., 222.

49. "Aquarius," "Thought at Niagara," *Knickerbocker* 22 (Sept. 1843): 195.

50. José Barreiro, ed., *Indian Roots of American Democracy* (Ithaca, N.Y., 1992), viii. Donald A. Grinde Jr., "Iroquoian Political Concept and the Genesis of American Government," in Barreiro, *Indian Roots*, 47–66.

51. Dwight W. Hoover, *The Red and the Black* (Chicago, 1976), 56–57.

Conclusion

1. Roach, *Cities of the Dead*, 2–3.

2. Fenton, *The Great Law and the Longhouse: A Political History of the Iroquois Confederacy* (Norman, Okla., 1998), 713.

3. http://www.9-11commission.gov/family/index.htm (accessed August 2004).

4. Polly Summar, *Albuquerque Journal*, July 27, 2004.

5. *The 9/11 Investigations: Staff Reports of the 9/11 Commission; Excerpts from the House-Senate Joint Inquiry Report on 9/11*, ed. Steven Strasser, intro. Craig R. Whitney (New York, 2004).

6. National Commission on Terrorist Attacks Upon the United States, Al Felzenberg, Deputy for Communications, Media Advisory, May 19, 2004. http://www.9-11commission .gov/press/pr_2004–05–19b.pdf.

7. *New York Post*, July 25, 2004.

8. *New York Times*, May 25, 2004.

9. *Baltimore Sun*, May 30, 2004.

10. http://www.usatoday.com/news/washington/2004-07-22-report-book-buyers_x.htm.

11. Heidi Benson, "9/11 Report Creates a Stir in Bookstores," *San Francisco Chronicle*, August 1, 2004 (www.sfgate.com). Ernest R. May, *The Kennedy Tapes: Inside the White House During the Cuban Missile Crisis* (New York, 1998).

Introduction

On the history of social investigations in Britain, see *Retrieved Riches: Social Investigation in Britain, 1840–1914,* ed. David Englander and Rosemary O'Day (London, 1995). A useful survey of antebellum reform is Ronald G. Walters, *American Reformers, 1815–1860* (New York, 1978). Also see Steven Mintz, *Moralists and Modernizers: America's Pre–Civil War Reformers* (Baltimore, 1995). On utilitarianism, political economy, and scientific legislation, see Eric Stokes, *The English Utilitarians and India* (Oxford, 1959); L. J. Hume, *Bentham and Bureaucracy* (Cambridge, 1981); and Donald Winch, "The Science of the Legislature: The Enlightenment Heritage," in *The State and Social Investigation,* ed. Michael J. Lacey and Mary O. Furner (Washington, D.C., 1993), 63–94. The *State and Social Investigation* is a fine anthology that focuses on a later period and supports a rather monolithic view of the state which all but ignores the role of legislatures in generating social knowledge. On the history of sociology, see Bruce Mazlish, *A New Science: The Breakdown of Connections and the Birth of Sociology* (New York, 1989); Randal Collins and Michael Makowsky, *The Discovery of Society* (New York, 1972); *The Social in Question: New Bearings in History and the Social Sciences,* ed. Patrick Joyce (London, 2002), Part 1; Robert C. Davis, "Social Research in America Before the Civil War," *Journal of the History of the Behavioral Sciences* 8 (1972): 69–85; and Selwyn K. Troen, "The Diffusion of an Urban Social Science: France, England, and the United States in the Nineteenth Century," *Comparative Social Research* 9 (1986): 247–66. On knowledge and social control, see Stanley Cohen and Andrew Scull, *Social Control and the State* (Oxford, 1983); *Social Control in Nineteenth Century Britain,* ed. A. P. Donajgrodski (Totowa, N.J., 1977); and David J. Rothman, *The Discovery of the Asylum; Social Order and Disorder in the New Republic* (Boston, 1971).

On the feud over the comparative benefits of the two systems of incarceration in antebellum America, see Negley K. Teeter and John D. Shearer, *The Prison at Philadelphia, Cherry Hill: The Separate System of Penal Discipline, 1829–1913* (New York, 1957). For individual states' engagement in social research see, for example, Pennsylvania Senate, *Report of the Select Committee Appointed to Visit the Manufacturing Districts of the Commonwealth for the Purpose of Investigating the Employment of Children in Manufactories* (Harrisburg, 1838); *Report of Select Committee Appointed to Examine into the Condition of Tenant Houses in New*

York and Brooklyn, New York Assembly Document 205 (March 9, 1857); and *Report of the Commissioners of Alien Passengers and Foreign Paupers,* Massachusetts House Document 18 (Boston, 1853). On Dorothea Dix's campaign for asylum reform, see Dix, *On Behalf of the Insane Poor, Selected Reports* (1843–52; New York, 1971). In the wake of the Civil War, many states established institutions for social research; see William R. Brock, *Investigation and Responsibility: Public Responsibility in the United States, 1865–1900* (Cambridge, 1984). A good survey of antebellum politics is Joel Silbey, *The Partisan Imperative: The Dynamics of American Politics Before the Civil War* (New York, 1985). On the Reform Act as a watershed in British politics, see J. A. Phillips and C. Wetherell, "The Great Reform Act of 1832 and the Political Modernization of England," *American Historical Review* 100 (Apr. 1995): 411–36, and "The Great Reform Bill of 1832 and the Rise of Partisanship," *Journal of Modern History* 63 (Dec. 1991): 621–46. Frederick Law Olmsted's project was titled *A Journey in the Seaboard Slave States, with Remarks on Their Economy* (New York, 1856). On the visits by agents of statistical societies to the domiciles of the poor, see M. J. Cullen, *The Statistical Movement in Early Victorian Britain* (New York, 1975), 135–37. On the contribution of religious revivals (rather than the marketplace) to the making of modern American print culture and mass media, see David Paul Nord, *Faith in Reading: Religious Publishing and the Birth of Mass Media in America* (New York, 2004).

Along with Hanna Fenichel Pitkin, *The Concept of Representation* (Berkeley, 1967), I found helpful Brian Seitz, *The Trace of Political Representation* (Albany, 1995). An important analysis of the emergence of the American public sphere and its relationship with print culture is Michael Warner, *The Letters of the Republic: Publication and the Public Sphere in Eighteenth Century America* (Cambridge, Mass., 1990). On citizenship and the public sphere, see Michael Schudson, *The Good Citizen: A History of American Civic Life* (New York, 1998); Mary Ryan, *Civic Wars, Democracy and Public Life in the American City during the Nineteenth Century* (Berkeley, 1997); and James Vernon, *Politics and the People: A Study in English Political Culture, 1815–1867* (Cambridge, 1993). On print culture in historical perspectives, see Roger Chartier, *The Order of Books: Readers, Authors, and Libraries in Europe between the Fourteenth and Eighteenth Centuries,* trans. Lydia G. Cochrane (Stanford, 1992); Elizabeth L. Eisenstein, *The Printing Revolution as an Agent of Change* (Cambridge, 1980); Ronald J. Zboray, *A Fictive People: Antebellum Economic Development and the American Reading Pubic* (New York, 1993); and Adrian Johns, *The Nature of the Book: Print and Knowledge in the Making* (Chicago, 2000).

The concept of the archive has been widely used in postcolonial literature to designate, in a rather loose manner, bodies of knowledge, scholarly disciplines, and other types of discourse, administrative records, official publications, and brick-and-mortar-archives. See, for example, Thomas Richard, *The Imperial Archive: Knowledge and the Fantasy of Empire* (London, 1993); Ann Laura Stoler, "Colonial Archives and the Art of Governance," *Archival Science* 2, nos. 1–2 (2002): 87–109; and Tony Ballantyne, *Orientalism and Race: Aryanism in the British Empire* (New York, 2002). Also see Jacques Derrida, *Archive Fever,* trans. Eric Prenowitz (Chicago, 1996); Michel Foucault, *The Archeology of Knowledge* (1972; New York, 1982), part 3, and Carolyn Steedman, *Dust: The Archive and Cultural History* (New Brunswick, N.J., 2002). On the gap between the panoptic desire (and the attempt to create a total archive) and the reality of knowledge production and circulation, see Ballantyne, *Orientalism and Race,* 9. Ann Stoler remarked recently that colonial regimes were "imperfect, and even indifferent knowledge-acquiring machines. Omniscience and omnipotence were not, as is so often assumed, their defining goals" ("Tense and Tender Ties: The Politics of Comparison in North American History and (Post) Colonial Studies," *Journal of American History* 88 (Dec. 2001): 829– 66). Since the early 1980s, "new historicist" literary scholars have offered fresh ways of contextualizing literary texts historically; see Catherine Gallagher and Stephen Greenblatt, *Practicing New Historicism* (Chicago, 2001); Gallagher, *The Industrial Reformation of English Fiction: Social Discourse and Narrative Form, 1832–1867* (Chicago, 1985); and *The New Historicism*, ed. H. Aram Veeser (New York, 1989). On the social sciences and the question of objectivity, see Mary O. Furner, *Advocacy and Objectivity: A Crisis in the Professionalization of American Social Science. 1865–1905* (Lexington, Ky., 1975); Linda Gordon, "Social Insurance and Public Assistance: The Influence of Gender in Welfare Thought in the United States, 1890–1935," *American Historical Review* 97 (Feb. 1992): 41–43.

PART I • *Monuments in Print*

The famous report on child labor in the mines was published as *First Report of the Royal Commission on Children's Employment (Mines)* 1842 (380) 15, and in private editions, for instance, by William Clowes and Son. John Charles Frémont's first report was issued in 1843 as *A Report of an Exploration of the Country Lying between the Missouri River and the Rocky Mountains on the Line of the Kansas and Great Platte River,* Senate Document 243, 27th Cong., 3d sess., serial 416. It was later coupled with the report of his 1843–44 expedition and published in separate editions by the printers of the House and the Senate; see *Report of the Exploring Expedition to the Rocky Mountains in the Year 1842, and to Oregon and North California in the Years 1843–44* (Washington, D.C., 1845).

The prominence given to minute details in natural history, on the one hand, and in social reportage, on the other, has received diverse scholarly attention. Susan Cannon views the bumblebee episode in Frémont's account and similar detailed descriptions as a demonstration of the influence of "Humboldtian Science" (instead of a Baconian aggregation of facts) on antebellum American science. Thomas Laqueur argues that detailed descriptions of human bodies are constitutive of the post-Enlightenment humanitarian sensibility. See Susan Faye Cannon, *Science in Culture: The Early Victorian Period* (New York, 1978), especially chapter 3, and Thomas W. Laqueur, "Bodies, Details, and the Humanitarian Narrative," in *The New Cultural History,* ed. Lynn Hunt (Berkeley, 1989), 176–204. On the motif of the sublime in mid-nineteenth-century American paintings and geology, see Barbara Novak, *Nature and Culture: American Landscape and Painting, 1825–1875* (New York, 1980), 18–77.

On the imaginary work that sustains national communities, see Benedict Anderson, *Imagined Communities: Reflections on the Origins and Spread of Nationalism* (1983; London, 1991). Geoffrey Nunberg's views on the historicity and materiality of information is influenced by the writing of Walter Benjamin, especially "The Storyteller," and "The Work of Art in the Age of Mechanical Reproduction," in *Illuminations,* ed. H. Arendt (New York, 1969). On issues of copyright in state publications in historical perspectives, see William F. Party, *Copyright Law and Practice,* vol. 1 (Washington, D.C., 1994), 338–58; Neil Davenport, *United Kingdom Copyright and Design Protection: A Brief History* (Emsworth, Hampshire, 1993), 157–64.

On the production and diffusion of books as a "circuit of communication," see Robert Darnton, "What is the History of Books?" in *Kiss of Lamourette: Reflections in Cultural History* (New York, 1990), 107–35. Also see D. F. McKenzie, *Bibliography and the Sociology of Texts* (Cambridge, 1999). On authorship, see, for instance, Michel Foucault, "What is an Author?" in *The Foucault Reader*, ed. Paul Rabinow (New York, 1984), 101–20; Carla Hesse, "Enlightenment Epistemology and Laws of Authorship in Revolutionary France, 1777–1793," *Representations* 30 (Spring 1990): 109–37; John Brewer, "Authors, Publishers and the Making of Literary Culture," in *The Pleasures of the Imagination: English Culture in the Eighteenth Century* (New York, 1997), 125–66; and Mark Rose, "Literary Property Determined," in *Books and Owners: The Invention of Copyright* (Cambridge, Mass., 1993), 92–112. A good example of literary criticism that incorporates the physical aspects of books is *Reading Books: Essays on the Material Text and Literature in America*, ed. Michele Moylan and Lane Stiles (Amherst, 1996), and Robert Patten, "When is a Book Not a Book," *Biblion: The Bulletin of the New York Public Library* (Spring 1996): 35–63. On reading, see Michel de Certeau, "Reading as Poaching," in *The Practice of Everyday Life*, trans. Steven Rendall (Berkeley, 1984), 165–76; Jonathan Rose, *The Intellectual Life of the British Working Classes* (New Haven, 2001); Richard Altick, *The English Common Reader: A Social History of the Mass Reading Public, 1800–1900* (1957; Columbus, Ohio, 1998); William J. Gilmore, *Reading Becomes a Necessity of Life: Material and Cultural Life in Rural New England, 1780–1835* (Knoxville, Tenn., 1989); and Roger Chartier, "Text, Printing, Readings," in *The New Cultural History*, ed. Hunt, 154–175. On the "information age" in historical perspectives, see, for instance, *A Nation Transformed by Information: How Information Has Shaped the United States from Colonial Times to the Present*, ed. Alfred D. Chandler and James W. Cortada (New York, 2000). On the documentary style, see William Stott's classic *Documentary Expression and Thirties America* (New York, 1973), and Paula Rabinowitz, *They Must be Represented: The Politics of Documentary* (New York, 1994). On the literariness of official state documents, see Robert A. Ferguson, "The Literature of Public Documents," in *The Cambridge History of American Literature*, vol. 1, *1590–1820*, ed. Sacvan Bercovitch (New York, 1994), 470–95. For orality and print in the colonial period, see Sandra M. Gustafson, *Eloquence is Power: Oratory and Performance in Early America* (Chapel Hill, 2000).

Chapter One • Blue Books and the Market of Information

A. V. Dicey's late-nineteenth-century confidence in the might of "public opinion" was challenged in the 1960s by Oliver Macdonagh, who demonstrated that important reforms (namely the Passenger Acts) rested on bureaucratic initiatives without any previous public campaign. Macdonagh's conception was known as the "Tory thesis" of government growth. The entire Tory/Whig debate over public opinion was displaced in the historical literature by the ascendance of the Gramscian notion of "hegemony" and by the growing emphasis on pervasive public culture or an omnipotent "discourse." Both approaches reject a mechanistic view of power, opinion, and political action. In addition, the "Benthamite" category itself has lost much of its explanatory appeal. There were strong divisions among Bentham's followers as to the role of government in allocating documents and diffusing information. Moreover, some of the utilitarians' publication strategies were employed by other factions as well. See A. V. Dicey, *Lectures on the Relation Between Law and Public Opinion in England* (London, 1905), and Oliver Macdonagh, *A Pattern of Government Growth, 1800–1860: The Passenger Acts and*

Their Enforcement (London, 1961). On Chadwick's circle's publicizing techniques, see S. E. Finer, "The Transmission of Benthamite Ideas 1820–50," in *Studies in the Growth of Nineteenth-Century Government,* ed. Gillian Sutherland (London, 1972), 27. On the New Poor Law, see Anthony Brundage, *The Making of the New Poor Law: The Politics of Inquiry, Enactment, and Implementation, 1832–1839* (New Brunswick, N.J., 1978), and Peter Mandler, "The Making of the New Poor Law *Redivivus,*" *Past and Present* 117 (Nov. 1987): 131–57. On working-class publications against the New Poor Law, see R. K. Webb, *The British Working Class Reader, 1790–1848* (London, 1955), 123–36. Harriet Martineau's book was titled *Poor Laws and Paupers Illustrated: The Parish; The Hamlet; The Town; The Land's End* (London, 1833). On the centralization of information at the hands of the British government, see David Eastwood's excellent "'Amplifying the Province of the Legislature': The Flow of Information and the English State in the Early Nineteenth Century," *Historical Research* 62 (Oct. 1989): 276–94.

The best archival record for an early Victorian royal commission of inquiry is that of the Constabulary Force Commission (1836–39). The commission issued a thin report in 1839 but never completed its work or published the lengthy document its commissioners had envisaged. Many of its records (questionnaires, letters, notes) are still in the Public Record Office (HO 73/2–9) and sections 5–4 of the Edwin Chadwick Papers, University College, London. On the history of public-record legislation, see Winston Churchill's *First Report of the Royal Commission on Public Record,* 1912 (cd. 6361) 44, Appendix 1. See also Hilary Jenkinson, *Guide to the Public Record* (London, 1949), 7–10, 12–14; *The British Public Record Office* (Richmond, Va., 1960), 17–21; and Philippa Levine, "History in the Archives: The Public Record Office and Its Staff, 1838–1886," *English Historical Review* 101 (1986): 20–41.

Library scholar Margaret Steig conducted pioneering work on the informational functions of the Victorian state in "The Nineteenth Century Information Revolution," *Journal of Library History* 15 (Winter 1980): 22–52. On Stationery Office history, see David Bucher, *Official Publications in Britain* (London, 1991); Hugh Barty-King, *Her Majesty's Stationery Office: The Story of the First 200 Years, 1786–1986* (Norwich, England, 1986); James G. Ollé, *An Introduction to British Government Publications* (London, 1965); and P. Ford and G. Ford, *A Guide to Parliamentary Papers* (Oxford, 1956). A good anthology on Habermasian scholarship is *Habermas and the Public Sphere,* ed. Craig Calhoun (Cambridge, Mass., 1992). Another valuable collection is *The Phantom Public Sphere,* ed. Bruce Robbins (Minneapolis, 1993). For an early critique of Habermas's work, see Oskar Negt and Alexander Kluge, *Public Sphere and Experience: Toward an Analysis of the Bourgeois and Proletarian Public Sphere,* trans. Peter Labanyi, Jamie Owen Daniel, and Assenka Oksiloff (Minneapolis, 1993). On the "plebian public sphere," see Kevin Gilmartin, *Print Politics: The Press and Radical Opposition in Early Nineteenth-Century England* (Cambridge, 1996). Also see Jürgen Habermas, *The Structural Transformation of the Public Sphere: An Inquiry into a Category of Bourgeois Society,* trans. Thomas Burger (1962; Cambridge, Mass., 1991), and Robert C. Holub, *Jürgen Habermas: Critic in the Public Sphere* (London, 1991).

Chapter Two • The Battle of the Books

On the New York State geological project, see Michele L. Aldrich, "New York Natural History Survey, 1836–1845" (Ph.D. diss., University of Texas at Austin, 1974). For post–Civil War congressional investigation of the conditions in the South, see, for example, *Memphis Riots and Massacre*, House Report 101, 39th Cong., 1st sess., serial 1274; and *Affairs in the Late Insurrectionary States*, 13 vols., House Report 22, 42d Cong., 2d sess., serial 1529–41. On congressional investigative powers, see Allan Barth, *Government by Investigation* (New York, 1955); James Hamilton, *The Power to Probe: A Study of Congressional Investigations* (New York, 1976); and *Congress Investigates: A Documentary History, 1792–1974*, ed. Arthur M. Schlesinger Jr. and Roger Burns, 5 vols. (New York, 1975). Carl Schurz's report was titled *Report of Carl Schurz on the States of South Carolina, Georgia, Alabama, Mississippi, and Louisiana, in Message of the President of the United States*, Senate Exec. Doc. 2, 39th Cong., 1st sess., serial 1237. Also see Hans L. Trefousse, *Carl Schurz: A Biography* (Knoxville, Tenn., 1982), 158–60. An important source on government printing and patronage is Culver H. Smith, *The Press, Politics, and Patronage: The American Government's Use of Newspapers, 1789–1875* (Athens, Ga., 1977). On press coverage of Washington politics, see Samuel Kernell and Gary C. Jacobson, "Congress and the Presidency as News in the Nineteenth Century," *The Journal of Politics* 49 (Nov. 1987): 1016–37; and Thomas C. Leonard, *The Power of the Press: The Birth of American Political Reporting* (New York, 1986). On the circulation of information and the early version of the "informed citizen," see Richard D. Brown, *Knowledge is Power: The Diffusion of Information in Early America, 1700–1865* (New York, 1989), and *The Strength of the People: The Idea of an Informed Citizenry in America, 1650–1870* (Chapel Hill, 1996). On antebellum newspapers, see Michael Schudson, *Discovering the News: A Social History of American Newspapers* (New York, 1967); Dan Schiller, *Objectivity and the News: The Public and the Rise of Commercial Journalism* (Philadelphia, 1981); and David T. Z. Mindich, *Just the Facts: How "Objectivity" Came to Define American Journalism* (New York, 1998). For histories of the Government Printing Office, see James L. Harrison, *100 GPO Years, 1861–1961* (Washington, D.C., 1961); Robert Washington Kerr, *History of the Government Printing Office* (Lancaster, Pa., 1881); and Laurence F. Schmeckebier, *The Government Printing Office: Its History, Activities and Organization* (Baltimore, 1925).

On circular letters and their relationship to other forms of information, including official publications, see Noble E. Cunningham's introduction to *Circular Letters of Congressmen to Their Constituents*, ed. Cunningham, vol. 1 (Chapel Hill, 1978). On Gales and Seaton as congressional reporters, see Donald A. Ritchie, *Press Gallery: Congress and the Washington Correspondents* (Cambridge, Mass., 1991), 7–34. Jonathan Swift's famous tale is "A Full and True Account of the Battel fought last Friday between the Antient and the Modern books in St. James's Library" in *Selected Prose and Poetry*, ed. Edward Rosenheim Jr. (New York, 1959), 150–82.

Government publications have been of interest predominantly for bibliographers. Thus, for a pioneering overview of federal publications in the early republic, see J. H. Powell, *The Books of a New Nation: United States Government Publications, 1774–1814* (Philadelphia, 1957). On government publications during the first half of the twentieth century, see Leroy Charles Merrit, *The United States Government As Publisher* (Chicago, 1943), and Paul Bixler, "Uncle Sam's Best Sellers," *Saturday Review of Literature* 18 (May 28, 1938): 3–4, 16. On the War of the Rebellion project, see Dallas D. Irvine, "The Genesis of the *Official Records*," *Mississippi Valley Historical Review* 24 (Sept. 1937): 221–29. On the nexus of culture and the state, see Mathew Arnold, *Culture and Anarchy*, ed. R. H. Super (Ann Arbor, 1965); Ian Hunter, *Culture and Government: The Emergence of Literary Education* (London, 1988); David Lloyd and Paul Thomas, *Culture and the State* (New York, 1998); and *State/Culture: State Formation after the Cultural Turn,* ed. George Steinmetz (Ithaca, 1999). On "Saxon eloquence," see Kenneth Cmiel, *Democratic Eloquence: The Fight over Popular Speech in Nineteenth Century America* (Berkeley, 1991), 111–20. On reconciliation as the predominant theme of Civil War memory, see David W. Blight, *Race and Reunion: The Civil War in American Memory* (Cambridge, Mass., 2002).

Chapter Three • The Bee in the Book

John Higham, *From Boundlessness to Consolidation: The Transformation of American Culture, 1848–1860* (Ann Arbor, 1969). Allan Nevins claimed that too much was made of Jessie Benton's contributions to Frémont's reports (*Frémont: Pathmaker of the West* [1928; New York, 1955], 117–18). Frémont's reports were reprinted, for example, by D. Appleton and Co. in New York City (1846 and 1856, when Frémont was the Republican party's candidate for presidency), G. H. Derby and Co. in Buffalo (1849 and 1850), by Hall and Dickson in Syracuse in conjunction with Hall and Dickson in New York (1847), and by H. Polkinhorn in Washington (1845). On John C. Frémont's explorations, see Tom Chaffin, *Pathfinder: John Charles Frémont and the Course of American Empire* (New York, 2002), 95–366. See also William Goetzmann, *Explorations and Empire: The Explorer and the Scientist in the Winning of the American West* (1966; New York, 1993), 240–52. On the exploring expedition, see Nathaniel Philbrick, *Sea of Glory: America's Voyage of Discovery: The U.S. Exploring Expedition, 1838–1842* (New York, 2003); William Stanton, *The Great United States Exploring Expedition of 1838–1842* (Berkeley, 1975); and *Magnificent Voyagers,* ed. Herman J. Viola and Carolyn Margolis (Washington, D.C., 1985). Anita Hibler's research on the publication of the exploring expedition reports is particularly detailed and useful. Anita M. Hibler, "The Publication of the Wilkes Reports, 1842–1877" (Ph.D. diss., George Washington University, 1989). For a bibliographical history of each volume, see Daniel C. Haskell, *U.S. Exploring Expedition, 1838–1842, and Its Publications, 1844–1874* (New York, 1940). Charles Wilkes's narrative account was issued as *Narrative of the United States Exploring Expedition, During the Years 1838, 1839, 1840, 1841, 1842,* 5 vols. (Philadelphia, 1844).

On the border dispute with Mexico, see William Goetzmann, *Army Exploration in the American West, 1803–1863* (New Haven, 1959), 175–78; L. David Norris, James C. Milligan, and Odie B. Faulk, *William H. Emory: Soldier-Scientist* (Tucson, 1998), chap. 3; and Odie B. Faulk, Introduction to the reprint of John Russell Bartlett's *Personal Narrative of Explorations* (1854; Chicago, 1965). David Dale Owen's geological report was issued as *Report of a Geological Reconnaissance, of the Chippewa Land District of Wisconsin, and the Northern Part of Iowa,* Senate Exec. Doc. 57, 30th Cong., 1st sess., serial 509. On mid-nineteenth-century science, see Robert V. Bruce, *The Launching of Modern American Science, 1846–1876* (New York, 1987), 201–68; Howard S. Miller, *Dollars for Research: Science and Its Patrons in Nineteenth Century America* (Seattle, 1970); and Lillian B. Miller, *The Lazzaroni: Science and Scientists in Mid-Nineteenth Century America* (Washington, D.C., 1972). On the dispute over the route to the pacific, see Robert Royal Russel, *Improvement of Communication with the Pacific Coast as an Issue in American Politics, 1783–1864* (Cedar Rapids, Iowa, 1948), 168–201. For bibliographical details of antebellum western reporting, see Henry R. Wagner and Charles L. Camp, *The Plains and the Rockies: A Critical Bibliography of Exploration, Adventure and Travel in the American West, 1800–1865,* ed. Robert H. Becker (San Francisco, 1982).

On dedicating books in early modern Europe, see Natalie Z. Davis, "Beyond the Market: Books as Gifts in Sixteenth Century France," *Transactions of the Royal Historical Society,* ser. 5, 33 (1983): 69–88. On authorship in antebellum America, see William Charvat, *The Profession of Authorship in America, 1800–1870,* ed. Matthew J. Bruccoli (1968; New York, 1992), and Meredith L. McGill, *American Literature and the Culture of Reprinting, 1834–1853* (Philadelphia, 2002). McGill provides an exceedingly valuable analysis of antebellum debates about intellectual rights (especially the international copyright law) in which market-driven and republican notions about authorship and publishing clashed. Her discussion, together with recent work on the publication might of antebellum religious societies, and this book's emphasis on the role of government in circulation of texts demonstrate, in different contexts, that the antebellum literary arena was not entirely governed by the modalities and ideologies of the liberal, profit-driven marketplace.

PART II • *The Culture of the Social Fact*

Chapter Four • *Scenes of Commission*

For useful details on royal commissions and their personnel, see *Officials of Royal Commissions of Inquiry 1815–1870,* ed. J. M. Collinge, in vol. 9 of *Office Holders in Modern Britain* (London, 1984). The only monograph on the topic is still H. M. Clokie and Joseph F. Robinson, *Royal Commissions of Inquiry: The Significance of Investigations in British Politics* (Stanford, 1937). Also see H. F. Gosnell, "British Royal Commissions of Inquiry," *Political Science Quarterly* 49 (1934): 84–118. Two biographies of Chadwick stand out: S. E. Finer, *The Life and Times of Sir Edwin Chadwick* (London, 1952), and Anthony Brundage, *England's "Prussian Minister": Edwin Chadwick and the Politics of Government Growth, 1832–1854* (University Park, Pa., 1988). On the debate over the expansion of Victorian government, see *The Victorian Revolution-Government and society in Victoria's Britain,* ed. Peter Stansky (New York, 1973). On the early history of royal commissions, see T. J. Cartwright, *Royal Commissions and Departmental Committees in Britain* (London, 1975), 32–48. For details on the work of the Factory Commission, see T. J. Ward, *The Factory Movement, 1830–1855* (London, 1962), 81–134. A good analysis of the politics of Whig governments is Peter Mandler, *Aristocratic Government in the Age of Reform: Whigs and Liberals, 1830–1852* (Oxford, 1990). The Irish Poor Law Commission's recommendation not to legislate a poor law for Ireland was rejected outright by the British cabinet; see Helen Burk, *The People and the Poor Law in Nineteenth Century Ireland* (Littlehampton, England, 1987), 17–46. The version of the Irish Poor Law Commission's report employed in this chapter is the privately published *The Miseries and Misfortunes of Ireland and the Irish People from the Evidence Taken by the Commissioners for Inquiring into the Condition of the Poorer Classes in Ireland* (London, 1836). For the tension between scientific and local knowledge, see Hugh Raffles, "Intimate Knowledge," *International Social Science Journal* 54, no. 3 (2002): 325–35. On nineteenth-century statistical imagination, see Mary Poovey, "Figures of Arithmetic, Figures of Speech—The Discourse of Statistics in the 1830s,"

Critical Inquiry 19 (Winter 1993): 256—76; Mary Poovey, *Making a Social Body: British Cultural Formation, 1830—1864* (Chicago, 1995); Theodore M. Porter, *The Rise of Statistical Thinking, 1820—1900* (Princeton, 1986); and Ian Hacking, *The Taming of Chance* (Cambridge, 1990).

Michel Foucault explored the panopticon to great effect in *Discipline and Punish: The Birth of the Prison*, trans. Alan Sheridan (New York, 1979), 195—308. Also see Foucault, "The Eye of Power," in *Power/Knowledge: Selected Interviews and Other Writings, 1972—1977*, ed. Colin Gordon (New York, 1980), 146—65. Foucault's earlier work, especially his description of the "medical gaze" in the *Birth of the Clinic*, acknowledged more complicated movements and arrangements of the eye than in the Panopticon; see *The Birth of the Clinic: An Archaeology of Medical Perception*, trans. Alan M. Sheridan (London, 1973), 107—23. Also see Martin Jay, *Downcast Eyes: The Denigration of Vision in Twentieth-Century French Thought* (Berkeley, 1993), 381—416 (esp. 411—416); John Rajchman, "Foucault's Art of Seeing," *October* 44 (Spring 1988): 89—119; and Thomas R. Flynn, "Foucault and the Eclipse of Vision," in *Modernity and the Hegemony of Vision*, ed. David Michael Levin (Berkeley, 1993), 273—86. Nick Crossley contends that the Panopticon presupposes an intersubjective rather than objectifying gaze in "The Politics of the Gaze: Between Foucault and Merleau-Ponty," *Human Studies* 16 (October 1993): 399—419. For other critical approaches to the role of royal commissions in British political life, see Adam Ashforth, "Reckoning Schemes of Legitimation: On Commissions of Inquiry as Power/Knowledge Form," *Journal of Historical Sociology* 3 (Mar. 1990): 1—22; Frank Burton and Pat Carlen, *Official Discourse: On Discourse Analysis, Government Publications, Ideology and the State* (London, 1979); and P. Corrigan and D. Sayer, *The Great Arch: English State Formation as Cultural Revolution* (Oxford, 1985).

On the factory movement's exposure of factory conditions, see *The Poor Man's Advocate; or, A Full and Fearless Exposure of the Horrors and Abominations of the Factory System in England*, 50 vols. (Manchester, 1830), and R. G. Kirby and A. E. Musson, *The Voice of the People: John Doherty, 1798—1854: Trade Unionist, Radical and Factory Reformer* (Manchester, 1975). On the counterinvestigation conducted by the Glasgow operatives, see *Sixth Report from the Select Committee on the Operation of the Factory Acts*, HC 1840 (504) 10, pp. 27—28. For William Dodd's work as a social investigator, see Dodd, *The Factory System Illustrated: In a Series of Letters to the Right Hon. Lord Ashley Together with A Narrative of the Experience and Sufferings of William Dodd* (1842; London, 1968). On tourism to factories, see R. Boyson, *The Ashworth Cotton Enterprise. The Rise and Fall of a Family Firm, 1818—1880* (Oxford, 1970), 181—83. For an example of a delegation of laborers that traveled abroad to conduct a social investigation, see *Report of the Coventry Independent Deputation of Workmen Appointed to Visit the Ribbon-weaving Districts of France and Switzerland* (Coventry: Taunton's Free Press Office [1860]). On Inspector Stuart's career, see Ursula Henriques, "An Early Factory Inspector," *Scottish Historical Review* 1 (1971): 18—46. For a critique of the power of law to affix social categories, see Wendy Brown, *States of Injury: Power and Freedom in Modernity* (Princeton, 1995).

Chapter Five • Facts Speak for Themselves

An important summary of Bakhtin's theories is Tzvetan Todorov, *Mikhail Bakhtin; The Dialogical Principle*, trans. Wlad Godzich (Minneapolis, 1984). On the 1840s language of discovery, see Gertrude Himmelfarb, *The Idea of Poverty: England in the Early Industrial Age*

(New York, 1983), 356–57. On the sexual voyeurism of post-Enlightenment reform literature, see Karen Halttunen, "Humanitarianism and the Pornography of Pain in Anglo-American Culture," *The American Historical Review* 50 (Apr. 1995): 303–34. Victorian authors drew on parliamentary reports to build scenes and characters in their narratives. See, for example, Sheila M. Smith, "Wilenhall and Wodgate: Disraeli's Use of Blue Books Evidence," *Review of English Studies* 13 (Nov. 1962): 368–84.

For the antislavery appropriation of the parliamentary hearings, see the Society for the Abolition of Slavery, *Analysis of the Report of a Committee of the House of Commons on the Extinction of Slavery* (London: S. Bagster Printer, 1833); The Society for the Abolition of Slavery, *Abstract of the Report of the Lords Committee on the Condition and Treatment of Colonial Slaves* (London: S. Bagster Printer, 1833); "Legion," *A Letter from Legion to… the Duke of Richmond… on the Slavery Committee of the House of Lords: Containing an Exposure of the Character of the Evidence on the Colonial Side Produced Before the Committee* (London: S. Bagster Printer, [1833]); and "Legion," *A Second Letter from Legion to… the Duke of Richmond… Containing an Analysis of the Anti-slavery Evidence Produced Before the Committee* (London: S. Bagster, 1833). In all likelihood, the two pairs of documents were produced by the same organization.

On metonymy and representation of social reality, see Jonathan Arac, *Commissioned Spirits: The Shaping of Social Motion in Dickens, Carlyle, Melville, and Hawthorne* (New York, 1989), 34–47; Stephen J. Spector, "Monsters of Metonymy: *Hard Times* and Knowing the Working Class," *English Literary History* 51 (Summer 1984): 365–84; Roman Jakobson, "Two Aspects of Language and Two Types of Aphasic Disturbances," in Jakobson and Morris Halle, *Fundamentals of Language* (The Hague, 1956), 53–82. The notion of the implied reader was elaborated by Wolfgang Iser; see his *The Act of Reading: A Theory of Aesthetic Response* (Baltimore, 1978). In recent decades, the social sciences (anthropology in particular) have engaged in self-critique that centers on the dynamics and ethics of fieldwork (especially the relationship between researcher and informant) as well as the textuality of social scientific texts. The literature is enormous. Standing out is the compilation *Writing Culture: The Poetics and Politics of Ethnography*, ed. James Clifford and George E. Marcus (Berkeley, 1986), especially Clifford, "Introduction: Partial Truths," 1–26, and Renato Rosaldo, "From the Door of His Tent: The Fieldworker and the Inquisitor," 77–97.

Chapter Six • *Can Freedmen Be Citizens?*

The Emancipation League commenced collecting information about freedmen by sending questionnaires to superintendents and supervisors of freedmen's affair. See *Facts Concerning the Freedmen, Their Capacity and Their Destiny, Collected by and Published by the Emancipation League* (Boston: Press of Commercial Printing House, 1863). On the history of the American Freedmen's Inquiry Commission (AFIC), see John G. Sproat, "Blue Print for Radical Reconstruction," *Journal of Southern History* 23 (Feb. 1957): 25–44; and James M. McPherson, *The Struggle for Equality: Abolitionists and the Negro in the Civil War and Reconstruction* (Princeton, 1964), 178–91. On the federal government and the freedmen, see Louis S. Gerteis, *From Contraband to Freedman: Federal Policy Toward Southern Blacks, 1861–1865* (Westport, Conn., 1973); Mary Frances Berry, *Military Necessity and Civil Rights Policy:*

Black Citizenship and the Constitution, 1861–1868 (London, 1977); and *Freedom: A Documentary History of Emancipation, 1861–1867,* ed. Ira Berlin et al. ser. 1, vol. 1, *The Destruction of Slavery* (Cambridge, 1985), and vol. 2, *The Wartime Genesis of Free Labor: The Upper South* (Cambridge, 1993).

The AFIC's official reports were published together as Senate Exec. Doc. 53, 38th Cong., 1st sess., serial 1176. Also see *Official Records,* ser. 3, 3:430–54; ser. 3, 4:289–82. The two supplementary reports were published privately. See Samuel Gridley Howe, *The Refugees From Slavery in Canada West: Report to the Freedmen's Inquiry Commission* (Boston, 1864), and James McKaye, "The Mastership and Its Fruits: The Emancipated Slave Face to Face with His Old Master: A Supplemental Report" (New York: Loyal Publication Society, no. 58, 1864). Robert Dale Owen published a book based on the commission's final report, *The Wrong of Slavery, The Right of Emancipation, and the Future of the African Race in the United States* (Philadelphia: J. B. Lippincott and Co., 1864). Abridged versions of the reports were published in the abolitionist and the general press. See, for example, *National Anti-Slavery Standard,* August 15, 1863.

On the Sanitary Commission, see William Quentin Maxwell, *Lincoln's Fifth Wheel: The Political History of the United States Sanitary Commission* (New York, 1956). The Sanitary Commission also engaged in social research; see Benjamin Apthorp Gould, *Investigations in the Military and Anthropological Statistics of American Soldiers* (New York: US Sanitary Commission, 1869). For an account on a politically charged congressional investigation (the Thompson Committee) of the war effort, see Bruce Tap, *Over Lincoln's Shoulder: The Committee on the Conduct of the War* (Lawrence, Kans., 1998). For biographical material on Robert Dale Owen, see Elinor Pancoast and Anne E. Lincoln, *The Incorrigible Idealist: Robert Dale Owen in America* (Bloomington, 1940), and Richard W. Leopold, *Robert Dale Owen: A Biography* (Cambridge, Mass., 1940). On Samuel Gridley Howe, see Harold Schwartz, *Samuel Gridley Howe: Social Reformer, 1801–1876* (Cambridge, Mass., 1956). For Robert Dale Owen's Civil War propaganda, see, for example, Robert Dale Owen, *The Policy of Emancipation: In Three Letters* (Philadelphia, 1863). For information on the Sea Islands experiment, see Willie Lee Rose, *Rehearsal for Reconstruction: The Port Royal Experiment* (Indianapolis, 1964). On the invention of "miscegenation," see Sidney Kaplan, "The Miscegenation Issue in the Election of 1864," in Kaplan, *American Studies in Black and White: Selected Essays, 1949–1989* (Amherst, Mass., 1991), 47–100. Also see Elise Lemire, *"Miscegenation": Making Race in America* (Philadelphia, 2002), 115–44. On the history of U.S racial thinking, see Bruce R. Dain, *A Hideous Monster of the Mind: American Race Theory in the Early Republic* (Cambridge, Mass., 2002).

De Bow's statistical research is described in Ottis Clark Skipper, *J. D. B. De Bow: Magazinist for the South* (Athens, Ga., 1958); and H. G. and Winnie Leach Duncan, "The Development of Sociology in the Old South," *American Journal of Sociology* 39 (1934): 649–56. The first American book to include *sociology* in its title was George Fitzhugh, *Sociology for the South or the Failure of Free Society* (Richmond: A. Morris, 1854). On spiritualism, see Ann Braude, *Radical Spirits: Spiritualism and Women's Rights in Nineteenth-Century America* (Boston, 1989). On the rise of professional social science after the Civil War, see Thomas Haskell, *The Emergence of Professional Social Science: The American Social Science Association and the Nineteenth Century Crisis of Authority* (Urbana, Ill., 1977). For the relations between the war experience and public awareness of the social sphere, see, for instance, Ellen E. Guilot, *Social Factors in Crime as Explained by American Writers of the Civil War and Post Civil War Period* (Philadelphia, 1943). On the prejudice against former American slaves in Canada, see Jason H. Silverman, "The American Fugitive Slave in Canada: Myths and Realities," *Southern Studies* 19 (Spring 1980): 215–27.

PART III • *Totem Envy*

Henry Rowe Schoolcraft submitted his survey of the Iroquois to the New York senate as *Report of Mr. Schoolcraft, to the Secretary of State, Transmitting the Census Returns in Relation to the Indians*, New York, Senate Doc. 24, 1846. The ethnologist-publisher John R. Bartlett (see chap. 3) co-published the report under the title *Notes on the Iroquois: or, Contributions to the Statistics, Aboriginal History, Antiquities, and General Ethnology of Western New York* (New York: Bartlett and Welford, 1846). The following year it was republished in expanded form as *Notes on the Iroquois; or Contributions to American History, Antiquities, and General Ethnology* (Albany: Erastus H. Pease and Co., 1847). Schoolcraft's congressional project on the Indian tribes was titled *Historical and Statistical Information Respecting the History, Present and Prospects of the Indian Tribes of the United States,* 6 vols. (Philadelphia: Lippincott, Grambo and Co., 1851–57). It was also published as *Archives of Aboriginal Knowledge: Containing All the Original Papers Laid Before Congress Respecting the History, Antiquities, Language, Ethnology, Pictography, Rites, Superstitions, and Mythology, of the Indian Tribes of the United States,* 6 vols. (Philadelphia: Lippincott, 1860). Lewis Henry Morgan's study of the Iroquois was published as *League of the Ho-Dé-No-Sau-Nee or Iroquois* (Rochester: Sage and Brother, 1851).

On congressional publications that address Indian nations, see Steven L. Johnson, *Guide to American Indian Documents in the Congressional Serial Set: 1817–1899* (New York, 1977). On the history of the perception that the Indians were fated to disappear, see Brian W. Dippie, *The Vanishing American: White Attitudes and U.S. Indian Policy* (Middletown, Conn., 1982). On Indian federal policy, see Christine Bolt, *American Indian Policy and American Reform: Case Studies of the Campaign to Assimilate the American Indians* (London, 1987). On the contributions of the Smithsonian to American ethnology, see Curtis M. Hinsley, *The Smithsonian and the American Indian: Making a Moral Anthropology in Victorian America* (Washington, D.C., 1981). On the Office of Indian Affairs, see Edward E. Hill, *The Office of Indian Affairs, 1824–1880: Historical Sketches* (New York, 1974). For insightful analysis of the removal policy and the haunting Indian ghost in literature, see Lucy Maddox, *Removals: Nineteenth Century American Literature and the Politics of American Indian Affairs* (New York, 1991), and Reneé L. Bergland, *The National Uncanny: Indian Ghosts and American Subjects* (Hanover, N.H., 2000).

Samuel G. Morton's book is *Crania Americana; Or, a Comparative View of the Skulls of Various Aboriginal Nations of North and South America: To Which is Prefixed an Essay on the Varieties of the Human Species* (Philadelphia: J. Dobson, 1839). For a remarkably useful description of the anthropological projects of Gallatin, Schoolcraft, Morton, Morgan, and Squire, see Robert E. Beider, *Science Encounters the Indian, 1820–1880* (Norman, Okla., 1986). Also, see Reginald Horsman, "Scientific Racism and the American Indian in the Mid-Nineteenth Century," *American Quarterly* 27 (May 1975): 152–68; and *Race and Manifest Destiny* (Cambridge, Mass., 1981). For federal documents that were used to justify the removal of Indians, see, for example, *Correspondence on Removal of Indians West of Mississippi River, 1831–33*, Senate Doc. 90, 29th Cong., 2d sess., serial 494. The Doolittle Commission's report was published as U.S. Congress, *Condition of the Indian Tribes: Report of the Joint Special Committee* (Washington, D.C.: Government Printing Office, 1867). On the Pottawatomie leaders visit to Washington, D.C., see Richard Smith Elliot, *Notes Taken in Sixty Years* (St. Louis: R. P. Studley and Co., 1883). Homi Bhabha's observations are offered in *The Location of Culture* (London, 1993), 93–101. On temporality and the anthropological subject, see Johannes Fabian, *Time and the Other: How Anthropology Makes Its Object* (New York, 1983).

Chapter Seven • *Archives of Indian Knowledge*

The most detailed biography of Schoolcraft is Richard G. Bremer, *Indian Agent and Wilderness Scholar: The Life of Henry Rowe Schoolcraft* (Mount Pleasant, Mich., 1987). For secondary literature on "savagery" and "civilization," see Robert F. Berkhofer Jr., *The White Man's Indian: Images the American Indian from Columbus to the Present* (New York, 1978), and Ronald L. Meek, *Social Science and the Ignoble Savage* (Cambridge, 1976). On Schoolcraft and Hiawatha, see Chase S. Osborn and Stellanova Osborn, *Schoolcraft—Longfellow—Hiawatha* (Lancaster, Pa., 1942). On Seth Eastman's life and artistry, see John Francis McDermott, *Seth Eastman: Pictorial Historian of the Indian* (Norman, Okla., 1961).

For Squier's archeology, see Thomas G. Tax, "E. George Squier and the Mounds, 1845–1850," in *Toward a Science of Man: Essays in the History of Anthropology,* ed. Timothy H. H. Thoresen (The Hague, 1973), 99–124; and Gordon Willey and Jeremy Sabloff, *A History of American Archaeology* (San Francisco, 1974), 42–87. The mystery of the mounds also inspired poetic production, such as William Cullen Bryant's "The Prairies," *Poems* (1832). For a highly detailed account on Catlin's and Schoolcraft's efforts to seek congressional patronage, see Brian W. Dippie, *Catlin and His Contemporaries: The Politics of Patronage* (Lincoln, Nebr., 1990). On chromolithography and Schoolcraft's project, see Peter C. Marzio, *The Democratic Art: Chromolithography, 1840–1900, Pictures for a Nineteenth Century America* (Boston, 1979), 27–31.

Chapter Eight • *The Purloined Indian*

For biographical details, see Carl Resek, *Lewis Henry Morgan: American Scholar* (Chicago, 1960), and "How Morgan Came to Write *Systems of Consanguinity and Affinity*," ed. Leslie A. White, *Papers of the Michigan Academy of Science, Arts and Letters* 42 (1957). Thomas Trautmann's *Lewis Henry Morgan and the Invention of Kinship* (Berkeley, 1987) is the most important scholarship on Morgan's work on kinship. Herbert M. Lloyd's edition of *League of the HO-DE'-NO-SAU-NEE or Iroquois,* 2 vols. (New York, 1904) also contains useful documents. On Morgan and Marxism see, William H. Shaw, "Marx and Morgan," *History & Theory* 23 (1984): 215–28. Elisabeth Tooker explores more comprehensively than most other Morgan scholars do the importance of the New Order for his ethnological output; see "The Structure of the Iroquois League: Lewis H. Morgan's Research and Observations," *Ethnohistory* 30 (Spring 1983): 141–54; and "Lewis H. Morgan and His Contemporaries," *American Anthropologist* 94 (June 1992): 357–75.

On American masculinity and the Indian motif, see E. Anthony Rutondo, *American Manhood: Transformation in Masculinity from the Revolution to the Modern Era* (New York, 1993), 227–28. For a different psychological interpretation of Morgan's Indian games, see Mark C. Carnes, *Secret Ritual and Manhood in Victorian America* (New Haven, 1989). On antebellum minstrelsy, see Eric Lott, *Love and Theft: Blackface Minstrelsy and the American Working Class* (New York, 1993). On Indians as the children of the Great Father in Washington, see Michael Paul Rogin, *Fathers and Children: Andrew Jackson and the Subjugation of the American Indian* (New York, 1975). On the history of mimicking Indians in the United States, see Philip J. Deloria, *Playing Indian* (New Haven, 1998).

Edgar Allan Poe's story "The Purloined Letter" was republished in *The Complete Poems and Stories of Edgar Allan Poe, with Selections from his Critical Writings*, ed. Edward H. O'Neill, vol. 2 (New York, 1946), 593–607. For the Lacanian *mirror stage*, see Jacques Lacan, "The Mirror Stage as Formative of the Function of the I as Revealed in Psychoanalytic Experience," *Ecrits: A Selection*, trans. Alan Sheridan (New York, 1977), 1–7; and Shoshana Felman, *Jacques Lacan and the Adventure of Insight: Psychoanalysis in Contemporary Culture* (Cambridge, Mass., 1987). On Franz Fanon's work, see Ronald A. T. Judy, "Fanon's Body of Black Experience," in *Fanon: A Critical Reader*, ed. Lewis R. Gordon, T. Denean Sharpley-Whiting, and Reneé T. White (Oxford, 1996), 53–73. On womanhood as a performance, see Joan Rivier, "Womanliness as a Masquerade" (1929), in *Formations of Fantasy*, ed. Victor Burgin, James Donald, and Cora Caplan (London, 1986), 35–44. For analyses of the social turmoil in antebellum western New York, see Mary Ryan, *Cradle of the Middle Class: The Family in Oneida County, New York, 1790–1865* (Cambridge, 1981), and Paul E. Johnson, *A Shopkeeper's Millennium: Society and Revivals in Rochester, New York, 1815–1837* (New York, 1978).

Morgan's reports on material culture were incorporated into the annual report of the Regents of the University of the State of New York: *Second Annual Report of the Regents of the University, on the Condition of the State Cabinet of Natural History*, New York Senate Doc. No. 20, 1848 (Albany: Charles Van Benthuysen, 1848), 84–91; *Third Annual Report of the Regents of the University*, New York Senate Doc. No. 75, 1849 (Albany: Weed, Parsons, 1850), 65–97 (63–95 in the rev. ed.); and *Fifth Annual Report of the Regents of the University*, New York Assembly Doc. No. 122, 1851 (Albany: Charles Van Benthuysen, 1852), 67–117. For a great example of Morgan's ability to tie together domestic arrangements and political regimes, see Morgan, "Montezuma's Dinner," review of Hubert Howe Bancroft's *Native Races of the Pacific States*, vol. 2, *Civilized Nations*, North American Review 122 (Apr. 1876): 265–308.

For sites and environments of memory, see Pierre Nora, "Between Memory and History: Les Lieux de Memoire," *Representations* 26 (Spring 1989): 7–24. On the affinity between the League of Iroquois and the American federal structure, see Bruce Johansen, *Forgotten Founders: Benjamin Franklin, the Iroquois and the Rationale for the American Revolution* (Ipswich, Mass., 1982); *Exiled in the Land of the Free: Democracy, Indian Nations and the U.S. Constitution*, eds. John Mohawk, Oren Lyons, and Bruce Johansen (Santa Fe, 1992); and Donald Grinde Jr. and Bruce E. Johansen, *Exemplar of Liberty: Native America and the Evolution of American Democracy* (Berkeley, 1991). For a critique of the notion that the Iroquois inspired American federalism, see Elisabeth Tooker, "The United States Constitution and the Iroquois League," in *The Invented Indian: Cultural Fictions and Government Policies*, ed. James A. Clifton (New Brunswick, N.J., 1990), 107–28. A few years after the appearance of *League of the Iroquois*, Minnie Myrtle (pseudonym for Anna Johnson) published *The Iroquois: The Bright Side of the Indian Character* (New York, 1855), in which she popularized Morgan's research in a further attempt to defend the character of the Indian against prejudice.

Conclusion

For information about the Commission to Strengthen Social Security, see *http://www .csss.gov*. Daniel Patrick Moynihan's Report was published as United States Department of Labor, Office of Policy Planning and Research, *The Negro Family: The Case for National Action* (Washington, D.C., 1965). On the Left reaction to Moynihan's report and similar social studies, see, for example, William Ryan, *Blaming the Victim* (New York, 1970). On President Clinton's health reform plans, see Jacob S. Hacker, *The Road to Nowhere: The Genesis of President Clinton's Plan for Health Security* (Princeton, 1997), and Theda Skocpol, *Boomerang: Clinton's Health Security Effort and the Turn Against Government in U.S. Politics* (New York, 1996). On the replacement of scientific neutrality with advocacy and other aspects of victims' representation, see Alyson M. Cole, *The Cult of True Victimhood* (Stanford, 2006). Historian Gertrude Himmelfarb's 1990s writings are a good example of neo-Victorian moralism; see, for example, her *The De-Moralization of Society: From Victorian Virtues to Modern Values* (New York, 1995).

Page numbers in *italics* refer to illustrations.